Strategies for Teachers

Third Edition

Strategies for Teachers

Teaching Content and Thinking Skills

Paul D. Eggen
University of North Florida

Donald P. Kauchak
University of Utah

Allyn and Bacon
Boston • London • Toronto • Sydney • Tokyo • Singapore

Series Editor: Virginia Lanigan
Editorial Assistant: Nihad Farooq
Marketing Manager: Kathy Hunter
Editorial-Production Administrator: Donna Simons
Editorial-Production Service: Shepherd, Inc.
Composition Buyer: Linda Cox
Manufacturing Buyer: Aloka Rathnam
Cover Administrator: Suzanne Harbison

Copyright © 1996 by Allyn & Bacon
A Simon & Schuster Company
Needham Heights, MA 02194

Library of Congress Cataloging-in-Publication Data

Eggen, Paul D., 1940–
   Strategies for teachers : teaching content and thinking skills /
  Paul D. Eggen, Donald P. Kauchak.—3rd ed.
     p. cm.
   Includes bibliographical references and index.
   ISBN 0–205–15011–X
   1. Teaching.   2. Education—Experimental methods.   3. Thought and
thinking—Study and teaching.   4. Learning, Psychology of.
I. Kauchak, Donald P., 1946–   . II. Title.
LB1027.3.E44   1995
371.1'02—dc20   95–21070
                                         CIP

Printed in the United States of America

10 9 8 7 6 5 4 3   00 99 98 97

Photo Credits: p. 1, p. 21, p. 103, p. 180: Jim Pickerell; p. 58, p. 134, p. 313: Brian Smith; p. 205,
p. 235, p. 276: Stephen Marks

Contents

Preface

Major changes have occurred since the second edition of *Strategies for Teachers* was written, and we continue to be immersed in one of the most exciting periods in the recent history of education. The "cognitive revolution" is acquiring increasing momentum, and our understanding of learning has improved dramatically since the late 1980s. This awareness is reflected in greater understanding of the social nature of learning, the impact of context on understanding, the need for domain-specific knowledge in higher-order thinking, expert-novice differences in thinking and problem solving, and the belief that learners construct their own understanding of the topics they study. Teachers now use the effective teaching literature popular in the seventies and eighties as a foundation, going beyond it to focus on helping their students acquire a deep understanding of the topics they study while at the same time developing higher-order and critical-thinking abilities. We have attempted to reflect these advances as we revised the text.

In writing the third edition we relied on three sources. The first is the continuing advance of cognitive psychology that we referred to in the last paragraph. This advance has important implications for teachers, which are reflected in the suggested teacher actions integral to the models in the text. The second is the effective teaching literature, which continues to provide a foundation that all teachers should possess—the basic abilities and dispositions of teaching.

The third source is experience. Since we wrote the second edition we have spent a great deal of time in classrooms, observing teachers, working with students, and studying the complex interactions that take place in teaching-learning activities. This experience has also helped us understand that while the cognitive revolution is in full swing, teaching continues to be eclectic, reflecting a variety of conceptions of effective instruction. This experience is reflected in the scope of the text.

As with the second edition, this book focuses on instruction, using a *models approach.* A models approach links prescriptive teaching strategies to specific content and thinking goals, while acknowledging that no approach to instruction replaces the ability and wisdom of an effective teacher. Reflecting research suggesting that coverage in depth of carefully selected content is preferable to broad, superficial coverage, we have consciously avoided dealing with every topic commonly presented in a general methods text. Instead, we have attempted to present and illustrate the models in detail, including suggestions for modifications that can make them flexible, allowing teachers to express their own styles and preferences.

The book exists in two main parts. The first two chapters provide a frame of reference by outlining advances in effective teaching and the teaching of thinking. The remaining chapters are devoted to detailed coverage of the individual models, including suggestions for modifications that make them adaptable to a variety of teaching-learning situations.

In preparing the third edition, we have made three important changes. First, the scope has been increased to include models ranging from those reflecting constructivist views of learning to direct instruction and lecture-recitation. Readers using the book will now leave with a wider array of strategies than existed in the second edition, from which they can choose those most appropriate for meeting their needs and preferences.

Second, in addition to beginning each chapter with one or more detailed case studies, the discussion includes a number of short vignettes designed to fully illustrate the information in the chapter. All cases and examples are taken from lessons we've taught or observed, our only concession to authenticity being the shortening of the episodes in the interest of space and clarity.

Third, changes have also been made in the presentation of each model. The Inductive Model in Chapter 3 and the Integrative Model in Chapter 5 are now framed by constructivist views of learning. In Chapter 4 the Concept-Attainment Model reflects increased emphasis on hypothesis testing and the ability to teach the scientific method in a variety of contexts. Chapter 6, a new chapter, presents the Direct-Instruction Model, which reflects a research-based alternative to the inductively oriented models in Chapters 3, 4, and 5. The Lecture-Discussion Model in Chapter 7 is also new and provides a second alternative to inductively oriented models while retaining high levels of teacher-student interaction. The Inquiry Model in Chapter 8 has been broadened to include a greater variety of applications. Chapter 9 is an addition that describes three cooperative learning models that are based on our improved understanding of the social nature of learning. The book closes with Chapter 10, in which suggestions for combining and synthesizing the models are made.

In making our revision, we have attempted to ground the models in the most recent theory and research, making it a conceptually sound yet highly applicable text. We hope it provides you with opportunity for professional growth.

In preparing this manuscript we want to thank the people who have supported its development, particularly Virginia Lanigan, Nihad Farooq, and Kelly Bechen. We want to especially thank the many teachers in whose classrooms we've worked and visited, and on whose instruction several of the case studies in the text are based. This experience has brought to the book an authenticity that would have been otherwise impossible.

P.E.
D.K.

Information Processing and Models of Teaching

This is a book about teaching strategy. As you study the text, you will examine a number of conceptually related strategies designed to increase your students' achievement and higher-order and critical-thinking abilities. The strategies are based on the premise that students learn more effectively when they are actively involved in organizing and finding relationships in the information they study than they would if they passively received teacher-delivered bodies of knowledge. This active involvement results both in deeper understanding of the content studied and in an improved ability to think. The teaching models presented in this book are intended to actively involve students in the processes of taking in information and mentally transforming it into more organized and comprehensible forms.

When you have completed your study of this chapter, you should be able to meet the following objectives:

- Identify the significant elements of the teacher-effectiveness research.
- Describe what is meant by active teaching.
- Describe the differences between a models approach to instruction and other approaches.
- Identify the three major factors influencing the choice of a teaching model.
- Outline the differences between a behaviorist and an information-processing approach to learning.
- Describe the two major approaches to organizing internal knowledge.

To introduce these strategies, let's look at two teachers involved in learning activities with their students.

Carol Rand began her junior high English class by welcoming students and saying, "Today we're going to approach the way we think about the things we've read a little bit differently. To see what I mean, look up at the screen and describe the two passages that you see."

She then displayed the following information on the overhead projector:

1. On Friday, September 13, 1973, I was born to JoAnn and Bob Cheever. My mother said I smiled soon after arriving.
2. Robert H. Cheever, Jr. was born to JoAnn and Bob Cheever on Friday, September 13, 1973. The nurse told his mother that he smiled after making a hesitant cry.
3. As I place the carefully wrapped package on the park bench, I look up and see Molly walking across the street. I hope that she doesn't see me.
4. As George placed the carefully wrapped package on the park bench, he looked up and saw Molly walking across the street. He hoped that she didn't see him.

Carol then asked the students to look at the four passages and tell how the second and fourth items were similar and different from the first and third. "Simply tell us some of the things that are the same or different," she directed.

Individual students made a number of statements such as, "One and three have 'I' in them, but two and four have a person's name instead of 'I'," "All four passages describe an event," and "People are involved in all four passages."

Based on the students' observations, Carol asked a number of directed questions that guided the students to an understanding of first- and third-person perspective in writing. She showed the students two more examples of each, the students discussed them, and as a homework assignment Carol asked the students to write a short narrative paragraph in both the first and third person.

Let's look now at another area and topic. As you read the second example, think about what the two lessons have in common.

Dan Harris was beginning a unit on immigration and its effect on America's development. He remembered from past experiences with this topic that it was sometimes hard to get his history class to appreciate and understand that immigration is a dynamic process that has shaped and is continuing to shape the American experience. To try to capture its ever-changing nature, he began the first lesson of the unit by saying, "All right everyone, I thought we might try a slightly different approach to begin our unit on immigration in America. Rather than just reading about the history of immigration and the different immigrant groups, I'd like each of you to go out into your neighborhoods and interview someone who has actually immigrated. If you have trouble finding someone, I'll help. When you locate this person, ask the following questions:

1. Why did you decide to come to America?
2. What were the major problems that you encountered in the move?
3. What was the biggest difference between this country and the one that you left?

TABLE 1.1

	Reasons For Coming	Hardships Encountered	Differences Between U.S. and Country of Origin
European Immigrants			
Central and South American Immigrants			
Asian Immigrants			

Write down the responses that you get, summarize them, and bring them to class, and we'll put them on the chart that I've attached to the board." The chart appeared as shown in Table 1.1.

After pausing for a minute to allow students to read, he went on, "When we have all the information on the chart, we will analyze the data for the similarities and differences we find, and we'll see if we can explain the differences."

What features do the two lessons have in common? Are there important differences between them? Please keep the lessons in mind as you study this chapter, and we'll see how they relate to the themes of the text.

Learning: A Cognitive Perspective

Let's think about the two lessons again. First, the teaching in each case was based on cognitive descriptions of learning, which view learners as active investigators of their environment (Resnick and Klopfer, 1989). This view is grounded in the premise that people instinctively strive to make sense of the world around them. In an effort to achieve the order they need, they investigate and structure the experiences they have. As a simple example, imagine walking down the hall of a school building, meeting a person, and saying, "Hi" or "Good morning." Because of our past experiences, we expect a similar response in return. If the person walks by us without saying anything, we're inclined to wonder, "What's wrong with her?" or "Sheesh, unfriendly person." (Probably nothing is wrong with her. We will look at this example again in Chapter 2.) Our understanding of the way the world works—particularly social graces in the professional world—is that we expect responses when we greet people. This is the way we've mentally structured our past experiences.

Similar processes are involved in academic learning experiences, which means that teaching strategies based on these views require that learners are active participants in the

learning process. These strategies ask students to examine the information they're studying, find relationships, and build understanding based on them. These relationships can be
as simple as seeing a pattern in rules for forming plural nouns to as complex as understanding how the Muslim domination of the Indian Ocean contributed to Columbus's voy-
age to the Americas.

If students are to be drawn into and involved in the process of meaning making, they
must be provided with information, which is a second characteristic of this approach to
instruction. Learners cannot think in a vacuum. Both Carol Rand and Dan Harris displayed
for the students information to be used as the basis for analysis.

A third similarity between the two activities is that both were thoroughly grounded in
research. Carol used examples to illustrate first- and third-person points of view, which are
potentially difficult ideas for junior high students. She dealt with the problem by first providing examples of these ideas and then asking students to provide their own. The value of
this practice in student learning is well documented in research literature (Tennyson and
Cocchiarella, 1986). Dan dealt with the need for illustrations and representations by asking the members of the class to bring in individual case study data to analyze. These case
studies then served as the basis for further analysis and discussion.

Fourth, Carol and Dan both actively directed and guided the students' analysis of the
information. Good (1983) coined the term **active teaching,** *which is a positive and proactive approach to teaching in which teachers are directly involved in guiding learning
through questioning and discussion.* It describes a basic philosophy and orientation in
which teachers play a major role in encouraging students to analyze and think about the
content they are learning.

Finally, both episodes were oriented toward problem solving. In both instances students were asked to find patterns in the information through their own investigation and
analysis. With practice in these processes, students learn not only the content of the lesson
but also develop the ability to solve academic problems (Bransford, 1993).

The similarities in the lessons are summarized as follows:

- The instruction was based on cognitive descriptions of learning which view learners
  as actively involved in making sense of their experiences.
- The teachers provided the students with information which the students analyzed dur-
  ing the lessons.
- The strategies were based on research.
- The teachers actively directed the students' analysis of the information they studied.
- The lessons had a problem-solving orientation.

Finally, while the lessons were related in many ways, the specific strategy each
teacher used was different. The goals of each lesson were different, and each teacher
chose a strategy most appropriate to reach the goal. This text is based on the view that
there is no single, most appropriate method for reaching every educational goal, and the
strategies we present in the following chapters are developed with that premise as a
framework.

To this point we have suggested that the text is developed from a research-based foundation of cognitive learning theory, which requires a direct and active teacher guiding the students' learning. Through the learning activities, students acquire a deep understanding of the topics they're studying while at the same time developing their higher-order thinking and their ability to solve problems. However, specific strategies vary according to the goals and style of the teacher. Let's examine each of these themes in more detail.

Research and the Teacher's Role in Learning

A large body of educational research underscores the importance of the teacher in helping students learn (Gage, 1985; Brophy and Good, 1986). The findings consistently indicate that the teacher is the single most important factor outside the home in affecting student learning and development. Teachers who have clear goals, actively strive for learning, and use effective methods produce results. This research also reinforces the idea that teaching and learning are enormously complex, and teachers must have a great deal of knowledge, understanding, and skill. In this section of the chapter we explore this research, place it in an historical perspective and discuss its implications for the teaching strategies that are most effective.

Educators haven't always been optimistic about the ability of research to guide classroom practice. In fact, during a period in the 1960s and 1970s both research and teachers themselves were given little credit for contributing to student learning. This pessimism was caused by a number of factors including faulty research designs and inefficient research procedures (Rosenshine, 1979; Gage and Giaconia, 1981).

One of the oldest traditions in research on teaching focused on teacher characteristics, which was based on the implicit assumption that teachers were "born and not made." (This idea is dying but not completely dead today.) The strategy that followed this assumption looked at teacher characteristics, such as warmth and humor, and investigated whether the presence or absence of these characteristics made any differences in student learning. However, the researchers often failed to determine whether these characteristics, typically measured on paper-and-pencil tests, produced any differences in actual teaching behaviors, let alone differences in student achievement. As we would expect, this approach proved unproductive and was ultimately abandoned.

Another line of research originating in the 1960s and extending into the 1970s focused on the relationship between home- and school-related factors and student learning (Coleman et al., 1966; Jencks et al., 1972). Largely refinements of earlier work, these studies searched for factors that correlated with student achievement. They suggested that the most important variables impacting school learning were outside the classroom and even the school; they included factors such as parents' income and educational background, which were unalterable and outside education's sphere of influence. Needless to say, both researchers and teachers were discouraged by the results. The data seemed to suggest that the most important variables in learning were beyond educators' control. In addition, these results led to sharply reduced national and state funding for educational research. With reduced economic support, research efforts were made even more difficult.

Teachers Do Make a Difference:
The Teacher-Effectiveness Research

However, from this discouragement a new and productive paradigm—one focusing on teacher actions in the classroom—emerged. It resulted from the convergence of two separate lines of research. One was a re-analysis of the Coleman et al. (1966) data we described earlier. This re-analysis focused on individual schools and individual teachers and found that there were large differences in the effectiveness of both. When the effects of home variables were held statistically constant, researchers found striking differences in student achievement at both the school and teacher levels. Certain schools and teachers were much more effective in producing student learning than were others (Brophy and Good, 1986; Good and Brophy, 1986). The logical questions to be asked were, "Why?" and "How?"

Answers came from subsequent research that focused on observing teachers. These observational studies took investigators into classrooms and attempted to link teacher actions to student learning. Unfortunately, the first studies were guided by speculation and researcher beliefs about good teaching. For example, a theme that generated literally hundreds of studies was based on the idea that the more indirect a teacher was in asking questions and using student ideas the more students would learn (Dunkin and Biddle, 1974). However, the realities of the classroom as measured by the data collected did not match the hypotheses of the investigators.

It was not until the observational studies were combined with an additional model that the efforts became productive. This research model, which attempted to document the effects of teacher behaviors on student learning, is called effectiveness research; it became an important focus of attention in education. A major factor setting the effectiveness paradigm apart from the earlier efforts was the lack of any predisposition or preconceived notions on the part of the researchers as they conducted their investigations.

This research began with investigators identifying samples of teachers whose students scored higher than expected for their grade and ability levels on standardized achievement measures, as compared to teachers whose students scored as expected or below. They then analyzed the teachers' classrooms in both groups to see if any differences existed. The results were striking. Investigators found wide variation in the actions of the two groups, and *a description of these patterns—the patterns of teacher behavior that influence student learning—makes up the body of knowledge that we now call the* **teacher-effectiveness research.**

Although initially correlational in nature, the model was later advanced to include experimental investigations in which effective teaching behaviors identified by the correlational studies were then taught to new groups of teachers and their effects were measured (Gage and Giaconia, 1981; Gage, 1985). The behaviors of these teachers, and more importantly, the achievement of their students were compared to control groups of teachers and students; the results indicated that the effective teachers acted differently and their students learned more. These teacher-effectiveness studies have focused on a diverse spectrum of behaviors ranging from classroom management strategies to homework and seatwork practices. The overriding conclusion from this research is that teachers *do* indeed make a difference. (We will examine specific teacher-effectiveness behaviors in Chapter 2.)

Beyond Effective Teaching

The literature on effective teaching made an invaluable contribution to education because it both confirmed the critical role teachers play in student learning and provided "education with a knowledge base capable of moving the field beyond testimonials and unsupported claims toward scientific statements based on credible data" (Brophy, 1992, p. 5). It provides, however, only a threshold or a base line above which all teachers should be. Expert teachers go beyond this threshold to construct lessons that help students learn content in a meaningful way. Further, critics have argued that the behaviors specified in the teacher-effectiveness research are too fragmented and simplistic in their orientation, focusing on isolated skills that students are reinforced for demonstrating, instead of aiming at conceptual growth. Actual understanding may or may not occur (Marshall, 1992).

Teaching for Understanding

How do we know if we're teaching for understanding, and what do we mean by "understanding?" The answer is not as simple as it appears. Perkins and Blythe (1994) describe understanding as ". . . being able to do a variety of thought-demanding things with a topic—like explaining, finding evidence and examples, generalizing, applying, analogizing, and representing the topic in a new way" (pp. 5–6). The teaching models described in this text are designed to help teachers ensure that their students' learning is at the level of understanding and not at the level of memorization, which is so prevalent in schools today.

Teacher questioning provides a beginning to this process, with questions such as:

"Why?"
"How do these compare?" ("How are they alike or different?")
"What would happen if . . . ?"

and particularly,

"How do you know?"

These questions can do much to promote student understanding. Surprisingly, teachers ask questions such as these less than 1 percent of the time (Boyer, 1983).

Teaching for understanding requires a concept consistent with both the teacher-effectiveness research and the movements that have extended this research. It is called *active teaching,* and we turn to it now.

Active Teaching

The term active teaching was created by Thomas Good (1983) to refer not only to a category of teaching behaviors but also a philosophical orientation to teaching. As the name implies, an active teacher is directly involved in student learning through the process of providing examples and other representations, asking questions that require more than mere recall, providing explanations, and monitoring student progress. It is based on the documented premise that teachers do indeed have an important impact on student learning.

Active teaching can be summarized as follows. Active teachers:

- Identify clear learning goals for their students.
- Select teaching strategies that will most effectively reach the learning goals.
- Provide examples and representations that help students acquire a deep understanding of the topics they study.
- Require that students are actively involved in the learning process.
- Guide students as they construct their understanding of the topics being studied.
- Carefully monitor students for evidence of learning.

A thread that runs through all of these characteristics is the central involvement of the teacher in the learning process.

A repertoire of effective teaching strategies is essential for active teachers. This is the topic of the next section of the chapter. If teachers are to help students learn, they must be able to select and use teaching strategies that produce learning. In doing this, the inevitable question concerning the best way to teach arises.

The Need for Instructional Alternatives

Arguments over questions about the best way to teach have absorbed educators' energies since the beginning of formal education. Attempts to answer this question have focused on authoritarian versus democratic techniques (Anderson, 1959), discovery-oriented versus expository approaches (Keislar and Shulman, 1966), teacher versus student centeredness (Dunkin and Biddle, 1974) and direct versus indirect approaches to teaching (Peterson and Walberg, 1979). Thousands of studies have been conducted in an attempt to answer this question in its various forms. The overriding conclusion from this research is: *there is no one best way to teach.*

Bruce Joyce and Marsha Weil first formalized the notion of varying procedures for different teaching situations when their book *Models of Teaching* was published in 1972. At that time the idea was quite new and perhaps even controversial. However, since then the logic of teachers being able to use different instructional strategies to meet different goals has become so widely accepted that it is no longer an issue. In fact, the need for teachers to be able to use different strategies is even more important today since learners are now more diverse (Villegas, 1991).

Teaching can be viewed as a task in which someone (the teacher) attempts to help one or more persons (the students) acquire understanding, skills, or attitudes (the subject matter). Each of these components influences the form of the teaching act. The models approach to teaching recognizes the importance of these components and integrates them into a decision-making framework based on three factors. These factors are:

- the teacher
- the students
- the content

We discuss these factors in the following sections.

Selecting Teaching Strategies: The Role of the Teacher

Teachers are probably the most important factors influencing the question of how to teach. Directing student learning at any level is a very personal and idiosyncratic enterprise. How we teach depends to a large extent on who we are (Kagan, 1992b). The goals that we select, the strategies that we use to reach the goals, and the way that we relate to students all depend on what we bring to the classroom as human beings.

Attempts to identify an ideal teacher type have proved fruitless. Hundreds of research studies investigating different types of teachers have indicated that there is no best personality pattern. Our own experiences in the classroom confirm these findings. Energetic, thoughtful, humorous, serious, traditional, and unorthodox teachers have all proven effective in different situations. Much of teachers' effectiveness lies in understanding their own personal strengths and preferences and adopting compatible teaching strategies.

Selecting Teaching Strategies: The Impact of Learners

Students are a second factor influencing the choice of a particular teaching strategy. Individual students respond differently to various instructional strategies (Corno and Snow, 1986). This effect has been called by some researchers an "aptitude-treatment interaction," with aptitude reflecting what students bring to a learning situation, and treatment describing our attempts to accommodate these differences (Cronbach and Snow, 1977). Studies indicate that in some cases practices found effective with one type of student are actually ineffective with others (Coker et al., 1980). Researchers in this area have found that what a student brings to the classroom may be as important as any other factor in determining the effectiveness of a given method.

Students differ in a number of important ways, varying in academic abilities, background, interest, and motivation. In addition, a student's culture, including the values, attitudes, and traditions of a particular group can also have an important influence on learning (Cushner et al., 1992). All of these individual differences influence the effectiveness of a particular instructional strategy.

Content and Teaching Strategies

A third factor influencing a teacher's choice of teaching strategy is the content being taught. For example, a social studies teacher may want the class to remember basic facts concerning the American Revolution in one lesson, to understand the assimilation problems encountered by immigrants to a country in a later unit, and to analyze the strengths of a democracy compared to a communist society in a third case. Though these tasks are similar in that they all involve American history, the goal in each case is different. The teacher is trying to teach factual information to one class, have the students understand the process of assimilation in the second, and develop analytical skills in the third. Since the goals are different, the strategies needed to reach the goals are also different; you don't, for example, teach factual information in the same way that you teach analytical skills.

Teachers' goals vary even within a single class period. A literature teacher discussing *The Raven,* for example, might want students to remember the poem's author, to relate the poem to the author's life, and to learn the concepts of *meter, rhyme,* and *imagery*. These goals are related but different, and each requires a different teaching strategy.

Similar situations exist in elementary schools. In teaching reading, for instance, the teacher will want students to be able to correctly pronounce words, identify the major theme of a story, explain cause-and-effect relationships, and predict the consequences of certain events in the story. Again, the teacher's goals are related, but different. Trying to reach all of the goals in the same way is impossible.

This text is based on the premise that no single approach to teaching is appropriate in all situations, and consequently, effective teaching requires different strategies to reach different goals. The best strategy is the one that is most effective for reaching a particular goal in a specific situation. Only when teachers are aware of different types of content can they identify the most effective strategy, and the actual selection and use of a strategy can occur only if the teacher possesses a repertoire of techniques. The use of optimal strategies demands knowledge of alternatives. This book is designed to provide the alternatives in the form of teaching models.

The Models Approach to Teaching

Teaching models *are prescriptive teaching strategies designed to accomplish particular instructional goals.* They are prescriptive in that the teacher's responsibilities during the planning, implementing, and assessment stages of instruction are clearly defined. The models described in this book are designed for active teaching, but they could also be used as a guide for curriculum design or for choosing and constructing instructional materials.

Models differ from general teaching strategies in that models are designed to reach specific goals. The use of models requires an ability to specify precise learner outcomes so that a specific model can be selected to match a particular goal.

To better understand this process and how a teaching model relates to it, let us compare the role of a teacher using a model to that of an engineer. In considering a project, an engineer first identifies the type of structure to be built, such as a building, a bridge, or a road. Having done so, an appropriate design or blueprint is selected. The specifications of the blueprint determine the actions the builder takes and the kind of building that will result. The type of blueprint depends on the type of structure to be built. Similarly, teachers considering a model first identify what is to be taught and then select a strategy to reach that goal. The model is specifically designed to achieve a specified goal and will determine in large part the actions of the teacher.

A teaching model, then, is a type of blueprint for teaching. Extending this analogy, other similarities between a teaching model and a blueprint can be seen. Several disciplines, such as physics, structural engineering, and architecture, influence the design of a building. Similarly, many disciplines influence the design of teaching models. Anthropology, sociology, linguistics, and psychology have all impacted the models currently used in schools. Psychology is probably the most significant of these influences.

Each of the models discussed in this text is based on learning theory. The theories focus on different aspects of the learner, and as a result, their implications for teaching vary. The implications are then translated to the teacher through the teaching model. In a similar manner, the procedures to be followed in building a structure are translated to the engineer through the blueprint, based upon architectural theories of design.

The teacher is analogous to the builder; just as the builder is ultimately responsible for the structure, the teacher is ultimately responsible for accomplishing the goals of a lesson. Further, just as a blueprint provides structure and direction for the builder, the model provides structure and direction for the teacher. However, a blueprint does not dictate all of the actions of a builder, and a model cannot dictate all of the actions taken by a teacher.

A blueprint is not a substitute for basic engineering skill, and a teaching model is not a substitute for basic teaching skills. A model cannot take the place of fundamental qualities in a teacher, such as knowledge of subject matter, creativity, and sensitivity to people. It is, instead, a tool to help good teachers teach more effectively by making their teaching more systematic and efficient. Models provide sufficient flexibility to allow teachers to use their own creativity, just as the builder uses creativity in the act of construction. As with a blueprint, a teaching model is a design for teaching within which the teacher uses all of the skill and insights at his or her command.

The number of possible teaching goals is so large and diverse that it is impossible to discuss them all in depth in one book. As indicated in the introductory section of this chapter, this text will focus on one set of related tasks called *information processing*. We now turn to discussion of these strategies.

Information Processing

Educational goals are typically divided into three families or domains: affective, psychomotor, and cognitive. Emotional and social development goals are in the affective domain; the acquisition of manipulative and movement skills is classified as psychomotor; and cognitive goals address the development of the student's intellect. Each family is important and will be described briefly in the paragraphs that follow.

The affective domain considers a student's self-concept, personal growth, and emotional development. Teachers who work in this area need skill in helping students diagnose and find solutions to personal and social problems. Goals such as the "ability to work with peers," "consideration of the elderly," or "willingness to listen to other people's ideas" all fall within this domain. Affective goals are attitudinal in nature and do not have students' intellectual growth as their primary focus.

The psychomotor family, by comparison, is concerned with the development of muscular skill and coordination. This area includes goals such as "learning how to sew a buttonhole," "developing a good tennis serve," or "learning to operate a wood lathe." While intellectual skills enter into each of the psychomotor tasks, the primary focus is on the development of manipulative skills rather than on the growth of intellectual capability.

Cognitive goals center on the intellectual growth of the individual. Growth in this area includes the acquisition of basic skills such as reading, writing, and mathematics, as well as the learning of facts, concepts, and generalizations. The explicit focus of schools is primarily in this domain.

Within the cognitive family is an important set of goals called information processing. While admittedly oversimplified, **information processing** *can be thought of as the way* *people gather and organize information from the environment in order to form useful patterns that can be used to explain and predict events in their experience.* Information-processing goals focus on the acquisition of knowledge through an analysis of information from the world around us. They are aimed at intellectual growth achieved by students' active investigation of their environment rather than the emotional or social development of the individual.

Teachers who focus on information-processing goals have two sets of objectives. One helps students develop a deep understanding of specific topics taught in schools; the other helps them develop the cognitive skills that will allow them to learn on their own. Information-processing strategies designed to teach specific topics and develop learners' cognitive skills help teachers reach both sets of objectives.

Information-processing teaching strategies are based on a movement in psychological thinking that views the learner as an active investigator of the environment rather than a passive recipient of stimuli and rewards. This emphasis can be described as ". . . a view that treats man as a searcher after, processor of, and indeed, creator of, information" (Farnham-Diggory, 1972, p. xiii). The brain is considered to be an organ whose primary function is "to actively seek, select, acquire, organize, store, and, at appropriate times, retrieve and utilize information about the world" (Smith, 1975, p. 2).

In a more recent quote, Brophy (1992) puts the learner at the center of the learning process by stating:

> *Current research . . . focuses on the role of the student. It recognizes that students do not merely passively receive or copy input from teachers, but instead actively mediate it by trying to make sense of it and to relate it to what they already know (or think they know) about the topic. Thus, students develop new knowledge through a process of active construction (p. 5).*

This is the essence of information processing. It stresses the importance of meaningful learning versus rote memorization of content.

Dissatisfaction with Behaviorism: The Growth of Information Processing

Information-processing psychology developed from a dissatisfaction with behaviorism (Mayer, 1987). The behaviorist approach describes learning in terms of conditioning and stimulus-response pairing. For example, a teacher question is a stimulus and a memorized answer is the response. A common procedure in investigating learning within the behaviorist tradition was the serial learning task (Murdock, 1992). As an example of serial learning, consider the following:

> Examine the following list of words for about three seconds each and then cover the list with a piece of paper. Then count backwards from twenty by twos. (In formal learning studies the words would be presented one at a time for a fixed period of time. Other aspects of the study such as counting backwards—designed to keep you from rehearsing the information—and the recall task itself would be more tightly controlled.) When

you've finished counting, try to recall the words in any order and compare your list with the original one.

Serial Learning List

Apple	Hammer	Banana
Cat	Pear	Hamster
Shovel	Parrot	Vice
Dog	Saw	Orange

In the behaviorist learning paradigm, the serial list that you encountered was the stimulus (or stimuli), and the list that you remembered was the response.

However, as researchers studied the learning process they encountered something unanticipated; learners did not reproduce the lists in the way they were presented. Instead, when given the freedom to recall these lists in any form they preferred, they would often produce reorganized lists such as the following:

Apple	Shovel	Cat
Pear	Hammer	Dog
Banana	Saw	Parrot
Orange	Vice	Hamster

It was obvious from these lists that something was going on in the learners' heads while they were attempting to memorize these words. They were using a memorization strategy that linked the new material to information they already had stored in their memories. Learners grouped words into categories, such as fruits or animals, and used these categories to retrieve the information. Rather than *passively* facing the learning tasks, learners *actively* restructured the information to take advantage of existing categories of knowledge.

These experiments led psychologists to believe that the most interesting components in a learning experiment were not the stimuli or the responses, but rather what was going on in learners' heads when they were faced with the tasks. This emphasis on mental processes and cognitive structures stressed the importance of the way people process information. The central goal of this processing is to make the world more comprehensible.

Information-processing psychologists think about the cognitive structure in learners' minds in one of two major ways. Let's look at them now.

Cognitive Structures as Conceptual Frameworks

One way of viewing the information we have stored in our memories is to think of it as *an organized and interconnected network of ideas often called a* **conceptual framework.** For example, the framework for a child's concept of *dog* might be represented as shown in Figure 1.1.

Each person's conceptual framework around an idea is personal and idiosyncratic, and reflects that person's exposure to the concept. The framework for a child who has or raises dogs is quite different from that of a child who has not been around them. More impor-

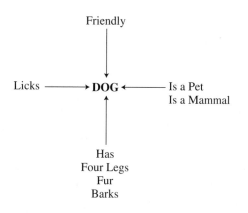

FIGURE 1.1   A Conceptual Framework

tantly, each person's conceptual framework determines how new information will be encoded. A complex framework has many points to which new information can be connected, resulting in more information being stored in memory; a simple framework's number is limited, so less information is stored. The patterns we see in schools support this notion. Students who come to us with a wealth of past experiences typically learn more and faster than those who have not had such experiences. They have more elaborate mental frameworks to which new information can be attached, which makes their learning more meaningful. This premise is a fundamental principle that undergirds early enrichment programs for at-risk students.

Cognitive Structures as Schemas

A second way of thinking about cognitive structures is to describe them as scripts or **schemas,** *which describe knowledge as dynamic and useful sets of interconnected ideas, relationships, and procedures.* Schemas not only organize information and tell us what to expect from the world; they also tell us how to operate within it. Each of us has a schema for driving cars, for example. Our schemas allow us to get into a strange car, put the key in the ignition, and with a minimum of fuss, start it and drive away. Schemas allow us to store past information in usable forms and to integrate new information into existing ones. For example, if we understand how to drive a car with an automatic transmission, learning how to drive with a stick shift is much easier than if we've had no experience with driving. New information about the stick shift is incorporated into the existing schema for driving, which includes starting the car, obeying traffic regulations, and other aspects of driving.

Storing Knowledge: The Role of Information Processing

As new information is attached to knowledge that already exists in our memories, whether viewed as networks or schemas, both short-term and long-term memory are involved. Short-term memory is limited in capacity and duration. It functions, for example, when we look up a telephone number. We retain it long enough to dial the number, and it is then forgotten. In contrast, long-term memory is virtually unlimited in capacity and duration; through it we are able to remember things that occurred years ago (Eggen and Kauchak, 1994).

Information processing moves the information from short-term to long-term memory. The quality of that processing determines how effectively the information is stored in long-term memory and how easily we can retrieve it at some later time.

To illustrate this process, let's look at a fourth grader's developing understanding of the concepts of *mass, volume,* and *density.* Suppose the child sees a balance with blocks of unequal volume, such as the one shown in Figure 1.2.

The child's observations of the balance and blocks enters her short-term memory. If her thinking is typical of fourth graders, the child will initially conclude that the mass of block A is greater than that of block B (Eggen and McDonald, 1987). If not corrected, the information about the blocks will enter her long-term memory in this form, consistent with the common misconception that large objects (objects with greater volume) have more mass than smaller objects (objects with less volume).

With guidance, however, the child will see that the balance is equalized, and therefore the masses of the two blocks must be the same. With further guidance and discussion, the child will recognize that block A must be less dense than block B, since its volume is greater than the volume of block B, and the masses of the two blocks are equal. To develop this understanding the child has *processed the information.* (We should point out, however, that a misconception doesn't mean that no information has been processed. The results of the processing are simply invalid.)

The point in this illustration is that a learner has taken information from the environment, transformed it into ideas that made sense to the child, and stored this information in his or her long-term memory. The process of transforming information into meaningful ideas is the essence of information processing. The strategies described in this text are designed to take advantage of our ability as learners to actively investigate the environment and make sense of our experiences.

Processing that emphasizes meaningfulness is superior to rote memory as a way of storing information in memory (Eggen and Kauchak, 1994; Rosenshine and Stevens, 1986). **Meaningfulness,** while overused in the educational literature, has a precise definition; *it refers to the number of links or associations between an idea and other ideas.* The more links, the more meaningful the idea. For example, we have made an effort to make the concept of *teaching model* more meaningful for you by associating it with engineering. As you continue the study of this text, we hope the meaningfulness will increase as you begin to make associations between the models and various forms of content, thinking abilities, types of reasoning, and modifications.

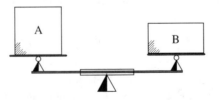

FIGURE 1.2   Balance with Blocks of Unequal Volume

As noted earlier in this section, information processing involves a dual relationship that includes the acquisition of organized bodies of knowledge and the intellectual skills necessary to learn independently. We turn now to a discussion of these skills.

Cognitive Skills in the Classroom

In recent years considerable emphasis has been placed on the school's role in the development of students' higher-order and critical thinking (Bransford et al., 1991; Nickerson, 1988; Resnick and Klopfer, 1989). Educators are recognizing that it is no longer sufficient to simply teach students *what* they should know, but in addition they must be taught *how* to know. Psychology in general and information processing specifically provide one framework for addressing the development of students' thinking skills and abilities (Steinberg, 1985; Rosenshine and Stevens, 1986).

Students' higher-order and critical thinking abilities develop when they are provided opportunities to practice these skills across diverse areas of curriculum. As illustrations of activities that develop students' cognitive skills, consider the following:

- A teacher wants her class to understand the concept of *participatory democracy*. She begins the lesson by providing the students with descriptions that range from their student government to the United Nations. She also includes cases of nonparticipatory governments for contrast. Students examine and discuss the similarities in the examples and identify the ways they are different from those that are nonparticipatory. They continue until they can specify the features of participatory democracy that are consistent with the examples.
- A field trip to the zoo is followed by the teacher asking the class to list all of the animals seen. The class then groups the members of the list in terms of similarities, and they discuss the basis for the groups.
- A biology teacher wants students to know how the human circulatory system operates. To reinforce the idea students are asked to form an analogy with the sanitary system of a city. Students make comparisons between analogous parts such as large water mains, pumping stations, and sewage-treatment plants.
- As an introductory activity in the reading of *Silas Marner,* a freshman literature class is given a handout describing two seemingly dissimilar characters. When told the descriptions are of the same person, students attempt to explain the disparity. The teacher uses these explanations as a basis for discussing the book.

Let's look now at the similarities in the examples. First, each teacher wanted the students to acquire a deep understanding of a particular topic. The topics ranged from understanding participatory democracy and the circulatory system to identifying the similarities among zoo animals and characters within a novel. Acquiring understanding was a central goal in each of the lessons. Development of higher-order and critical thinking was not pursued at the expense of content.

A second similarity is the *way* the students developed their understanding of the topics. They were presented with information and were involved in making comparisons, finding patterns, forming and documenting conclusions, and developing generalizations.

Rather than being passive listeners, they found their own relationships in the topics they studied with active guidance from the teacher.

It is our opinion, as well as the opinion of others working in the area (Bransford et al., 1991), that the most logical and productive way to teach students cognitive skills is to provide them with ongoing opportunities for practice. Students are given enormous amounts of experience in developing the basic skills of reading, writing, and various components of math. It should be no less the case with cognitive skills and strategies.

The most efficient way to provide this experience is by integrating the skills into the regular curriculum. This approach allows teachers to help students develop cognitive strategies without sacrificing content.

An alternate approach is to deal with thinking as a separate part of the curriculum, such as a course in "thinking." This approach has two important drawbacks. First, thinking and content are literally inseparable (Bransford, 1993). When students practice the skills, they must practice them on some form of knowledge. As we said earlier in the chapter, thinking is not done in a vacuum. Second, a separate approach to thinking skills also is less likely to succeed. Because thinking skills compete with other areas for time, a win-lose relationship develops. As more time is devoted to one area, less time is devoted to the other. The models presented in this book avoid this pitfall by integrating content and the development of cognitive strategies into comprehensive teaching models.

We will examine higher-order and critical thinking in more detail in Chapter 2.

Summary

In this chapter we discussed four separate but interrelated themes. Perhaps the most important of these is the idea developed from the teacher-effectiveness research that teachers make a difference in student learning and achievement. The book is based on the idea that an active teacher is a primary factor influencing learning in the classroom. A major goal of the text is to empower teachers with the knowledge, understanding, and strategies that will allow them to first acquire and then go beyond effective teaching to acquire genuine expertise in the processes of instruction.

Two additional themes of information processing and higher-order and critical thinking were also introduced in the chapter. Information processing as a major school of cognitive psychology provides the framework for the design of the effective teaching strategies described in Chapters 3–9 of the text.

Higher-order and critical thinking involve the ability to use information to find order in the world and solve problems. These goals are an essential part of the modern school curriculum. Information-processing teaching strategies provide an effective means of teaching these cognitive goals without sacrificing content.

The fourth theme presented was the models approach to instruction. Teaching models are specific teaching strategies designed to achieve specific goals. The models described in this text were developed to help students acquire a deep understanding of content while they simultaneously practice higher-order and critical thinking. These two interrelated goals are the focus of Chapter 2.

The themes and organization of the text are represented in the outline in Figure 1.3. We will develop these ideas as the text evolves.

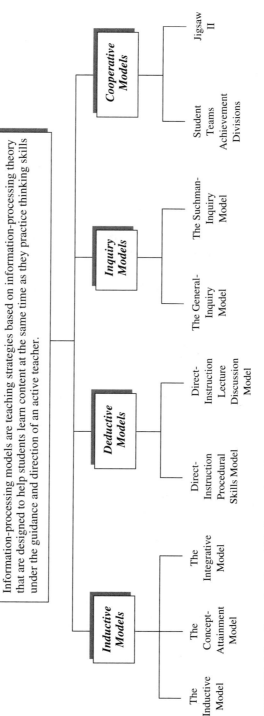

FIGURE 1.3 Organization of Information-Processing Models

Important Concepts

Active teaching (p. 5)

Conceptual framework (p. 14)

Information processing (p. 12)

Meaningfulness (p. 16)

Schemas (p. 15)

Teacher-effectiveness research (p. 7)

Teaching models (p. 11)

Discussion Questions

1. Refer to the short teaching episodes at the beginning of the chapter. How might the same content have been taught differently? What would be the advantages and disadvantages of the alternative approaches?

2. Describe a specific class you've been in that used an information-processing approach. In your description, explain how the three characteristics of information processing discussed in the first section of the chapter were either present or missing.

3. One criticism made of the effectiveness research is that teaching effectiveness was defined in terms of student performance on standardized achievement tests. What other important school outcomes might be missed or ignored by these tests?

4. Describe a particularly effective teacher that you've had in terms of the characteristics of active teaching described in this chapter. Do all of these characteristics apply? Are there some behaviors displayed by this teacher that were not described by the definition of active teaching?

5. Are there some times when a teacher doesn't want to take an active teaching role? If so, when would this be and what would the alternate role be?

6. Choose two different content areas of the curriculum (e.g., science versus language arts). Discuss how the content in each area might influence the choice of teaching methods.

7. Briefly describe your own personal goals for teaching and discuss how these might influence your choice of teaching methods.

8. How does the age or ability of a student influence the choice of a teaching strategy? Imagine that you are responsible for teaching the same basic content to three different classes ranging from remedial to accelerated. How would your teaching methods differ? (See Corno and Snow [1986] and Rosenshine and Stevens [1986] for excellent discussions of this problem.)

9. Describe a type of higher-order or critical thinking that you believe is important at your level or in your area of the curriculum. How would you go about teaching this type of thinking? How would you measure whether or not students adopted it?

C h a p t e r 2

Essential Teaching Skills and the Teaching of Thinking

I. Essential Teaching Skills: The Foundation for Teacher Effectiveness
   A. *Essential Teaching Skills: What Are They?*
   B. *Essential Teaching Skills: A Theoretical Perspective*

II. Beyond Effective Teaching: Thinking for Thinking and Understanding
   A. *Teaching Thinking: An Enduring Concern*
   B. *Teaching Thinking: Increasing Learner Motivation*
   C. *A Climate for Thinking*

III. Higher-Order and Critical Thinking
   A. *Higher-Order Thinking*
   B. *Critical Thinking*
   C. *Higher-Order and Critical Thinking: The Role of Metacognition*
   D. *Higher-Order and Critical Thinking: Attitudes and Dispositions*

In Chapter 1, you examined the history of the teacher effectiveness research and its most important finding—teachers have a major impact on the amount their students learn. The teacher-effectiveness research describes abilities that all teachers should have; it identifies the foundation for teaching expertise. Building on that foundation, we now move beyond effective teaching to examine instruction that results in learners' deep understanding of content and the acquisition of higher-order and critical thinking abilities.

The 1980s and 1990s have marked an unprecedented interest in student thinking and the ability to teach it (Presseisen, 1986). Poor performance on standardized tests by American students compared to students from other countries, concerns expressed by business leaders, and predictions of rapid technological change for the future have all contributed to this increasing interest.

A great deal about teaching thinking has been learned in the last fifteen years. Conceptions of intelligence and the nature of student development have changed, the significance of background knowledge for thinking is now accepted, and the importance of active learner involvement is emphasized as never before. These factors have contributed to more well-informed views of effective instruction for teaching thinking. Our goal for this chapter is to explain these views and examine their implications for teaching.

When you've completed your study of this chapter, you should be able to meet the following objectives:

- Identify in case studies examples of teachers displaying essential teaching skills.
- Demonstrate essential teaching skills in your own instruction.
- Describe factors that have contributed to educators' continued interest in teaching thinking.
- Identify characteristics of higher-order thinking.
- Identify characteristics of critical thinking.
- Describe the role that metacognition plays in utilizing higher-order and critical thinking.
- Describe the impact of attitudes and dispositions on the application of higher-order and critical thinking.

To begin our discussion of essential teaching skills and higher-order and critical thinking, let's observe an American History class.

Teri Bowden is beginning a unit on the colonization of North America with her American History students. We join her class as she is standing at the door greeting the students at 10:13 A.M. as they file into class for her third period.

"Good morning Suzanne, nice haircut. . . . Hey José, are you going to do as well today as you did yesterday?" she interjects as Suzanne and José walk into the room.

"David, that goes in your locker. . . . Hurry up. You have two minutes," she directs as he starts through the door with a basketball in his hand.

"Awe, Mrs. Bowden," David protests, walking away with a little grin on his face.

"Get to your seats quickly," Teri reminds them. "You have five minutes to answer the questions on the overhead."

As the bell stops ringing at 10:16, the students are peering at the overhead and hunching over their desks as Teri takes roll.

At 10:20 Teri asks, "How are you all coming?" Amidst "Fine," "Okay," and "Just about done," Teri says, "Okay, one more minute."

The students finish and pass their papers forward. Teri quickly goes over the exercises and says, "Get these out of your folders as you come in tomorrow morning."

"Now," she announces, turning to the class and shaking her finger for emphasis, "let's shift our thinking a little and begin to focus on the colonial period, which began in the 1600s. This is a very important part of American History, but what's most interesting about all of this is what we're studying has ramifications for the entire world, even today. Today's topic is one of the most important ideas of the entire colonial period, so let's see what kind of job we can do in figuring it out."

Damon smiled wryly and whispered to Charlene, "Bowden thinks *everything* is interesting."

Teri then continued, "To get us started I want you to look at the three short passages that I'm going to display on the overhead, and I want you to read them carefully and look for any patterns that might exist in them. So . . . our goal in this lesson is to look for patterns, and then we'll relate these patterns to the events we've been studying in American History."

She then displayed the following information:

In the mid-1600s the American colonists were encouraged to grow tobacco, since it wasn't grown in England. The colonists wanted to sell it to France and other countries but were forbidden to do so. In return, the colonists were allowed to import textiles from England, but were forbidden from making their own. All of the materials were carried on British ships.

Early French colonists in the New World were avid fur trappers and traders. They got in trouble with the French monarchy, however, when they attempted to make fur garments and sell them to Spain, England, and others. They were told that the produced garments would be sent to them from Paris instead. The monarchy also told them that traps and weapons must be made in France and sent to them as well. Jean Forge complied with the monarchy's wishes but was fined when he hired a Dutch ship to carry some of the furs back to Nice.

India was a "Jewel in the Crown" of the 19th-century British Empire. India produced large quantities of materials such as raw linens, foodstuffs, and salt. As the Indians became more nationalistic, however, trouble began. England wanted to produce the clothing from the raw materials in the home islands, and when the Indians tried to establish stronger ties with other countries to increase the scope of their trade, their endeavors were quickly squelched. England argued that the British homeland was more than capable of providing for India's needs, and further, it had a large and efficient fleet. This policy eventually led to Indian protest and ultimately to independence.

"Now let's take a look," Teri went on. "What kinds of reactions do you have? . . . Ann?"

Ann began hesitantly, "Each of the examples deals with some type of colony."

"Good start, Ann," Teri smiled. "And what, specifically, were the colonies? . . . Lenore?"

"There were the French and British colonies in North America, and the British colony in India."

"Looks like there were some problems," Rufus volunteered.

"Good observation, Rufus. What do you mean?"

". . . In each case the colony wanted to do something, but England and France wouldn't let colonists do it."

"Give us some specific examples if you can, . . . Eric?"

"The colonists produced something the parent country wanted, such as tobacco, or furs, or raw linen."

"Very observant, Eric!" Teri enthused. "Go on Pam."

". . . They sent the stuff to their parent country," Pam responded after carefully inspecting the information.

"And they couldn't send it anywhere else!" Steve jumped in, adding to the idea.

"That's very good, both of you. Where do you suppose Steve got that idea? Connie?"

". . . It says it right in the first two examples," Connie responded, "And in the third one it says that when India tried to establish stronger ties with other countries to expand the scope of its trade, colonists got in trouble."

"Excellent, everyone! Connie, good use of information to support your ideas. You've all improved a great deal in that regard. Keep going, . . . Mary."

". . ."

"What did they get in return in each case?"

". . . They got textiles from England, . . . and fur garments, traps, and stuff from France, . . . and clothing from England," Mary responded as she looked from case to case.

"And what did each get from other countries? Liz?"

". . . Nothing."

"They weren't allowed to," Bob jumped in.

"And what made you say that, Bob?"

"It says in the second example that they were told that their traps and weapons would be sent from France, and in the third example it says that the British argued that the homeland was more than capable of providing for India's needs."

"Does this tell us for certain that they weren't allowed to import goods from other countries?"

". . . Not exactly," Jill added. "We're sort of assuming it from the information, although it's really implied in the description."

"Very good, Jill. Class, notice that Jill used the word 'assume.' Actually she made a conclusion, and the term we use for that kind of conclusion is *infer*. Here the information wasn't directly in the data; she had to go beyond the data to form her conclusion. That's an inference. Nice job," Teri smiled gesturing with her arms to the class.

"Now let's go a bit farther. What other patterns do you see in the descriptions? Kim?"

". . ."

"How were the goods shipped, Kim?"

"On ships," Kim returned, bringing laughter from her classmates.

"Yes, good, Kim!" Teri laughed with them. "What ships, or whose ships?"

". . . In each case it was the ships from the parent country. It says that directly in the first case and in the second one it says that Jean Forge got into trouble when he hired a Dutch ship to carry some furs back to Nice."

"What evidence is there in the third case? Melinda?"

"They argued that they had a large and efficient fleet," Melinda quickly responded.

"OK, good, Melinda. Now anything else? . . . What do you think? Cherrie?"

". . . I think that they also couldn't make their own manufactured goods. It says in each case that when the colonists tried to make their own materials from the raw materials that they couldn't do it."

"They couldn't make *any* manufactured goods, not just those from the raw materials they provided," Kathy added.

"What made you say that?" Teri queried.

"The British colonists grew tobacco, but they weren't allowed to manufacture anything, not just something that you might make out of tobacco," Kathy answered.

"Yes, but you can't make anything out of tobacco," Gregg retorted.

"Oh yes you can," Kathy responded. "They could have made cigars and stuff."

"Those are both good points," Teri interjected. "Everyone, remember this," Teri noted, raising her voice. "This is important. Do you see how both Kathy and Gregg used information to support their arguments? Nice job!"

She then went on, "Do we have some other evidence that supports either Kathy's or Gregg's position, even though they're not really at odds?"

"I think so," Jack volunteered. "In the second case the French colonists were told not to manufacture traps and weapons, and they produced furs, so it wasn't just fur coats that were not allowed.

"That's excellent, everyone! Very good analysis of the information we have here. Now let's look back and see what we've found."

At that point Teri had the class look back at what they had done, summarized the common characteristics, and then continued. "We've examined the three cases, and now we want to take a broader look at the information in general. Let's begin. We have a situation where . . .? Toni?"

". . . Colonists related to a country producing only raw materials, no manufactured stuff," Toni began hesitantly.

"Good," Teri smiled, as she wrote what Toni had said on the board. "Go on."

". . . And they can only be sold to the mother country."

"Who in turn provided the manufacturing and the shipping," Gregg jumped in.

"Excellent!" Teri praised. "Very clear, succinct description of what we've been discussing."

"Now we know the features of this policy," she went on. "Does anyone know what it's called?"

". . ."

"This is called *mercantilism*. It was a colonial economic policy designed to make money for the parent country by taking colonial raw materials in exchange for manufactured products."

She then went on, "What other countries besides England and France have been *guilty* of mercantilism?"

The class then analyzed some additional examples, such as Belgium and the Netherlands, and discussed their mercantile policies.

Teri then continued, "Let's look again at the question I asked 'What other countries have been *guilty* of mercantilism?' What assumption is being made in that question?"

". . . It looks like you're suggesting that mercantilism is bad," Anthony offered tentatively.

"Good thinking," Teri smiled and gestured for emphasis. "That's exactly what it implies. Now, mercantilism may very well have been bad . . . exploitation of colonialized lands and that kind of thing. However, the question I asked had in it an *unstated* assumption. Recognizing unstated assumptions is part of the thinking process, and we all need to be on the lookout for that kind of thing. . . . Again, that's good thinking, Anthony."

She then continued, "Now look at another case and see if it illustrates mercantilism or not. Remember, be ready to explain why or why not when you've made your decision." She then displayed the following description on the screen:

> *Canada is a member of the British commonwealth. Canada is a large grain producer and exporter, deriving considerable income from selling grain to Great Britain, France, Russia, and other countries. This trade has also enhanced the shipping business for Greece, Norway, and Liberia, which carry most of the products. Canada, however, doesn't rely on grain alone. It is now a major producer of clothing, high tech equipment, and heavy-industry equipment.*

"What do you think? Is this mercantilism? . . . Someone? Amy, we haven't heard from you," she continued.

". . . I would say no," Amy responded after a few seconds of studying the description.

"OK, now tell us why."

". . . Well, there are several reasons," Amy went on. "Canada trades with several countries according to the information, uses a variety of ships to carry the goods, and produces a lot besides raw materials."

"Excellent analysis, Amy," Teri smiled. "Now that we're comfortable with that part, let's go a step farther and examine our thinking in this activity. What are some things you had to do in order to arrive at the conclusion? Start us off, Conchita."

". . . First we had to observe, so we would eventually recognize the essential characteristics," she responded.

"Good beginning! What else? Bob?"

"We hunted for a pattern in the three paragraphs."

"And we had to make comparisons before we could find the patterns," Amy added.

"Good. All of you! What else? Jack?"

"We had to separate out the relevant from the irrelevant information," Jack answered.

"For example?" Teri probed.

". . . Well, whether it was guns, or traps, or clothing, or whatever, really didn't matter. The important point was that the colonists weren't allowed to manufacture anything."

"Excellent, Jack! Now, go on. Patty?"

". . . We didn't see everything in the examples, so we had to infer some of it, and then you asked us for evidence to support our inference."

"Very good, Patty. Can you remember an example of where we did this?"

". . ."

"Can anyone think of an example of where we made an inference and then had to back it up?"

"I . . . think so," Patty volunteered. "Bob said that he bet that the colonies weren't allowed to get materials from other countries, and then used the example where France said the traps and weapons would be sent from there."

". . . Jill also said that it didn't tell us for sure, but that it was strongly implied and we inferred it from the information that we were given," Becky added.

"We also generalized when we formed the definition of mercantilism," Lisa Jo added. "We talked about those parts of mercantilism working in all cases, so that's generalizing, isn't it?"

"Yes it is. Your point is a good one; generalizing is a form of inference. Very well done, Lisa Jo," Teri responded.

"Let's move on," Teri continued. "We now want to examine the impact of mercantilism on other events during the colonial period, and we want to think about mercantilism in other parts of the world, such as Africa. . . . So, for tomorrow, I want you to read this article that I copied from one of the news magazines awhile back. As you read the article, think about how the information in it relates to what we discussed today. Your warm-up activity at the beginning of the class will ask you about some of the information in the article."

She then concluded, "You did a very nice job today. Your analysis of your own thinking is getting better and better. I'm proud of all of you."

To begin our discussion, let's look back at Teri Bowden's lesson and examine its implications for teaching. Three important features were demonstrated in the lesson:

1. She displayed teaching skills that all teachers—regardless of content area, grade level, or topic—should be able to demonstrate. We call these skills "essential teaching skills."
2. Her goal for developing higher-order and critical thinking and her content goal were integrated. Neither was "tacked on" to the other, and her instruction throughout the lesson was directed at both goals simultaneously.
3. Her lesson focused on deep understanding of a particular topic—the role of mercantilism in colonialization.

We examine each of these elements in detail in the following sections of the chapter. We begin with a discussion of essential teaching skills that all teachers should possess.

Essential Teaching Skills: The Foundation for Teacher Effectiveness

Imagine that you're sitting unnoticed at the back of a classroom. This could be a first-grade class studying basic math facts taught by a veteran teacher; a junior high life-science class studying different types of worms taught by a first-year teacher; or a high school English class reading and discussing one of Shakespeare's plays taught by a teacher with several years of experience. Regardless of the teacher's personality or background, the grade level of the students, or the topic being studied, some teacher behaviors increase the amount students learn more than other patterns. We call these patterns "essential teaching skills," and they are derived from the teacher-effectiveness research described in Chapter 1. Let's look at these patterns.

Essential Teaching Skills: What Are They?

We are all familiar with the notion of basic skills. These are the essential abilities in reading, writing, and mathematics that all learners must possess to function effectively in the world. (Increasing evidence indicates that in order to function in the 1990s and beyond, basic skills must include higher-order and critical thinking [Bransford et al., 1991]. We discuss this evidence later in the chapter.) **Essential teaching skills** are analogous to basic skills and can be described as *the critical teacher attitudes, skills, and strategies necessary to promote student learning.*

While we will discuss the skills separately for the sake of clarity, they are interdependent, and none is as effective alone as it is in concert with the others. The blend and appropriate application of the skills—in the context of particular lessons—are critical.

These essential teaching skills are outlined in Figure 2.1.

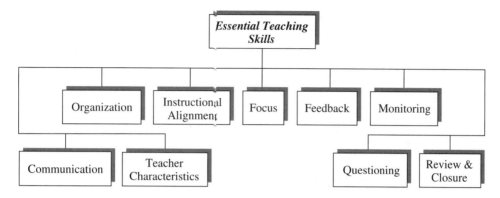

FIGURE 2.1   Essential Teaching Skills

Teacher Characteristics

While teacher characteristics are admittedly not skills, we want to begin with them anyway to emphasize how important they are to teaching. Teachers set the emotional tone for the classroom, design instruction, implement learning activities, and assess student progress. Their orientation toward teaching is critical in these processes.

With this as a frame of reference, let's turn again to Teri Bowden and her teaching. She identified clear goals and an effective strategy to reach the goals, she provided examples to help students acquire a deep understanding of her topic (her cases illustrating mercantilism), and she promoted and guided the students' active involvement throughout the learning activity. Hers was a positive, proactive orientation, based on the belief that all students can learn, and that it's her responsibility to try her hardest to be sure that all reach their maximum potential. These are the characteristics of active teaching (Good, 1983) that we described in Chapter 1.

In addition, Teri displayed four other characteristics essential for promoting a climate that increases learning and motivation. These characteristics are:

- Enthusiasm
- Modeling
- Warmth and empathy
- Positive expectations

Teacher Enthusiasm.   One of the characteristics of effective teachers is enthusiasm.

They care about what they teach and communicate to their students that what they are learning is important. Such teachers offer living proof of this and are apt models whose intensity beckons identification and inspiration (Wlodkowski and Jaynes, 1990, p. 19).

We see the effect of Teri's enthusiasm in Damon's comment, "Bowden thinks *everything* is interesting." While no one can suggest that teacher enthusiasm will make eager learners out of "turned-off" students, we have nothing to lose. If even a few students are more motivated and learn more because of our enthusiasm, we are ahead of where we would be if we were neutral or even unenthusiastic.

Teachers demonstrate enthusiasm in the way they use their voice, eyes, hand gestures, and body movements, in addition to the words they select (Collins, 1978). Some examples are:

- Varying pitch, loudness, and rate of delivery
- Making eye contact with students; having animated eyes
- Gesturing frequently with head and arms
- Moving from place to place; having an energetic manner
- Using descriptive language; varying word selection

Teri demonstrated each of these characteristics in her teaching.

Teacher Modeling.   Modeling *occurs when people imitate behaviors they observe in others* (Bandura, 1986). Teachers communicate a great deal about their attitudes toward what they're teaching and beliefs about what is important through modeling. It is nearly impossible to be effective if teachers model distaste or lack of interest in the topics they teach. In contrast, if teachers display a pattern of statements such as Teri's, ". . . but what's most interesting about all of this is that what we're studying has ramifications for the entire world, even today," motivation and learning—over time—can be increased.

Teacher Warmth and Empathy.   Let's look again at how Teri began her class period. She made an attempt to greet the students personally as they walked in the door, and even when she told David that he had to take his basketball back to his locker, she did it in a nonpunitive way.

Warmth *refers to teachers' abilities to demonstrate that they care for students as people;* **empathy** *is teachers' capacities for understanding how students feel, what their points of view might be, or where they're "coming from."*

Research documents the importance of these qualities (Blumenfeld, 1992; Wlodkowski and Jaynes, 1990). It is difficult to be a truly effective teacher without caring about students. Even young children are able to perceive differences in the caring of their teachers (Robinson et al., 1981), and a negative emotional climate is associated with lowered achievement (Soar and Soar, 1978).

One of the best indicators of caring is a teacher's willingness to give time. Let's look at a letter a ninth-grade student wrote to her geography teacher to see an example taken from an actual classroom. (The teacher's name has been changed, but the student's note is verbatim.)

Mrs. Hanson,
I want to thank you for everything you have done for me this year. I think that you're the only teacher I've had who believed in me and gave me the confidence I really needed.

In a sense, I went to you when I couldn't turn to my own family and I want to thank you for always having time for me and my problems.

I don't want this letter to sound "cheesy" or "sucking up." It's just that I would have never gotten through the year without you and your advice.

You never treated me just as a student, but as a person unlike most teachers have and that's what makes a great teacher, and Mrs. Hanson you certainly are a great teacher.

Sincerely,

Lisa Zahorchak

All students need the support and caring of teachers, and students having personal, adjustment, or behavior problems have an even greater need for this support. Warmth and empathy are often communicated by a teacher's willingness to take that extra minute with students.

Positive Teacher Expectations.

Mrs. Cummings watched as her new fifth-grade class filed into her room. She noticed a girl named Nicole and recalled that she had had Nicole's brother Mike two years earlier. Mike had been an above-average student with excellent study habits, and he was a pleasure to work with in class. Their parents were very involved in the children's schoolwork, and the home environment was positive.

Mrs. Cummings didn't know, however, that Nicole had few of her brother's study habits. She was a happy-go-lucky girl interested in socializing, and she was already developing an interest in boys. Schoolwork was not a high priority for her.

Mrs. Cummings greeted Nicole with a big smile, told her it was nice to have her in class, and that she was sure that they would have a very good year.

Partway through the grading period, Mrs. Cummings was scoring some math papers and noticed that Nicole's was missing. In checking her book, she found that two other assignments were also missing and that Nicole had been scoring a bit lower on the tests than Mrs. Cummings had anticipated.

The next day she called Nicole to her desk before class, put her arm around her, and said, "Honey, I can't imagine what happened to your homework papers. Please find them and turn them in. If you get them in by tomorrow, you'll get credit."

To be on the safe side, she called Nicole's parents that evening. They had been unaware of the missing homework and commented that Nicole had been rather vague when they asked if she had any homework for the next day.

Nicole's parents took immediate action. They postponed TV and telephone conversations until they saw that all her homework was finished and correct, and they called Mrs. Cummings—at Mrs. Cummings's request—to check on Nicole's progress. Mrs. Cummings reported that things were much better and that Nicole had improved considerably on the last test (adapted from Kauchak and Eggen, 1993).

Consider Mrs. Cummings's responses to Nicole. Because of her positive experiences with Nicole's brother, she had similar positive expectations for Nicole and her behavior. Because of these expectations she greeted Nicole warmly, and when Nicole's behavior was

TABLE 2.1   Characteristics of Differential Teacher Expectations

Characteristic	Teacher Behavior Favoring Perceived High Achievers
Emotional support	More interactions; more positive interactions; more eye contact and smiles; stand closer; more direct orientation to student
Teacher effort and demands	Clearer and more thorough explanations; more enthusiastic instruction; require more complete and accurate student answers
Questioning	Call on more often; allow more time to answer; prompt more
Feedback and evaluation	More praise; less criticism; provide more complete and lengthier feedback; more conceptual evaluations

less industrious than Mike's had been, she acted immediately. As a result, Nicole's work improved. Mrs. Cummings expected Nicole to learn and she behaved in a way that promoted that learning.

Teacher expectations *are inferences that teachers make about the future behavior or academic achievement of their students, based on what they know about these students now* (Good and Brophy, 1994, p. 83). They exert a powerful influence on teachers' behaviors. Believing that students can and will learn (positive teacher expectations) is a key variable that separates teachers who produce high student achievement from those who don't (Good, 1987).

Unfortunately, teachers are often unconsciously discriminatory, treating students they perceive to be high achievers more favorably than those they perceive to be lower achievers. Students quickly recognize these differences. "After ten seconds of seeing and/or hearing a teacher, even very young students could detect whether the teacher talked about or to an excellent or a weak student and could determine the extent to which that student was loved by the teacher" (Babad et al., 1991, p. 230).

Differential treatment falls into four dimensions: emotional support, teacher effort and demands, questioning, and feedback and evaluation. These four areas are summarized in Table 2.1 (based on reviews by Good, 1987; and Good and Brophy, 1994. Adapted from Eggen and Kauchak, 1994).

Good and Brophy (1994) observe, "Sometimes our expectations about people cause us to treat them in ways that make them respond just as we expected they would" (p. 87). This statement illustrates the self-fulfilling nature of teacher expectations.

Being treated differently affects the way learners feel about themselves. Students "learn" that they have lower ability or are less worthy if they are consistently left out of discussions or have interactions with teachers that are brief and superficial. Students are very aware of differences in treatment, and these differences can have a powerful effect on both motivation and achievement. High expectations communicate that the teacher believes students can learn and cares enough to make the effort to promote that learning. Over time, learning is increased.

Communication
The importance of teachers being able to communicate clearly is intuitively sensible, and research documents a strong link between communication and student achievement

(Cruickshank, 1985; Snyder et al., 1991), as well as student satisfaction with instruction (Snyder et al., 1991).

Clear communication can be classified into four elements:

- Precise terminology
- Connected discourse
- Transition signals
- Emphasis

Precise Terminology.   If we look again at Teri Bowden's instruction, we see that she described her ideas clearly, and her explanations and answers to questions avoided the use of terms such as *perhaps, maybe, might, and so on, probably, and usually.* These vague phrases leave students with a sense of uncertainty, resulting in lowered achievement (Smith and Cotten, 1980).

Precise terminology *means that teachers define ideas clearly and eliminate vague terms from presentations and answers to students' questions.* While it's impossible to eliminate all vague terms from presentations, with effort teachers can make their language much more precise, which in turn contributes to increased achievement by students.

Connected Discourse.   **Connected discourse** *means the teacher's lesson is thematic and leads to a point.* Teri Bowden's lesson is a clear example of connected discourse. The theme of the lesson was the concept *mercantilism,* and the entire lesson was developed around that theme.

In contrast, let's look at another example.

A teacher is beginning a lesson on the Civil War with a group of fifth graders. She tells the students that the goals of the lesson are to understand the dynamics of the war, to understand what caused the war, and why the North won. Prior to the lesson she lists several terms on the chalkboard, such as "Appomattox," "amendment," "free state," "Underground Railroad," "sectionalism," "abolitionists," and "secede."

After she states her goal she begins by explaining the concept of sectionalism and shows the students different sections of the United States on a small map. She then goes on with a question-and-answer activity in which she asks the students how they think it would feel to be a slave, continues with a brief discussion of Abraham Lincoln, an equally brief discussion of why they think the North won the war, and some information on reconstruction.

Here we see that the teacher discussed sectionalism, what it would feel like to be a slave, Abraham Lincoln, why the North won the war, and reconstruction, all in the same lesson. The lesson was not thematic and it didn't lead to a particular point. Her instruction would be described as disconnected or "scrambled" discourse.

There are two major obstacles to the goal of connected lessons: the presentation can be sequenced inappropriately, or information can be added to the discussion without clearly indicating how it relates to the topic. Both problems existed in the lesson on the Civil War, while neither was a problem in Teri Bowden's instruction.

Transition Signals.   Transition signals also contribute to clear communication. A **transition signal** *is a verbal statement that communicates that one idea is ending and another is beginning.* As an illustration, let's look again at Teri Bowden's comment, "Now let's shift our thinking a little and begin to focus on the colonial period, which began in the 1600s." This comment prepared the students to move from the warm-up exercises to the lesson for the day.

During any lesson, students are at different places mentally. Transition signals focus students' attention, increasing the likelihood that they will be concentrating on the appropriate topic.

Emphasis.   A fourth aspect of clear classroom communication is emphasis. **Emphasis** *alerts students to important information in a lesson and can occur through vocal and verbal behavior or repetition* (Eggen and Kauchak, 1994). Research indicates that each form of emphasis increases achievement by focusing student attention on important information (Mayer, 1983). When Teri said, "Those are both good points. Everyone, remember this, . . . [raising her voice] . . . This is important. Do you see how both Kathy and Gregg used information to support their arguments? Nice job!" she was emphasizing the fact that providing evidence was important in the lesson. Use of this type of emphasis increases the clarity of communication and helps students follow the theme of the lesson.

Repeating a point also signals that an idea is important. For instance, statements such as, "Remember when Juanita said that amphibians have a three-chambered heart? That tells about their position in the chain of evolution," or "What did Juanita say about the structure of the heart of amphibians?" Both the statement and the question are forms of repetition, which in turn are a part of emphasis.

Language and Knowledge of Content.   Our discussion of clear language has two important implications for teachers. First, we must try to monitor our own speech to ensure that our presentations are as clear and logical as possible. Videotaping lessons and developing lessons with many questions are simple and effective ways to check on the clarity of our speech. Second, we must thoroughly understand the content we teach. If the content is unfamiliar, or our own grasp of it is uncertain, we should spend more time studying and preparing. Teachers whose understanding of topics is thorough use clearer language and form better explanations than those whose background is weaker (Carlsen, 1987; Cruickshank, 1985).

Clear understanding is particularly important when using instructional models that emphasize teachers guiding learners rather than lecturing to them. Guiding learning requires that teachers keep their goals constantly in mind, keep students involved, and ask appropriate questions at the right times. These are sophisticated abilities that require that the teacher's understanding of the topics be deep and thorough.

Organization

Organization is intuitively sensible. We have all complained at one time or another about our lack of organization, and many of us have probably made conscious efforts to improve it. It affects the way we live, and also, of course, our teaching. Teachers who are "organized" have students who learn more than their less organized counterparts (Bennett, 1978; Rutter et al., 1979).

TABLE 2.2   Characteristics of Effective Organization

Characteristic	Example
Starting on time	Teri's students were in their desks and working on her "warmup" activity when the bell rang to begin the period.
Materials prepared in advance	Teri's materials were displayed on the overhead as her students walked in the door. The examples for her lesson were at her fingertips.
Established routines	The students knew how to pick up their papers from their folders without being told.

A key factor in organization is time. Effective teachers manage to squeeze more minutes of instruction into the amount of time they have allocated than do less effective teachers, and organization is a key factor in this wise use of time.

Important characteristics of effective organization are outlined and illustrated in Table 2.2.

Each of the characteristics in Table 2.2 allows teachers to maximize the time available for instruction. Beginning classes promptly, having materials prepared in advance, using warm-up activities at the beginning of classes, and having students trained to perform routine tasks without being told all help teachers use their time well.

Organization and Classroom Order.   A large body of research indicates that teachers' ability to maintain orderly classrooms is one of the most important factors influencing student achievement (Blumenfeld et al., 1987; Evertson, 1987). Good (1979), in a review of this research, observed, "Teachers' managerial abilities have been found to relate positively to achievement in every process-product study conducted to date" (p. 54).

Classroom order is also closely related to the quality of instruction—to which the remaining chapters in this book are devoted—and teacher organization. In looking again at Teri Bowden's organization, we see that students had a task waiting for them when they walked in the room, which they completed while Teri took roll. This prevents "down time" at the beginning of the period—one of the times that management problems are most likely to occur. Further, her well-established routines allowed her to devote more of her energy to instruction instead of having to spend both physical and mental energy maintaining order.

It should be emphasized that classroom order doesn't mean teacher lecture and passive students. We saw that Teri's class was very orderly, but that a great deal of interaction took place throughout the lesson. Order implies that the students are spending as much of their time focused on learning as possible; it doesn't mean that they sit quietly while a teacher does all the talking.

Classroom order also increases student motivation. Brophy (1987), in describing what he calls "essential preconditions for motivating students," concluded, "Nor is such motivation likely to develop in a chaotic classroom. Thus we assume that: . . . the teacher uses classroom organization and management skills that successfully establish the classroom as an effective learning environment" (p. 208). Classroom order is an essential ingredient of effective teaching, and it is virtually impossible to be a truly effective teacher without being an effective manager.

Instructional Alignment

Instructional alignment *refers to the match between objectives and learning activities* (Cohen, 1987). In looking again at Teri Bowden's instruction, we see that her goals were clear and concise; she wanted students to understand the concept of mercantilism while at the same time practice higher-order and critical thinking. Her instruction was pointed directly toward those goals, and her assignment for the next day—to read a news article and relate the information to mercantilism—was also directly related to her goals.

While the notion of instructional alignment seems simple, a surprising number of teachers have goals and learning activities that are not congruent. Even worse, in some cases the instruction doesn't seem to be pointed to any particular goal.

As a contrasting example, let's look again at the teacher in the lesson on the Civil War. We said earlier that she described her goals as understanding the dynamics of the war—to understand what caused the war, and why the North won. We found that she also listed several terms on the chalkboard and then discussed sectionalism, what the students thought it would feel like to be a slave, Abraham Lincoln, why students think the North won the war, and some information on reconstruction. After the discussion, the teacher assigned an in-class essay on the war using the terms she had listed on the chalkboard. Finally, she gave the students a homework assignment in which they were supposed to write a paragraph describing what the term *indivisible* meant to them, and the lesson was ended.

This is a case of instruction that was almost completely out of alignment. The only part of the learning activity that related to her goal was the brief discussion of reasons why the North had won the war. At no point in the lesson did she use or refer to any of the terms on the chalkboard, yet her seatwork assignment focused on those terms. Then, her homework assignment dealt with the concept *indivisible,* to which no part of her instruction referred.

Instructional alignment is more sophisticated and subtle than it appears. For example, on the surface, the teacher's instruction looked acceptable, perhaps even good. Her students were orderly and the teacher involved the students in a question-and-answer activity. The lack of alignment wasn't obvious or apparent. In fact, in a research study examining preservice, first-year, and veteran teachers' concepts of effective instruction, most of the pre-service and first-year teachers missed the fact that the instruction in this lesson—which was on videotape—was not aligned, while veteran teachers quickly identified the alignment problem (Harris and Eggen, 1993).

Focus

In reviewing what we've discussed to this point, we see that we have examined teacher attitudes, effective communication, teacher organization, and the need for instruction to be aligned if student achievement is to be as high as possible.

For these elements of instruction to be most effective, students must be engaged or "with us" in the lesson. Lesson **focus** *attracts and holds students' attention throughout the learning activity.*

Learning begins with attention, and attention must be maintained for continued learning. Focus is the process teachers use to attract and maintain attention throughout the lesson. Focus exists in two forms:

- Introductory focus
- Sensory focus

Though the two forms are interrelated, we discuss them separately for the sake of clarity.

Introductory Focus.   To help understand introductory focus, let's look again at Teri Bowden's lesson. As soon as students finished their warm-up activity, she said,

> . . . let's shift our thinking a little and begin to focus on the colonial period, which began in the 1600s. This is a very important part of American History, but what's most interesting about all of this is that what we're studying has ramifications for the entire world, even today. Today's topic is one of the most important ideas of the entire colonial period, so let's see what kind of job we can do in figuring it out.

Teri used this statement as her **introductory focus,** *which is the set of teacher actions at the beginning of a lesson designed to attract students' attention and pull them into the lesson.* While similar to an "advance organizer" (Ausubel, 1968; Corkill, 1992), the function of introductory focus is more attention getting and motivational, while the function of an advance organizer is more of a conceptual introduction. Introductory focus is designed to enhance motivation by arousing curiosity and making lesson content attractive.

Sensory Focus.   **Sensory focus** is *the use of stimuli—concrete objects, pictures, models, materials displayed on the overhead, and even information written on the chalkboard—to maintain attention.* The more concrete and attractive the materials, the better they serve as forms of sensory focus. In addition to supplementing her introductory focus, the examples Teri displayed on the overhead helped maintain attention by giving students something to observe visually.

The chalkboard is probably the simplest form of sensory focus that exists. It is often underused, however, particularly in elementary schools. Teachers often deliver their lessons verbally instead of using the board as a supplement; as a result, lessons lose focus, and students become inattentive. This is a particular problem for students with special needs or for those who have trouble focusing their attention on verbal information.

Feedback

Feedback *is information about current behavior that can be used to improve future performance* (Eggen and Kauchak, 1994). Feedback has been thoroughly researched and its importance in improving learning is clear (Good and Brophy, 1994; Rosenshine and Stevens, 1986). Feedback is so important that it is sometimes cited as a learning principle. Regardless of the topic, grade level, or task, learners need information about their performance.

Effective feedback has five characteristics, which are illustrated in Figure 2.2. These characteristics are equally important for both written and verbal feedback.

In providing verbal feedback, the informational value of the teacher's response is crucial. Let's look at the following example:

> A teacher is working with students on simplifying arithmetic expressions, and displays the following expression on the board:

$$4 + 3(6 - 2) - 5$$

> The teacher asks, "What must we do first to simplify the expression? Leroy?"
> "Add the four and the three."
> "Not quite, Leroy. Can someone help out?"

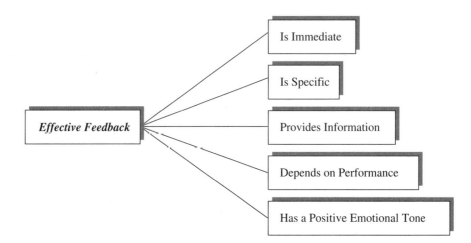

FIGURE 2.2   Characteristics of Effective Feedback

Even though the feedback was immediate, it was not specific, and it provided Leroy with no additional information. Contrast that response to the following exchange:

"What is the first step in simplifying the expression? Emilio?"
"Add the four and the three."
"Look again, Emilio. If we first add the four and the three, we then would have seven times the six minus two in parentheses. What does the expression imply?"
". . . That it's three times the numbers in parentheses."

In the second example, the teacher gave a specific response based on Emilio's answer and provided information that allowed him to answer correctly, both of which enhance learning through effective feedback. In contrast to Leroy, Emilio not only understands why his first answer was incorrect, but has also been given the opportunity to answer correctly. (As we saw in our discussion of teacher expectations, the quality of the teacher's feedback often depends on the teacher's expectations for the student involved. It's easy to slide into lowered expectations, which result in superficial feedback, which in the long run lowers achievement.)

In addition to the characteristics we've already described, the emotional tone of feedback is important. To be motivated, students must feel safe. Feedback in the form of criticism, sarcasm, or ridicule detracts from this safety, destroys motivation, and decreases learning (Murphy et al., 1986).

Monitoring
Monitoring *is the process of constantly checking students' verbal and nonverbal behavior for evidence of learning progress.* It is important during all learning activities, and particularly during seatwork, when students may be making repeated errors.

Monitoring extends beyond seatwork, however, and also includes being aware of students' reactions during learning activities. Monitoring, in short, is the ability to be flexible and responsive to students (O'Keefe and Johnston, 1987).

Alert teachers immediately recognize when students become inattentive; they move near them or call on them to bring them back into lessons. Less alert teachers don't notice the inattention. A sensitive teacher also responds to students' nonverbal behaviors and makes statements (or asks questions) such as, "José, I see your eyes crinkled up. Do you want me to repeat what I just said?" Careful monitoring followed by appropriate responses can strongly contribute to a climate of support while simultaneously demonstrating high expectations both for behavior and learning. Unless teachers are constantly aware of their students' behaviors, the effectiveness of the other essential skills is greatly reduced.

Review and Closure

Review *summarizes previous work and forms a link between what has been learned and what is coming.* **Closure** *is a form of review that occurs at the end of a lesson.* Review emphasizes important points and can occur at any point in a learning activity, although it most commonly occurs at the beginning and end of a lesson.

The value of review is well documented by research (Emmer et al., 1979; Rosenshine and Stevens, 1986). Dempster (1991) goes further in saying that ". . . reviews may do more than simply increase the amount learned; they may shift the learner's attention away from verbatim details of the material being studied to its deeper conceptual structure" (p. 71). This deeper conceptual structure is especially important when we teach for understanding.

When a topic comes to closure, it is summarized, structured, and completed. The notion of closure is intuitively sensible and it is often used in everyday discussions, for example, "Let's try to get to closure on this." In learning activities, it pulls together the lesson content and signals the end of a lesson.

Teri's closure was thorough and extensive. Let's look again at a portion of the dialogue in the lesson.

Teri: That's excellent everyone! Very good analysis of the information we have here. Now let's look back and see what we've found. [She then goes on] We've examined the three cases, and now we want to take a broader look at the information in general. Let's begin. We have a situation where . . .? Toni?

Toni: . . . Colonists related to a country produce only raw materials, no manufactured stuff.

Teri: Good. . . . Go on.

Toni: . . . And they can only be sold to the mother country.

Gregg: Which in turn provides the manufacturing and the shipping.

Teri: Excellent! Very clear, succinct description of what we've been discussing. . . . Now we know the features of this policy. Does anyone know what it's called?

At this point, Teri provided the term *mercantilism,* since the students had identified the essential characteristics of the concept.

The process of coming to closure at the end of a lesson is important. This is the last of the information that the students take away from the class, and if the ideas aren't clear, they may develop misconceptions that can be difficult to eliminate.

Questioning

Questioning is one of the most important skills in effective teaching. (It is arguably the *most* important skill.) Through questioning a teacher can help students form relationships, ensure success, involve reluctant students, induce the involvement of an inattentive student, and enhance students' self-esteem.

Becoming skilled at questioning is difficult because it involves several things at once (Eggen and Kauchak, 1994):

- Remembering the goals of the lesson.
- Monitoring students' verbal and nonverbal behaviors.
- Maintaining the flow and development of the lesson.
- Preparing the next question.

With practice, however, teachers can become skilled with questioning, and this skill is highly developed in expert teachers.

Effective questioning has four characteristics:

- Frequency
- Equitable distribution
- Prompting
- Wait-time

Frequency.   In thinking back to Teri Bowden's lesson, we see that she asked a large number of questions. In fact, she developed much of her lesson with questioning.

Questioning frequency *refers to the number of questions teachers ask,* and research indicates that effective teachers ask a large number of questions (Brophy and Evertson, 1976; Coker et al., 1980). Being asked questions increases student involvement, which in turn increases achievement (Morine-Dershimer, 1985; Pratton and Hales, 1986).

Questioning also helps students maintain sensory focus, provides communication of important concepts through repetition, and is an effective way of informally assessing student understanding.

Equitable Distribution.   Merely asking a lot of questions isn't enough, however. If the same students are answering all of the questions, others become inattentive, and overall achievement is lowered. Kerman (1979) used the term **equitable distribution** *to describe a questioning pattern in which all students in the class are called on as equally as possible.* We saw earlier in the chapter that teachers sometimes discriminate among students based on their expectations of students' abilities to answer. Because teachers expect less from lower than from higher achievers, they call on them less—often unconsciously. Further, most teacher questions are not directed to particular students (McGreal, 1985). This means that a student who wants to volunteer, or even "shout out" an answer is allowed to do so, and those who don't are allowed to remain passive. This practice results in lowered achievement (Brophy and Evertson, 1974), which is easy to understand. Students fall into a pattern of not responding, they become inattentive, and achievement suffers.

One solution is to call on all students as equally as possible, and direct questions to students by name. This method concurrently promotes equitable distribution and prevents a vocal minority from dominating the activity. Equitable distribution communicates to students that the teacher expects them to be actively involved and able to answer. When this becomes a pattern, both achievement and motivation improve (Kerman, 1979).

To make the process work, however, the classroom must be managed to prevent student **call-outs,** *which are answers given by students before the students have been recognized by the teacher.* Call-outs usually come from the higher achieving or more aggressive students in the class, and if this becomes a pattern, the less aggressive and lower achieving students are often left out, equitable distribution is reduced, and general achievement is lowered.

In looking again at Teri Bowden's teaching, we see that she was effective in applying this research in her lesson. She directed her questions to specific students by name, and her instruction never strayed from the goal of her lesson.

Equitable distribution is a simple idea but sometimes difficult to put into practice. It requires careful monitoring of students and a great deal of teacher energy. Unfortunately, we don't often see it practiced in classrooms. However, its effects can be very powerful for both learning and motivation, and we strongly encourage you to persevere and to pursue it rigorously.

Prompting. At this point an important question arises. In an effort to achieve equitable distribution, what do you do when the student you call on either doesn't answer or answers incorrectly? The answer is prompting. A **prompt** *is any teacher question or directive that elicits a student response after the student has failed to answer or has given an incorrect or incomplete answer.* As an illustration, let's look again at some dialogue from Teri's lesson.

Teri: That's very good, both of you. Where do you suppose Steve got that idea [that the colonists couldn't send goods anywhere other than the parent country]? Connie?

Connie: It says it right in the first two examples, and in the third one it says that when India tried to establish stronger ties with other countries to expand the scope of its trade, it got in trouble.

Teri: Excellent, everyone! Connie, good use of information to support your ideas. You've all improved a great deal in that regard. Keep going. . . . Mary?

Mary: (No response)

Teri: What did they get in return in each case?

Mary: . . . They got textiles from England, . . . and fur garments, traps, and stuff from France, . . . and clothing from England.

When Mary was unable to respond, Teri asked another question that helped Mary successfully answer. Let's look at one more example.

Teri: Now let's go a bit farther. What other patterns do you see in the descriptions? Kim?

Kim: (No response)

Teri: How were the goods shipped, Kim?

Kim: On ships.

Teri: Yes, good, Kim! What ships, or whose ships?

Kim: . . . In each case it was the ships from the parent country.

As with Mary in the earlier exchange, when Kim was unable to respond correctly, Teri provided a cue in the form of another question, and then asked Kim for an expansion of her answer with an additional question. This is the essence of prompting.

Prompting and Classroom Climate.   Consider the effects on students if a pattern of prompting is established. It communicates that the teacher expects a successful answer and will provide assistance to ensure success. As a result, on succeeding questions students are likely to increase their effort.

In contrast, consider again Kim's response, "on ships," which drew laughter from the other students. If a climate of accountability and support had not been established, Kim might have been embarrassed. However, since everyone in the class was being called on, and Teri was prompting each student who didn't answer correctly, Kim was not uniquely "on the spot," so the likelihood of being embarrassed was greatly reduced.

Wait-Time.   Let's look again at Teri's lesson. While it's hard to see in a written case study, after asking a student a question Teri waited a few seconds for an answer, giving students time to think. *This period of silence, both before and after a student responds, is called* **wait-time**, and research indicates that in most classrooms, it is too short, typically less than one second (Rowe, 1986).

Perhaps a more intuitively sensible label for wait time might be "think time," because in reality waiting actually gives the student a little time—ideally about three to five seconds—to think. There are at least three benefits to this practice (Rowe, 1974, 1986):

- Equitable distribution improves, and responses from cultural minorities increase as teachers become more responsive to students.
- Students give longer and better responses.
- Voluntary participation increases, and fewer students fail to respond.

Wait-time must be implemented judiciously, however. For example, if students are involved in a form of drill and practice, such as with multiplication facts, quick answers are desirable and wait-times should be short (Rosenshine and Stevens, 1986). Also, if a student appears uneasy, we may choose to intervene earlier. On the other hand, students need time to respond to questions asking them to apply, analyze, or evaluate information. In general, increasing wait-time reduces student anxiety rather than increasing it, because a climate of support is established. All students are expected to participate, they're given time to think about their responses, and they know that the teacher will help them if they're unable to answer.

Essential Teaching Skills: A Theoretical Perspective

In the last section we described essential teaching skills as the abilities that all teachers should possess—an essential foundation upon which all other skills are based. This implies that a first-year teacher should possess each of these abilities, which is not a simple task.

To understand the challenges that teachers face we need to understand how we all take in information from the environment, process it, and store it in our memories. Our processing systems include two important memory stores: **working memory,** *which is the portion of our memory in which conscious processing of information occurs,* and **long-term memory,** *which is our permanent memory store* (Eggen and Kauchak, 1994). Working memory is our consciousness; it is the workbench or working space that we use to consider information from the environment and solve problems.

An important aspect of our processing system is that working memory is limited in capacity. This limitation means that we are able to consciously process only a certain amount of information, and if we attempt to cope with too much information at a time, some will be lost or ignored in an effort to simplify the amount we have to process.

This problem is common in schools with students who have not mastered, for example, basic operations in math, or skills in reading. When required to solve a math word problem, too much of the working memory's limited capacity is required to simply read the problem or perform the basic mathematical operations, leaving an inadequate amount of thinking space to figure out the more sophisticated aspects of the problem. As a result, students can't solve the problem.

Automaticity: Saving Memory for Decision Making

The solution to this problem is **automaticity** (Bloom, 1986; Case, 1978), *which is the overlearning of information and skills to the point where they can be accessed or used with little mental effort.* Skills that are automatic take up virtually no working memory space. For example, consider learning to drive a car with a stick shift. Initially, the process is quite mechanical, and a great deal of conscious effort is spent on simply depressing the clutch, shifting, and releasing the clutch without killing the motor. In time, however, the process is nearly effortless, and people can be engrossed in conversation while smoothly shifting through the gears; the process of driving and shifting has become "automatic."

So, what does this have to do with essential teaching skills? The process of teaching is very complex and demanding. Teachers are expected to maintain order, have high levels of student involvement in learning activities, teach creatively, treat students as individuals, and complete a seemingly endless stream of paperwork. This is difficult if not impossible unless essential teaching skills are virtually automatic. Unless teachers' questioning skills become automatic, for example, the models that are presented in Chapters 3 through 9 will be difficult if not impossible to use. As another example, if teachers are using considerable portions of their working memory to simply maintain order in their classrooms, they will also find it difficult to implement these strategies.

Lack of automaticity helps explain why we see so much lecture and seatwork in schools. Lecture is simple; the teacher has to focus only on organizing and delivering content. Since students are passive, management problems are usually minimal. Seatwork is similar. The teacher only needs to monitor students for signs of confusion or disruption— the demands on working memory and energy are low.

In contrast, involving students through interactive questioning is much more complex and demanding. The teacher must not only organize the content, he or she must be able to ask the right question at the appropriate time in order to help a floundering student, or refocus the class when it has drifted away from the original goal. All of this must be done while calling on all students equally, asking the question before identifying the student, watching for signs of confusion, and maintaining classroom order.

The solution is conceptually simple, but demanding in reality. Developing automaticity becomes a matter of practice. These abilities are easy enough to learn if the teacher is willing to expend the effort, and the outcomes can be enormously rewarding. Both learning and motivation increase, and the sense of satisfaction that comes with truly guiding student learning can be tremendous.

This completes our discussion of essential teaching skills. We now want to go beyond effective teaching to examine higher-order and critical thinking and what teachers can do to develop these capabilities in students.

Beyond Effective Teaching: Teaching for Thinking and Understanding

In Chapter 1, and earlier in this chapter, we said that effective teaching provides only a foundation upon which excellence is built, and that expert teachers go beyond this threshold to construct lessons that help students acquire a deep and thorough understanding of the topics they study. Resnick and Klopfer (1989) use the term **generative knowledge,** *which is "knowledge that can be used to interpret new situations, to solve problems, to think and reason, and to learn"* (p. 5), to describe this deep understanding.

Generative knowledge involves learning both content and thinking skills. Acquiring generative knowledge means, " to teach content and the skills of thinking at the same time. . . . There is no choice to be made between a content emphasis and a thinking-skill emphasis. No depth in either is possible without the other" (Resnick and Klopfer, 1989, p. 6). David Perkins (1992) underscores the relationship between thinking and knowledge of content by saying, *"Learning is a consequence of thinking.* Retention, understanding, and the active use of knowledge can be brought about only by learning experiences in which learners think about and think with what they are learning" (p. 8). The interrelationship between thinking and understanding is captured in the following quote:

> *Cognitive research is revealing that even with what is taken to be good instruction, many students, including academically talented ones, understand less than we think they do. With determination, students taking an examination are commonly able to identify what they have been told or what they have read; careful probing, however, often shows that their understanding is limited or distorted, if not altogether wrong. This finding suggests that parsimony is essential in setting out educational goals: Schools should pick the most important concepts and skills to emphasize so that they can concentrate on the quality of understanding rather than on the quantity of information presented (Science for all Americans, 1989, p. 145).*

The implications for teaching are clear—if deep understanding of content is a goal, emphasis on thinking must also be a goal. The models presented in Chapters 3 through 9 of this text are designed to capitalize on these two interrelated goals.

Teaching Thinking: An Enduring Concern

Education tends to be a "trendy" profession, and we've all seen the "latest" come and go. Concerns about whether or not the teaching of thinking might be one more example of a brief, transitory trend have been expressed in comments such as, "It was easy to believe that the 'let's teach thinking' spirit might be a short-term fad that would soon change to some other trendy notion" (Bransford et al., 1991, p. 148). However, the interest in teaching thinking during the 1980s was unprecedented (Presseisen, 1986), and the trends in the 1990s suggest, if anything, even greater attention to the topic.

Several factors have contributed to this enduring interest. They are outlined in Table 2.3 (based on work by Bransford et al., 1991).

The crucial need for teaching also arises from current practice in today's schools. One comprehensive study concluded,

> *Only rarely did we find evidence to suggest instruction (in reading and math) likely to go much beyond merely possession of information to a level of understanding its implications and either applying it or exploring its possible applications. Nor did we see activities likely to arouse students' curiosity or to involve them in seeking a solution to some problem not already laid bare by teacher or textbook.*
>
> *And it appears that this preoccupation with the lower intellectual processes pervades social studies and science as well. An analysis of topics studied and materials used gives not an impression of students studying human adaptations and exploration, but of facts to be learned (Goodlad, 1984, p. 236).*

Another study found,

> *Many students are unable to give evidence of a more than superficial understanding of concepts and relationships that are fundamental to the subjects they have studied, or of an ability to apply the content knowledge they have acquired to real-world problems. The general picture of the thinking ability of U.S. students*

TABLE 2.3   Factors Contributing to the Interest in Teaching Thinking

Factor	Description
Poor test scores	American students score poorly on tests that require thinking, (e.g., writing persuasive essays, solving word problems in math, using formal and informal reasoning).
Concerns of business leaders	Business leaders perceive that high school and college graduates cannot speak and write effectively, learn on the job, and use quantitative skills.
Increased need for thinking in the future	Many future jobs will require complex learning skills, and the ability to adapt to rapid change. Thinking will no longer be in the domain of a select few.
National needs and personal rights	The primary weapon against being exploited by selfish leaders is their ability to think (Machado, 1980). The major impediment to peace in the world is irrational behavior (Nickerson, 1986).

> *that is painted by these reports [national assessments of education progress, and studies from the National Commission on Excellence in Education] is a disturbing one (Nickerson, 1988, p. 5).*

Teaching Thinking: Increasing Learner Motivation

The need for teaching thinking is well documented. Without an emphasis on thinking, deep understanding of content is virtually impossible. The reverse is also true. In order to think effectively in an area, a person must possess a great deal of generative knowledge about the area (Bransford et al., 1991; Nickerson, 1988; Resnick and Klopfer, 1989).

What receives much less emphasis, however, is the fact that goals that increase higher-order and critical thinking also lead to increased learner motivation (Brown, 1988; Stipek, 1993). Teaching for thinking emphasizes learner autonomy and independent inquiry. Because of this emphasis, students' needs for control, competence, and achievement are more likely to be met than they are when passive approaches focusing on teacher lecture and student memorization are used. Autonomy, student self-direction, and self-regulated learning are all factors that increase students' motivation to learn (Atkinson, 1983; Deci, 1981; White, 1959).

To see the motivational effects of teaching for thinking we can look again at Teri Bowden's instruction. The students were in a learning environment where their answers were based on their own thoughts as they interpreted information, not what they thought Teri wanted to hear or what they had memorized. Being allowed the freedom to say what you actually think rather than what you believe someone expects to hear is intellectually liberating. This freedom, combined with learning to defend your position based on evidence provided, can lead to a personal sense of power and satisfaction. The combination can be intellectually exciting and motivating.

A Climate for Thinking

As with other aspects of teaching, teaching for thinking requires some supporting elements. To illustrate these elements, let's look again at Teri Bowden and the intellectual climate that she established with her students:

- She provided students with information and began the lesson in an open-ended and nonthreatening way.
- She promoted a spirit of cooperation rather than competition and avoided any comparisons of performance among the students.
- She focused on improvement rather than displays of ability, as indicated by her comments, "Excellent, everyone! Connie, good use of information to support your ideas. You've all improved a great deal in that regard. . . ."
- She emphasized that success was evidenced by improvement and progress rather than high grades and performance compared to others.

Each of these factors created a climate in which the students felt safe and willing to take risks. This type of classroom climate is critical for both thinking and learner motivation (Maehr, 1992).

Higher-Order and Critical Thinking

We have discussed the need for teaching thinking, and the relationships between teaching for thinking, deep understanding of content, and learner motivation. We now want to look at what *higher-order thinking* and *critical thinking* mean. As with many other aspects of human functioning, thinking is complex, and we readily acknowledge that what you are about to read may oversimplify the processes. However, we offer this description of thinking as a starting point and foundation for your growth in this area.

Let's look now at higher-order and critical thinking.

Higher-Order Thinking

Higher-order thinking *is the forming of conclusions based on evidence.* Conclusions exist in two primary forms—finding patterns (inductive conclusions), and making judgments based on those patterns (deductive conclusions). These forms are outlined in Figure 2.3.

Evidence for a conclusion refers to data or proof. The most common form of evidence is fact or observation. If an individual observes an incident, the observation is considered to be evidence for a conclusion based on that observation. Evidence answers the question, "How do you know?" We conclude, for example, that a person is asleep. How do we know that she is asleep? The evidence we have for our conclusion is that the person's eyes are closed, she is breathing regularly, and perhaps even snoring. Notice that we don't observe that the person is asleep; we conclude that she is asleep. In response to our statement, "You sure had a nice nap," she may even protest, "I wasn't asleep. I heard everything that was going on."

If higher-order thinking is the forming of conclusions based on evidence, what is *not* higher-order thinking? Information obtained through memorization, and conclusions formed on the basis of belief, authority, or emotion—without supporting evidence—is not higher-order thinking. Nickerson's (1986) notion of irrational behavior, which we cited earlier in the chapter, is another example of thinking that is not higher-order. Let's look at the different kinds of conclusions in more detail now.

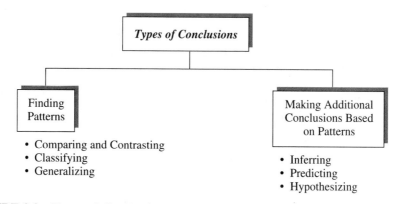

FIGURE 2.3   Types of Conclusions

Inductively Formed Conclusions:
Finding Patterns Based on Specific Cases

Searching for and describing patterns is perhaps the most fundamental process that exists in the world of science. The laws that we have learned in physics, such as "Moving objects tend to keep moving in a straight line unless a force acts on them," which describes part of Newton's Law of Inertia, is one example of the many patterns that have been found and described.

Daily examples are common and regularly appear in newspapers and magazines. For instance, the famous aspirin study reported a few years ago concluded that people who take an aspirin every other day have less chance of having a heart attack than people who don't. This conclusion described a pattern found in people who took an aspirin every other day compared to people who took a placebo. The investigators found that the aspirin takers had fewer heart attacks after a five-year period than the non-aspirin-takers, and, based on these results, articulated a pattern relating aspirin taking and heart attacks. (We will critically examine this study in the next section.)

Patterns in the health professions abound. The following are a few additional examples:

- People who have high levels of blood cholesterol—particularly low-density lipoproteins, or "bad cholesterol"—have a greater incidence of heart disease than do those with lower cholesterol levels.
- People who smoke have a higher incidence of heart disease and cancer than those who don't smoke.
- People who get regular aerobic exercise have a lower incidence of heart disease than people who don't exercise.
- Women who become moderately overweight in their thirties have a higher incidence of breast cancer than women who maintain their ideal body weights.

Each of these examples describes a pattern, and the pattern is based on a series of specific observations.

The process of searching for patterns extends across all disciplines. In addition to the laws we study in physics and chemistry, examples such as, "Students of effective teachers are on task a greater percentage of their time in school than students of less effective teachers," describe a pattern in the teacher-effectiveness literature. "Intermittently reinforced behaviors are more enduring than are continually reinforced behaviors," is a pattern found in behaviorism, one school of psychology. "Writers tend to write from their own experiences," is a pattern found in the study of literature. These are all patterns that are based on specific observations of people and objects.

Teri Bowden capitalized on the process of finding patterns by presenting her students with the three written examples illustrating the concept *mercantilism.* Then, based on the pattern found in the examples, they constructed—with Teri's guidance—an understanding of the concept.

In the process, Teri capitalized on the need for evidence in forming conclusions. To clarify this emphasis, let's look again at some of the dialogue in the lesson.

Steve: And they couldn't send it anywhere else!

Teri: That's very good, both of you. Where do you suppose Steve got that idea? Connie?

Connie: It says it right in the first two examples. . . . And in the third one it says that when India tried to establish stronger ties with other countries to expand the scope of their trade, they got in trouble.

By making direct reference to the information in the case study, Connie provided evidence that supported Steve's conclusion. Teri capitalized on this process at several points in the lesson.
    Let's look at another example.

Bob: They weren't allowed to [get finished goods from other countries].

Teri: And what made you say that, Bob?

Bob: It says in the second example that they were told that their traps and weapons would be sent from France, and in the third example it says that the British argued that the homeland was more than capable of providing for India's needs.

Teri's lesson focused on a deep understanding of the concept of *mercantilism* while simultaneously giving students practice in finding patterns based on evidence. Her instruction illustrates the integral relationship between content and thinking that is so important for both a thorough understanding of content and the gradual development of students' thinking abilities (Resnick and Klopfer, 1989; Perkins, 1992).

Deductively Formed Conclusions:
Making Inferences, Predictions, and Hypotheses
Forming patterns is valuable both in understanding the world and in the processes of thinking because patterns provide the basis for specific conclusions. As an illustration, let's look once more at Teri's lesson.

Teri: What do you think? [Does the example with Canada illustrate mercantilism?]. . . Someone? Amy, we haven't heard from you.

Amy: . . . I would say no.

Teri: OK, now tell us why.

Amy: . . . Well, several reasons. Canada trades with several countries according to the information, uses a variety of ships to carry the goods, and produces a lot besides raw materials.

Amy concluded or inferred that the example with Canada did not illustrate the concept *mercantilism* and her statements about trade, shipping, and finished products were the evidence that she provided for her conclusion. The conclusion was based on the pattern—the characteristics of *mercantilism*—that students found earlier in Teri's first three examples.
    The process of making conclusions based on patterns is also common in the everyday world. Table 2.4 provides some illustrations.
    Teacher questioning is a powerful tool that can be used to promote student formation of specific, defensible conclusions. Questions such as "Why?" "How do you know?" "On what are you basing that?" "What made you say that?" and "What would happen if . . . ?"

TABLE 2.4   Conclusions, Evidence, and Patterns

Conclusion	Evidence	Pattern
Grape Nuts is better for you than Cheerios. (an *inference*)	Grape Nuts has 0 grams of fat/serving. Cheerios has 2 grams of fat/serving. Grape Nuts has 170 mg of sodium/serving. Cheerios has 290 mg of sodium/serving.	Diets low in fat and sodium are healthier than are diets higher in fat and sodium.
It will rain this afternoon. (a *prediction*)	The humidity is 98%. The barometric pressure is low.	Rain is likely under conditions of high humidity and low pressure.
If the economy is "down" an incumbent president will lose the presidential election. (an *hypothesis*)	The American economy was "down" in 1991–1992. George Bush lost the presidential election in 1992. The economy was "down" in 1979–1980. Jimmy Carter lost the election in 1980.	People tend to "vote their pocketbooks" in presidential elections.

are all questions that ask students to provide evidence for their conclusions. Unfortunately, these questions are uncommon in classrooms. Boyer (1983) reported that less than 1 percent of all teacher questions ask students to do more than recall memorized information.

Critical Thinking

Critical thinking *is the process of assessing conclusions based on evidence.* Assessing conclusions with evidence takes several forms. Some of them include:

- Confirming conclusions with facts
- Identifying bias, stereotypes, cliches, and propaganda
- Identifying unstated assumptions
- Recognizing overgeneralizations and undergeneralizations
- Identifying relevant and irrelevant information.

Confirming conclusions with facts was the critical-thinking process that was demonstrated the most in Teri's lesson. Of course not all of the processes can be practiced in every lesson; however, being aware of them can help teachers capitalize on the processes when opportunities present themselves. For example, the specific raw materials that each colony produced were irrelevant, and Teri capitalized on that aspect of the examples as illustrated in the following excerpt from her lesson.

Jack: We had to separate out the relevant from the irrelevant information.

Teri: For example?

Jack: . . . Well, whether it was guns, or traps, or clothing, or whatever, really didn't matter. The important point was that the colonists weren't allowed to manufacture anything.

Teri further capitalized on an opportunity to promote critical thinking by helping her students recognize an unstated assumption in her question about countries being "guilty" of mercantilism. It takes an alert teacher to recognize these opportunities when they arise, and Teri demonstrated her expertise by doing so in her lesson. Her alertness further illustrates the need for automaticity in the essential teaching skills and the basic processes of thinking. Otherwise, teachers won't have enough working memory space available to recognize opportunities to practice critical thinking when they arise.

Critical Thinking in Day-to-Day Living

As with making conclusions based on evidence, opportunities to practice critical thinking are common in everyday living. In fact, the term opportunity is an understatement; critical thinking is important if people are to function effectively in their environments.

As an example, let's look again at the aspirin study we referred to earlier. As a result of the publicity generated by the study's results, many people started taking aspirin. Less publicized, however, was the fact that less than 1 percent of the aspirin takers in the study had a heart attack, and less than 2 percent of the placebo takers had a heart attack. Based on the results of the study, both aspirin takers and non-aspirin takers have less than a 2 percent chance of having a heart attack. Also, the population was select—male physicians— and the study only ran five years. These limitations at least suggest the possibility that the results were overgeneralized. With all of this data, we should have some skepticism about taking aspirin, particularly if we have sensitive stomachs.

Many other examples exist. We must look for the evidence that an advertiser's claims are valid, that comments about other people are based on fact rather than innuendo, and a host of others. Opportunities to utilize critical thinking abound in everyday life; teaching critical thinking prepares students for these opportunities.

Basic Processes

As we look at Teri Bowden's teaching and other examples from our daily lives we see that a number of basic cognitive processes (Nickerson, 1988; Presseisen, 1986) were used. **Basic cognitive processes** *are the fundamental constituents of thinking.* They are our thinking "tools" (Eggen and Kauchak, 1994). The basic processes that have been illustrated to this point in the chapter can be summarized as shown in Table 2.5.

Using these basic processes and developing critical thinking skills requires high levels of judgment and awareness on our parts and certain attitudes and dispositions or "habits of mind." We discuss these elements in the next sections.

Higher-Order and Critical Thinking: The Role of Metacognition

Metacognition *is the awareness of and control over our cognitive processes.* Nickerson (1988) characterizes the role of metacognition in higher-order and critical thinking in this way: "The fact that an individual has some knowledge that would be useful in a given situation does not guarantee that it will be accessed and applied in that situation" (p. 19). To increase the likelihood that learners will apply their thinking appropriately, they need to be aware of the thinking they're doing. To illustrate these processes, let's look at another piece of Teri Bowden's lesson.

TABLE 2.5   Basic Processes in Thinking

Process	Subprocesses
Observing	
Finding patterns and generalizing	Comparing and contrasting Classifying
Form conclusions based on patterns	Inferring Predicting Hypothesizing

Assessing conclusions based
   on evidence
   (Critical thinking)
	Confirming conclusions with facts/observations
	Checking consistency
	Identifying bias, stereotypes, cliches, and propaganda
	Identifying unstated assumptions
	Recognizing overgeneralizations and
	   undergeneralizations
	Identifying relevant and irrelevant information

Teri: Does this tell us for certain that they weren't allowed to import goods from other countries?

Jill: Not exactly. . . . We're sort of assuming it from the information, although it's really implied in the description.

Teri: Very good conclusion, Jill. Class, notice Jill used the word "assume." Actually, she made a conclusion, and the term we use for that kind of conclusion is *infer*. Here the information wasn't directly in the data; she had to go beyond the data to form her conclusion. That's an inference. Nice job.

In this part of her lesson she helped students not only practice making inferences, but she also made them *aware* of the fact that they were forming inferences. This is a form of metacognition. She then reinforced the processes as she summarized the lesson.

Teri: Excellent analysis, Amy. . . . Now that we're comfortable with that part, let's go a step farther and examine our thinking in this activity. What are some things you had to do in order to arrive at the conclusion? Start us off, Conchita.

Conchita: . . . First we had to observe, so we would eventually recognize the essential characteristics.

Teri: Good beginning! What else? Bob?

Bob: We hunted for a pattern in the three paragraphs.

Amy: And we had to make comparisons before we could find the patterns.

Teri: Good. All of you! What else? Jack?

Jack: We had to separate out the relevant from the irrelevant information.

Teri: For example?

Jack: . . . Well, whether it was guns, or traps, or clothing, or whatever, really didn't matter. The important point was that the colonists weren't allowed to manufacture anything.

Teri: Excellent, Jack! Now, go on. Patty?

Patty: . . . We didn't see everything in the examples, so we had to infer some of it, and then you asked us for evidence to support our inference.

Teri: Very good, Patty. Can you remember an example of where we did this?

Patty: I think so. . . . Bob said that he bet that the colonies weren't allowed to get materials from other countries and then used the example where France said the traps and weapons would be sent from there.

Becky: Jill also said that it didn't tell us for sure, but that it was strongly implied and we inferred it from the information we were given.

Lisa Jo: We also generalized when we formed the definition of mercantilism. . . . We talked about those parts of mercantilism working in all cases, so that's generalizing, isn't it?"

Teri's discussion and analysis of students' thought processes provided a foundation for metacognition to develop in her students, and if this emphasis became part of her instructional routine, the thinking of her students would soon become quite sophisticated.

Higher-Order and Critical Thinking: Attitudes and Dispositions

Perhaps the most important parts of the thinking processes are the attitudes, dispositions, inclinations, or "habits of mind" that we hope to develop in our students. The ability to use evidence, for example, is strongly limited if learners have to be continually reminded that evidence is required. Ultimately, our goals are for students to be "inclined" to use evidence without being reminded. These inclinations develop in time if students have repeated experiences in which evidence is required. A periodic lesson won't do the trick. Teaching for thinking must be infused throughout the regular curriculum. Just as Teri Bowden demonstrated in her teaching, teachers must emphasize thinking as a theme for their instruction.

The following simple example illustrates how such an inclination operates in everyday life.

Terry and Tabatha were walking down the hall when they met Andrea coming the other way.

"Hi Andrea," Terry and Tabatha said in unison.

Andrea barely glanced at the two girls and kept walking.

"Sheesh, is she stuck up or what?" Terry grumbled.

"We don't know that," Tabatha replied. "Maybe she isn't feeling well, or maybe something happened to her this morning."

Tabatha demonstrated the inclination to look for evidence, remain open-minded, and reserve judgment. Opportunities to promote and encourage these inclinations show up in classrooms all of the time. Teachers need to be aware of the possibilities, and to capitalize on them when they occur.

A number of attitudes and inclinations associated with higher-order and critical thinking have been identified. Some of them include:

- A desire to be informed
- An inclination to be reflective
- The tendency to look for evidence
- An inclination to look for relationships (versus isolated pieces of information)
- A desire to know both sides of an issue
- An attitude of open-mindedness
- Healthy skepticism
- The tendency to reserve judgment
- Respect for others' opinions
- Tolerance for ambiguity

Extending our earlier example with breakfast cereals, our goal is to get kids to develop an inclination to select a cereal on the basis of evidence about its nutrients instead of simply not thinking about it, or deciding on the basis of taste alone or the endorsement of a professional athlete. If they look at the nutrient information and make a decision on the basis of evidence, they're demonstrating both the inclination and the ability to do critical thinking.

We have now seen that higher-order and critical thinking involve the combination of deep understanding of specific topics, the ability to use basic cognitive processes effectively, understanding of and control over our basic cognitive processes (metacognition), and attitudes and dispositions. The relationship among these elements of thinking are illustrated in Figure 2.4.

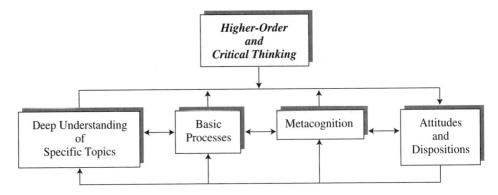

FIGURE 2.4   Elements of Thinking

This completes our discussion of essential teaching skills, and introduces you to higher-order and critical thinking. As you study the specific teaching models in Chapters 3 through 9, you will find additional examples of the skills and thinking abilities in these strategies.

Summary

Teacher effectiveness describes patterns of teacher actions that result in increased student achievement as measured on standardized tests. Based on the teacher-effectiveness research, essential teaching skills, which specify the abilities that all teachers should possess, have been identified. These skills represent a foundation upon which other teaching strategies are based.

Expert teachers go beyond essential teaching skills to promote higher-order and critical thinking in their students. Teaching for thinking and deep understanding of content cannot be separated, and expert teachers simultaneously teach both.

In addition to acquiring a deep understanding of specific content together with using basic cognitive processes, developing thinking includes training in metacognition and developing the attitudes and dispositions associated with thinking. Teaching for thinking and deep understanding of content emphasizes high levels of student involvement and classroom discussion, the process of acquiring knowledge as well as the knowledge itself, and learning in context. It deemphasizes learning based on memorization, teacher lecture, passive students, and knowledge learned as isolated concepts.

Important Concepts

Automaticity (p. 43)
Basic cognitive processes (p. 51)
Call-out (p. 41)
Closure (p. 39)
Connected discourse (p. 33)
Critical thinking (p. 50)
Empathy (p. 30)
Emphasis (p. 34)
Equitable distribution (p. 40)
Essential teaching skills (p. 28)
Feedback (p. 37)
Focus (p. 36)
Generative knowledge (p. 44)
Higher-order thinking (p. 47)
Instructional alignment (p. 36)

Introductory focus (p. 37)
Long-term memory (p. 43)
Metacognition (p. 51)
Modeling (p. 30)
Monitoring (p. 38)
Precise terminology (p. 33)
Prompt (p. 41)
Questioning frequency (p. 40)
Review (p. 39)
Sensory focus (p. 37)
Teacher expectations (p. 32)
Transition signals (p. 34)
Wait-time (p. 42)
Warmth (p. 30)
Working memory (p. 43)

Exercises

Read this passage and answer the questions that follow.

Technology is the knowledge and skill that humanity has for using, making, and controlling our environment. In the United States we have a high level of technology. One of its indications is our heavy dependence on time.

Think for a moment about how you use time. When do classes begin at your school? At what time do you go to lunch? How many minutes are there in a quarter of a football game? We have ways of measuring time very accurately.

Most of us wear watches on our wrists. This shows how great a value we place on knowing what time it is. We even refer to "split-second timing." For some purposes, we need to measure time in split seconds. What is the record for the 100-meter dash? Can you think of other occasions when split-second timing is important?

Anthropologists know about other less technological societies as well. In these societies the time of day is often measured by the height of the sun in the sky. The changes in the shape of the moon are another way of measuring time. For some societies the slow change of the seasons is an exact enough measure of time.

We know that hundreds of planes land and take off from a busy airport each day. The arrival and departure of these planes cannot be controlled by the height of the sun in the sky. By consulting a schedule, we can learn that the plane leaves at 1:50 P.M. We had better be on time.

1. Based on the information in the passage, which of the following statements is most accurate?
   a. The higher the level of technology, the more important precise time is.
   b. Technology exists to a high degree in the United States.
   c. While time is measured in many ways, it is valued to a greater extent in this country than in others.
   d. Anthropology and history are the ways we learn about ourselves and other countries.

2. Of the following, the best description of your performance in Item 1 is:
   a. You demonstrated higher-order thinking by forming a general conclusion based on specific information.
   b. You demonstrated critical thinking by assessing a conclusion based on evidence.
   c. You demonstrated higher-order thinking by forming a specific conclusion based on a general pattern.

3. Look at the following graph. Based on the information in the graph, estimate the animal population in the year 2000.

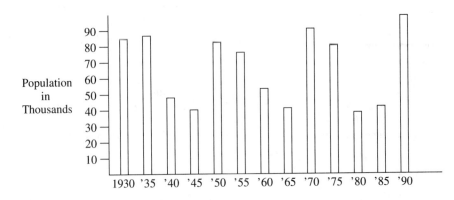

4. Of the following, the best description of your performance in Item 3 is:
   a. You demonstrated higher-order thinking by describing a general pattern based on specific information.
   b. You demonstrated critical thinking by assessing a conclusion based on evidence.
   c. You demonstrated higher-order thinking by making a specific conclusion based on a general pattern.

5. Of the following, the statement that best describes what was required in your thinking *prior* to answering Item 3 is:
   a. You engaged in higher-order thinking by describing a general pattern based on specific information.
   b. You engaged in critical thinking by assessing a conclusion based on evidence.
   c. You engaged in higher-order thinking by making a specific conclusion based on a general pattern.

Discussion Questions

1. According to the Goodlad (1984) quote, teachers tend to conduct most of their instruction at a knowledge/recall level. What explanation would you offer for that tendency?

2. Why do you suppose that teachers ask very few higher-order questions as Boyer (1983) found in his research?

3. In the early 1980s and before, the emphasis was on "context-free" thinking, or in other words, higher-order and critical thinking that deemphasized knowledge of specific content. Why do you suppose there is now a much greater emphasis on specific knowledge in thinking?

4. What implications does the emphasis on thinking have for scope and sequence in curriculum design?

5. What implications does the limited capacity of people's working memories and the concept of automaticity have for the teaching of higher-order and critical thinking?

6. When do you think teachers should begin focusing on higher-order and critical thinking in students? Should it begin in kindergarten or some time later? If later, why? If later, when?

7. The essential teaching skills were described as a foundation for the learning of other teaching strategies. This description implies that first-year teachers should be knowledgeable and proficient in all of the essential teaching skills. Is this realistic? Why or why not?

C h a p t e r *3*

The Inductive Model: A Constructivist View of Learning

I. The Inductive Model: An Overview
A. *Social Structure of the Model*
B. *The Inductive Model: Theoretical Perspectives*

II. Goals for the Inductive Model
A. *Concepts: Categories with Common Characteristics*
B. *Relationships among Concepts: Principles, Generalizations, and Academic Rules*

III. Planning Lessons with the Inductive Model
A. *Identifying Topics*
B. *Specifying Objectives*
C. *Selecting Examples*

IV. Implementing Lessons Using the Inductive Model
A. *Phase 1: Lesson Introduction*
B. *Phase 2: The Open-Ended Phase*
C. *Phase 3: The Convergent Phase*
D. *Phase 4: Closure*
E. *Phase 5: The Application Phase*

V. The Inductive Model: Emphasis on Thinking

VI. The Inductive Model: Options
A. *Examples*
B. *Length of Lessons*
C. *Fostering Cooperation*
D. *Efficiency in Planning*

VII. Assessing Student Learning
A. *Measuring Content Outcomes*
B. *Measuring Thinking Skills*

The Inductive Model is a straightforward but powerful strategy designed to help students develop higher-order- and critical-thinking abilities while at the same time teaching specific content topics. Teachers present students with information that illustrates topics and then guide the students as they search for patterns in the information. Grounded in the view that learners construct their own understanding of the world, rather than consuming it in an already-organized form, the model requires that teachers are skilled with questioning and guiding student thinking. Its effectiveness depends on the teacher as an active leader in helping students process information. The model is effective for promoting high levels of student involvement and increasing student motivation while creating a safe and supportive learning environment.

When you've completed your study of this chapter, you should be able to meet the following objectives:

• Classify topics in the school curriculum as concepts, generalizations, principles, or academic rules.

- Describe the characteristics of concepts, generalizations, principles, and academic rules.
- Plan and implement lessons using the Inductive Model.
- Adapt the Inductive Model for learners at different ages and with varying backgrounds.
- Assess student understanding of content objectives taught using the Inductive Model.
- Assess the development of higher-order- and critical-thinking abilities developed with the Inductive Model.

To begin our discussion, let's look at three teachers, each using the Inductive Model in a slightly different way to help students reach both content and thinking-skills goals.

Judy Nelson is beginning the study of longitude and latitude in social studies with her fifth graders. Knowing that some of her students have limited backgrounds, she plans as if they have virtually no experience with these ideas. In preparation, she buys a beach ball, finds an old tennis ball, and checks her wall maps and globes.

After conducting her beginning-of-class routines, she has students identify where they live on the wall map. She then introduces the lesson by asking students, "Now suppose you made some new friends on your summer vacation and you want to describe for them exactly where you live. How might we do that?"

After getting a number of suggestions from her students, she notes that all are good ideas, but none are precise enough to pinpoint their exact location. She then says, "Today, we are going to figure out a way to identify where we live precisely. When we're done, we'll be so good at this that we'll be able to pinpoint any city in the world. Keep this in mind as we work today. OK, ready to go?"

She then holds up the beach ball and globe and asks her students to compare the two, calling on individual students in each case.

After several comparisons, Judy asks them to identify north, south, east, and west on the beach ball, and draws a circle around the center of the ball. She continues by asking, "Now what can you tell us about this line? Let's begin. Tara?"

"It's a circle."

"Good, Tara," Judy smiled. "What else? Andy?"

"It's in the middle of the ball."

"Fine, Andy. . . . Now look at the tennis ball. Amy?"

"It's also in the middle of the ball."

Judy then cuts the ball in half, leading the students to conclude that the center line divides the ball into two hemispheres as illustrated in Figure 3.1.

Judy identifies the lines as "equators," and she continues by drawing other lines on the beach ball, and says, "Now compare the lines to each other. Kathy?"

". . . They're all even."

"Go ahead Kathy. What do you mean by even?" Judy encourages.

". . . They don't cross each other," Kathy explains motioning with her hands.

"Excellent, Kathy!" Judy nods smiling.

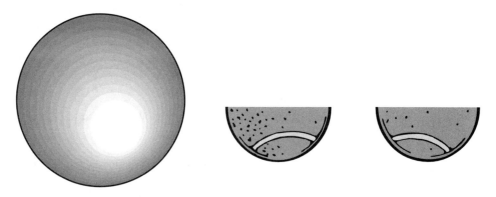

FIGURE 3.1 Beach Ball and Tennis Ball

She then continues with her questioning, guiding the students to additional comparisons such as the lines all run east and west, and they get shorter as they move away from the equator. Judy then writes them on the chalkboard. When the class is done making comparisons, Judy introduces the term "latitude," to describe the lines they have been discussing.

She continues by drawing lines of longitude on the beach ball, as shown in Figure 3.2.

She continues by asking, "How do these lines compare to the lines of latitude? David?"

". . . They go all around the ball."

"Yes they do," Judy smiled. "What else? Tricia?"

". . . You have the same number of each on the ball."

"Yes I do," Judy nodded, realizing that she had drawn three lines of latitude and three lines of longitude on the ball.

"How do the lengths of the longitude lines compare to the lengths of the latitude lines? Chris?"

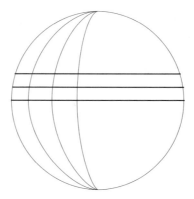

FIGURE 3.2 Beach Ball with Lines of Longitude and Latitude

". . . It looks like they're the same."

"Same as each other?"

"Yes."

"Let's take another look. What do all of the longitude lines do here?" Judy asked pointing the top of the ball toward Chris.

"They all cross there."

"Good," Judy smiles, "So what do we know about the lengths of the longitude lines?"

". . . They're . . . I don't know."

"OK, wrap this string around the ball," Judy suggests, handing Chris a piece of string that she had on her desk.

Chris then measures the circumference of the ball through the poles with the string.

Judy has Jennifer repeat the process with another piece of string at a different point on the ball but still going through the poles, and has Andy and Karen measure the ball simulating lines of latitude to demonstrate that the latitude lines get shorter near the poles.

"So, what do we know about the lengths of the strings? Chris?"

"They're the same," Chris responds pointing to the longitude strings, "But these got shorter," pointing to the latitude strings.

"And what do these represent?"

"Lines of longitude."

"Excellent! So, what do we know about the lines of longitude?"

". . . They're all the same length."

"And how do we know?

"The strings were all the same length."

"Great! Good thinking," Judy responds enthusiastically.

Finally, Judy reviews by asking students to compare the characteristics of latitude and longitude, and relates both to the globe and her flat wall maps. Some of their conclusions include:

1. Longitude lines are farthest apart at the equator, while latitude lines are the same distance apart everywhere.
2. Lines of longitude are the same length; latitude lines get shorter north and south of the equator.
3. Lines of longitude intersect each other at the poles, and lines of latitude and longitude intersect each other.
4. Lines of longitude run north and south and measure distance east and west, and lines of latitude run east and west and measure distance north and south.

   Students then identify the latitude and longitude of different locations on the maps, and practice finding the exact location of cities around the world using longitude and latitude.

Sue Grant is beginning a study of Charles's Law with her chemistry students, and begins by stating, "We've been studying the kinetic theory of gases, and today we are going to examine another law describing the behavior of gases. This law was originally formed by a French man named Jacques Charles, so the law was named after him. When we're finished today, you'll be able to solve problems using his law."

She then continues by taking three identical balloons, inflating each with as close to an equal amount of air as possible. She holds them up and asks her students to compare them; the class concludes that they're the same size. As her students watch, she puts the first in a beaker of boiling water, the second in a beaker of water at room temperature, and the third in a beaker of ice, as shown in Figure 3.3.

She then displays three drawings for the students as shown in Figure 3.4, and a graph as shown in Figure 3.5.

She then puts the students in pairs and says, "Now, work with your partner, and let's carefully observe and compare. Compare the balloons to each other, compare the three drawings to each other and to the balloons, and compare both to the graph. I want you to make as many conclusions as you can, and I want you to be ready to support your conclusions with evidence. I'll give you five minutes. Write your conclusions and evidence on your paper."

The classroom quickly becomes a buzz of voices as students study the balloons, drawings, and graph. As they work, Sue walks among them, periodically making a comment or offering a few words of encouragement.

At the end of the five minutes, she stops them and begins, "OK, what have we concluded? . . . Steve and Barbara?"

". . . We decided that the masses in each of the balloons were the same."

"Good," Sue nods. "And why did you say that?"

"The number of molecules—dots—in each balloon is the same."

"Excellent. Good thinking you two."

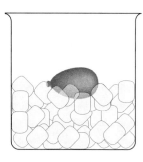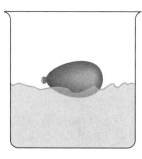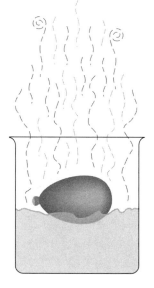

FIGURE 3.3 Beakers with Inflated Balloons

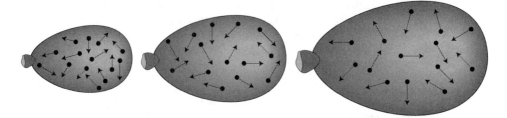

FIGURE 3.4   Models of Balloons at Different Temperatures

She then continues this process, calling on other pairs.
The following are some of their conclusions and supporting evidence:

The masses of air in the balloons are equal.

The number of "dots" in the three drawings is equal.

The molecular movement increased in the heated balloon.

The arrows in the third balloon are longest.

The volume of the heated balloon increased and the volume of the cooled balloon decreased.

The molecules are closest together in the first drawing and farthest apart in the third drawing.

Temperature and volume appear to be directly proportional.

The graph shows that the volume is proportional to the temperature.

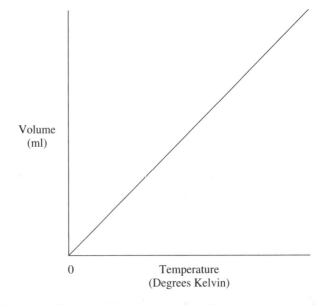

FIGURE 3.5   Graph Relating Temperature and Volume

Sue then continues, "Look again at the graph. We found that the volume is proportional to the temperature, but what temperature? . . . Greg?"

". . . I'm not sure what you mean."

"Look at the graph. Is the volume proportional to the Celsius temperature or the absolute temperature?"

". . . It looks like the absolute temperature."

"Yes it does. That's what we see in the graph. Very good."

Sue then continues by writing $T_1 \propto V_1$, and $T_2 \propto V_2$, on the chalkboard, and saying, "What do the ones and twos mean? Debbie?"

". . . The ones mean some temperature and some volume, and the twos mean another temperature and another volume."

"Good, so if we know they're proportional, what do we know about their ratios? Mike?"

". . . They're equal."

"Excellent, so how can we write the relationship? Tony?"

". . . It would be $T_1/T_2 = V_1/V_2$."

"Outstanding, everyone. That's Charles's Law, and that's what we're after today."

Sue continues saying, "We see from Charles's Law how temperature affects volume. Let's think about how what we just learned relates to what we already know about mass and density. . . . As the temperature increases, what happens to the mass of the gas? Randy?" Sue went on.

". . . Nothing."

"Good. And how do you know?"

". . . The amount didn't change, only the volume."

"Excellent. And how about the density? Jo?"

". . . It . . . it gets . . . less."

"Super. Explain that for us."

". . . The air is expanding, but the mass is the same, so it must be less dense."

"Bravo! Good explanation, Jo."

Sue then went on to give the students several problems in which temperatures changed and they had to determine the change in volume, or a change in volume occurred and they had to determine what temperature caused the change.

Jim Rooney is a teacher in Lakeside Middle School, one of two middle schools in Brooksville, a small town in Florida. Jim is a bit frustrated that his eighth graders seem to be confused and unable to properly punctuate singular and plural possessive nouns in their own writing. He decides he has nothing to lose by trying to help them develop their own understanding of the rules, so he prepares a passage in which the rules are illustrated.

Jim begins the class by saying, "Today, we're going to practice finding patterns. The goal for today's lesson is to identify some patterns in the way words are used in passages. When we're finished, this should help us in our writing. . . . OK, let's go."

He then begins his lesson by displaying the passage, which appears as follows.

*Jefferson, a rural county in Central Florida, has six **schools**—one high **school**, two middle schools, and three elementary schools. Five of the schools* *are in Brooksville, the largest **city** in Jefferson **county**. The* city's *schools and the schools in three other **counties** hold an annual scholastic and athletic competition, and students in the* counties' *schools met this year in Brooksville. In all, students from five **cities** were involved, and the* cities' *students did very well.*

*The two **women** advisors of* Brooksville's *debate teams were particularly proud, because the* women's *teams won both of their debates. The members of Debate-1 swept the competition. The members of Debate-2 also squeaked out a win, and* theirs *was perhaps a greater accomplishment, since they haven't competed as long.*

*Four **girls** and three **boys** won both athletic and scholastic honors. The* girls' *accomplishments were noteworthy in math on the academic side and tennis on the athletic side. The* boys' *achievements were in writing and track. One **boy** set a new school record in the 100-meter dash; the* boy's *time was a new school record.*

*Many **children** from the elementary schools participated as well, and the* children's *accomplishments were equally impressive. Several of the children wrote short **stories**. One **child** wrote a **story** involving a **woman** and the* woman's *struggle to keep her farm in the face of hardship. The* child's *story and the* story's *plot were very sophisticated. Several* stories' *plots and characters were interesting and well developed. The stories were put in a **display**, and three of the **displays** were photographed for the local newspaper. The* displays' *contents included the stories as well as some background information on the author. Lakesha Jefferson had her story published in the paper, and* hers *was the first of its type to be presented this way.*

He asks the students to look at all of the bold-faced terms and see if they have anything in common. They make a number of observations and in the process recognize that they're all either singular or plural nouns. As part of the process, he leads them to conclude that plural nouns are formed by merely adding an -*s* if the noun ends in a consonant or in -*y* preceded by a vowel, but removes the -*y* and adds -*ies* if the noun ending in -*y* is preceded by a consonant. They also see that some nouns, such as woman and child, become plural by changing the form of the word.

Jim continues the lesson the next day by first reviewing the rules for forming plural nouns, and then turns to the nonitalicized words in the passage, following a procedure similar to the one he used with the bold-faced terms. He asks the students what the nonitalicized terms have in common and leads the students to the rules for forming singular and plural possessive nouns based on their observations of the information in the passage.

The Inductive Model: An Overview

Let's begin our study of the Inductive Model by looking back at the episodes we've just read and seeing what they have in common. This will give us a concrete reference point from which to develop our discussion.

TABLE 3.1   Examples Leading to General Conclusions

Specific Examples	General Conclusions
Drawings of latitude and longitude on the beachball, and lines on maps.	Latitude lines are parallel, run east-west, and measure distance north and south of the equator. Longitude lines intersect at the poles, run north-south, and measure distance east and west of the prime meridian.
Demonstration with balloons and drawings of containers and molecules.	When pressure is constant, volume is directly proportional to absolute temperature. $$\frac{T_1}{V_1} = \frac{T_2}{V_2}$$
Passage containing illustrations of singular and plural possessive nouns.	To make singular nouns possessive we add apostrophe 's', and to make plural nouns possessive we add an apostrophe (if the plural ends in 's').

- First, the topics the teachers focused on were well-defined—longitude and latitude in Judy Nelson's lesson, the relationship between temperature and volume in Sue Grant's, and the rules for forming singular and plural possessives in Jim Rooney's.
- Second, each teacher started with a specific example or set of examples—Judy's beach ball, tennis ball, and maps; Sue's demonstration and drawings; and Jim's passage.
- Third, the students practiced the basic processes of observing, comparing and contrasting, finding patterns, and generalizing as they processed the information in the examples.
- Fourth, the teachers guided the students from the specific examples to the conclusions in each case. These processes are outlined in Table 3.1.

The conclusions were the content goals the teachers had identified when they planned their lessons.

Social Structure of the Model

Social structure refers to the characteristics of the classroom environment necessary for learning to take place, and the roles of the teacher and students in the environment. The Inductive Model requires a classroom environment in which the students feel free to take risks and offer their conclusions, conjectures, and evidence without fear of criticism or embarrassment. We will discuss specific ways of promoting a safe and supportive climate in the section on implementing lessons using the Inductive Model.

The Teacher's Role

As we saw in our introductory examples, the teacher sets the tone for the activity by encouraging students to make observations and focusing these observations through questioning. The teacher actively leads the learning activity (Good, 1983), keeps the students on task (Doyle, 1983), and establishes positive expectations (Good and Brophy, 1994), all of which are positively related to student achievement.

The success of a lesson depends on the quality of the examples that teachers use and their ability to guide the students' analysis of the information. When the Inductive Model is used, the teacher does not display or demonstrate information for students and then explain it, as would be typical in a lecture or demonstration. Rather, the teacher presents carefully chosen examples, and guides the students as they form their own understanding of the topic. This doesn't imply in any way that the teacher is intentionally vague or withholds information from the students. Clear goals are as critical with the Inductive Model as they are with a lecture or any other format. The major difference is that instead of merely telling students, the teacher guides them. To effectively use the Inductive Model, teachers must be experts with questioning.

The essence of the Inductive Model from the teacher's perspective is the process of presenting learners with examples that illustrate the topic you want them to learn and then guiding their thinking until the objective is reached. Each of the teachers in our introductory episodes followed this basic procedure.

From the learner's perspective, the essence of the learning activity is the process of analyzing the examples to find their essential common elements, ultimately creating meaning from them. Let's look now at the learner's role in a bit more detail.

The Inductive Model: Theoretical Perspectives

The Inductive Model is grounded in the principles of **constructivism**, a view of learning that says that learners develop their own understanding of the way the world works rather than having it delivered to them by others (most commonly teachers) in an already-organized form. Constructivism places the learner in the center of the learning process.

> *Current research . . . focuses on the role of the student. It recognizes that students do not merely passively receive or copy input from teachers, but instead actively mediate it by trying to make sense of it and to relate it to what they already know (or think they know) about the topic. Thus, students develop new knowledge through a process of* active construction *(Brophy, 1992, p. 5).*

Constructivism is rooted in the work of Jean Piaget, the famed Swiss researcher who pioneered the examination of children's intellectual development and so strongly influenced curriculum and instruction in this country.

> *Piaget alerted us that "real learning" is not simply the parroting back of information. Real learning involves personal invention or construction, and the teacher's role in this process is a difficult one. On the one hand, the teacher must honor students' "inventions," or they will not share them. On the other hand, the teacher needs to guide students toward a more mature understanding (Prawat, 1992, p. 11).*

In contrast, Brown and Campione (1990) describe instruction not informed by constructivist thought.

> *The teacher lectures and the students listen. Children assume the role of passive, rather than active participants. It is as if the knowledge the teacher has can be*

transmitted directly to the students; the metaphor is that of pouring information from one container (the teacher's head) to another (the student's head) (p. 112).

The Inductive Model places students at the center of the learning process, yet prescribes a critical role for teachers. It acknowledges that learners are active and will construct understanding that makes sense to them, and at the same time it calls for a specific and critical role for teachers in guiding the students toward valid understandings of the topics they study. We will describe these roles in detail in the sections that follow, but first, let's look at a more detailed discussion of the content the teachers in our introductory episodes taught.

Goals for the Inductive Model

The Inductive Model is designed to accomplish several interrelated goals. The first of these objectives is to help students construct a deep and thorough understanding of specific topics, such as longitude and latitude, Charles's Law, or the rules for forming possessives, as we saw in the three episodes that introduced the chapter.

Second, the Inductive Model is designed to put students in an active role in the process of constructing their understanding. Each of the teachers provided the students with data— the balls with drawings on them in Judy's case, the demonstration, models, and graphs in Sue's, and the passage in Jim's. As students actively work to make sense of this data—with the guidance of the teacher—they not only construct a thorough understanding of the topics, but they also gain skill and confidence in making sense of their environment.

As we look at the lessons, we see that the procedures the teachers used were similar, but the specific content they taught was different. Judy focused on single, specific ideas— latitude and longitude, which are called concepts, while Sue and Jim dealt with relationships between concepts—a principle in Sue's case and an academic rule in Jim's. Generalizations, which are closely related to principles, are a third type of relationship among concepts. The types of content are outlined in Figure 3.6.

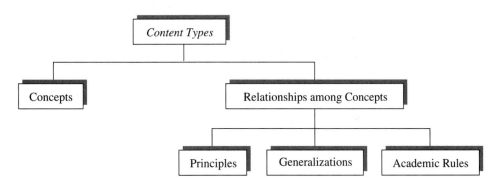

FIGURE 3.6   Goals for the Inductive Model

Concepts: Categories with Common Characteristics

Concepts *are categories, sets, or classes with common characteristics.* For example, whenever Judy Nelson's students encounter parallel, imaginary lines on a map that run east-west, but measure distance north and south, they know they are dealing with latitude. *Latitude* is a concept.

As another example, suppose small children saw the following blocks.

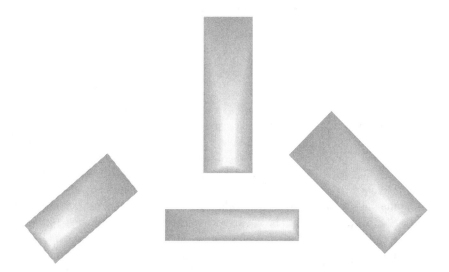

Even though they vary in size, relative dimension, and orientation, the blocks would be classified as rectangles because they all have opposite sides equal and parallel, with angles of 90°. *Rectangle* is also a concept.

The number of concepts taught in the school curriculum is nearly endless. Some are listed in Table 3.2.

Similar lists could be generated for other areas, such as *major scale* and *tempo* in music, *perspective* and *balance* in art, or *aerobic exercise* and *isotonic exercise* in physical education. In addition, many other concepts exist that don't neatly fit into a particular content area such as *honesty, bias, love,* and *internal conflict.*

TABLE 3.2   Concepts in Different Content Areas

Language Arts	Social Studies	Science	Math
Infinitive	Culture	Monocot	Quadratic
Pronoun	Republican	Conifer	Pyramid
Plot	Liberal	Arthropod	Triangle
Hyperbole	Pork Barrel	Work	Division
Indirect Object	Community Helper	Digestion	Equivalent Fraction

Characteristics

A concept's **characteristics** *are its defining features,* and concept learning depends on the students' ability to identify the essential characteristics in the teacher's examples. For instance, in Judy Nelson's lesson, she helped her students identify the following characteristics of latitude:

- parallel lines
- lines run east and west
- lines measure distance north and south of the equator

The students then generalized to conclude that latitude always has those characteristics. Similarly, the concept rectangle has the characteristics:

- opposite sides equal in length
- opposite sides parallel
- all angles 90°

Other characteristics, such as the size, color, or orientation are not essential, and an important part of concept learning is the ability to discriminate between the essential and nonessential characteristics.

Learners "construct" the concept through the process of generalizing. For instance, in the case with the *concept rectangle,* we saw four examples, each with 90° angles and opposite sides equal and parallel. Students then generalized to conclude that all rectangles have these characteristics.

Many concepts, such as *latitude, longitude,* and *rectangle,* have well-defined characteristics. Others, such as *democracy* or *liberal,* are less precise. For instance, some democracies are more "democratic" or more "democracy-like" than others.

For concepts such as these, the characteristics are much harder to specify, and some researchers believe they are better represented with a **prototype**, *a case that is a good illustration of the concept* rather than trying to specify characteristics (Schwarz and Reisberg, 1991). In this case, learners generalize from the prototype in "constructing" the concept.

Concepts: Ease of Learning

The ease of learning a concept depends on the number of characteristics it has and to what degree they are tangible (Tennyson and Cocciarella, 1986). *The concept rectangle* is easy to learn, because it has only three essential characteristics, all of which are concrete and observable. *Democracy,* in contrast, is much more difficult because of its complexity.

These differences are reflected in the school curriculum. Shapes, such as rectangle, are taught at the kindergarten level or before, while democracy rarely appears until the middle-school years. Further, if you asked people on the street to give you a precise description of democracy, few could give you more than vague notions, which demonstrates how difficult some concepts such as democracy are to learn.

Concept Analysis: Clarifying Meaning

Learners don't understand concepts in isolation; rather, their understanding connects the concept to other, related concepts. Concept analysis is a useful tool in helping develop

TABLE 3.3   Concept Analysis

Definition	A part of speech that modifies verbs, adjectives, or other verbs.
Characteristics	Modifies verbs Modifies adverbs Modifies adjectives
Examples	Susan <u>quickly</u> jumped to her feet. Kelly revealed her feelings <u>very openly</u>. David, a weightlifter, is <u>incredibly</u> strong.
Superordinate Concept	Part of speech, modifier
Subordinate Concept	Adverb that modifies another adverb
Coordinate Concept	Adjective

these connections. **Concept analysis** *is the process of describing a concept in terms of its characteristics, related concepts, examples, and definition.* A concept analysis for the concept adverb is illustrated in Table 3.3.

From Table 3.3 we see that the concept analysis includes a **definition**—*a statement including a* **superordinate concept**, *which is a larger category into which the concept fits, and its characteristics.* The definition helps link the concept to a larger class of which it is a member.

A concept analysis also includes **subordinate concepts**, *which are subsets or examples of the concept,* and **coordinate concepts**, *which are also members of a larger category.* The role of the subordinate and coordinate concepts are outlined in the next section.

Examples: The Key to Concept Learning

Whether concepts are specified by their characteristics or by prototypes, the key to concept learning is a carefully selected set of **examples**, *which are cases that illustrate the concept,* together with a definition (Tennyson and Cocciarella, 1986). In cases where the concept may be confused with a closely related concept, both positive and negative examples are necessary. For instance, when learning the concept *insect,* students should also be shown spiders—which are arachnids—so they won't conclude that spiders are insects. By pointing out differences between the two, such as eight legs for spiders instead of the six found in insects, learners are less likely to confuse the two.

Using concept analysis as a tool for thinking about examples, we see that subordinate concepts provide the positive examples, and coordinate concepts help us select the negative examples. For instance, in the case of the concept *insect,* positive examples—subordinate concepts—would include beetles, butterflies, ants, and others, while the negative examples—coordinate concepts—would include examples of arachnids, such as spiders.

Judy Nelson actually used positive and negative examples in her lesson on longitude and latitude. In effect, her examples of longitude served as negative examples for latitude and vice versa.

Quality of Examples.   In order to make learning most effective, teachers want to use the best examples possible. What makes an example a good one? In the case of concept learning, the best examples are those in which the characteristics of the concept are observable in the examples. For example, in teaching the concept *mammal* we would want to use examples that would help students learn that mammals have fur, are warm-blooded, and give live birth to their young. In the real world teachers will have to compromise in some cases, but this criterion is the ideal for which we always strive. This is why Judy Nelson began her lesson with the beach ball. Drawing lines on it allowed her to illustrate the characteristics of longitude and latitude more clearly than would have been possible with a flat wall map or even the globe. Judy then elaborated on the students' initial understanding when she used the globe and her flat wall maps.

Relationships among Concepts: Principles, Generalizations, and Academic Rules

We said that concepts are categories with common characteristics. When we find an object, event, or idea that fits the category, we classify the single instance into it. This helps us simplify our experiences by allowing us to remember the large categories instead of each particular instance. Imagine, for example, how bewildering the world would be if we had to try to identify and understand each individual insect among the billions that exist rather than understand the broad classes. Some very practical aspects of our lives, such as pest control, would be literally impossible.

We also said that we form the concepts through the process of generalizing. We see patterns among the characteristics in the specific examples and we generalize on those patterns. The process of generalizing can be even more powerful, however. Individual concepts can be linked to each other through this process to find broader patterns than the concepts themselves.

These broad patterns exist as principles, generalizations, and academic rules. Each is a relationship between two or more concepts as we saw in Figure 3.6 and we now see highlighted in Figure 3.7.

Principles: Relationships Accepted as True
Principles *are relationships among concepts accepted as true or valid for all known cases.* The terms principles and laws are often used interchangeably, and we saw that the term law was used in Sue Grant's lesson topic. The statement "When pressure is constant, an

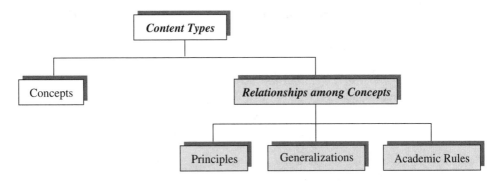

FIGURE 3.7   Relationships among Concepts

increase in temperature results in an increase in volume," is a principle. It describes a relationship between the concept temperature and the concept volume, and we accept it as true.

Some other examples of principles are the following:

- The greater the unbalanced force on an object, the greater its acceleration.
- Like magnetic poles repel and unlike poles attract.
- Change is inevitable.

Principles are an important part of the school curriculum, particularly in the sciences. Much of the content of courses such as chemistry and physics is an examination of principles and their applications.

Generalizations: Relationships with Exceptions

Many of the patterns we observe in the world have obvious exceptions, however, and **generalizations** *are relationships between concepts that describe patterns that have exceptions.* For example, look at the following statements.

- People immigrate for economic reasons.
- A diet high in saturated fat raises a person's cholesterol level.
- Teachers increase achievement by calling on all students equally.

As with principles, each statement describes a relationship between two concepts, but in contrast with principles, each has obvious exceptions. For example, people have also immigrated for religious or political reasons; for some fortunate people a high-saturated-fat diet has no impact on their cholesterol; and highly motivated students achieve whether they're called on or not.

Much of what we know about human behavior in general and teaching and learning in particular exists in the form of generalizations, as is most of the health-related information that we acquire from the media. For instance, the famous study suggesting that an aspirin every other day helps reduce the danger of heart attack is a rough generalization at best, and the even more problematic belief that vitamin C helps prevent colds may not even be valid.

The value in understanding the difference between principles and generalizations relates to helping students think about the validity of different assertions. The validity of the explanations and predictions that are based on generalizations depends on the validity of the generalizations themselves. The ability to make and assess these conclusions are basic critical thinking skills.

Academic Rules: Relationships Arbitrarily Derived by Humankind

Consider statements such as the following:

- A pronoun must agree with its antecedent in number and gender.
- In rounding off a number, if the last digit is 5 or more, you round up, and if it is 4 or less, you round down.
- In English, an adjective precedes the noun it modifies.

Each of the statements is an **academic rule**, *which is a relationship between concepts arbitrarily derived by people.* For instance, in both Spanish and French, adjectives follow the nouns they modify, which demonstrates the arbitrary nature of the rule. In the case of rounding, it would be equally valid to round up if the last digit were six or more, but it has been arbitrarily set at five.

While arbitrary, rules are important for consistency, particularly in the areas of communication. For example, if we didn't have a rule to consistently communicate both singular and plural possessives—the goal in Jim Rooney's lesson—our writing would be very confusing and communication would be difficult.

Examples and Applications

As with concepts, learners "construct" their understanding of principles, generalizations, and academic rules by working with examples. The teacher's role is to provide the best examples possible, and to guide students as they attempt to construct meaning from the examples. In the case of principles, generalizations, and rules, a good example is one in which the relationship between the concepts is observable. For instance, Sue Grant was careful to illustrate the relationship between temperature and volume, both with her demonstration and with her model. She didn't illustrate differences in temperature or differences in volume alone. She illustrated the relationship between the two. Jim Rooney first illustrated possessives for singular and plural nouns, and then linked them to the use of apostrophes. In both cases, the teachers did an excellent job of illustrating the relationship they wanted their students to understand.

Having analyzed the content taught with the Inductive Model, we now turn to a discussion of planning, implementing, and evaluating lessons in which the model is used.

Planning Lessons with the Inductive Model

The planning process for using the Inductive Model is straightforward, involving three essential steps. They are illustrated in Figure 3.8.

Identifying Topics

The planning process can have a number of beginning points, one of which is identification of the content being taught (Peterson, Marx, and Clark, 1978). This is a practical and intuitively sensible beginning point. For example, the teachers in our opening episodes focused on longitude and latitude, Charles's Law, and the rule for forming singular and plural possessives. These topics then became the beginning or focal points for the planning process. Topics may come from textbooks, curriculum guides, or any other sources, including teachers themselves. When the topics are concepts, principles, generalizations, or rules, the Inductive Model can be used effectively.

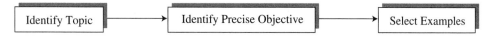

FIGURE 3.8   Planning with the Inductive Model

Specifying Objectives

Content Objectives

Having identified the topic, we must then decide exactly what we want students to know about it. This means our objective is explicit to the point that we can identify what we want our students to be able to say or do. Effective teachers have very clear objectives in mind and teach directly toward them (Berliner, 1985). For example, Judy Nelson wanted her students to be able to do each of the following:

- State the characteristics of longitude and latitude.
- Identify the longitude and latitude of cities and other specified locations on a map.
- Identify a city or landmark nearest a given longitude and latitude.

Judy's objectives were clear, as were Sue Grant's and Jim Rooney's, and this conceptual clarity provides focus during the lesson. Beginning teachers often specify their objectives in writing, while veterans do so less often, instead relying on their past experience and thought processes (Clark and Peterson, 1986).

Clear objectives—whether or not they're stated in writing—are critical because they provide the framework for teachers' thinking as they guide their students' "constructions" of the topics they're teaching. If the teachers' objectives aren't clear, they won't know what questions to ask, their responses to students' questions will be vague, and they will be less able to offer suggestions to students working collaboratively. Also, clear objectives guide teachers in their selection of examples. If objectives aren't clear, the teacher doesn't know what he or she is trying to illustrate, and the likelihood of selecting the best possible examples is reduced.

Our experience in working with teachers indicates that their questioning effectiveness is closely related to the clarity of their objectives. In asking teachers what they were trying to accomplish after watching vague and uncertain lessons, they usually have difficulty precisely describing their objectives. Teachers must be clear about their objectives to effectively guide their students' thinking.

Developing Higher-Order and Critical Thinking

The second part of specifying objectives is slightly different from the first. While content objectives focus on *outcomes*, such as identifying the relationships between an animal's characteristics and its habitat, or immigration and economics, higher-order and critical thinking focus on the *process* of finding patterns, forming explanations, hypothesizing, generalizing, and documenting each of these conclusions with evidence. Planning for thinking means that teachers consciously intend to have learners observe, compare, search for patterns, generalize, predict, and explain *while* they are actively "constructing" their understanding of the topic. Teaching for thinking doesn't change the content objective; rather, it changes the way the teacher and students operate as they move toward it.

We saw in Chapter 2 that "Learning is a consequence of thinking" (Perkins, 1992, p. 8), which means that content goals and goals for thinking are inextricably interwoven. Learners will automatically use the processes, since they are involved in constructing deep understandings of the topics they are studying. The teacher helps make this use conscious and systematic.

Selecting Examples

The third step in the planning process is the selection of examples. Once teachers know exactly what they want students to be able to say or do, they must find examples that will illustrate those characteristics. From our earlier discussion, we know that, ideally, examples include observable characteristics if a concept is being taught, or an observable relationship in the case of a principle, generalization, or rule. Selecting the examples can be as simple as drawing on a beach ball as Judy Nelson did, or as demanding as creating a complex simulation and role play to illustrate a concept such as *discrimination* or *relative deprivation*. The importance of good examples is impossible to overstate. Let's briefly look at some different forms examples can take.

Realia

Realia is nothing more than a substitute word for "the real thing." This is the most fundamental form of example and it should be used wherever possible. For instance, an ideal example of an arthropod would be a live lobster purchased from a fish store. The children could see and touch the animal, feel its hard and cold shell, and notice its jointed legs and three body parts. The essential characteristics of the concept would be illustrated in this example.

Demonstrations and hands-on activities are another form of realia. Sue Grant's balloons in three different conditions allowed the students to observe the relationship between temperature and volume. When students connect two wires to a battery and make a bulb light up, they are seeing an actual complete circuit, not a simulation, model, role play, or other indirect method of illustrating the concept.

Pictures

When realia are impossible, pictures are often an acceptable compromise. Since we can't bring young and mature mountains into the classroom, and it is difficult to go to where we can observe them directly, pictures of the Rocky Mountains and Appalachian Mountains would be an appropriate way of illustrating these concepts. The key is to come as close as possible to reality. Detailed colored slides or photographs are better than black and white pictures, which are, in turn, better than outline drawings.

Models

Some content—particularly in science—is impossible to observe directly. In these cases, **models**, *which allow us to visualize what we can't observe directly,* are effective. Sue Grant's drawings were a type of model because they allowed her students to visualize the spacing and motion of the molecules under three different temperature conditions. The molecular motion was impossible to illustrate in any other way.

As another example, look at the model of a water molecule shown in Figure 3.9. While the model is obviously not reality, it illustrates accepted characteristics of the water molecule. One atom (the oxygen) is larger than the other two (the hydrogens), which are both equidistant from the oxygen, and the shape is accurate. From this we can see that while models do not actually illustrate reality, they can help us identify essential characteristics of reality.

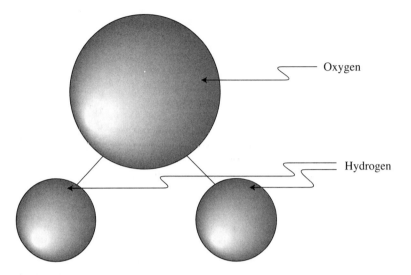

FIGURE 3.9   Model of a Water Molecule

Case Studies
Case studies, particularly mini case studies, can be powerful tools in illustrating topics difficult to illustrate in other ways. For example, consider the following illustration.

> Mary's dream had come true. John, a boy she had wanted to date for some time, had asked her to go to the movies. However, as she thought about her homework assignments for that night, she remembered the term paper that was due on Friday. She had been putting off work on the paper until the last moment, and now she didn't know what to do.
>
> Johnny knew if he cheated off Bill's paper, he'd pass the test, but he also knew if he got caught cheating, he'd be suspended.
>
> Although Mary hated to leave her hometown friends and family, and even her room, which she had lived in since a child, she wanted to go to college in Boston, 500 miles away.

Notice that in each of the three anecdotes, the character is faced with two alternatives that are antagonistic to each other. The brief case studies illustrate the concept *internal conflict*. We can see how hard the concept would be to describe, and a definition such as "To come into collision, clash, or be at variance within oneself," would also do little to clarify the concept for the learner. The brief scenarios, however, provide a clear picture of the characteristics of the concept. Skill in developing case studies can help teachers communicate many difficult concepts to their learners. Case studies are powerful teaching aids in areas such as social studies or literature where other forms of illustration are often difficult to find.

Simulation and Role Play
Simulation and role play are forms of examples used when concepts are hard to illustrate in any other way. Because they are often found together, we discuss them at the same time.

For instance, consider a concept such as *discrimination* in a social studies class. While students hear a great deal about it, many have little first-hand experience. A simulation where some members of the class are discriminated against because of eye or hair color, height, or some other arbitrary characteristic provides powerful illustrations of an important concept.

Social studies teachers have also used simulations to illustrate our court system, the ways bills become laws, and the drudgery of assembly-line jobs.

We have devoted this space to a discussion of the various forms of examples because they are critical in learning concepts, principles, and generalizations. Without examples, learning is often reduced to mere memorization (Tennyson and Cocciarella, 1986).

Quality of Examples: Teaching At-Risk Students

We hear a great deal about **at-risk students**—*students in danger of failing to complete their education with the skills necessary to survive in modern society* (Slavin, Karweit, and Madden, 1989). At-risk students are characterized by high drop-out rates, low achievement and low self-esteem (Vito and Connell, 1988). They are often experientially deprived, meaning they lack experiences that more advantaged students enjoy. For example, we referred to the concepts *young* and *mature mountains* in the last section. Students with advantaged backgrounds may have traveled through the Rocky Mountains or Appalachian Mountains, or both, so a verbal reference to them would be meaningful. In contrast, for a student without these experiences, a simple verbal description would be meaningless.

A major way teachers can accommodate these differences is by providing the experience the students need; this is why the quality of examples is so important. If the examples are good enough, all of the information that the student needs to understand the topic is contained in the example. In essence, the example becomes the student's experience in the case of the disadvantaged learner. Realistically, high-quality examples won't eliminate all of the background differences between disadvantaged and advantaged students, but using these examples is an important step a teacher can take to help narrow the gap. For other students, excellent examples make their understanding richer and more meaningful. It is the nearest thing that exists to a win-win situation for everyone.

Implementing Lessons Using the Inductive Model

You have identified your topic, carefully specified your objectives, and have selected or created your examples. You're now ready to enter the classroom with your students and begin the lesson. Implementing a lesson using the Inductive Model combines five interrelated phases. They are illustrated in Figure 3.10.

Phase 1: Lesson Introduction

During the lesson introduction, the teacher tells the students that he is going to present them with some examples and their task is to look for patterns and differences in them. The teacher can introduce the lesson in a variety of ways. A simple statement can be used such as, "Today, I'm going to show you some examples. I want you to be very good

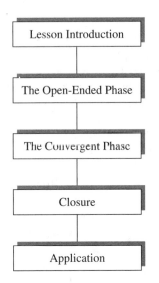

FIGURE 3.10   Steps in Implementing Inductive-Model Lessons

observers and try and see what kind of pattern exists in them." Alternately, the lesson can begin as Judy Nelson did when she posed the problem of specifying for a new friend exactly where the students lived. Sue Grant identified Charles's Law by name, linked it to kinetic theory, and told the students that they would be able to solve problems with it when they finished the lesson. Jim Rooney began his lesson by simply elaborating on a review of the previous day's work. Each of these introductions provides a conceptual framework for the lesson in which students understand that their task is to analyze the examples and look for patterns.

Phase 2: The Open-Ended Phase

During the open-ended phase, the students actually begin the process of constructing meaning from the presented examples. The teacher begins this phase by presenting examples to the students and asking them to observe, describe, and compare them. The teachers have several choices:

- They can present an example and ask students to observe and describe it. This is what Judy Nelson did with her beach ball, and what Sue Grant did with her demonstration.
- They can present two or more examples and ask the students what they have in common (search for patterns). This was Jim Rooney's choice in his activity.
- They can present an example and a nonexample and ask the students to contrast the two.
- Depending on the activity, the teachers can even begin with a negative example and have the students describe it.

Whichever option the teacher chooses, students begin their analysis by responding to open-ended questions—questions that ask them to simply describe or compare (and contrast), and as a result, have a variety of acceptable answers. For example, the following are some of the questions Judy Nelson asked during this phase:

"Now what can you tell us about this line? Let's begin. Tara?"

and later she said,

"Now compare the lines to each other. Kathy?"

Open-ended questions have several advantages compared to typical convergent questions (questions requiring a single correct answer):

- They are easy to construct and ask. Teachers can ask students to describe or compare and then use students' responses as the basis for further questions. As a result, questioning becomes less labor-intensive for teachers.
- Because a variety of responses are acceptable, the questions are "safe," meaning shy or reluctant learners are virtually assured of success in answering them. As a result, they are excellent for promoting student motivation and a supportive classroom climate (Eggen and Kauchak, 1994).
- Since the questions can be asked and answered quickly, it is easy for teachers to call on several different students in a short time period. As a result, student involvement and equitable distribution are easier to achieve. Research indicates that larger numbers of classroom questions are related to increased achievement (Pratton and Hales, 1986).
- The questions allow for brisk lesson pacing, which results in greater student attention than in slower paced lessons.
- Open-ended questions have been found effective with cultural minorities and students with limited English language proficiency because they provide safe opportunities for these students to demonstrate what they know (Langer, Bartolome, Vasques, and Lucas, 1990).
- Open-ended questions allow teachers to diagnose students' backgrounds. What the students "observe" in the examples will reflect their backgrounds and perceptions of the examples.

The last point is particularly important. As we said earlier in the chapter, students "construct" new understanding based on their background, so diagnosis of their present level of understanding is important. Asking open-ended questions is a simple, efficient way of obtaining this information.

Learning to keep questions open-ended requires some adjustment at first. Because teachers are concerned with time, lesson momentum, and pace, they tend to be very directive and want to "hone in" on the idea they're after almost immediately. To increase student participation and give students time to think, we're encouraging you to "loosen up" a little and remain open-ended a little longer.

For instance, suppose you are teaching the concept of direct object and you have illustrated the concept with the following sentences:

Kelly threw the ball to Jamey.
Jim dumped the cans in the recycle bin.

Teachers—knowing that their objective is for students to understand direct objects—tend to want to ask questions such as, "What did Kelly throw?" or "What did the people do in each sentence?" While not technically wrong, they narrow the opportunity for students to respond, and many of the advantages of open-ended questions are eliminated. A better beginning question in the open-ended phase would be, "What do you notice about the sentences?" or "What are some things that the sentences have in common?" This type of questioning provides opportunities for students to think about the sentences and share their thoughts with the rest of the class.

As another example, consider a teacher who wants students to understand the following rule: "Nonessential clauses in a sentence are set off by commas." A sentence might be displayed on the board or overhead as the following:

The boys in this class, who are among the most hard working in the school, did very well on the last test.

The teacher would then continue by saying, "What do you notice about the sentence?" "Tell me something about the sentence." "Describe this sentence for me," or some similar directive. At this point in the activity, these questions are better than: "What is the subject of the sentence?" or other questions that have a specific right or wrong answer.

There is no rule suggesting a specific number of open-ended questions to ask. With practice, teachers become comfortable with the process and use their professional judgement as to when to move on. Monitoring students' behavior is important here. If they appear eager to continue describing or comparing the examples, the teacher may continue a bit longer; if they appear "antsy" or eager to "get on with it," the teacher can move on more quickly. This is when Phase 3 begins.

Phase 3: The Convergent Phase

The open-ended phase is characterized by observations, descriptions, and comparisons where virtually all answers are acceptable. In that a specific content goal exists, the lesson must progress to an explicit description of the relationship in a principle, generalization, or rule, or the characteristics of a concept. To reach that goal, the teacher narrows the range of student responses and leads them to verbally identify the relationship or characteristics. Because the students' processing results in or converges on a specific answer, it is called the "convergent phase."

The open-ended phase flows naturally into the convergent phase, and the line between the two is often blurred. You shouldn't be concerned if you don't see a sharp distinction between the two in the activity.

Let's return to Judy Nelson's lesson for a moment to see how she made the transition from the open-ended phase to the convergent phase.

She continues by asking, "How do these lines compare to the lines of latitude? David?"

"... They go all around the ball."

"Yes they do," Judy smiled. "What else? Tricia?"

"... You have the same number of each on the ball."

"Yes I did," Judy nodded, realizing that she had drawn three lines of latitude and three lines of longitude on the ball.

"How do the lengths of the longitude lines compare to the lengths of the latitude lines? Chris?"

Judy began the convergent phase with the previous question. This question, while still calling for a comparison, referred the students to the lengths of the lines, rather than referring to lines of latitude and longitude in general, so it was narrower than the earlier ones had been, and required a more specific answer. This narrowing of possible student responses occurs during the convergent phase.

As we saw in Judy's lesson, however, the process of converging on the content objective doesn't always go as planned. When Judy asked Chris to compare the lengths of the longitude and latitude lines, she wanted Chris to say that the longitude lines were all the same length, but he didn't. Let's look again at how she handled it.

"How do the lengths of the longitude lines compare to the lengths of the latitude lines? Chris?"

"... It looks like they're the same."

"Same as each other?"

"Yes."

"Let's take another look. What do all of the longitude lines do here?" Judy asks pointing the top of the ball toward Chris.

"They all cross there."

"Good," Judy smiles, "So what do we know about the lengths of the longitude lines?"

"... They're ... I don't know."

"OK, wrap this string around the ball," Judy suggests, handing Chris a piece of string that she had on her desk.

Chris then measures the circumference of the ball through the poles with the string.

Judy has Jennifer repeat the process with another piece of string at a different point on the ball but still going through the poles, and has Andy and Karen measure the ball simulating lines of latitude to demonstrate that the latitude lines get shorter near the poles.

"So, what do we know about the lengths of the strings? Chris?"

"They're the same," Chris responds pointing to the longitude strings, "But these got shorter," pointing to the latitude strings.

"And what do these represent?"

"Lines of longitude."

"Excellent! So, what do we know about the lines of longitude?"

". . . They're all the same length."

"Great! Good thinking," Judy responded enthusiastically, and she then went through a similar line of questioning to demonstrate that the latitude lines were shorter near the poles.

When Chris was unable to provide the correct answer, Judy might simply have told him that the lines were the same length and moved on. This is seemingly more efficient than the process Judy went through. However, Chris's conception of lines of longitude and latitude was that they were all the same length, and it is unlikely that merely telling him otherwise would be convincing. Instead, Judy confronted his misconception directly, and convincingly demonstrated the characteristics of both longitude and latitude. This tactic, together with her prompting questions, led Chris to an understanding of longitude and latitude that was much more meaningful than merely telling him about the concept.

This process of linking content to evidence is critical. For example, in spite of an eight-week unit on the topic of photosynthesis, over 90 percent of fifth graders retained the original belief that instead of making their own food, plants get their food from the outside, just as people do (Roth and Anderson, 1991). In another study with eighth graders who had completed a course in physical science, over 75 percent of the students retained the belief that larger objects (objects with greater volume) have more mass and are more dense than smaller objects, in spite of considerable experience in solving problems with the formula $D = M/V$ (Eggen and McDonald, 1987). While these two studies were both done with science content, we see from Judy Nelson's lesson that misconceptions can exist in all content areas.

As we said earlier in the chapter, even low-achieving and experientially deprived students bring a great deal of background knowledge with them to the learning situation, and this knowledge will have an important impact on their learning. Merely "telling" students has little influence in changing previous conceptions. They must have clear examples combined with teacher-student and student-student interaction that helps them "reconstruct" misconceptions and accurately construct new conceptions. This is what Judy Nelson did in her work with her class in general, and Chris in particular.

For another example, let's look again at the episode with Dawn Adams, the teacher in the lesson on nonessential clauses.

She had displayed three sentences for the students that appeared as follows:

The boys in this class, who are among the most hard working in school, did very well on the last test.

Mrs. Adams's salary, which isn't enough to live on, is paid twice a month.

The school that is located on the south side of town is only two years old.

Dawn has asked for several observations and comparisons. Now let's see how she handles the convergent phase of the activity.

"Look at the information set off by commas in the first two sentences. What can you tell us about this information in each case? Dan?"

". . . It tells us something about the people," Dan responds after studying the sentences.

"And what is this information called? Ginger?"

". . . A clause?"

"Yes, good. How do you know?"

"It has both a subject and a verb part."

"Very good Ginger. Now, look at the first sentence. What is it basically about? Mary?"

". . ."

"What is the sentence primarily about, the boys doing well on the test, or the boys being good looking?"

". . . Doing well on the test."

"Yes, excellent," Dawn smiles. "And how about the second one? Lori?"

". . . Getting paid every two weeks."

"All right!" Dawn waves enthusiastically. "So, what does that tell us about the information set off by the commas? Roger?"

". . . It's sort of added stuff in the sentence."

"OK, and what do you mean by that?"

". . . The sentence would still mean about the same thing if that information wasn't there."

"Good! Now look at this part of the third sentence," and she then underlined the clause 'that is located on the south side of town.' "How is it different from the first two? Ken?"

". . . It looks like we need that part of the sentence for it to mean what we want it to mean."

"Good, Ken. And what else do we see in the first two sentences that we don't see in the third one? Sue?"

". . . The commas."

From this episode we see how Dawn skillfully led the students to a conclusion about the nonessential nature of the information in the first two sentences. Just as Judy Nelson had done when one of her students was unable to answer, Dawn prompted Mary when she was unsure of the answer. This kind of guidance both helps students understand the topic and assures success, producing a climate of support. This is characteristic of teaching in the convergent phase.

Phase 4: Closure

Closure is the point at which students identify the characteristics of the concept or can state the principle, generalization, or rule. Judy Nelson reached closure when her students were able to summarize the characteristics of longitude and latitude. Sue Grant reached closure when the students were able to state Charles's Law, and Jim Rooney reached closure when his students could state the rule for punctuating singular and plural possessive nouns.

Let's look now at how Dawn Adams reached closure and see how it flowed directly from the convergent phase of her lesson.

> "Very good. So describe what we've found in a general statement. Cal?"
>
> ". . . When we have information in a sentence that isn't really important to its meaning, we set it off with commas. If it is important, we don't put any commas in the sentence."
>
> "Very good, Cal. And what do we call this information?"
>
> "A clause."
>
> "Good. Just to be sure you've got it, go ahead and describe it once more in your own words. Kerri?"
>
> ". . . If the clause is necessary to the meaning of the sentence it isn't set off by commas, and if it isn't, we do set it off."

While a formal statement of closure is generally important and contributes to students clearly understanding the lesson (Brophy and Good, 1986), certain exceptions will exist. For example, suppose the concept of "above" is being taught to a group of young children. It could be defined as "A position in space where one object is at a higher altitude than another." Obviously, young students would be unlikely to generate such a statement even with considerable prompting. In this case, the teacher would move directly to the application phase in lieu of a formal statement of closure.

Phase 4 also provides opportunities to help students develop thinking skills related to recognizing irrelevant information. For instance, in the case with the nonessential clauses, they could be prompted to notice that the pronoun at the beginning of the clause is *not relevant* because the clause in each example began with different pronouns. In Jim Rooney's case the content of the sentences in each case is irrelevant to the rule. The essential information was that the words were singular and plural possessive nouns ending in -*y*. With any topic, it is quite easy to assess the examples for nonessential information, which in turn sensitizes students to this important thinking skill.

Phase 5: The Application Phase

While being able to state a definition of a concept or describe a principle, generalization, or rule reflects understanding at one level, to make the topic meaningful, students must be able to apply it in a "real-world" setting. Judy Nelson's students, for example, must be able to find the longitude and latitude of different locations around the world, Sue Grant's must be able to solve problems with Charles's Law, and Jim Rooney's must be able to correctly punctuate singular and plural possessive nouns in their writing. Developing these abilities occurs in the application phase.

The application phase typically includes a seatwork or homework assignment. However, in spite of careful development of the concept, principle, generalization, or rule, application still requires a transition for the student that often requires additional help from the teacher. Let's see how Judy Nelson handled this part of the learning activity.

"OK, everyone. Suppose now that you were trying to tell someone exactly how to locate Denver, Colorado. How would we do that? Connie?"

". . . We would find its longitude and latitude."

"Good, Connie. Everyone, do that with your maps." (All the students have maps in front of them.)

Judy walks among the students watching them work. After about a minute she begins, "All right. What did you find? Kim?"

". . . Its about 40°."

"North or south?"

". . . North."

"How do you know?"

". . . Because it's north of the equator."

"Yes. Excellent, Kim." Judy then continues by identifying Denver's longitude.

This process of carefully monitoring students' initial efforts at application and then discussing them helps solidify ideas in the students' minds, makes the topic more meaningful for them, and helps bridge the gap between the teacher-led learning activity and independent practice.

When the teacher is satisfied that most of the students can comfortably apply the information on their own, the teacher can give an assignment that requires further application. While most of the students work independently, she can help those individuals who haven't fully grasped the idea or who are not yet ready for application on their own.

Application: The Role of Context

The application phase is most effective when students are required to apply their understanding in a realistic context. Judy Nelson capitalized on the role of context with her initial problem of trying to specify exactly where the students lived. Jim Rooney used paragraphs that related to the students' experience as the context for applying his rule. This tactic is much more effective that having the students apply the rule to isolated sentences. Dawn Adams had her students write a paragraph and required that it contain at least three examples of nonessential clauses and two other examples of clauses that were essential. She also required that the paragraphs make sense; the students couldn't merely tack several sentences together and call it a paragraph.

As another example, Sue Grant gave her students the following problem.

You have a balloon filled with 1,620 ml of air at room temperature—72°F. Suppose that you put it in the freezer, which is 10°F. What will its volume be? What assumptions are we making when we solve this problem?

Here Sue provided a common, household context for her problem, measuring whether or not the students realized that they had to first convert to Celsius and then to absolute temperature. Her problem was easy to write, but powerful in its ability to make Charles's Law meaningful to students.

Application: Linking New and Old Learning

The application phase also includes helping learners link new learning with prior understanding. For example, Sue Grant's students connected Charles's Law to their earlier understanding of mass, volume, and density, Jim Rooney's students linked possessives to earlier understanding of singular and plural nouns, and Judy Nelson's students linked their understanding of latitude and longitude to earlier knowledge about the earth.

If these links don't spontaneously develop during the course of the lesson, the teacher should formally link the information through review. For example, Sue Grant said to her students,

> "We see from Charles's Law how temperature affects volume. Let's think about how what we just learned relates to what we already know about mass and density."

In this way, she helped link their understanding of Charles's Law to their earlier understanding of mass and density.

The Inductive Model: Emphasis on Thinking

As we've studied each of the phases to this point, we've seen that the explicit focus was on the content objectives. The planning started with content topics, specific content objects were identified, and examples that illustrated the topics were created.

As we saw in our discussion of planning for using the Inductive Model, the thinking skills objectives are not an outcome in the same sense as are the content objectives; rather, they're processes the students are involved in as they move to the content objective. For example, in each of our episodes we saw the teachers promote thinking in their students in the following ways:

- Each teacher emphasized comparing (and contrasting). This is one of the most important and fundamental of thinking skills.
- By asking students to identify the characteristics of longitude and latitude (Judy Nelson), verbally state Charles's Law (Sue Grant), and verbally state the rule for punctuating possessives or nonessential clauses (Jim Rooney and Dawn Adams), the students were required to find patterns and generalize.
- In each case the students were required to apply the information they learned in a realistic context.

These are all important thinking skills, the development of which is inherent in the structure of the Inductive Model.

In addition, the teachers capitalized on other opportunities to involve their students in thinking processes. For instance, Judy Nelson asked the following questions during her activity:

> "Go ahead Kathy. What do you mean by even?"

"Excellent! So, what do we know about the lines of longitude?"

". . . They're all the same length."

"And how do we know?

Sue Grant's students worked in pairs; she required them to write conclusions (inferences) in one column and the supporting observations in another. The following are some of her examples.

Inference	*Observation*
The masses of air in the balloons are equal.	The number of "dots" in the three drawings is equal.
The volume of the heated balloon increased and the volume of the cooled balloon decreased.	The molecules are farthest apart in the first drawing and closest together in the third drawing.

Learning to recognize the opportunity to ask questions such as, "How do you know?" "Why?" and "What would happen if?" requires practice. With effort, teachers develop the inclination to ask these questions, and recognizing opportunities gets easier and easier. The payoff is a much higher level of student thinking with little extra class time.

Unfortunately, teachers rarely ask questions, such as "Why?" or "How do you know?" Our belief is that it is more a matter of awareness and practice than consciously choosing not to ask them. We hope that your study of this material will change those patterns.

The Inductive Model: Options

To this point we have illustrated and discussed the planning and implementation of Inductive-Model lessons. However, in applying the model in different content areas and at different levels of the curriculum, variations will occur. We discuss some of these in this section.

Examples

We have emphasized the role of examples as Inductive Model lessons are planned. Again, the importance of high-quality examples cannot be overstated. Several considerations in the creation or selection of examples exist, however.

Number of Examples

How many examples do you need? The precise answer is as many as you need to illustrate the scope of the topic. For instance, if you were teaching the concept of *adverb,* a minimum number would be at least one example each of an adverb modifying a verb, an adjective, and another adverb, plus one or two adjectives as nonexamples.

As another case, if you were teaching the concept *reptile,* you would need at least one example each of an alligator (or crocodile), snake, lizard, and turtle, and a sea turtle (so the students don't conclude that sea turtles are some kind of fish because they live in the water), together with a frog (which is an amphibian) as a nonexample.

In the case of topics with a narrower scope, such as nonessential clauses, we saw that Dawn Adams used two examples of nonessential clauses set off by commas and one example (a nonexample) of an essential clause not set off. While a third positive example would have been good, Dawn provided enough information so that the students could identify a pattern in it, which allowed them to practice finding patterns and generalizing.

Accommodating Individual Differences

Adapting the Inductive Model for use with students at different levels of development and experience depends on two factors—the background of the students and the examples that teachers choose. For example, Sue Grant's students had experience with concepts such as mass, volume, temperature, and pressure, evidenced by the fact that they incorporated these concepts into their conclusions and supporting observations. Had they lacked those concepts, Sue would have had to back up and begin by developing them. (Because the Inductive Model begins open-endedly, informal diagnosis of the students' background is built into the process.) Also, the students were able to deal with the abstraction involved in Sue's models of molecular motion and the information in the graph she presented. The illustrations that Sue used were more abstract than those that would be effective with younger students. In comparison, Judy Nelson used a very concrete beginning—the beach ball with the lines on it—for her lesson because she knew that several of her students had no experience in this area.

The decisions that teachers make about the kind of examples to use depends upon students' backgrounds. In Judy's case, abstract illustrations would have been less effective because of the students' lack of background. In general, the younger the students or the less experience they have had with the topic, the greater the need for high-quality examples. High-quality examples are the ideal for everyone; with young children and learners lacking experience, they are a must.

Creativity in Teaching

We have all heard about creative teachers and the need for teachers to be creative. In fact, while often difficult to implement, creativity can be quite simple conceptually. It is simply how eye catching, attractive, and clever we are in preparing our examples. A prime example of this is the Children's Television Workshop's work on *Sesame Street*. *Sesame Street* teaches a number of concepts and rules, which are most cleverly illustrated. For instance, a muppet who runs off into the distance and announces, "Now I'm far," then comes closer and says, "Now I'm near," is doing nothing more than illustrating the concepts far and near. However, the illustrations are attractive, eye catching, and clever. They are creative.

Judy Nelson was quite creative in using the beach ball for her initial illustration of longitude and latitude. It was reasonably eye catching and very clear. This is the essence of creativity.

Teaching "Off the Top of Your Head"

Teaching "off the top of your head" means generating examples on the spot and guiding your students toward an idea that appears spontaneously during the course of a lesson. As your expertise with the model develops, your ability to guide your students will require less conscious effort on your part, and you will be able to recognize opportunities to use mini inductive lessons in the context of larger topics. Let's look at some examples of this idea.

In the middle of a class discussion, one of Sandy Clark's students raised her hand and said, "I don't get this 'division by zero is undefined.' I just don't understand what they mean by 'undefined.'"

Sandy paused, thought a moment, and said, "OK, look," and she then wrote the number 12 on the chalkboard.

"Now, I'm going to give you each a number to divide into 12, and when I call your name, you give me the answer. Roy, divide by 2; Eddie, 0.03; Karen, 0.01; Jeff, 0.002; Judy, 0.0004; Kelly, 0.000006; John, 0.000000002; Donna, 0.0000000000003."

"We'll go ahead and make a table," and she then wrote the following on the board as the students gave their answers.

Divided by	Answer
2.0	6
0.03	400
0.01	1,200
0.002	6,000
0.0004	30,000
0.000006	2,000,000
0.000000002	6,000,000,000
0.0000000000003	40,000,000,000,000

"So, let's look at the patterns we have here," Sandy directed. "What do you notice about the left column? Terry?"

"The numbers are getting smaller and smaller."

"Good. So imagine now that we kept going with those numbers. Eventually we would be approaching what? Leah?"

". . . I'm not following you."

"Imagine that we have many more numbers in the column," Sandy continued, "and they continued to get smaller and smaller. Eventually, they would be nearly what?"

". . . Zero."

"Yes, exactly, good," she smiled at Terry.

"Now look at the right column. What pattern do you see there? Rene?"

"They're getting bigger and bigger."

"Now imagine that the numbers in the left column got incredibly small, so small that we can hardly imagine. What would happen to the numbers on the right?"

"They would be huge," Brent volunteered.

"And ultimately if we actually got to zero, what would happen to those on the right? . . . They would sort of what?" Sandy gestured openly as if illustrating an explosion with her arms.

". . . They would sort of explode?" Dennis responded uncertainly, reacting to both the pattern and Sandy's gestures.

"Yes, exactly," Sandy nodded. "That's what we mean by 'undefined.'"

Several points should be made about this example. First, Sandy had the insight to be able to generate her examples "on the spot." This required clear understanding of her subject matter and what it would take to illustrate this topic for her students in a meaningful way. The interface between teachers' own understanding of a topic and their understanding of what it takes to help learners understand the topic is described in various ways, but most sensibly as "subject matter knowledge for teaching" (Grossman, Wilson, and Shulman, 1989).

Second, Sandy's illustration and development of the idea that "Division by zero is undefined" took less than ten minutes. This is what we mean by mini inductive lessons in the context of larger discussions.

Third, and perhaps most importantly, Sandy could have simply tried to explain division by zero using a verbal description, and it would have taken less time. However, the likelihood of the explanation being as meaningful to the students as Sandy's illustration is also much less.

An important trend suggested by the research on teaching is "in-depth study of fewer topics." This approach to teaching suggests that in-depth investigation of fewer topics is preferable to superficial coverage of many and that students need time and opportunities to think about the topics they're learning. Brophy (1992) describes this movement in this way:

> *Embedded in this approach to teaching is the notion of "complete" lessons carried through to include higher-order applications of content. The breadth of content addressed, thus, is limited to allow for more in-depth teaching of the content. Unfortunately, typical state and district curriculum guidelines feature long lists of items and subskills to be "covered," and typical curriculum packages supplied by educational publishers respond to these guidelines by emphasizing breadth over depth of coverage (p. 6).*

Inductive lessons that provide opportunities for students to analyze examples and apply new content in realistic settings are one solution to this problem.

Length of Lessons

In working with teachers, we're often asked, "How long should the lesson be?" The answer is the same for all lessons—as long as it takes the students to reach the objective. In some cases, it may be rather long; for example, it took Judy Nelson's students about thirty minutes to develop valid characteristics of latitude and longitude, and they spent the rest of the class period practicing identifying the longitude and latitude of various locations around the world. In comparison, it took Dawn Adams's students less than ten minutes to develop the rule for punctuating nonessential clauses, and we saw that Sandy Clark's "spontaneous" lesson also took less than ten minutes.

Fostering Cooperation

Lessons taught with the Inductive Model are excellent vehicles for promoting cooperation among students. For example, in the open-ended phase of the activity, Sue Grant had her students work in pairs as they made comparisons of the balloons, her models, and the graph. Jim Rooney had individual students write comparisons on a piece of paper, but he could have as easily had students work in pairs as well.

Using the open-ended phase of the Inductive Model is a good way to introduce students to working together. Since they are only required to make observations and comparisons in most cases, the cognitive task isn't so demanding that the process is frustrating for them. With some practice, students can then be introduced to more demanding tasks, such as making and defending conclusions, as Sue Grant's students did.

Efficiency in Planning

Expert teachers can often use the Inductive Model nearly as spontaneously as we saw Sandy Clark use it here. As teachers acquire increased confidence in "thinking on their feet," their preparation for Inductive-Model lessons can become very efficient. Each of the teachers in our examples spent only a matter of minutes in gathering their materials.

This doesn't imply in any way, however, that the teachers were unprepared. They had very specific objectives in mind and they were clear in how they intended to help their students reach the objectives. Admittedly, beginning teachers will probably have to commit more information to paper, since they don't have the experience that veterans have in teaching. However, with practice and effort they, too, can acquire the expertise to efficiently guide student learning in the ways that we saw illustrated in this chapter.

Assessing Student Learning

Measuring Content Outcomes

The content outcomes of a lesson conducted using the Inductive Model can be measured in a variety of ways, ranging from standard paper-and-pencil objective tests, to performance measures and portfolios.

Regardless of the measure, teachers must be very clear in their thinking to be sure that their objectives, learning activities, and assessments are consistent with each other. Each of the teachers in the examples we presented in the chapter had learning activities that were consistent with their objectives.

Maintaining this consistency through the assessment phase of teaching can be a difficult task. It's easy to fall into the trap of thinking you're measuring one level of understanding when in fact you're measuring another. For example, consider the following test item designed to measure students' understanding of the concept arthropod.

Circle all of the following that are arthropods.

  a. alligator
  b. shrimp
  c. oyster
  d. dragonfly

In order to respond correctly to the item, students must know how each of the animals appear. If not, they could understand the concept and still respond incorrectly. This invalidates the item. While the item is intended to measure students' understanding of the concept, it more nearly measures the students' knowledge of each of the individual animals.

Pictures would be much better. If pictures are used (assuming the characteristics are displayed in detail), students could respond to the item without knowing the names of the animals, and those with less experience are not disadvantaged compared to the rest of the class.

Better yet, although admittedly more demanding, would be for the teacher to display two examples, such as a grasshopper and a clam, and have the students explain in writing why the grasshopper is an arthropod and the clam is not. This provides students with an opportunity to apply the knowledge they have acquired and also gives the teacher insight into students' thinking.

As another example, suppose that Sue Grant wanted to measure her students' understanding of Charles's Law and she presented the following problem.

$$T_1 = 50°C, T_2 = 40°C, V_1 = 100 \text{ ml. Find } V_2.$$

The problem presented in this way measures little more than recall of the procedure. In situations such as this, students commonly memorize formulas, plug in numbers without understanding, and find answers that have virtually no meaning for them. Further, regardless of the way a lesson is taught, if the measurement is essentially knowledge and recall, mature students, such as those in junior high and high school, will study more in response to the way they're tested than to the way they're taught (Crooks, 1988).

Much better problems would be the following:

It's July 15, and extremely hot outside. You have three closed containers, each filled with 250 ml of air in your kitchen, which is 23°C. (Imagine that the containers are made of an elastic that can expand and contract without changing the pressure.) You put container A in the freezing compartment of your refrigerator, B in the other part of the refrigerator, and C outside your house.

1. Which of the following best describes the volume of each container after they have been in these conditions for an hour?
   a. Since the mass of air for each doesn't change, each container will have 250 ml of air in it.
   b. All three containers will have more than 250 ml of air in them.
   c. A will have less than 250 ml of air, the volume of B will not change, and C will have more than 250 ml of air.
   d. A and B will have less than 250 ml of air, and C will have more than 250 ml of air.
   e. We don't have enough information to make conclusions about the volume of the air in each case.
2. If the freezing compartment of your refrigerator is –6°C, what will be the volume of air in the container placed there?

Notice that the first example is qualitative. This measures a different kind of understanding than does the quantitative problem. Both measurements are necessary. Students often learn to put numbers in formulas and get answers with little actual understanding of the concepts and principles involved. Qualitative measurements help assure that this doesn't happen.

In both Judy Nelson's and Jim Rooney's cases, simple performance measures would be the most effective form of assessment. For instance, Jim could have his students write paragraphs—just as he did in the application phase of the lesson—to determine the extent to which his students could correctly punctuate singular and plural possessive nouns in the context of one or more paragraphs. Judy could simply have the students find the longitude and latitude of several locations, and also find cities and landmarks when given the coordinates. She could personalize the process by having the students find the longitude and latitude of the city they came from if they lived somewhere else, the city their grandparents live in, a city they visited, or a variety of others.

Measuring Thinking Skills

When assessing thinking, the same item formats available to measure content mastery can be used to assess the development of thinking skills (Norris and Ennis, 1989). Formats such as multiple-choice and essay tests—if properly designed—as well as performance measures can be effectively used for assessing thinking. While the use of multiple-choice tests is controversial, experts believe "that multiple-choice tests do have a role in collecting information on students' critical thinking. . . . If information is desired on how well, in general, a group of students can use certain critical thinking abilities, then multiple-choice tests are valuable" (Norris and Ennis, 1989, p. 29).

When the Inductive Model is used, these abilities are comparing and contrasting, inferring, predicting, generalizing, and applying. However, as we saw in Chapter 2, domain-specific knowledge is an integral part of the thinking process, which means that there is no such thing as a content-free assessment of thinking. For example, if Judy Nelson were attempting to assess her students' thinking, she would prepare items that would require her students to use the processes in the context of geography in general, and longitude and latitude in particular. The same would be true for the other teachers.

As an example, suppose Judy Nelson displayed a map of the world with no lines of latitude or longitude shown on it and presented the following paper-and-pencil item.

Look at the map displayed on the overhead and find Chicago. Which of the following is the best predictor of Chicago's longitude and latitude?

  a. 40° N. latitude, 90° E. longitude
  b. 40° S. latitude, 90° W. longitude
  c. 40° N. longitude, 60° E. latitude
  d. 40° S. longitude, 60° W. latitude
  e. 40° N. latitude, 90° W. longitude

Explain the reasons for your choice.

_____
_____
_____
_____

An item such as the preceding one assumes that the latitude and longitude of Chicago have never been discussed in class. The item would require the following of students:

- Know that latitude measures distance north and south of the equator.
- Know that longitude measures distance east and west of the prime meridian.
- Recognize that Chicago is north of the equator.
- Recognize that Chicago is west of the prime meridian.

As another example, consider the following item (again based on an unmarked map).

Look at Lisbon, Portugal on the map. Its latitude is approximately 10° W. Now look at Madrid, Spain. Based on our understanding of latitude and the location of Lisbon, which of the following is the best predictor of Madrid's latitude.

   a. 4° W.
   b. 4° E.
   c. 14° W.
   d. 6° E.

This item would merely require that students recognize that Madrid is east of Lisbon but still west of the prime meridian. It is easy to write, but requires that students both apply previous understanding to a new problem and predict an outcome.

As a third example, consider the following item related to Dawn Adams's lesson on punctuating nonessential clauses.

Look at the following information.

   1. The American flag is colored red, white, and blue.
   2. Harrison Ford starred in a number of action films including *Star Wars, Indiana Jones,* and *Patriot Games.*
   3. The United States, Russia, Great Britain, and France all have United Nations veto powers.
   4. To most conveniently get to New York from Los Angeles you would go through St. Louis and Indianapolis.

Write a generalization about the use of commas based on the sentences.

This form of item would be useful in the context of a unit on punctuation, and it is an extension of the students' work on nonessential clauses. Assuming that the students haven't already been taught a rule about punctuating elements in a series, they would be encouraged to look at the information, find a pattern, and generalize from it. The item could be used as an introduction to a lesson on the rule. If the teacher includes one or more examples on each exercise that the students are required to complete, their analytical thinking can be improved significantly. With practice they become skilled at searching for patterns, and that inclination to search will transfer to new situations.

As shown in each item, assessing thinking skills is an extension of the process that would be used in the lesson itself; the only difference lies in the individual nature of the item. In the lesson the information is processed through a group effort, but is processed individually as the students respond to the item.

While not commonly used, even true-false items can be valuable in assessing student thinking. For example, consider the following item based on Sue Grant's lesson on gas pressure.

Look at the three closed containers. The pressures in all containers are equal. The mass of the air in each container is 3 grams. Container A was heated and container B was left at room temperature. The three containers then appear as follows:

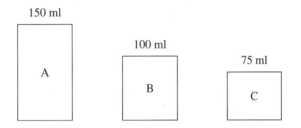

Mark T if the statement is true, F if the statement is false, or X if we cannot tell based on the information given.

_____ **1.** The mass of the air in A is greater than the mass of the air in B.
_____ **2.** The mass of the air in B is greater than the mass of the air in C.
_____ **3.** The temperature of B is greater than the temperature of C.
_____ **4.** The density of A is greater than the density of B.
_____ **5.** The density of B is greater than the density of C.
_____ **6.** The gas particles in B are moving faster than the gas particles in C.

An item such as this assesses students' ability to apply their understanding as well as their ability to make inferences based on the information they have. For example, students commonly conclude that not enough information is given to respond to statement 3, but this isn't the case. They were told the pressures and original masses were equal. Under these conditions, the temperature of C must have been lowered in order for its volume to be smaller.

In each of these examples, we see that domain-specific knowledge and the cognitive processes are both brought to bear on the items. Because of these requirements, the assessment process is more complex and teachers should be constantly aware of possibilities for error. A combination of paper-and-pencil items, performance measures, and teacher observation during learning activities is the best insurance against invalid evaluation, and we encourage you to use all of these in your assessments.

This concludes our discussion of the Inductive Model. Please turn now to the following exercises, designed to measure your understanding of the content of the chapter.

Summary

The Inductive Model is a powerful strategy that can be used to teach concepts, generalizations, principles, and academic rules, while at the same time emphasizing higher-order and critical thinking. The model, based on constructivist views of learning, emphasizes learners' active involvement and the construction of their own understanding of specific topics.

The Inductive Model begins when the teacher arranges for the students to be presented with information, in which they search for patterns. Their search provides them with practice in higher-order thinking and the process of constructing understanding. The teacher's role is to provide enough guidance to prevent the students from veering too far from the central theme of the lesson, and to ensure that the learners' constructions are valid.

The success of lessons in which the Inductive Model is used depends on the quality of the examples used to illustrate the topics being taught. High-quality examples have the characteristics of the concept or the relationship in the generalization, principle, or academic rule observable within them.

The Inductive Model, while more time consuming than other direct-instruction models, has the advantage of promoting high levels of student involvement and motivation. Because of the emphasis on high-quality examples, the model is very effective with low achievers, at-risk students, and second-language learners.

Important Concepts

Academic rule (p. 75)

At-risk students (p. 79)

Characteristics (p. 71)

Concept analysis (p. 72)

Concepts (p. 70)

Constructivism (p. 68)

Coordinate concepts (p. 72)

Definition (p. 72)

Examples (p. 72)

Generalizations (p. 74)

Models (p. 77)

Principles (p. 73)

Prototype (p. 71)

Social structure (p. 67)

Subordinate concepts (p. 72)

Superordinate concept (p. 72)

Exercises

1. "Active teaching" was illustrated in each of the episodes that introduced the chapter. Give an example of teaching that isn't active.

2. Identify an instance in her lesson where Judy Nelson was attempting to establish positive expectations for her class.

3. Examine each of the following statements and classify each as a generalization, principle, or rule.
   a. People immigrate for economic reasons.
   b. Subjects and verbs in sentences agree with each other in number.
   c. A diet high in saturated fat raises a person's cholesterol level.
   d. Like magnetic poles repel and unlike poles attract.

4. Identify the concepts being related in each of the statements in Item 3.

5. For each of the statements in Item 3, describe one or more examples that could be used to effectively illustrate the relationship.

6. Do a concept analysis of the concept rectangle.

7. Classify each of the following according to type of example: (realia, pictures, models, case studies, or simulation and role play).
   a. Jim Rooney's passage.
   b. Judy Nelson's beach ball with lines drawn on it.
   c. Judy Nelson's maps.
   d. Sue Grant's balloons.
   e. Sue Grant's drawings of the balloons and molecules.
   f. Dawn Adams's sentences.

8. A teacher is teaching a lesson on equivalent fractions and has the students fold two pieces of duplicating paper so they appear as follows:

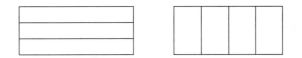

She then has the students shade in one of the three portions on the first paper and one of the four portions on the second. The teacher has the choice of beginning the activity by asking:

"What do you notice about the two pieces of paper?" or
"How many parts are shaded in each paper?"

   a. Which of the two questions is more desirable for beginning a lesson with the Inductive Model? Why?

The teacher then has the students fold the first paper into fourths and the second one into thirds so they appear as follows:

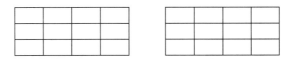

She again has the choice of at least two different questions, such as:

"How do the two papers compare now?"
"Now how many parts of each paper are shaded?"

   b. Which of the two questions is more desirable when using the Inductive Model? Why?

9. The following scenario is based on an actual classroom lesson where the Inductive Model was used to teach a rule. Read the anecdote and answer the questions that follow. (The paragraphs in the case study are numbered to make references easier.)

Tony Reed wanted his students to learn the rule: "When adding -*ing* to words the final consonant is doubled if preceded by a short vowel sound but not if preceded by a long vowel sound."

1. He began his lesson by saying, "We're going to see how good at thinking you've become. I'm going to write some words on the board and I want you to observe and compare them carefully. Then we'll see if we can find a pattern in them. OK?"

2. He then wrote the following words on the board.

   get   fight
   mat   hope

3. He continued by saying, "Look at the words I've written on the chalkboard. Tell me something about them. Sonya?"

4. ". . . They're all words," Sonya responded.

5. "Indeed they are," Tony smiled. "What else? Pat?"

6. ". . . Those have three letters," Pat answered pointing to the words in the left column.

7. "Yes, good! Something else. Jim?"

8. ". . . The ones on the right begin with different letters."

9. "Yes they do," Tony acknowledged. "Bill?"

10. "They're all one-syllable words."

11. "Some are verbs and some are nouns," George volunteered.

12. "Yes, all good observations," Tony praised. "Now let me show you some more," and with that he wrote the following words on the board.

    cut   bite
    tip   boat

13. "Now tell me about these. Gail?"

14. "They're also verbs and nouns," Gail answered.

15. "Good! . . . Betty?"

16. "Some have three letters and some have four."

    "OK, Betty. . . . Now let me show you a few more," and he then wrote additional words on the board so his list appeared as follows:

    get   getting   fight   fighting
    mat   matting   hope   hoping

    "Now, what do you notice here? Mike?"

17. "You added *-ing* to all the words," Mike said instantly.

18. "Good, Mike. Now, let's do it once more," and he added *-ing* to the words in his second list, so his total list appeared as follows:

    get   getting   fight   fighting
    mat   matting   hope   hoping
    cut   cutting   bite   biting
    tip   tipping   boat   boating

19. "Now let's look at all the words," Tony requested. "Look at the first two columns in each case and compare them to those in the last two columns," he directed, pointing to the columns in each case. "Nikki?"

20. ". . . The words in the first column all have three letters and those in the third column all have four letters," Nikki replied.

21. "Good. And what do you see, about in the middle of each word? . . . Roger?"

22. ". . . I'm not sure what you mean."

23. "Look," Tony directed, pointing to the vowel in each word.

24. "Oh, those are all vowels. Each of the words has a vowel in the middle."

25. "Now compare the sounds of the vowels in the two lists. Roy?"

26. ". . ."

27. "Say the words in the first column, Roy."

28. ". . . Get, mat, cut, tip," Roy responded, pronouncing the words correctly in each case.

29. "Yes, good. Now say the words in the third column. Karen?"

30. "Fight, hope, bite, boat," Karen responded, again pronouncing the words correctly.

31. "Yes, good, Karen. What did you notice about the sounds of the vowels? Kim?"

32. ". . . The ones in the first column had a short sound."

33. "Exactly! And how about the ones in the third column, Jill?"

34. ". . . They weren't short. They said their name."

35. "Good observation, Jill. . . . Now look at the words in the second and fourth columns. What do you notice about the spelling of those words? Keith?"

36. ". . . They all have *-ing* added to them."

37. "Yes. Now look a bit more closely. What kind of pattern do you notice? Kareem?

38. ". . ."

39. "Look at the consonants at the ends of the words, Kareem. What do you notice?"

40. ". . . They're doubled here, but not over there."

41. "Yes, good thinking, Kareem."

42. "Outstanding, everyone. . . . Now what did Kim and Jill say about the sounds of the vowels in the words? Kathy?"

43. ". . . Well," Kathy said hesitantly. "The ones in the first column were short and the ones in the third column were long."

44. "Yes, excellent, Kathy. And what did we add to each of the words? Alysia?"

45. "We added *-ing*," Alysia replied quickly.

46. "Now try and relate what we've found here, someone?"

47. ". . . Go ahead, Dominic."

48. ". . . The words in the first column had short vowels, . . . and their consonants were doubled."

49. "Excellent, Dominic! You've identified the relationship between the vowel sound and the spelling. Now how about the other words? Charlotte?"

50. ". . . Their vowel sounds were long and the consonant wasn't doubled," she replied.

51. "Now let's put this together and try and state it in a rule," Tony probed. ". . . I'll get you started. . . . When adding *-ing* to words . . . Trang?"

52. ". . . You double the consonant at the end if the vowel sound is short, but you don't if the vowel sound is long."

53. "Very well done, Trang. You've identified the relationship between vowel sounds and spelling when adding *-ing*."

54. "Now, give me a word, add *-ing* to it, and explain why the spelling is the way it is. Suzanne?"

55. Tony went on to ask the students for several more examples of adding the suffix to words with long and short vowel sounds. He then told the students to write a short paragraph using at least two examples of adding *-ing* where they would have to double the final consonant and two other examples where they would not double the final consonant, and underline the words in each case. He then directed the students to begin writing their paragraphs.

    a. Identify each of the phases in the lesson, including the points where the lesson shifts from one phase to another.

    b. Identify five examples of open-ended questions in the activity.

      c. Locate two prompting sequences in the lesson by identifying the first question of the sequence.

      d. Identify a repetition question in the lesson.

      e. Identify two basic thinking processes that the students used in the lesson.

10. Consider a teacher wanting to teach the principle: "Less-dense materials float on more dense materials if they don't mix." The lesson is introduced by displaying two vials of the same volume, one containing water and the other containing cooking oil, and placing them on a balance. The mass of the water is measurably greater than that of the cooking oil. The water and oil are then poured together into a third vial and the oil floats. Answer the following questions based on the information.

      a. How many examples did the teacher use?

      b. What kind of examples were they? (realia, pictures, etc.)

      c. What specific information would the teacher have to prompt the students to identify?

      d. What might the teacher do in Phase 5 of this lesson for application of the principle?

Discussion Questions

1. Consider the motivational features of Tony Reed's lesson. What did he do that promoted student motivation, and what might he have done to increase it? Compare the lesson to Judy Nelson's, Sue Grant's, Jim Rooney's, and Dawn Adams's. What motivational advantages did each have? How could the student motivation be increased in each case?

2. Teachers obviously do not have time to develop an inductive lesson for every concept and generalization existing in curriculum materials. How do they decide what concepts and generalizations to select?

3. Are some concepts and generalizations more conducive than others to being taught using the Inductive Model? If so, what characteristics do they have in common?

4. Are there instances when verbal examples would be sufficient for teaching a concept, generalization, principle, or rule? If so, what would these instances be?

5. What are the major advantages of inductive teaching? The major disadvantages?

6. We have briefly discussed options for using the Inductive Model with different age groups. What other factors would have to be considered in using the model with younger elementary students? With advanced high school students?

7. An Inductive-Model lesson can begin with little or no introduction to the content being taught. How important is this?

C h a p t e r *4*

The Concept-Attainment Model

The Concept-Attainment Model is an inductive teaching strategy designed to help students of all ages reinforce their understanding of concepts and practice hypothesis testing. Developed from concept-learning research (Klausmeier, 1985; Tennyson and Cocchiarella, 1986), the model uses positive and negative examples to illustrate concepts as simple as square or dog and as sophisticated as oxymoron or socialism.

The design of this model, first suggested by Joyce and Weil (1972), is based on the work of Bruner, Goodnow, and Austin (1956) who investigated how different variables affect the concept-learning process. The model is consistent with the views of constructivism—discussed in Chapter 3—which suggest that learners "construct" their own understanding of the way the world works rather than having it presented to them in an already-organized form. When the Concept-Attainment Model is used, positive and negative examples of concepts become the basis for students' constructions.

The Concept-Attainment Model is also useful for giving students experience with the scientific method and particularly with hypothesis testing, experiences that are often hard to provide in content areas other than science.

When you've completed your study of this chapter, you should be able to meet the following objectives:

- Identify topics most appropriately taught with the Concept-Attainment Model.
- Prepare a list of examples that effectively illustrate a concept.
- Sequence a list of examples to promote analytical thinking and hypothesis testing.
- Implement lessons using the Concept-Attainment Model.
- Adapt the Concept-Attainment Model for learners of different developmental levels.
- Assess student understanding of content objectives taught with the Concept-Attainment Model.
- Assess the development of students' analytical thinking based on the Concept-Attainment Model.

To begin our discussion, let's look at a teacher using the Concept-Attainment Model to help students reinforce their understanding of a concept and develop their analytical thinking.

Karl Haynes, a fifth-grade teacher, began a science lesson by calling students' attention to a bag he held in his hand.

He said, "Today, we're going to do something a little different than what we've been doing. I have an idea in mind, and you are going to figure out what it is. To help you figure it out, I'm going to show you some things that *are* examples of the idea, and I'm also going to show you some things that *are not* examples of the idea. Then, based on the things that are examples of the idea and the others that are not examples of the idea, you will figure out what the idea is. This is sort of a game and it will give us all some practice in being good thinkers. If you're not quite sure of what we're doing, you will catch on once we get started. OK, ready? . . . Here we go."

Karl then reached into the bag, pulled out an apple that had been cut in half, and put it on the table in front of a cardboard sign that said, "Examples." He also took a rock out of the bag and placed it in front of a sign that said "Nonexamples."

"Now," he continued, "the apple is an example of the idea I have in mind, and the rock is not an example of the idea. . . . What do you think the idea might be? . . ."

"We eat apples," Rufus volunteered.

"Good," Karl smiled, "so the idea might be . . . ?"

". . ."

". . . Things . . . we . . .?" Karl prompted.

". . . Eat?" Rufus continued hesitantly.

With that, Karl wrote the word "HYPOTHESES" on the board, underlined it, and asked, "What do we mean by the term hypotheses? Anyone?"

". . . It's kind of a guess," Mike volunteered after a few seconds.

"Yes," Karl nodded to Mike. "For our purposes that's a good definition. Our *hypotheses* will be our educated guesses as to what the idea might be." He then wrote 'things we eat' under the word HYPOTHESES.

"What else might be a possibility?" Karl went on. ". . . Jim?"

"It could also be things that are alive—or at least were alive."

"Fine," Karl replied, writing the words 'living things' on the board under the list of hypotheses. "Any others? . . . Meg?"

"Well, this is sort of like Jim's idea but it's a little different. How about things that grow on plants?"

"Okay. . . . Does everyone see how living things and things that grow on plants are different? No? Karen, can you explain that to the class?"

"Well, there are some living things that don't grow on plants. Like animals."

"Excellent thinking, Karen. Do we have any other ideas?"

After pausing for a few seconds he continued, "Well then, let's look at a few more examples," and he then took out a sliced tomato and put it under the positive example sign and placed a carrot that had been sliced in half under the negative example sign.

He continued, "What does this new information tell us? Let's first look at the hypotheses we have. Are they still all acceptable? . . . Serena?"

"It can't be things to eat," Serena responded.

"Explain why Serena," Karl encouraged.

". . . Well, . . . we eat carrots, . . . and carrot is not an example."

"Good, Serena," Karl smiled. "Very good, clear explanation. The added information that we have has required that we eliminate that hypothesis."

"Now, let's look at the rest of the hypotheses. . . . How about 'things that grow on plants'? . . . Sherry?"

". . . Things that grow on plants is out."

"Why? Explain," Karl smiled.

". . . A carrot grows from a plant."

"And?" Karl probed.

". . . It's not an example," Sherry added quickly.

"Excellent, Sherry. Good thinking and good explanation. "Now, how about living things?"

"Also out," Jaime volunteered.

"Go on."

". . . Carrot is living and it's not an example," Jaime quickly explained, seeing how the process is intended to work.

"Yes! That's fine," Karl waved enthusiastically. "You are really catching on to this."

"How about things that we eat that grow above the ground?" Renita offered.

"Are you suggesting another hypothesis?" Karl asked.

"Yes."

"Very good. Perhaps I should have pointed that out in the beginning. We can always add hypotheses as long as the data support them. . . . Now, how will we know if the data do indeed support them? . . . Anyone?"

". . ."

"This is a little tough to describe, so I'll try to help you. An hypothesis is supported if all of the examples fit the hypothesis, and if none of the nonexamples fit the hypothesis. For example, do both an apple and a tomato grow above the ground?"

"Yes," the class said in unison.

"Do either a rock or a carrot grow above the ground?"

"Part of the carrot does," Heidi noted.

"Good thinking," Karl nodded. "What is your reaction to Heidi's point, Renita?"

"I meant the part that we eat."

"OK, is that all right with you, Heidi?"

Heidi nodded her head, "I think we should say, 'plant parts we eat that are above ground.'"

"Excellent, Heidi. We can also modify hypotheses so that they better fit our data. This is the kind of thinking that we're after. Very well done!"

"Now, . . . is the hypothesis, 'plant parts we eat that are above ground,' acceptable? . . . Remember, all the examples must fit the hypothesis, and none of the nonexamples can fit the hypothesis."

Among a chorus of nods, "yes's," and "OKs," Karl continued with the process. Shawn offered the hypothesis things we eat with seeds in them, and Marsha offered red foods, to the giggles of the class.

Karl then asked in seeming admonishment, "Are apples and tomatoes both red, and are either the rock or the carrot red?"

"No," the students responded.

"Hmm. . . . Now, I want us to have fun with this, of course, but remember that the only thing that determines whether or not an hypothesis is acceptable is whether or not the data support it. . . . And do the data support red foods?"

The students nodded, a bit sheepishly.

"Good. Now, I know you didn't mean any harm, but keep that in mind."

Karl then added an avocado to the list of positive examples, a piece of celery to the negative examples list, and they again analyzed the hypotheses as they had done before.

Karl continued by adding and analyzing hypotheses with a peach, a squash, and an orange as positive examples, and a head of lettuce, artichoke, and potato as negative examples.

The students continued the process with Karl's guidance, narrowing their hypotheses to things with seeds in them and finally modifying the hypothesis to seeds in the edible part of the plant.

Karl then asked, "Does anyone know what we call foods that have seeds in the edible part of the plant, like the ones we have here?"

After hesitating a few seconds and hearing no response, he said, "We call these foods fruits," and wrote the word fruit on the board.

Karl then continued, "Excellent everyone. Now, we need a good clear definition of fruit. Someone give it a try. . . . Go ahead, Goeff."

"Okay, . . . Fruits are . . . things we eat . . . that have seeds in them."

"Seeds in what part?"

". . . In the part that we eat."

"Very good, Goeff. I'll revise this slightly to smooth it out a little, but we essentially have it."

Karl then wrote on the board, "Fruits are foods we eat with seeds in the edible part."

Karl then had the class take out a piece of paper and categorize additional examples as either positive or negative examples of the concept *fruit*.

Let's look now at another teacher using the Concept-Attainment Model to help high school students reinforce their understanding of the concept *metaphor*.

Tanya Adin, a ninth-grade English teacher, began her sixth-period class on Friday by saying, "I know that you're all anxious to start the weekend, so to break the routine we're going to do something a little different today. It will help us review some of the ideas we have briefly dealt with in the past, and it will give us some practice in being good critical thinkers."

"Now, this is what we're going to do. . . . I have a list of sentences on this transparency," she continued, motioning with the transparency in her hand. "Some of the sentences illustrate a concept I have in mind, and others do not illustrate the concept. The ones that do, I've marked with a Y, which stands for yes, meaning they illustrate the concept, and the others are marked with an N, meaning no, they do not illustrate the concept. Then, you need to figure out what the concept is based on the yes's—the examples—and the no's—the sentences that are not examples.

"Let's try it," she continued. "I'll show you an example and a nonexample to begin. Remember, the examples—yes's—illustrate the concept, and the nonexamples— no's—do not illustrate the concept."

Tanya then put the transparency on the overhead and uncovered the first two sentences, which appeared as follows:

1. John's Camaro is a lemon. (Y)
2. Hurricane Andrew did a great deal of damage in Florida. (N)

The students looked at the examples for a few seconds, and Dean then said, "Cars."

"Okay, good," Tanya nodded. "The example is about cars and the nonexample has nothing in it about cars, so cars could be the concept. . . . Any other possibilities?"

". . . I think linking verbs," Antonio added.

"You mean you think linking verbs is the concept?" Tanya asked.

"Yeh, there's a linking verb in the first sentence, but there isn't one in the second one."

"Very good, Antonio. Good thinking. . . . Now, this is the kind of thing we're trying to do. We see both a description of a car and a linking verb in the yes example, but we don't see either of them in the no example, so cars and linking verbs are both possibilities for the concept.

". . . Now, let's go on. Are there any other possibilities?"

"How about present tense?" Nancy wondered.

"Good thinking, Nancy. Is present tense acceptable?"

". . ."

Seeing the uncertainty on the students' faces, Tanya continued, "Does the yes example illustrate present tense?"

The students nodded that it did, and Tanya went on, "Is there anything about present tense in the no example."

"No," Bruce said quickly, beginning to see how the process worked.

"Very good," Tanya waved briskly. "You see how we do this? . . . Good. Now, let's go on."

Tanya then briefly explained that they were hypothesizing the possibilities that they had listed, so each was an hypothesis. She then noted that she would refer to the items on the list as hypotheses from that point on.

Tanya then uncovered two more sentences on the overhead, so her list appeared as follows:

1. John's Camaro is a lemon. (Y)
2. Hurricane Andrew did a great deal of damage in Florida. (N)
3. Mrs. Augilar's Lexus is a pearl. (Y)
4. My grandmother's hat is a garden of daisies. (Y)

"I know," Adam said eagerly after looking at the list for a few seconds. "It's possessives. Each of the yes's has a possessive in it."

"What does everyone else think?" Tanya queried. "Can we accept Adam's hypothesis?" Tanya wondered out loud, emphasizing the word hypothesis as she asked the question.

"How about number two?" Rachael wondered.

". . . It's a no," Karla pointed out.

". . . Oh, yes," Rachael nodded, recognizing Karla's point.

"Good, . . . any others?" Tanya continued. "Okay, let's look at our hypotheses so far. . . . How about cars? Is it still okay? . . . Heidi?"

". . . I don't think so?"

"Explain why for everyone."

". . . Well, . . . number four has nothing about a car in it."

"And . . ."

". . . It's a yes example," Heidi said after realizing what Tanya was after.

"Very good, Heidi," Tanya nodded, and she then continued, "How about present tense? Is it still acceptable? . . . Lisa?"

". . . I . . . think so."

"Please explain," Tanya encouraged.

". . . All of the yes examples are in the present tense."

"And?" Tanya probed.

". . . The no is in the past tense."

"Very good," Tanya nodded and smiled.

"Now," she went on, "is there anything else that we can add?"

". . . How about metaphors?" Ramona offered.

"Okay. . . . Is metaphor an acceptable hypothesis?" Tanya asked over her shoulder as she added metaphor to the list she was writing on the board.

The students looked at the examples uncertainly, and in response, Tanya continued, "Is each of the positive examples a metaphor?"

Tanya smiled as some of the students nodded that they were, and she went on, "Any other hypotheses?"

". . . How about figures of speech?" Frank suggested.

"Good! . . . Figures of speech okay?"

". . . Yes," several students said simultaneously beginning to get comfortable with the process.

"Any others?"

After waiting a few seconds, Tanya said, "Okay, let's look at another example."

She uncovered another example, so her list now appeared as follows:

1. John's Camaro is a lemon. (Y)
2. Hurricane Andrew did a great deal of damage in Florida. (N)

3. Mrs. Augilar's Lexus is a pearl. (Y)
4. My grandmother's hat is a garden of daisies. (Y)
5. My bedroom is green. (N)

"Now, anything else we can add to our list of hypotheses?" Tanya asked, looking at the following list.

~~cars~~
linking verbs
present tense
possessives
metaphor
figures of speech

Hearing nothing, she continued, "Okay, let's look at them. How about linking verbs? Is it still okay? Amanda?"

". . . No."

"Why not?"

". . . There's a linking verb in the last one, and it's a no."

"Very good analysis, and a good, complete explanation," Tanya responded, gesturing at the board. "So, how about present tense?"

"Also out," Shannon volunteered quickly. ". . . The nonexample is in the present tense," she added, responding as Tanya gestured for her to continue.

"Excellent. . . . How about possessives?"

"Out," Donalee offered.

"Explain why."

"There's no possessive in the last sentence."

"Wait. It's a no," David interjected.

"Go on, David," Tanya nodded.

". . . It's a nonexample, . . . and it doesn't have a possessive in it, . . . so possessive is still okay," David said slowly as he was describing his thoughts.

"Do you agree with that, Donalee?"

". . . I guess . . . I see now," she responded after looking at the examples again.

"Excellent. . . . Now, how about metaphor?"

The students concluded that metaphor was still acceptable, since the fifth sentence was not a metaphor and it also was not an example, and they went through similar reasoning with figures of speech.

Tanya then added the following example to her list.

6. Autumn leaves are the skin of trees, wrinkled with age. (Y)

The students decided that possessives must be rejected since the sentence did not illustrate possessives, and it was a positive example; they further concluded that metaphor and figures of speech were still acceptable.

Tanya then added a seventh example.

7. I had a million pages of homework last night. (N)

After some discussion the students concluded that metaphor was acceptable, but that figures of speech was unacceptable, since the seventh sentence was a figure of speech—a hyperbole—and it was a nonexample.

"Now," Tanya interjected, "let's stop for a moment and take a look at what we've been doing. Let's look back at the process that we've been in so far. Let's try and describe it. . . . Go ahead, someone."

". . . Well, we've been trying to guess what the concept is that you have in mind," Alandrea volunteered after several seconds.

"Actually, you haven't been guessing, and I want to emphasize that," Tanya responded, waving at the board. "You have made your decisions based on information. In this case the information is in the form of the examples that I've given you, but it can apply to nearly everything you do. For example, why did you decide that figures of speech wasn't an acceptable hypothesis?"

". . . That sentence—'I had a million pages of homework to do last night.'—is a figure of speech and you told us it was a nonexample," Sydney suggested.

"Exactly. You made the decision to reject figures of speech based on the data, not on a mere whim.

"The same thing applies to life in general," Tanya went on. "Now this may seem like a silly example, but it applies. Your dad decides to fix you cooked oatmeal for breakfast rather than Cream of Wheat. It says on the box that oatmeal has virtually no fat and no sodium, while Cream of Wheat has some of each, plus preservatives. Just as you used information in this exercise to direct your thinking, your dad used information about the fat and sodium content of the cereals, to reject Cream of Wheat on that basis.

"So, we're learning a very fundamental process here that helps us learn to live better as a result of thinking more clearly. Keep the oatmeal and Cream of Wheat example in mind, and we'll remind ourselves of it and others as we do lessons like these."

Tanya then went back to the theme of the lesson, displaying the following examples, one at a time, and asking the students to consider whether or not metaphor was still an acceptable hypothesis after each one.

8. At night you are the moonlight floating through my window, lifting the curtains. (Y)
9. So far my life has been like an unmarked chalkboard. (N)
10. He touched her cheek as the sun touches a rose. (N)
11. The blank sheet of paper reclined on my desk and stared at me with its blank eyes, waiting for me to tease it with my pencil. (N)
12. The guns cracked and the bullets squealed as the battle raged for hours. (N)

After displaying and analyzing the last example, Tanya asked, "Now, what do you think? Did we prove that the concept is metaphor?"

"Yes," several students said simultaneously, and others nodded in agreement.

"It looks promising, doesn't it?" Tanya smiled. "Suppose, for instance, though, that sometime later we found a sentence that we were told was an example, but it wasn't a metaphor. Then what?"

". . . I guess we'd have to cross off metaphor," Wendy offered uncertainly.

"Yes, that's exactly right," Tanya went on. "An hypothesis is acceptable as long as *all* the data—examples of the concept in our case—support it, but we have to reject an hypothesis if *only one* item of data does not support it. . . . So, technically, you never actually prove an hypothesis. You can only gather more and more data that support it.

"You'll understand the process of analyzing hypotheses better and better as we do more of these," Tanya assured the students, seeing uncertain looks on some of their faces.

Tanya then asked individual students to give additional examples of metaphors to reinforce the concept, discussing each as they were offered. After several examples, she closed the lesson.

The Concept-Attainment Model: An Overview

Let's begin our study of the Concept-Attainment Model by looking back at Karl Haynes's and Tanya Adin's lessons and identifying their key elements. We'll begin by focusing on the features they had in common, and then we'll examine the differences in their procedures, as well as the planning and implementation of lessons using the model. Let's turn to their common features:

- First, both lessons focused on a concept—*fruits* in Karl's case and *metaphors* in Tanya's—rather than a principle, generalization, rule, or other form of content.
- Second, the teachers began by carefully explaining the procedure for using the model.
- . Third, they began with an example and a nonexample of the topic—an apple and a rock for Karl and the first two sentences for Tanya.
- Fourth, the activity centered on the process of offering and analyzing hypotheses, which resulted in the elimination of some, modification of others, and finally the isolation of a single hypothesis.

Social Structure of the Model

In Chapter 3 we described social structure as the characteristics of the classroom environment necessary for learning to take place, and the roles of the teacher and the students in that environment. As with the Inductive Model, the Concept-Attainment Model requires a social structure in which students feel free to think and test their ideas. This was briefly illustrated by Karl's admonishment of the students for laughing when Marsha offered "red foods" as an hypothesis. If supported by the existing data, no hypothesis is silly or trivial, and Karl communicated this spirit with his comments. He also noted that he knew the students meant no harm, and that he wanted them to enjoy the activity. These elements of respect for each others' ideas are important in capturing the spirit of the process.

This social support was further illustrated in the exchange between Donalee and David in Tanya's lesson. Donalee suggested that possessives had to be rejected, and David offered a valid counterargument. Aware of the need for students to feel safe, Tanya returned to Donalee and asked her to respond to David's reasoning rather then merely accepting it and continuing. This type of sensitivity on the part of the teacher is crucial when using either the Inductive or the Concept-Attainment Models.

The Teacher's Role

As we've already said, one of the teacher's roles is to help create an environment in which students feel free to think and conjecture without fear of criticism or ridicule, and both teachers performed this role very well.

A second role is to explain and illustrate how the model "works" and to guide the process and help students state and analyze hypotheses, and articulate their thinking. Both teachers first carefully introduced the activity—Karl explaining that he had an idea that the students were to figure out based on the examples and nonexamples, and Tanya beginning by saying that she had a list of sentences, some of which illustrated a concept and some of which did not.

The teachers then guided the activity in three important ways.

- First, they encouraged students to state their thinking in the form of hypotheses rather than in the form of observations. In Karl's lesson, for example, Rufus essentially made an observation when he said, "We eat apples." Karl—rather than recording Rufus's statement—helped him reword it into the hypothesis "things we eat."
- Second, Karl and Tanya helped guide the students' thinking as they determined whether or not an hypothesis was acceptable.
- Third, they asked the students to explain *why* they accepted or rejected hypotheses— for example, Tanya asking Amanda why linking verbs was unacceptable after Tanya displayed the fifth sentence in her lesson.

A final element of the process should be noted. Periodically, students will disagree as to whether or not an hypothesis is acceptable or not, or whether a new hypothesis can be added. The teacher must monitor these disagreements to help maintain the spirit of accepting and rejecting hypotheses based on data, while keeping up the flow of the activity. We saw a brief example of this in Karl's lesson when Heidi disagreed with Renita's hypothesis, which resulted in its modification. When a disagreement can't be immediately resolved, the teacher can encourage students to leave it on the list of hypotheses and allow additional data to resolve the problem.

The essence of the process for students is to suggest hypotheses; accept, modify, or reject them; and ultimately isolate a single hypothesis that best accounts for the data in the form of examples. We saw this illustrated in both lessons.

Goals for the Concept-Attainment Model

Content Goals

Content goals for a Concept-Attainment and an Inductive-Model lesson are related but not identical. There are two important differences between the models.

- First, while the Inductive Model is designed to teach concepts, principles, generalizations, or academic rules, the Concept-Attainment Model—as the name implies— focuses exclusively on concepts.

- Second, while the Inductive Model can be used to teach a topic essentially from "scratch," the Concept-Attainment Model requires that the students have some background with the concept.

For example, Tanya's students had some experience with both metaphors and other figures of speech, or they wouldn't have been able to suggest either as hypotheses. For this reason, the Concept-Attainment Model is often most effective for enrichment of a concept rather than for initial learning. It can be effectively used as a form of review and to help students understand the relationships between closely related concepts, as was the case in Tanya's lesson. She wanted the students to reinforce the relationships among the concepts of *metaphor, simile, personification,* and *hyperbole.*

However, as we saw in Karl's lesson, students don't necessarily have to know the label for the concept. His students identified the essential characteristic of the concept fruit, and he then supplied the label.

Developing Students' Critical Thinking

The Inductive Model and Concept-Attainment Model also differ in their emphasis. Unlike the Inductive Model, which emphasizes students' deep understanding of specific topics, the Concept-Attainment Model strongly focuses on the development of critical thinking in the form of hypothesis testing. As we saw in both lessons, much of the emphasis was on the students' analysis of the hypotheses and why they were accepted, modified, or rejected. The kinds of conclusions students practice making, such as, "The nonexample is in the present tense," as an explanation for why the hypothesis *present tense* had to be rejected, are as important as understanding the concepts themselves. While Tanya's lesson helped reinforce the relationships among metaphors, similes, and other figures of speech, her goal to develop students' critical thinking was equally important. If her primary goal had focused on the concept *metaphor* as a topic, she probably would have chosen a different model.

Planning Lessons with the Concept-Attainment Model

Identifying Topics

Research indicates that teachers usually begin the planning process by identifying a topic (Morine-Dershimer and Vallance, 1976; Peterson, Marx, and Clark, 1978). This was an appropriate beginning point when the Inductive Model was used, and it is also appropriate when using the Concept-Attainment Model. When the Concept-Attainment Model is used, the topic will be a concept and, as we've already said, this model is most effective if students have had some experience with the concept.

The Importance of Clear Goals

As we saw in the last section, goals for the Concept-Attainment Model include helping students develop concepts and the relationships among them and giving them practice with critical thinking processes—primarily stating and testing hypotheses. We also saw that the development of critical thinking strategies can be the dominant goal.

In Chapter 3 we emphasized that the teacher must know exactly what he or she is trying to accomplish by using the Inductive Model. In using the Concept-Attainment Model, while the goals are a bit different, being clear about goals is no less important. Karl Haynes was teaching a group of elementary students, so he had identified "seed contained in the edible part of the plant" as the essential characteristic of the concept *fruit*. A biology teacher would attach a more sophisticated set of characteristics to the concept, such as the fruit being an enlarged and ripened ovary, but Karl was teaching a valid concept for fifth graders. The important aspect of his planning was that he knew exactly what he wanted from his students.

The same was true in Tanya's case. She had clearly specified "a nonliteral comparison that avoids the words *like* and *as*" as the main characteristic of the concept metaphor, and she had these characteristics clearly in mind as she planned and conducted her lesson.

Both teachers were also clear in their intent to provide students with practice in developing their critical thinking abilities. Had practice with critical thinking not been an important goal for them, they would probably have chosen a different model.

Having a precise content goal in mind and knowing that emphasis will be placed on critical thinking, we are now ready to prepare and sequence examples.

Selecting Examples

The principles involved in selecting examples to teach a concept are the same regardless of the model selected. As we saw with the Inductive Model, the most important factor in selecting examples is identifying those that best illustrate the characteristics of the concept. Karl Haynes chose good examples when he used the apple, tomato, squash, peach and orange. In each case, the students could see the essential characteristic—the seeds in the edible part of the plant—in the examples. The same was true in Tanya Adin's case. The students could see a nonliteral comparison in each of the positive examples.

The teachers were also clever in their choices of examples. Karl, for example, used as examples tomato and squash—fruits commonly thought of as vegetables. Using them as examples encouraged students to broaden their thinking to include them in the concept *fruit*. As a result, even though the students may have had experience with the concept, their understanding of fruits was enriched.

Examples are selected so that each contains the combination of essential characteristics, and none of the nonexamples contain the same combination. To further illustrate this process, consider the characteristics of the concept *proper noun* and then analyze the following positive examples in terms of your list:

1. Mary
2. New York
3. John
4. Chicago
5. United States
6. George Washington

Two things are wrong with this list. First, the examples should have included the idea that a proper noun names a specific person, place or thing; there are no specific *things* in the list of positive examples. To ensure that the concept is complete, we would need to add positive examples such as *German Shepherd, Honda,* and *Old Testament.*

The second problem with these examples is that they exist in isolation rather than being presented in a meaningful context. In Chapter 3 we found that examples in context result in more meaningful learning than examples that are isolated and abstract. Putting the proper nouns in the context of sentences would be easy to do. For instance, the examples could be presented as follows:

1. Mary is one of the most common names that girls are given, and John is one of the most common for boys.
2. New York is the largest city in the United States, and Chicago is the second largest.
3. George Washington is often called the father of our country.
4. The German Shepherd is one of the smartest working dogs.
5. One of the first Japanese cars to be sold in this country was the Honda.
6. The Old Testament is strongly related to the Koran in many ways.

While presenting the examples in the context of a passage would be even better than providing sentences, the sentences are much better than offering only words in isolation.

Preparing Nonexamples

In selecting negative examples (or nonexamples), an attempt should be made to vary the nonessential characteristics and to represent all of the things that the concept is not. For instance, Tanya Adin used the following sentences (in addition to the simple statements, "Hurricane Andrew did a great deal of damage in Florida," and "My bedroom is green") as nonexamples in her lesson on metaphors.

I had a million pages of homework last night. (hyperbole)

So far I think my life has been like an unmarked chalkboard. (a simile using the word *like*)

He touched her cheek as the sun touches a rose. (a simile using the word *as*)

The blank sheet of paper reclined on my desk and stared at me with its blank eyes, waiting for me to tease it with my pencil. (personification)

The guns cracked and the bullets squealed as the battle raged for hours. (onomatopoeia)

From the list, we see that the negative examples served to differentiate *metaphor* from other figures of speech. When both the positive and negative examples are used, the learner can construct a valid concept that is not confused with closely related concepts.

As we see, each of the nonexamples—examples of *hyperbole, simile, personification,* and *onomatopoeia*—illustrated a concept coordinate to the concept *metaphor.* Thinking of concepts that are coordinate to the concept being taught is often helpful as the list of examples and nonexamples is being prepared.

Sequencing Examples

Having selected the examples and nonexamples, the final planning task is to put them in sequence. If the development of critical thinking is an important goal for the teacher, the examples should be arranged so the students are given the best opportunity to develop their critical-thinking abilities. The shortest route to a concept may not give students this opportunity, and it may not result in the deepest student understanding. Tanya, for example, purposely sequenced her examples so the students could initially offer *cars, possessives, present tense* and *linking verbs* as valid hypotheses—all of which ultimately had to be rejected—which gave the students considerable practice in analyzing hypotheses during the lesson.

Notice also that the teachers don't necessarily have to alternate examples and nonexamples in their sequences. They may choose to present two or even three positive examples in a row, which might be followed by two or more negative examples. This is a matter of teacher judgment. Karl's and Tanya's sequences, for instance, appear as shown in Figure 4.1.

To further illustrate this point, let's look at a simpler example.

Suppose the concept is "numbers with perfect square roots." Consider the sequences illustrated in Figure 4.2.

In sequence A the pattern is quickly and clearly established. Many students would probably hypothesize the concept after two positive examples. On the other hand, the concept is less obvious in sequence B, providing the students with a greater opportunity for hypothesizing and analysis of hypotheses. In preparing sequence B, the teacher was not trying to hide information from the students nor trying to trick them. Instead, the teacher wanted to maximize the students' opportunity to practice critical thinking. For any set of

Karl Haynes's Sequence	Tanya Adin's Sequence
1. Apple (Y)	1. John's Camaro is a lemon. (Y)
2. Rock (N)	2. Hurricane Andrew did a great deal of damage in Florida. (N)
3. Tomato (Y)	3. Mrs. Augilar's Lexus is a pearl. (Y)
4. Carrot (N)	4. My grandmother's hat is a garden of daisies. (Y)
5. Avocado (Y)	5. My bedroom is green. (N)
6. Celery (N)	6. Autumn leaves are the skin of trees, wrinkled with age. (Y)
7. Peach (Y)	7. I had a million pages of homework last night. (N)
8. Squash (Y)	8. At night you are the moonlight floating through my window, lifting the curtain. (Y)
9. Orange (Y)	9. So far my life has been like an unmarked chalkboard. (N)
10. Lettuce (N)	10. He touched her cheek as the sun touches a rose. (N)
11. Artichoke (N)	11. The blank sheet of paper reclined on my desk and stared at me with its blank eyes, waiting for me to tease it with my pencil. (N)
12. Potato (N)	12. The guns cracked and the bullets squealed as the battle raged for hours. (N)

FIGURE 4.1   Karl Haynes's and Tanya Adin's Sequences of Examples

Sequence A		Sequence B	
4	Yes	1	Yes
5	No	1/2	No
9	Yes	81	Yes
15	No	7	No
16	Yes	64	Yes
2	No	12	No
25	Yes	9	Yes

FIGURE 4.2 Two Sequences of Examples for Numbers with Perfect Square Roots

examples a number of sequences could be designed. The organization depends on the judgment of the teacher, the goals of the lesson, and the backgrounds of the students.

Implementing Lessons Using the Concept-Attainment Model

The implementation phase of the Concept-Attainment Model is flexible and can be fun for both the teacher and the students. The process can be presented as a type of game in which the students try to identify the idea (concept) the teacher has in mind. This can result in student **arousal**—*a physical or psychological reaction to the environment* by capitalizing on a "sense of the unknown," which has been documented by research as intrinsically motivating (Berlyne, 1966; Kagan, 1972). Further, the model can be used to add variety to classroom activities, which also increases student motivation (Stipek, 1993).

Introducing Students to the Concept-Attainment Model

For young or inexperienced learners or those used to teacher-centered expository lessons, the procedure used with the Concept-Attainment Model may be confusing initially. Both Karl and Tanya addressed this problem by providing very clear and explicit directions for the activity and by initially prompting students to form hypotheses based on the examples. (For instance, we saw that Karl nearly put the words in Rufus's mouth as Rufus stated the first hypothesis of the activity.)

Teachers can also help students get used to "playing the game" by using a familiar topic the first time or two the model is used. Then students can focus on the procedure, rather than having to learn how the model works while at the same time coping with a demanding topic. For example, topics such as living things, mammals, wooden objects, prime numbers, or even something such as "students with red hair" are all simple, concrete topics that would help students get used to the procedure.

Using a simple topic to introduce students to the procedure can also give them some practice with the thinking skills involved with the model. As we saw in the two lessons that introduced the chapter, the students are required to do some "reversals" in their thinking (for example, after Tanya had presented her fifth sentence the students had to reason as follows: The fifth sentence did not illustrate a possessive, and it was not an example; therefore possessives was still an acceptable hypothesis). The ability to do this kind of reasoning takes some practice, and students won't automatically be good at it. This is one of the reasons that having the students articulate their thinking is so important and why using familiar topics to introduce students to the model can help get them started.

We also saw in both lessons that the teachers had to initially prompt students to fully explain why they accepted or rejected hypotheses. In practice, teachers may have to do even more prompting than was illustrated in the introductory episodes. We intentionally abbreviated them to avoid excessive length. We turn now to the specific phases of the Concept-Attainment Model.

Phases in the Concept-Attainment Model

The Concept-Attainment Model occurs in four phases. The model begins by presenting examples, which provides students with data to begin the hypothesis-generation process. During the second phase, the teacher encourages students to analyze hypotheses in terms of the positive and negative examples provided. This begins a cyclical process of data presentation and hypothesis examination, which terminates with lesson closure. During lesson closure the teacher uses the examples to help students explicitly state characteristics and refine their definition of the concept. In the final phase, application, students are encouraged to extend and generalize their definition to additional examples. These phases are summarized in Table 4.1 and described in more detail in the following paragraphs.

Phase 1: Presenting Examples
After the activity has been introduced or explained, or once students have gained some experience with the procedure, the lesson begins with the teacher presenting examples to the students. Typically, it will be an example and a nonexample as Karl and Tanya did in their lessons. However, there is nothing inherently "wrong" with only presenting a positive example; not including a nonexample will merely result in many more initial hypotheses.

Karl began his lesson by presenting an apple as an example and a rock as a nonexample. Using a nonexample that was so distant from the example was designed to keep the possibilities for hypothesizing quite open. A teacher could just as appropriately have chosen something more closely related to the concept, such as milk, or another food. This would have narrowed the possibilities for hypotheses for students significantly and would have reduced the emphasis on critical thinking.

TABLE 4.1 Phases in the Concept-Attainment Model

Phase	Description
Presenting of Examples	Positive and negative examples are presented and hypotheses generated.
Analysis of Hypotheses	Students are encouraged to analyze hypotheses in light of new examples.
Closure	Closure occurs as students analyze examples to generate critical characteristics and form a definition.
Application	Additional examples are provided and analyzed in terms of the definition formed.

Phase 2: Analysis of Hypotheses

After presenting the first example or examples the teacher asks the students to hypothesize possible categories (concept names) that are illustrated by the positive example. In Karl's lesson, for example, the students initially hypothesized *things we eat, living things,* and *things that grow on plants,* while Tanya's students initially hypothesized *cars, linking verbs,* and *present tense,* and then added *metaphors* and *figures of speech* after she presented her third and fourth sentences. These hypotheses help direct students' attention to critical attributes and focuses subsequent classroom dialogue on these characteristics.

As another case, let's consider possible hypotheses for the following examples.

Among others, some hypotheses might include:

  closed figures
  four-sided figures
  squares
  figures with equal sides and equal angles
  figures with straight lines

From the list, we see that the hypotheses vary in specificity; *square*, for example, is a more specific hypothesis than is *four-sided figure*. This isn't a problem, because they will be eliminated or modified as the hypotheses are analyzed, until the appropriate degree of specificity is reached.

The Cyclical Process.   Having presented the students with the initial examples and having solicited the first set of hypotheses, the teacher then cycles back through Phases 1 and 2 by alternately presenting examples and analyzing the hypotheses. This is what the two teachers in our introductory episodes did in their lessons. For instance, after presenting her first example and nonexample and calling for students' initial hypotheses, Tanya added two more examples and asked the students to assess the acceptability of each of the hypotheses, in the process asking the students to explain why they accepted or rejected the hypothesis.

The purposes in asking the students to explain why they accept or reject an hypothesis are twofold. First, it helps students develop their thinking by having them articulate their own reasoning, and other students benefit from hearing their reasoning described in words. Second, the verbal description aids uniformity of understanding. If one student decides that an hypothesis must be rejected, for instance, and the discussion immediately moves to a second hypothesis, others in the class may not understand why the first one was rejected. Asking individuals to explain their reasoning makes the thinking skills visible to all of the students rather than to only those who voluntarily participate, and it helps students who are uncertain understand and stay involved in the activity (Beyer, 1983, 1984).

Notice also that hypotheses can be revised instead of being totally rejected. For instance, in Karl's lesson, Heidi wasn't satisfied with the hypothesis *things we eat that grow above the ground*, based on the argument that part of a carrot grows above the ground and *carrot* had been given as a nonexample. As a result, the hypothesis was revised to *plant parts we eat that are above ground*. In this instance, the students had a concrete experience that was consistent with the philosophy of hypothesis testing.

It is important during the analysis of hypotheses that the teacher refrain from passing judgment. It would be inappropriate at this point to say, "You've got it!" or "That's it!" if a student should hypothesize the label the teacher has in mind. For example, in Tanya's lesson, Ramona offered metaphor as an hypothesis after Tanya had displayed two examples and two nonexamples. Tanya then added *metaphor* to the list with no more or less reaction than she gave to any other hypotheses. If Tanya had acknowledged that *metaphor* was the concept she had in mind, the lesson would have been a simple guessing game rather than a process where the students learn to make conclusions based on data. Acting as Tanya did in response to Ramona's hypothesis puts the responsibility for identifying and verifying the concept on students. Through the process of offering and analyzing hypotheses, students become not only more proficient in those thinking strategies but also more autonomous learners.

The cyclical process in Phases 1 and 2 can be summarized in a series of steps:

- The teacher presents positive and negative examples.
- Students examine examples and generate hypotheses.
- The teacher presents additional positive and/or negative example(s).
- Students analyze hypotheses and eliminate those not supported by the data (examples).
- Students offer additional hypotheses if the data support them.
- The process of analyzing hypotheses, eliminating those invalidated by new examples, and offering additional hypotheses is repeated until one hypothesis is isolated.

Once learned, this cyclical process becomes familiar to both the teacher and students, and provides an internal structure for the model.

Phase 3: Closure
Once students have isolated an hypothesis that is supported by all of the examples, the lesson is ready for closure. At that point the teacher asks the students to identify the critical

characteristics of the concept and state a definition. The definition reinforces the students' understanding of the concept by including within it an identification of a superordinate concept and the concept's characteristics. Karl, for example, helped his students form the definition, "Fruits are foods we eat (superordinate concept) with seeds in the edible part." (*Seeds in the edible part* is the essential characteristic of the concept.)

In the case of proper noun, the teacher would help students state a definition such as the following:

> A proper noun is a noun (superordinate concept) that names a particular person, particular place, or particular thing (characteristics).

For *regular polygon,* the definition might be: "A regular polygon is a straight-lined plane figure with all sides and angles equal."

Having stated the definition, the students are prepared for the application phase of the model.

Phase 4: Application

The application phase of the Concept-Attainment Model is designed to reinforce the concept and help students extend and generalize it to new examples. The concept is reinforced by having the students classify additional examples as positive or negative and/or generate additional unique examples of their own. In Karl's lesson, the students identified the fruits from additional examples of foods, and Tanya asked her students to supply additional examples of metaphors.

This phase of the model is important for both students and teacher. It provides students with opportunities to try out their new knowledge on examples familiar to them. For the teacher, this phase provides valuable opportunities for feedback as to how and whether students understand the concept.

Developing Metacognitive Abilities

Suppose that you are about to go to a class or a meeting and you say to yourself, "I'm really dragging. I'd better have a cup of coffee before I go in there, so I can stay awake." Being aware of your attention and doing something to control it is called *meta-attention.* Meta-attention is one type of **metacognition**, *which is awareness of and control over our mental processes*—attention being one of the mental processes.

Developing metacognitive abilities in students is a valuable educational goal, because it can help them to become self-regulated learners. **Self-regulation** *is an individual's conscious use of mental strategies for the purpose of improving thinking and learning.* Self-regulated learners take responsibility for their own learning progress and adapt their learning strategies to meet task demands. One possible outcome from the Concept-Attainment Model is the development of student self-regulation.

Tanya attempted to help her students develop their metacognitive abilities when she compared the process of hypothesis testing in her lesson to the simple decision-making process involved in selecting oatmeal instead of Cream of Wheat. This simple example was a first step in helping students become aware of making conclusions and decisions based on information, instead of whim, emotion, or something worse, such as stereotyping. In addition, encouraging students to think about their own thinking helped them to recognize that the processes they were involved in had utility beyond the classroom. Developing metacognitive abilities and self-regulation would take much more than the one example we saw in Tanya's lesson, of course, but if provided with continued experiences, students would gradually develop these abilities. The same applies to the construction of all forms of knowledge and skills.

This completes our discussion of implementing Concept-Attainment lessons; before moving to the next section, however, we want to briefly discuss two questions that are often asked about the procedure. The first is, "What do I do if I get to the end of my list of examples and students haven't isolated one specific hypothesis?" If your set of examples and nonexamples is complete, this possibility will only occur when one hypothesis is a synonym for another. In that case you can retain both and when all the others have been eliminated, note that the two are synonymous.

The second is, "What do I do if the students eliminate all the hypotheses but one before all the examples are used?" Here the answer is simple. Simply allow the lesson to come to closure, and use the remainder of the examples as part of the application phase.

Implementing Concept-Attainment Activities: Modifications

We have described the Concept-Attainment Model as a structured strategy consisting of four interrelated phases. However, the strategy should not be viewed as rigid and inflexible. In fact, it can be very flexible and adaptable to different goals and learning situations. In this section, we describe some of the modifications that can be used to make the model more adaptable to your own teaching situation.

Developmental Considerations

In order to most effectively implement a Concept-Attainment activity, we need to consider the developmental level of the students. In general, the younger the students, the more concrete the examples need to be. Karl's lesson, for example, would be more appropriate for young children than would Tanya's, because the notion of a "nonliteral comparison"—the key characteristic of the concept *metaphor*—is much more abstract than "seeds in the edible part of the plant"—the key characteristic of the concept *fruit*.

A second adaptation that makes the model more effective with young children is to increase the emphasis on the positive examples and reduce the number of negative examples. Young children have difficulty dealing with the notion that something is not an example (Berk, 1994). The practice of inferring categories and doing rudimentary analysis of hypotheses is excellent for young children, however, and with modification they can become skilled in the strategy.

As students' facility with the model develops, they usually like it and often ask if they can "play the game." Preschool and early-elementary teachers have found the model effective as a form of review and to add variety to classroom activities. Also, experienced learners become adept at generating their own sequences of examples and "playing the game" with each other.

Concept-Attainment and Student Groupwork

The Concept-Attainment Model can also be used effectively when students work in pairs or small groups. For example, let's consider Tanya Adin's lesson again. After she had presented her first two examples, she asked students to volunteer possible hypotheses, and she conducted the activity in a large-group setting. Instead, she could have had students work in pairs and have each pair brainstorm and write a list of all possible hypotheses. Allowing students to work in pairs increases student involvement, which can have a positive impact on motivation.

The process would take very little organization—the individuals in each pair could be seated beside each other, and each group encouraged to analyze examples and share their thinking with each other. The pairs could then report their hypotheses to the whole group, which could then compile an overall list.

Next, after Tanya presented her second pair of examples, the groups could be asked to decide which hypotheses were acceptable and which ones had to be rejected. They could also be directed to write the reason they accepted or rejected the hypothesis in each case. This would capitalize on the critical-thinking process and give students practice in working together. These benefits—increased involvement, motivation, practice in working together, and increased opportunities for critical thinking—would take little extra effort on the part of the teacher.

Practicing the Scientific Method

Finally, as we mentioned earlier in the chapter, the model can also be used to introduce or reinforce the scientific method. As most people who teach science have seen, texts introduce the scientific method in the first chapter and fail to mention it again. As a result, students memorize the steps with virtually no understanding of the way the scientific method works.

Much about the methods of science can be learned from doing concept-attainment activities. For example, students first encounter a question or problem—to figure out what the concept is. Then, they hypothesize answers to the question—they suggest possible labels for the concept. As the process unfolds they see that hypotheses are accepted or rejected on the basis of data (the additional examples) and not on the basis of authority or someone's emotional reaction. Learning to make conclusions and decisions based on evidence rather than emotion or authority lies at the core of the critical thinking process.

The process also helps students understand the nature of hypothesis testing. For instance, an hypothesis is acceptable only if all the data support it, and it must be rejected if only one item of data is inconsistent with it. We look at the scientific method again in Chapter 8 when we discuss the Inquiry Model.

Concept-Attainment II and Concept-Attainment III

To this point, we have discussed basic procedures in implementing concept-attainment lessons, modifications that can be made for young children, and adaptations for using the model with student groupwork. We have also seen how the model can be used to give learners experience with the scientific method.

The basic procedure can be further modified, however, to increase the emphasis on thinking, metacognition, and the scientific method. We discuss these modifications in the next two sections.

Concept-Attainment II

The Concept-Attainment Model can be modified to increase the emphasis the activity places on student thinking. By changing the procedure slightly, students are placed in a situation where they not only get practice in analyzing hypotheses, but also learn to improve the efficiency of their thinking.

Concept-Attainment II is a modification of the concept-attainment strategy that provides students with greater initiative in learning concepts. As illustrated in the previous sections, the basic concept-attainment activity (which for reference we'll call Concept-Attainment I, or C.A. I), only the first two examples are initially presented, and the subsequent ones are then presented sequentially and usually one at a time. Concept Attainment II (C.A. II) is similar to C.A. I in that the first two are presented and labeled positive and negative, respectively. However, C.A. II differs from C.A. I in one important respect. In a C.A. II lesson, all of the examples are displayed to the student from the beginning of the activity. This allows the students to select subsequent examples to test their hypotheses.

After presenting all of the examples and labeling the first two, the teacher asks the students to hypothesize concept names, which are listed on the chalk board. Students are then encouraged to scan the remaining list for those that might substantiate or refute the hypotheses on the board. Students next choose an example from the list and indicate whether they think it is positive or negative. They also state which hypotheses would have to be rejected if their classification is correct. The teacher then verifies the classification. If the classification is correct, the appropriate changes are made in the list of hypotheses; if incorrect, the hypotheses are reanalyzed in light of the new information. The students then select additional examples and repeat the analysis process until one hypothesis is isolated.

For example, a typical Concept-Attainment II lesson might begin something like this. The teacher, wanting to teach the concept of *carnivores* might provide pictures of the following.

Examples

dog—yes	chair	tiger
car—no	cat	hamster
tree	beaver	mouse
cow		

Students might respond to this information with the following hypotheses, which would be listed on the board.

Examples		*Hypotheses*
dog—yes	cat	living things
car—no	beaver	animals
tree	tiger	domestic animals
cow	hamster	mammals
chair	mouse	carnivores

One advantage of the Concept-Attainment II activities is for the students to develop efficiency in their hypothesis testing. Efficiency is achieved if the example can be used to test all, or at least several, of the hypotheses. For example, one way to test all of these hypotheses is with *cat*. If cat is a no, then all of the hypotheses would need to be rejected. However, in this lesson with carnivore as the target concept, cat is a *yes*, so this example provides no basis to reject any of the hypotheses. Even though this particular example didn't result in the elimination of hypotheses, it provided some excellent practice with the process.

The students might then decide to choose beaver as the next example. If beaver is a yes, all of the hypotheses except carnivores and domestic animals are acceptable, but if beaver is a no, carnivore and domestic animals would be the only acceptable hypotheses. The teacher would verify beaver as a no because beaver is not an example of the concept *carnivore*. Therefore, the hypotheses living things, animals, and mammals would have to be rejected. Domestic animals and carnivores would be retained as viable hypotheses because beaver was a negative example of the concept, and dog and cat have been classified as positive examples. Now look at the list and see if you can determine a way in which students could investigate the hypothesis *domestic animal*.

Examples		*Hypotheses*
dog—yes	cat—yes	domestic animals
car—no	beaver—no	carnivores
tree	tiger	
cow	hamster	
chair	mouse	

Consider the choices *cow* and *tiger*. The two choices provide slightly different information. The difference is enough to make one a more efficient choice. First, if tiger is a yes, *domestic animal* must be rejected because a tiger is not a domestic animal. If tiger is a no, it merely says that the category cannot be rejected but it actually isn't supported either. The data are "neutral" with respect to the hypothesis because tiger may be a no for reasons other than the fact that it's not a domestic animal. Remember that when students select examples and examine hypotheses, they do not know what the concept is; they must infer it from the information provided.

Now, consider cow as a test of the hypothesis *domestic animal*. If cow is a no, *domestic animal* is rejected, because cow is a domestic animal, and succinct information about the inference is obtained. However, if cow is yes, not only is the category not rejected, it is directly supported (again because cow is a domestic animal). The choice of cow as an example provides more information about the hypothesis than does the choice of tiger, so cow is the more efficient choice. The reverse would be true if we had wanted to test the hypothesis *carnivorous animal*. In that case, tiger would be a more efficient choice. With practice, students become efficient at gathering data, obtaining maximum information with each example. A major benefit to students in a C.A. II activity is the practice they get in the process of analysis. In a limited sense, students are designing their own investigation or experiment.

Concept-Attainment III

A second modification of the basic procedure is designed to further increase the cognitive initiative and responsibility for learners. As with C.A. II, C.A. III requires more sophisticated analysis by students and helps them improve their efficiency; it does this by providing students with the opportunity to generate their own examples to test hypotheses. The basic strategy and thinking processes are basically the same as in C.A. II. However, rather than seeing the first two examples identified and having the remainder displayed for them, students see the first two identified and must then supply their own examples. For example, consider the following activity designed to teach the concept *vegetables with edible roots*.

The teacher begins by showing the class:

carrot	yes
corn	no

Some possible hypotheses might be:

orange-colored vegetables
vegetables with edible roots
vegetables rich in vitamin A
vegetables that are eaten raw

The responsibility of providing an example to test these hypotheses now rests with the students. The students could test the hypotheses by selecting additional examples of vegetables. An efficient choice might be radish. If radish is a yes, orange-colored vegetables and vegetables rich in vitamin A are eliminated, but if radish is a no, vegetables with edible roots and vegetables that are eaten raw are eliminated. For this lesson, radish is a yes, which leaves *vegetables with edible roots* and *vegetables that are eaten raw* as possible concepts. The students' task would then be to examine these remaining hypotheses further. A choice now might be potato. Potato as a yes would further support *vegetables with edible roots* but would force rejection of *vegetables that are eaten raw*. Because of the concept being taught, potato would be a yes, causing the latter hypothesis to be rejected and lending further support to the hypothesis *vegetables with edible roots*. Students would then continue to test the hypothesis and, in so doing, would be both reinforcing and enlarging their notion of the concept.

In planning for a C.A. III activity, the teacher should have additional examples available for use if the students' examples do not provide for a complete picture of the concept. If their use is not necessary during the course of the lesson, the teacher's examples could be used at the end of the activity as a means of evaluating the concept learning.

One additional advantage of C.A. III is the opportunity it affords learners to actively gather data. C.A. III is more lifelike or realistic than the other two concept-attainment formats in that students can more actively pursue a concept that they do not fully understand. Because students are not limited to the examples the teacher provides, they can use more of their own background knowledge, initiative, and creativity to investigate hypotheses. In addition, thinking strategies are best developed through overt practice in which students share and explain the thinking processes they went through in arriving at their answers.

Assessing Student Outcomes of Concept-Attainment Activities

Two kinds of outcomes result from concept-attainment activities. One is a deeper understanding of concepts—often those with which students have had some experience—and the other is increased critical-thinking abilities. In this section, we will address the assessment of both of these outcomes.

Assessing Understanding of Concepts

Students' attainment of a concept can be measured in one or more of four primary ways:

1. They identify or supply additional examples of the concept not previously encountered.
2. They identify the concept's characteristics.
3. They relate the concept to other concepts.
4. They define the concept.

A simple and effective way of measuring concept attainment is by asking students to identify or provide additional examples of the concept. This type of measurement item is relatively easy to prepare; unlike a statement of definition or characteristics, if the teacher uses unique examples, it is a valid way of measuring whether or not the students have constructed a valid understanding of the concept. For instance, consider the following item designed to measure the concept *direct object.*

Read the following passage and underline all of the direct objects in it.

> Damon and Kerri were out riding. As they rode, Kerri spotted a funny-looking animal in the bushes.
> "Let's catch it," she suggested.
> "No way," Damon responded. "I'm not chasing any strange animal. It might bite me."
> "C'mon, chicken," she retorted. "I'll bet it's harmless."
> "Ohh, all right. But, if it jumps you, I'm out of here."
> The kids then chased the animal. Unfortunately for Kerri, but fortunately for Damon, they had no luck in catching it.

In addition to measuring students' understanding of the concept, an additional advantage of this exercise is that the examples of direct objects are presented in the context of a paragraph; presenting examples this way increases the likelihood that students will be able to transfer the information to new settings.

A variation of this format is to ask students to provide examples of the concept rather than identify examples from the list. In that case, the students would be asked to write their own passage containing a specified number of examples.

A second form of measurement is to ask students to identify characteristics of the concept. The disadvantage of this type of measurement is that the item generally measures little more than knowledge, since the characteristics will already have been identified during the activity.

An illustration of this type of item could be the following:

Circle all of the following that are characteristic of mammals:

a. Naked skin
b. Lays eggs
c. Four-chambered heart
d. Scaly skin
e. Regulated body temperature
f. Nurses young

Students' understanding of concepts can also be measured by having students relate them to other concepts. Here the teacher asks the students to identify coordinate, superordinate, or subordinate concepts, or a combination of them. The following item is an example of this type of format.

If figures of speech is superordinate to the concept metaphor, which of the following are coordinate to the concept metaphor?

a. Simile   c. Personification   e. Alliteration
b. Trope   d. Meter   f. Iambic pentameter

This item tests students' understanding of the relationship between metaphor and concepts that are also figures of speech. Similar items can be designed to measure superordinate and subordinate relationships. Use of items such as these assumes that the teacher has discussed these relationships in class.

A fourth alternative for measuring concept learning is to ask students to provide a definition of the concept or to identify the correct definition from a list of alternatives. The disadvantage of this type of measurement item is that it is most like items used to measure students' knowledge of characteristics because it typically involves recall of information.

As this discussion suggests, there is no one best way to measure students' attainment of a concept. Each of the various items described tells the teacher something different about students' understanding, and the best assessment strategy is to use a combination of them.

Assessing Students' Critical-Thinking Abilities

Perhaps even more important than the assessment of students' understanding of the concept is an assessment of their critical-thinking abilities. This type of assessment is difficult using a paper-and-pencil format, but it can be done. For example, consider the following item:

You have been given the following examples:

Yes	No
36	5
81	111

The following hypotheses have been listed:

Two-digit numbers
Composite (not prime) numbers
Perfect squares
Multiples of 3

1. Are all of the hypotheses acceptable? Yes No (Circle one) Explain.

_____

_____

_____

2. You are given two more examples, so your list now appears as follows:

Yes	No
36	5
81	111
49	45

Which hypotheses are now acceptable, and which ones must be rejected? Explain why in each case.

_____

_____

_____

_____

_____

As we see from these items, and as we discussed in Chapter 2, the ability to assess hypotheses requires that students understand the concepts *two-digit numbers, composite numbers, perfect squares,* and *multiples of three.* This is the domain-specific knowledge dimension of critical thinking, which is a necessary aspect of thinking abilities in all areas.

We have provided here a brief description of the measurement and evaluation process in concept learning. Any of the leading texts in the area of assessment can give you a detailed discussion of the process.

Please turn now to the following exercises, which are designed to measure your understanding of the Concept-Attainment Model.

Summary

The Concept-Attainment Model closely relates to the Inductive Model in that it is designed to teach concepts while strongly emphasizing higher-order and critical thinking. An important strength of the Concept-Attainment Model is its ability to help learners understand the process of hypothesis testing with a wide variety of topics in the context of a single learning activity.

Concept-attainment activities begin when the teachers present the problem of having to identify the concept they have in mind. The concept is then typically illustrated with a positive and negative example, following by the students hypothesizing possible concepts. The process continues as additional positive and negative examples are presented, followed by analysis of the hypotheses. The process comes to closure when the concept is isolated and tested with additional examples.

The Concept-Attainment Model is most appropriately used when the teacher's goals are strongly oriented toward the development of higher-order and critical thinking. It is a less efficient model than the Inductive Model if the goals are more content-oriented.

Important Concepts

Arousal (p. 118)
Metacognition (p. 122)

Self-regulation (p. 122)

Exercises

1. Look at the content goals listed below. Identify which are appropriately taught with the Concept-Attainment Model. For those that are inappropriate, explain why.

   GOALS
   a. An English teacher wants her students to understand *gerund.*
   b. An elementary teacher wants his students to understand *soft.*
   c. A science teacher wants her students to know why two coffee cans released at the top of an inclined plane roll down the plane at different speeds.
   d. A science teacher wants his students to understand what *miscible fluids* (that are capable of being mixed) are.
   e. A literature teacher wants her students to know the time period in which Poe did his writing.

2. For each of the content goals identified in Item 1 as appropriate for concept attainment, prepare and sequence a list of examples that would help the students attain the concept.

3. Select a topic of your choice and design a sequence of examples that will maximize the students' practice with thinking skills.

4. Read the following case study illustrating a concept-attainment activity and answer the questions using information from the scenario.

   Michele Scarritt wants her students to practice their ability to test hypotheses, and in order to provide practice with the process, she focuses on the concept *canine*. She has done a number of concept-attainment activities with her students, so they are familiar and comfortable with the process, viewing it as a "thinking game."

   She cuts pictures of various animals and plants from magazines and pastes them on poster paper.

   "Today we are going to do another concept-attainment activity, and I've thought up a really good one for you," she says in her introduction to the class. "You're going to have to really think about this one, so I'm curious to see how you'll do."

"You can't stump us, Mrs. Scarritt," the students retort. "We get 'em all."

"We'll see," Michele continues smiling. "Here we go. . . ."

Michele then shows a picture of a German Shepherd as a yes example and an oak tree as a no example.

1. "I know what you're thinking of," Mary volunteers. "It's an animal."
2. "It could be pet," Tabatha added.
3. "I think it's mammal," Phyllis put in.
4. "Let's take a quick look at those hypotheses, to be sure we're all in the same place. Phyllis, where did you get mammal?"
5. ". . . A German Shepherd's a dog, and dogs are mammals."
6. "Okay," Michele nods, "and I think we can all see where Mary and John got pet and animal. Let's go on and look at some more data." She then showed a collie (yes) and a magnolia tree (no).
7. "I think it's dogs," Judy added.
8. "Okay, let's put that on the board. Now let's go a bit further," Michele said. She then showed a beagle (yes) and a Siamese cat (no).
9. "It can't be pet," Kathy quickly said, "because Siamese cat is a no and it's a pet."
10. "It can't be animal or mammal either," Mike noted, "because a cat is both an animal and a mammal."
11. "Let's continue," Michele requested. She then showed a fox (yes) and a leopard (no).
12. "It can't be just dog," Don asserted. "Maybe it's dog family."
13. "I'll show you another picture," Michele said. Then she showed a picture of a wolf (yes).
14. "It must be dog family," Denny stated. "All the yes's support the idea of dog family."
15. Michele then added, "What do we call dog family?" After hearing no response she said, "Animals in the dog family are called 'canines.'"
16. Michele then suggested, "Let's look at these pictures again (the yes's) and see what they have in common."
17. "They all have four legs," Sharon noted.
18. "They bark," Ann added.
19. "They have sharp, prominent teeth," Jimmy said.
20. "They all have hair," Jane suggested.

The lesson continued as Michele helped the class form a definition for *canine.* Then she showed them some additional pictures and asked them to classify them as canine or not.

Using information from the anecdote, respond to the following:

a. Identify all of the positive examples of the concept.

b. Identify all of the characteristics of the concept that were presented in the anecdote.

c. Identify all of the statements in the anecdote that were statements of hypothesizing.

d. Explain how Michele's sequence of examples promoted the development of students' thinking abilities in the activity.

e. What could Michele have done to further enrich the concept that the children attained?

f. What did Michele do that did not quite follow the concept-attainment procedure?

g. Where in the anecdote did Michele make students' thinking processes explicit?

Discussion Questions

1. How does using the concept-attainment model compare to naturalistic concept learning? What are some reasons for these differences? Would there be any advantages to making early concept learning more structured? Any disadvantages?

2. In implementing concept-attainment activities in diverse classrooms, we have noticed that students who do not typically participate can become quite actively involved. What might be the reason for this?

3. What would a concept-attainment activity be like if only positive examples were used? Only negative? What is the optimal mix of positive and negative examples?

4. What are the advantages of using coordinate concepts as negative examples in concept-attainment activities? Disadvantages? What can be done to minimize these disadvantages?

5. The amount of time that a teacher waits after asking a question has been found to be an important determinant influencing the quality of student answers (Rowe, 1974). How important is wait time in a concept-attainment activity? When should it occur?

6. In what areas of the curriculum is it hardest to provide adequate examples for concept-attainment activities? Easiest?

7. In what order should C.A. I, C.A. II, and C.A. III activities be introduced to students? What can be done to help students understand similarities and differences between the different strategies?

8. In terms of C.A. I, II, and III:
   a. Which is easiest to implement in the classroom?
   b. Which is the most difficult to implement?
   c. Which require(s) the most prior planning?

9. How could the thinking skills developed in C.A. II and III be evaluated?

Chapter 5

Teaching Organized Bodies of Knowledge: The Integrative Model

The Integrative Model is an inductive strategy designed to help students develop a deep understanding of organized bodies of knowledge, while at the same time practice higher-order thinking about the information they're studying. The Integrative Model, as with the Inductive Model, views learners as actively constructing their own understanding of the topics they study.

The Integrative Model is closely related to the Inductive Model in its structure and execution. The primary differences relate to the topics taught with each. While the Inductive Model is designed to teach specific topics in the form of concepts, generalizations, principles, and academic rules, the Integrative Model is designed to teach combinations of those specific forms of content in large, organized bodies of information.

The foundations of the Integrative Model are based on the conceptions of Hilda Taba (1965, 1966, 1967), and we want to gratefully acknowledge her contributions to our work.

When you've completed your study of this chapter, you should be able to meet the following objectives:

- Describe the characteristics of organized bodies of knowledge.
- Identify topics that exist in the form of organized bodies of knowledge.

- Plan lessons using the Integrative Model.
- Implement lessons using the Integrative Model.
- Adapt the Integrative Model for learners at different ages and with varying backgrounds.
- Assess student attainment of content objectives taught with the Integrative Model.
- Assess the development of student higher-order- and critical-thinking abilities developed with the Integrative Model.

To begin our discussion, let's look at two teachers, each using the Integrative Model to help students understand organized bodies of information while simultaneously practicing higher-order and critical thinking. (The episodes are based on lessons we have personally observed teachers conduct, and we appreciate their contributions to this work. The case studies have been abbreviated for the sake of clarity, but they capture the essence of the lessons.)

Kim Soo is involved in a science unit on amphibians with her fourth graders. To this point, the class has read about amphibians and Kim has used her science videodisc to show a variety of amphibians. As a class project, groups of students found pictures of frogs and toads, and the foods they eat. They brought the pictures to class, and with Kim's help organized them in a matrix. Kim supplied some additional information for the matrix and the result is shown in Figure 5.1.

Kim then laminated the matrix, so she could use it again later and prepared to guide students' analysis of the information in it.

After directing the class to study the chart for a moment, she began the activity by saying, "First, let's look at the words at the top of the chart." Pointing to 'characteristics' she continued, "This is kind of a big one. What do you think it means?"

". . . It's sort of the way they look," Andrea responded uncertainly.

"Sure," Kim nodded. "It's a way of describing them. The way they look, their color, the way they're built."

Next Kim had the students describe what "habitat" meant to them and she then went on, "Let's start with food since we're all familiar with it. Look carefully at the part that tells what toads eat. What do you notice here? . . . Serena?"

"Well, they eat earthworms," Serena responded.

"And what else? . . . Dominique?"

"Spiders," Dominique answered.

"Also grasshoppers," David volunteered.

"Yes, very good, everyone," Kim smiled. "Now look at the frogs. Let's do the same with them. What can you tell me about what they eat? Judy?"

". . . They eat insects," Judy replied.

"Also earthworms," Bill added.

"Now, let's go a bit farther," Kim encouraged. "Look at both the frogs and the toads. How would you compare what they eat? Is there any kind of pattern there?"

"They both eat insects," Tim noticed.

"Leroy?"

"They both eat earthworms too," Leroy offered.

". . . The food for each seems to be almost the same," Kristy added tentatively.

"Why do you suppose that the food seems to be the same? . . . Fernando?" Kim continued, smiling in acknowledgement of Kristy's answer.

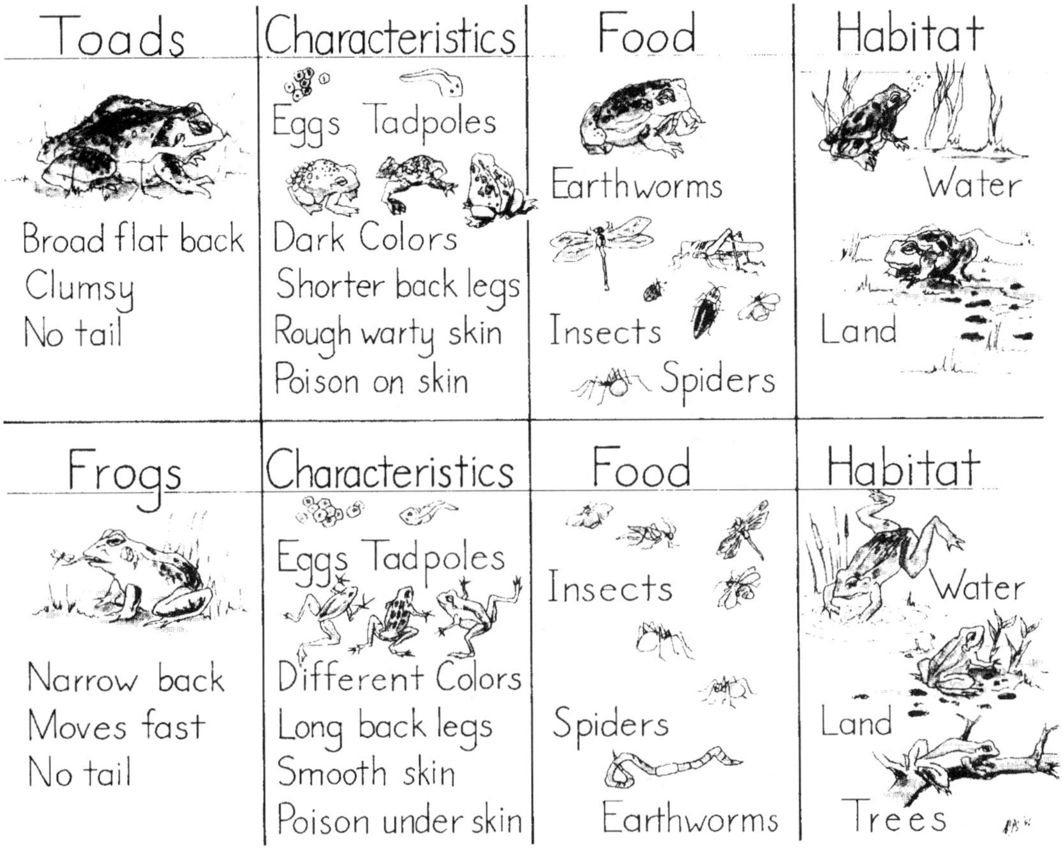

Toads	Characteristics	Food	Habitat
Broad flat back Clumsy No tail	Eggs Tadpoles Dark Colors Shorter back legs Rough warty skin Poison on skin	Earthworms Insects Spiders	Water Land
Frogs	Characteristics	Food	Habitat
Narrow back Moves fast No tail	Eggs Tadpoles Different Colors Long back legs Smooth skin Poison under skin	Insects Spiders Earthworms	Water Land Trees

FIGURE 5.1   Chart with Information about Frogs and Toads

". . . The frog and toad live in about the same places," Fernando responded after several seconds of studying the chart.

"How did you decide that?" Kim probed.

". . . It says on the chart that the frog lives on land, in water, and in trees, and it says that the toad lives on land and in water," Fernando responded, pointing to the chart.

"Yes, excellent, Fernando," Kim nodded. "Remember how we have talked about justifying our thinking in some of our work in math. This is exactly the same thing. Fernando provided evidence for his conclusion that their environments are about the same by pointing out where they live on the chart. This is the kind of thinking we're after."

"Also, the frog and toad are very much alike," Sonya added, turning back to the chart.

"What do you see that tells you that, Sonya?"

"From the pictures, we see that they look about the same," Sonya replied.

"Also, they both start from eggs and then become tadpoles. See where there are eggs and tadpoles on the chart?" Lakesha added.

"Very good everyone!" Kim enthused. "That is particularly good, Lakesha. You provided evidence for your comment without being asked for it. You're all thinking very well."

"Now here's a tough one," Kim continued. "Suppose that frogs and toads were quite different rather than being very similar. What kinds of conclusions might we make about them then? . . . Donna?"

". . . Maybe the food that they would eat would be different," Donna shrugged.

"Can you give us an example of where that would be the case, Donna?" Kim queried."

". . ."

"Think about some animals that we know about. What do they eat?"

". . . Dogs eat dog food and stuff."

"Sure. There's an example," Kim smiled. "Dogs are different from frogs and toads, and we see that they eat different kinds of foods."

"Wait," Emmitt waved. "Dogs and cats are different, but they eat the same kinds of foods."

"Excellent thought, Emmitt," Kim nodded. . . . "Now think about Emmitt's point everyone. Do you have some other thoughts?"

". . . Dogs and cats are different, but a cat is more like a dog than a toad," Tabatha added, to the giggles of some of the other students.

"Some of you are laughing," Kim smiled, "but consider what Tabatha said. What do you think?"

". . . I think she's right," Sylvia responded. "Cows and horses are different, but they eat the same food."

"Okay," Kim waved. "I think you've all come up with some good thoughts. . . . Now, let's think some more about all of this. Look again at the toad and frog in the first column of the chart. In what ways are they different? . . . Fred?"

". . . It says the toad is clumsy, but it doesn't say anything about the frog."

". . . Suppose that the toad wasn't clumsy," Kim continued, nodding in acknowledgement of Fred's answer. "How might that affect the food toads eat or where they live? . . . Anyone?"

". . ."

"Look over at the food column and the habitat column."

". . . Maybe toads could live in trees if they weren't clumsy," Marcy suggested.

"That's an interesting thought," Kim nodded. "Why do you think so?"

". . . They couldn't be clumsy and get up there; . . . if they were clumsy, they might fall out," Andre suggested after studying the chart for several seconds.

"Sounds sensible. What does anyone else think?"

The rest of the class nodded and murmured, and Kim went on, "How about food?"

"That would be different too," Kathy said quickly.

"Why do you think so, Kathy?" Kim probed.

". . . Well, . . . Well, maybe not?"

"Why not?"

"The frog and toad eat the same food."

"What does that have to do with it?"

". . . If the frog isn't clumsy, and the toad is, . . . and they eat the same food, . . . it doesn't matter."

"What doesn't matter?"

". . . Whether the toad is clumsy or not?"

"What do you think of Kathy's suggestions, anyone?"

The class discussed Kathy's ideas for a few more minutes and finally concluded that what she said made sense.

Kim then continued, "Now, let's summarize what we've found here, and let's think about animals in general. . . . I want you to try and extend beyond the toad and frog, and I'll help you if you need it.

"For instance," she went on, "what can we say about the characteristics of animals that look a lot alike?"

". . . They have mostly the same characteristics."

"So, how should we write that? Help me out," Kim urged as she moved up to the board.

". . ."

"I'll get us started." She then wrote, "Animals that look alike . . ." on the chalkboard.

". . . Will have similar characteristics," Carol offered.

"Okay," Kim replied, and she then wrote, Animals that look alike have similar characteristics, on the chalkboard.

"What else?" she urged.

"They also eat the same kind of food," Tonya offered.

"Good. So, . . . tell me what to write."

"Animals that look alike."

"And have the same characteristics," Nancy interjected.

"And have the same characteristics," Tonya repeated, "eat the same kind of food."

Kim then wrote the statement on the board, and asked the students for any additional summarizing statements.

Finally, they had a list of statements that appeared as follows:

1. Animals that look alike have similar characteristics.
2. Animals that look alike and have similar characteristics eat the same kind of food.
3. Animals that are similar live in similar habitats.

Finally, Kim asked the students if they could think of some examples that fit their statements, and they discussed animals such as deer and elk, different kinds of birds, and predators such as lions and leopards. They also discussed exceptions, such as the fact that deer and elk both live in the mountains, but some deer live on the plains as well, and then Kim closed the lesson.

Let's look now at another teacher using the Integrative Model in an eighth-grade history class. As you read through the second lesson, compare what the teacher is doing compared to what Kim Soo did in her lesson.

Tony Horton is beginning a unit on immigration with his American History students. He asked the students what *immigrant* meant and then asked them to suggest some representative immigrant groups from the late nineteenth century until the middle of the twentieth century, saying that they would look at immigration from the middle of the twentieth century to the present later in the unit. The students suggested that they study a group from Europe and another from the Far East. Tony also encouraged them to consider one or more groups closer to the United States as well, and at his suggestion they settled on Puerto Rico.

Just as he began again, Juan interjected, "What about Cuba? I have some relatives in Florida who came from Cuba."

"Sounds good to me," Tony nodded. "What do the rest of you think?"

The class agreed that it was a good idea, and Tony commented, "This will extend our study a bit past the middle of the century, but I really like your idea Juan. Also, everyone, we will extend what we're doing to consider Hispanic Americans in the Southwest, and many of the immigrant groups particular to California."

Tony then drew a matrix on the board that appeared as shown in Figure 5.2.

Next Tony organized the class into pairs and each pair was assigned to gather information about the four immigrant groups' reasons for coming, characteristics, and assimilation. The pairs turned in the notes they had gathered and Tony compiled the information, together with some of his own, into the chart that appears in Figure 5.3.

The next day Tony began the lesson by saying, "All right everyone, slide your desk next to your partner, and we'll analyze the information that we've put together in our chart," as he passed out a copy to each of the pairs.

After each pair had received a copy, he continued, "Now, here's your assignment. I want you to look in each column of the chart and look for patterns. For instance, when you look at the immigrants' reasons for coming, compare each group to see what they have in common. Then describe the commonalities in writing. Let's look at a sample. Everyone take a look at the first column for a minute and see if you find some things that the four groups have in common, or something that two or three of the groups have in common."

	Reasons for Coming	Characteristics	Assimilation
I T			
C H			
P R			
C			

FIGURE 5.2   Matrix Organized for Data Gathering

	Reasons for Coming	Characteristics	Assimilation
I T A L I A N S	Small farms couldn't support families Large estates controlled land Population increases Poor land, little irrigation, wooden plows Few factories, little industry Heavy taxes Stories of wealth in America	Many from low-income backgrounds Religious; Catholic Large families Tight family structure Many from farm occupations Most could not read or write English English language learned quickly by second generation	First generation did not mix Church schools Second generation moved away from home "Little Italy" in New York City Second generation "Americanized"
C H I N E S E	Large population Land controlled by war lords High taxes Crop failures Famine Promise of high wages in America	Many brought to U.S. initially as laborers Religious; Confucianism Most could not read or write English Retained many former customs Tight family structure	Men as job hunters initially lived together "China Towns" established in major cities Major influx from 1868–1890 Little social association with others Large population in western U.S. Eager to preserve customs
P U E R T O R I C A N S	Large population increases Few factories Little land Close to the United States Descriptions of "good life" in America	Many had low-income backgrounds Religious; Catholic Large families Most could not read or write English English language learned quickly by second generation Tight family structure	Major influx in 1940s and 1950s "Spanish Harlem" in New York Many stayed in northeastern U.S. Initially church, then public schools Second generation "Americanized"
C U B A N S	Batista overthrown Castro into power Promises of opportunity to return to Cuba	Many had upper-income backgrounds Religious; Catholic Tight family structure Many did not read or write English Politically powerful in South Florida Economically powerful in South Florida	Major influx in 1960s Large population in south Florida Adapted quickly to American politics Adapted quickly to American business practices

FIGURE 5.3 Matrix Containing Gathered Information

After about half a minute, Aurelia volunteered hesitantly, "It looks like the Italians, Chinese, and Puerto Ricans all had population problems, but that didn't seem to be the case for the Cubans."

"Excellent, Aurelia. That's exactly what we're trying to do," Tony praised, and he wrote "Population problems for the Italians, Chinese, and Puerto Ricans; not for the Cubans," on the board.

He then continued, "Now, I want you to work with your partner and find as many patterns as you have evidence for in each of the columns. Write them on your paper the way we did here with Aurelia's information. You have ten minutes."

"Do we turn these in, Mr. Horton?" James asked.

"Absolutely," Tony nodded. "Now get to work quickly and quietly."

The room soon became a buzz of voices as the students began studying the chart and writing information on their papers.

At the end of the ten minutes Tony said, "Okay, let's take a look. What do you have there?"

"Wait, we're not done," several of the students protested.

"All right. Five more minutes."

At the end of the five minutes, Tony said, "Now, here we go. What are some of the comparisons you made?"

Each of the pairs reported some of the comparisons that they found, and as they did Tony recorded them on the board. When they were finished, they had the following lists:

Reasons for Coming	*Characteristics*	*Assimilation*
Poor agriculture except for Cubans	Tended to come from lower classes except for Cubans	First generations stayed to themselves
Large populations except for Cubans	Most didn't speak English	Chinese assimilated more slowly than the others did
Promises of a better life in America	All were religious	At least initially, tended to stay where they first landed
Political problems in Cuba	All except Chinese quickly learned English	

"That's well done," Tony nodded, pointing to the lists. "Good work. . . . Now, let's look a little more closely at the information. Why do you suppose that the Italians, Chinese, and Puerto Ricans tended to come from the lower socioeconomic classes, while the Cubans did not? . . . Anyone?"

". . . I think it's because of why they came," Antonio offered. "The Italians, Chinese, and Puerto Ricans came so they could have a better life, but the Cubans were escaping from Fidel Castro's revolution."

"They wanted a better life too," Kevin interjected.

"Well, that's true, but the reasons were different. The others wanted to make a better living, and in Cuba it was politics mostly."

"Good thoughts everyone," Tony went on. "Is there anything that we can say in general about the reasons immigrants move from one country to another?"

". . . I think they think that they will have a better life in the new country," LaQuana put in. "It might be to make more money, or it might be for political reasons, but they all think they'll be better off in the new country than they are in the old one."

"Does everyone agree with that?" Tony asked, turning to the rest of the class.

Seeing several nods, Tony then wrote on the board, "Immigrants immigrate in search of a better life."

He then continued, "Let's look again at some of the comparisons we've made. We wrote that the Chinese assimilated less rapidly than did the other groups. Why do you suppose that was the case?"

". . . They were more different culturally than the others were," Christine volunteered finally.

"What information do we have on our chart that tells us they were more different culturally?"

". . . Their religion for one thing. The Italians, Puerto Ricans, and Cubans were mostly Catholic, which a lot of people in the United States are, but the Chinese were Confus . . . Confushist . . . whatever that religion is," Christine continued.

"Also, it says in the chart that the Chinese learned English slower than the others," Estella added.

"And why might that have been?"

"Their language is different. There are letters for each of the languages in the chart, and the Italians, Puerto Ricans, and Cubans use the same letters as English, but the Chinese letters are really different."

"Suppose they weren't different, meaning they used the same letters as we do. How do you suppose that would have affected how fast they assimilated?"

". . . It would have speeded it up," Dean offered.

"What do you think, Gayle? You've been sort of quiet," Tony encouraged.

". . . It might have speeded it up, but it still would have been slower than for the others."

"Why do you think so?"

"Well, the religion for one thing."

"And they retained many of their former customs," Shelli added.

Tony continued with the process of having students explain their comparisons and hypothesize outcomes until the information in the chart had been covered.

He then said, "Let's try and make some summary generalizations about the information we have here, and then we'll see if we think it applies to immigrant groups today."

With Tony's guidance the students offered some generalizations, which he wrote on the board. The list appeared as follows:

Immigrants immigrate in search of a better life.

Immigrants usually immigrate to make a better living. (Tony added, "Usually for economic reasons.")

Some immigrants immigrate for political reasons.

Immigrants usually hear stories of how good it will be in the new country.

If immigrants immigrate for economic reasons, they're usually in the lower economic classes in their native country.

Immigrants assimilate more easily if their language and customs are similar to the language and customs of the new country.

Immigrants tend to first settle where they initially land in the new country.

"Now let's take a look at our list as see if we think everything we've said is valid. How do they all look?"

". . . I don't think that 'economic reasons' is right," Troy said after several seconds.

"Go on, Troy. Why don't you think so?"

". . . It looks to me like both the Italians and Chinese also had political problems, sort of like the Cubans. The Puerto Ricans are the only ones that didn't seem to have political problems."

"What evidence do you have for that?"

Troy then referred to information on the chart, such as 'heavy taxes from government,' for the Italians and 'War lords' and 'heavy taxes' for the Chinese.

Tony acknowledged his point, asked the rest of the class if they thought the generalization should be revised, did so in response to their comments, and then analyzed each of the other generalizations in the same way.

Finally, he said, "We're going to keep this list on the board, and when we study immigrants further, we'll see if our generalizations are still valid. We'll ask ourselves, did we overgeneralize, or maybe even undergeneralize? Did we inappropriately stereotype any immigrant groups? Then, we'll look back at some of the early colonialization, such as the Jamestown and Plymouth Colonies. Can the people that settled then even be legitimately called immigrants? We'll start there tomorrow."

The Integrative Model: An Overview

As with the other models, we begin our discussion of the Integrative Model by looking again at the teaching episodes and identifying both their common elements and their differences. We then turn to a detailed discussion of planning and implementing lessons using the Integrative Model.

The lessons were similar in the following ways:

- First, the topics the teachers taught were organized bodies of information—the characteristics, food, and habitat of toads and frogs in Kim Soo's lesson, and the reasons for coming, characteristics, and assimilation of different immigrant groups in Tony Horton's.
- Both teachers began their lessons by displaying information that the teacher and students had gathered and compiled in a matrix.

- In each class students used the information in the matrix as a basis for increasing the depth of their understanding by searching for patterns, explaining similarities and differences, hypothesizing outcomes for changing conditions, and finally, generalizing of the results. The students practiced higher-order and critical thinking while simultaneously increasing the depth of their understanding of each topic.
- The teacher guided students' analysis—beginning with making observations and comparisons, proceeding through explanations and hypotheses, and ending with generalizations based on the comparisons, explanations, and hypotheses. The conclusions and general statements were the content goals of the lesson.
- Both teachers emphasized justifying their thinking by providing evidence for the conclusions they formed.

Because of the topics, ages of the students, and the teachers' goals, the lessons had some minor differences:

- Kim Soo began the lesson by having the students first observe and describe the information in a specific cell of the matrix, while Tony Horton had students make comparisons and search for patterns as the first part of the activity.
- Kim did her lesson as a large-group activity, while Tony had the students initially work in pairs, report their findings, and then analyze the findings in a whole group.
- Kim followed a sequence of having the students first make observations, which were then followed—pretty much in order—by making comparisons, forming explanations, hypothesizing, and generalizing. Tony had his students practice each of the processes as well, but they didn't follow a sequence in the same way Kim's students did.

The analysis in each lesson is summarized in Table 5.1.

TABLE 5.1   Comparison of Two Lessons

Similarities	Differences
Both teachers taught an organized body of information.	Kim's students began by describing information in a single cell. Tony's students began by making comparisons and looking for patterns.
The teachers displayed information in a matrix for the students.	
In both classes, the students' analysis was based on the information in the matrix rather than on information they recalled from reading or lecture.	Kim conducted her lesson as a whole-group activity. Tony's students began working in pairs followed by a whole-group discussion.
The teachers guided the students' analyses with directed questions.	Kim guided her students through the model's phases in order. Tony didn't follow a specific sequence.
Both lessons focused simultaneously on deep understanding of content and higher-order and critical thinking.	
Both lessons included all phases of the model.	

Social Structure of the Model

As with the Inductive and Concept-Attainment Models, the Integrative Model requires a classroom environment in which the students feel free to take risks and offer their conclusions, conjectures, and evidence without fear of criticism or embarrassment. Achieving a climate of support when using the Integrative Model is accomplished in much the same way as it is with the Inductive Model:

1. Providing virtually all the information students need to reach the content goals of the lesson. Kim Soo and Tony Horton used the information in their matrixes for this purpose.
2. Beginning the lesson open-endedly. Both teachers had the students respond to open-ended questions—the initial observations in Kim's lesson, and the comparisons the students recorded in Tony's.
3. Providing instructional support as the students did their analysis. In each case, the teachers guided the students, prompting when necessary and guiding the lesson toward the goal.

Providing all of the information that the students need to reach the goals of the lesson assures the students of success, because they can make their conclusions based on information they see rather than information that they may or may not remember. At the same time, open-ended questions and tasks allow students to respond to their own perceptions and thinking, also without fear of failure. In addition, open-ended questions have been documented as effective in eliciting participation from students who are cultural minorities and non-native English speakers who are developing their English proficiency (Langer, Bartolme, Vasques, and Lucas, 1990).

We are hearing a great deal in the 1990s about the apathy of many of our students; this apathy often manifests itself in students' unwillingness to participate in classroom discussions (Raffini, 1993). While it isn't a panacea, the combination of providing all of the information students need to reach a lesson goal—as Kim Soo and Tony Horton did—and the use of open-ended questions can do much to both promote a positive climate and increase students' willingness to participate in learning activities.

The Teacher's Role

As with the Inductive Model, the teacher guides students' analysis of the information displayed for them by starting open-endedly and continuing through a process of explaining, hypothesizing, and generalizing. The biggest task for the teacher is keeping the lesson's goal in mind while maintaining the flow of the discussion.

Similar to the Inductive Model, the success of a lesson depends on the quality of the representations the teachers use (the matrices in Kim's and Tony's lessons) and their ability to guide the students' analyses of the information. As with the Inductive Model, the teacher displays the information and guides the students as they construct their understanding of the topic. As with both the Inductive Model and the Concept-Attainment

Models, using the Integrative Model requires teachers who are skilled in questioning and can think on their feet.

The Integrative Model: Theoretical Perspectives

The Integrative Model is consistent with constructivist views of learning, which we introduced in Chapter 3. In both Kim's and Tony's lesson we saw the teachers guiding the students' thinking as they developed their understanding of the topics.

For example, Kim provided this guidance in her lesson:

T: Why do you suppose that the food seems to be the same?

S: . . . The frog and toad live in about the same places.

T: How did you decide that?

S: . . . It says on the chart that the frog lives on land, in water, and in trees, and it says that the toad lives on land and in water.

S: Also, the frog and toad are very much alike.

T: What do you see that tells you that?

S: From the pictures we see that they look about the same.

S: Also, they both start from eggs and then become tadpoles. See where there are eggs and tadpoles on the chart?

In Tony's lesson we also saw instances of the teacher assisting the process of constructing understanding. For example:

T: Why do you suppose that the Italians, Chinese, and Puerto Ricans tended to come from the lower socioeconomic classes, while the Cubans did not?

S: . . . I think it's because of why they came. . . . The Italians, Chinese, and Puerto Ricans came so they could have a better life, but the Cubans were escaping from Cuba.

S: They wanted a better life too.

S: Well, that's true, but the reasons were different. The others wanted to make a better living, and in Cuba it was politics mostly.

Both lessons were developed around students' evolving understanding of the topic, and at least a portion of the discussion broke away from the typical questioning pattern of teacher-student-teacher-student and toward a pattern where students were responding to each other rather than answering direct questions from the teacher. The approach the two teachers used capitalized on the social aspects of learning and the fact that understanding is constructed by learners based on what they already know. This captures some of the critical elements of instruction based on a constructivist view of learning (Brooks and Brooks, 1993; Clements and Battista, 1990).

Goals for the Integrative Model

The Integrative Model is designed to accomplish two interrelated goals. The first is to help students construct a deep and thorough understanding of organized bodies of information, and the second is to practice higher-order and critical thinking.

Accomplishing these goals within the model has three requirements:

1. Some information must be provided that students can analyze—for example, the data in Kim's and Tony's matrices.
2. Students must play an active role in the process of constructing their understanding.
3. Students must be allowed to practice higher-order and critical thinking, such as finding patterns, explaining, hypothesizing, generalizing, and assessing conclusions with evidence.

Reaching these goals requires that teachers have well-developed questioning skills. In looking back at the lessons, we see that the teachers asked virtually no questions that required the students to merely recall factual, memorized information; instead, they asked for comparisons, explanations, hypotheses, and generalizations.

Unfortunately, this type of teacher questioning is rare. John Goodlad (1984), in his well-known work *A Place Called School*, reported that only about 5 percent of class time, on average, was spent in discussion. He also reported:

> *Only rarely did we find evidence to suggest instruction (in reading and math) likely to go much beyond merely possession of information to a level of understanding its implications and either applying it or exploring its possible applications. Nor did we see activities likely to arouse students' curiosity or to involve them in seeking a solution to some problem not already laid bare by teacher or textbook.*
>
> *And it appears that this preoccupation with the lower intellectual processes pervades social studies and science as well. An analysis of topics studied and materials used gives not an impression of students studying human adaptations and exploration, but of facts to be learned (p. 236).*

Further, Boyer (1983) found that fewer than 1 percent of all teacher questions invite students to respond in a way that goes beyond factual questions or demonstrating a routine procedure. From the case studies, we see that Kim Soo's and Tony Horton's teaching behaviors were in direct contrast with the patterns identified by these studies.

While very different from the prevailing patterns in schools, the questioning and guidance Kim and Tony provided are not difficult to achieve. It takes a little adjustment in thinking—away from teaching as *telling* and toward teaching as *guiding*, and it also requires that students are provided with information to think with, such as Kim's and Tony's matrices.

Before we turn to planning and implementing lessons using the Integrative Model, let's look more closely at the topics Kim and Tony taught.

Organized Bodies of Knowledge: Relationships among Facts, Concepts, and Generalizations

To put our discussion in context, let's look back at the topics the teachers taught in the lessons presented in Chapters 3 and 4. In Chapter 3, the topics were longitude and latitude (concepts), Charles's Law, and the rules for forming singular and plural possessive nouns. In Chapter 4, the topics were fruit and metaphor (also concepts). The key feature that these topics have in common is the fact that they are all specific and well defined. Each has precisely described characteristics—parallel imaginary lines that measure distances north and south of the equator in the case of the concept latitude, for example, or a specific relationship, such as, as temperature increases, volume increases when pressure is constant in the case of Charles's Law. In contrast, the topics that Kim Soo and Tony Horton taught did not have specific characteristics, relationships, or boundaries. Instead they were **organized bodies of knowledge**, *which are topics that combine facts, concepts, generalizations, and the relationships among them* (Eggen and Kauchak, 1994). For instance, in Kim's lesson there were several facts—such as the kinds of foods frogs and toads eat; concepts—such as habitat; and generalizations—such as animals with similar characteristics tend to eat the same kinds of foods, and animals with similar characteristics tend to live in similar habitats.

Tony Horton's lesson was similar. There were facts, such as the major influx of Cubans was in the 1960s, and there was a place in New York called "Little Italy"; concepts— *socioeconomic status* (SES), *assimilation,* and *Confucianism*; and generalizations, such as the Chinese were eager to preserve their customs, second-generation Italians quickly learned English, and Puerto Ricans were primarily Catholic, among others.

In the lessons, however, the goal was to look for patterns in the facts, concepts, and generalizations, describe cause-and-effect relationships (explanations) among them, hypothesize additional possibilities, and form broad generalizations that encompassed all of the information. The goal was not to teach a single concept or generalization (or rule), as was the case when the Inductive Model was used.

Much of the content in schools exists in the form of organized bodies of knowledge. For example, geography teachers compare different cultural regions, such as the climate, culture, economics, geography, and economy of Brazil, Argentina, and Venezuela. English teachers compare the works of Faulkner, Fitzgerald, and Hemingway, or different Shakespearean plays. Life science teachers compare different body systems and the functions they provide. Primary teachers compare food, clothing, and foods for different seasons of the year. Each of these topics combines facts, concepts, and generalizations into organized bodies of knowledge just as Kim and Tony did in their lessons.

Additional examples of topics that are organized bodies of knowledge include the following:

- A comparison of different biomes, and the life forms and attributes of each in life science.
- A comparison of well-balanced and poorly balanced meals and the incorporation of the different food groups into each.
- A comparison of art forms in different historical periods.

- A comparison of the characteristics of country, jazz, folk, and rock music in a music class.
- A comparison of different community helpers in a primary class.
- A comparison of the settlement of the northern and southern colonies in a middle school history class.

Each of these topics combines facts, concepts, and generalizations, and the teacher would want students to identify and understand relationships among them in each case.

Planning Lessons with the Integrative Model

The planning process for using the Integrative Model is similar to that for using either the Inductive Model or the Concept-Attainment Model. The steps are outlined in Figure 5.4.

Identifying Topics

Research indicates that teacher planning most commonly begins with a topic (Morine-Dershimer and Vallance, 1976; Peterson, Marx, and Clark, 1978). This is a practical and intuitively sensible beginning point. The topics in the two lessons at the beginning of the chapter were frogs and toads and immigrants. These topics then became the focal point for the planning process. Topics come from textbooks, curriculum guides, and other sources including teachers themselves. When the topics are organized bodies of knowledge, the Integrative Model can be used effectively.

Specifying Objectives

The fact that planning typically begins with a topic doesn't imply that objectives are not important. In fact, effective teachers have very clear objectives in mind and teach directly to them (Berliner, 1985). This is true regardless of the topic being taught.

Content Objectives

Having identified the topic, we must then decide what we want students to know about it—the learner outcomes. Specifying student outcomes requires a bit more thought when the topics are organized bodies of knowledge, because they are defined less precisely than are concepts, generalizations, or rules. For example, merely knowing that he wanted his students to understand relationships among the "reasons for coming," "characteristics," and "assimilation" of the four immigrant groups wouldn't have been precise enough to help Tony Horton guide his students' analysis. He needed to anticipate some of the generalizations that

FIGURE 5.4   Planning with the Integrative Model

were summarized in his lesson, such as the relationships between immigration and economics, characteristics of immigrants and their reasons for coming, and characteristics of immigrants and their rates of assimilation. Other generalizations may arise as incidental information, which is very desirable, but having some of the outcomes in mind is critical to the flow and goals of the lesson.

Developing Higher-Order and Critical Thinking

The second part of specifying objectives is slightly different from the first. While content objectives focus on *outcomes* such as identifying the relationships between an animal's characteristics and its habitat, or immigration and economics, higher-order and critical thinking focus on the *process* of finding patterns, forming explanations, hypothesizing, generalizing, and documenting each of these conclusions with evidence. Planning for thinking means that teachers consciously intend to have learners observe, compare, search for patterns, generalize, predict, and explain while they are actively "constructing" their understanding of the topic. Teaching for thinking doesn't change the content objective; rather, it changes the way the teacher and students operate as they move toward it.

We saw in Chapter 2 that "Learning is a consequence of thinking" (Perkins, 1992, p. 8), which means that content goals and goals for thinking are inextricably interwoven. Learners will automatically use the processes as they are involved in constructing deep understandings of the topics they are studying. The teacher helps make this use conscious and systematic.

Preparing Data Representations

Having identified a topic and its related goals, the teacher is prepared to move to the third step, which is the capturing of information in a way that will allow students to process it. As we saw in Kim Soo's and Tony Horton's lessons, the data are often organized in the form of a matrix. We will first examine the use of matrices as forms of data retrieval, and later in the chapter we will show how other forms of displaying information can be used efficiently with the Integrative Model.

In each of the examples we've discussed, the topic involved a comparison—toads and frogs in Kim Soo's lesson and the four immigrant groups in Tony Horton's. We also see that two ideas were compared in Kim's lesson, while four were compared in Tony's. The number of ideas being compared depends on the developmental consideration as well as the teacher's goal.

Each of the other topics that we illustrated in the last section involved a comparison as well. However, the comparisons don't necessarily have to involve closely related concepts, such as toads and frogs, or different immigrant groups. For example, a teacher might want to compare arthropods to mammals to demonstrate—among other things—that animals with external skeletons are much smaller than animals with internal skeletons.

Student ideas and interests can be used as well. In Tony's lesson we saw that the choice of immigrant groups was made collaboratively between him and the students, while it appears that Kim alone made the decision to study toads and frogs. It also appears that Tony made the decision to include "reasons for coming," "characteristics," and "assimilation" as the dimensions on which the immigrant groups would be compared, and Kim made the decision to include their appearance, food, characteristics, and habitat as the dimensions to be examined. Although Tony and Kim made these decisions, they could have solicited student input if they had chosen to do so. Each of these decisions is a matter of teacher judgment.

Gathering Data

Once the ideas and dimensions have been identified, the next step is to gather the data that will appear in the matrix. Here the teacher has at least three options:

1. Assign individuals or teams of students to gather the data that will appear in each of the cells of the matrix. A teacher would choose this option if learning to do library research and/or organizing information was part of the teacher's goal.
2. Have the students gather some of the data, and add some additional data yourself. This is the option Kim and Tony chose.
3. Prepare the entire matrix yourself. This approach not only saves valuable classroom time, it also ensures that the matrix contains what the teacher wants. The disadvantage is that students aren't integrally involved in the process.

The gathering and organizing of data that are displayed in the matrix may appear time consuming, and it can be initially if you do all of the preparation yourself. However, if students help gather the initial information, your preparation time is reduced. Further, with the increasing use of technology, you can store the information in a computer and then quickly modify it the next time you teach the topic. So, while initial preparation can be demanding, once the matrix is prepared, any additional preparation is minimal. In the long run, your preparation is actually reduced, because you will have effective materials for involving students that can be used over and over. Let's turn now to a brief discussion of the most effective ways of displaying this data.

Effective Data Displays

While several means of presenting information can be used, some forms work much better than others. Two factors are important. The first is to display the information in as factual a form as possible. This provides optimal opportunities to process information and practice analytical and thinking skills. If this is impossible, next best is a series of relatively narrow generalizations, or a mixture of narrow generalizations and facts. Least desirable is a series of relatively broad generalizations. For example, let's consider Tony's lesson again, and compare the matrix he used to the one displayed in Table 5.2.

Because the information in Table 5.2 is already in the form of fairly broad generalizations, the opportunity for students to analyze information and form these generalizations themselves is lost. To be consistent with the principle "Learning is a consequence of thinking," students must be given the opportunity to think about the topics they're studying. Reducing this opportunity decreases the likelihood that they will develop the deep understanding that is so important.

TABLE 5.2   Matrix Containing Broad Generalizations

Reasons for Coming	Characteristics	Assimilation
Italians		
Economic problems Political problems Overpopulation	Lower socioeconomic class Religious	Relatively rapid assimilation
Chinese		
Overpopulation Economic opportunity Political problems	Religious Lower socioeconomic class	Relatively slow assimilation
Puerto Ricans		
Overpopulation Economic opportunity	Religious Lower socioeconomic class	Relatively rapid assimilation
Cubans		
Political problems	Higher socioeconomic class	Relatively rapid assimilation

Second, an effective data display includes enough information so that students can use data from one part of the matrix as evidence for a conclusion about another part. For example, Kim asked the students to explain why the frog and the toad would eat the same food, and she called on Fernando. He then noted that the animals live in essentially the same places. When he was asked to provide evidence for his response, he was able to point to the section of the chart that showed the habitat for each. If that section of the chart had not existed, Fernando would not have been able to use the matrix to provide the evidence for his conclusion.

We saw the same kind of processing in Tony's lesson. For instance, recall the following dialogue between Tony and his students:

T: Let's look again at some of the comparisons we've made. We wrote that the Chinese assimilated less rapidly than did the other groups. Why do you suppose that was the case?

S: They were more different than the others were.

T: What information do we have on our chart that tells us that they were more different?

S: Their religion for one thing. The Italians, Puerto Ricans, and Cubans were mostly Catholic, which a lot of people in the United States are, but the Chinese were Confus . . . Confushist . . . whatever that religion is.

S: Also, it says in the chart that the Chinese learned English slower than the others.

If the information about the immigrant groups' religions or the rate at which they learned English had not been included in the matrix, the students wouldn't have been able to provide evidence based on data they could observe.

Including enough information in the chart so students are able to verify their responses through observation is very important. We illustrate this process in greater detail as we discuss implementing Integrative Model lessons.

As an additional example, let's look at the matrix in Table 5.3. Here the teacher, as part of a unit on the solar system, assigned teams of students to gather the information that appears in the matrix. So, while gathering and organizing the data required guidance from the teacher, she didn't have to spend any of her planning time in actually gathering the information.

We see that the matrix contains a considerable amount of factual information that could promote analysis on the part of students. You will be asked to examine the information in these matrices again when you complete the exercises at the end of the chapter.

Implementing Lessons Using the Integrative Model

The Integrative Model is implemented in four closely related phases. They are:

- Phase 1: describe, compare, and search for patterns
- Phase 2: explain similarities and differences
- Phase 3: hypothesize outcomes for different conditions
- Phase 4: generalize to form broad relationships

There is an important aspect of the phases that should be emphasized. Though they are listed in order, and teachers will normally start with Phase 1, the phases are not hierarchical and they don't imply a rigid sequence. A teacher, for example, may move directly from a comparison in Phase 1 to an hypothesis in Phase 3, and then return to another comparison. Students' abilities to hypothesize in Phase 3 don't require that they have first formed explanations in Phase 2 that relate to the hypotheses. In many cases the phases will be conducted in sequence, and a sequence is more logical, but this is not a rigid requirement of the model. Each of the phases represents a form of higher-order thinking, so teachers want to give students a chance to practice these forms regardless of the sequence.

We saw illustrations of this flexibility in Kim's and Tony's lessons. Kim conducted her lesson so that the students went through the phases pretty much in order, while Tony Horton varied the sequence in the first three phases.

We also saw that Kim conducted her lesson as a large group, while Tony had the students complete the first phase in pairs. We will discuss additional modifications later in the chapter. For now let's turn to an analysis of each phase.

Phase 1: Describe, Compare, and Search for Patterns

Phase 1 marks the point where students begin their analysis of the information in the matrix. Looking again at Kim's and Tony's lessons, we see that Phase 1 can begin in one of two ways:

1. The teacher simply directs students' attention to a particular cell in the matrix and asks them to observe and describe the information. This is what Kim did in her lesson.
2. The teacher asks students to look for similarities and differences in two or more of the cells in a column of the matrix. This was Tony's approach.

TABLE 5.3 Matrix with Information about the Solar System

Name	Origin of Name	Diameter in miles	Distance from Sun in miles	Length of Year (orbit)	Length of Day (rotation)	Gravity Compared w/Earth's
Sun	Sol, Roman god of the Sun	865,000				
Mercury	Mercury, messenger of the Roman gods	3,030	35,900,000	88 Earth days	59 Earth days counterclockwise	0.38
Venus	Venus, Roman goddess of love and beauty	7,500	67,200,000	225 Earth days	243 Earth days counterclockwise	0.88
Earth	Terra Mater, Roman earth mother	7,900	93,000,000	365¼ days	24 hours counterclockwise	1
Mars	Mars, Roman god of war	4,200	141,500,000	687 Earth days	24½ hours counterclockwise	0.38
Jupiter	Jupiter, Roman king of all gods	88,700	483,400,000	12 Earth years	10 hours counterclockwise	2.34
Saturn	Saturn, Roman god of agriculture	75,000	914,000,000	30 Earth years	11 hours counterclockwise	0.92
Uranus	Uranus, Roman god, father of Saturn grandfather of Jupiter	31,566	1,782,400,000	84 Earth years	24 hours counterclockwise	0.79
Neptune	Neptune, Roman god of the sea	30,200	2,792,900,000	165 Earth years	17 hours counterclockwise	1.12
Pluto	Pluto, Greek god of the lower world	1,423	3,665,000,000	248 Earth years	6½ days counterclockwise	0.43

Continued

TABLE 5.3   *Continued*

Name	Moons	Average Surface Temperature (F)	Other Interesting Characteristics
Sun	0	10,000°	The sun is a star, Earth's star; a gigantic ball of glowing gases; more than 1 million Earths could fit inside the sun; sun's gravity keeps the 9 planets in orbit; sun gives planets light and heat
Mercury	0	300° below zero to 800° above zero	No atmosphere; no water; many craters
Venus	0	900° average	Atmosphere mostly carbon dioxide and poisonous sulfuric acid; no water; brightest planet; hottest planet; desert; huge lightning flashes; thick cloud cover; enormous winds
Earth	1	57° average	Atmosphere contains about 78% nitrogen, 21% oxygen, 1% other gases; water covers about 70% of surface; has plant life, animal life, and people
Mars	2	67° below zero average	Atmosphere—thin carbon dioxide; no water; white ice caps at poles; salmon sky; frequent dust storms; red, rocky surface (The Red Planet); appears to have no life; home of Earthlings' first space colony(?)
Jupiter	16 or more	162° below zero average	Atmosphere has hydrogen, helium, ammonia; no water; bands of color; Great Red Spot (hurricanes); faint horizontal ring; huge lightning bolts
Saturn	21 or more	208° below zero average	Atmosphere has hydrogen and helium; no water; has at least four rings tilted from horizontal position; mostly big ball of gas; clouds; some bands of color in shades of yellow. Mostly gas. Small solid core
Uranus	15 or more	355° below zero average	Atmosphere of hydrogen and helium; no water; greenish color; has at least nine verticle rings. Would float on water
Neptune	2 or more	266° below zero average	Atmosphere of hydrogen and helium; no water; bands of color in shades of blue
Pluto	1	460° below zero average	No oxygen; no water; extremely cold and dark; orbiting closer to the sun than Neptune from 1979–1999

*Matrix adapted by permission of Dr. June Main

The way you begin Phase 1 is a matter of preference and judgment. Kim's students were younger than Tony's and she chose to focus on a single cell to provide a task that better matched her students' developmental capabilities.

Using the matrix containing information about the solar system, the teacher could begin Phase 1 by having the students look for the trends in each of the columns.

This type of beginning has the same advantages that exist in the beginning of a lesson using the Inductive Model. Because Phase 1 is open-ended it breaks the ice for the students, assures success, promotes involvement, and allows the teacher to ask a large number of questions, a factor positively correlated with student achievement (Gall, 1984).

The point on the matrix where students begin the analysis is a matter of teacher discretion. Most commonly, the analysis begins with the top left cell, but this is probably more because we are in the habit of reading beginning with the upper left. There is no rule that says you must begin there, and if you have a reason to begin at another point, it would be perfectly appropriate.

The length of time you spend on a single cell (or column) is also a matter of judgment. You most likely wouldn't ask for a single observation or comparison and move on, but you don't want to overdwell on a single portion of the chart to the point where the momentum of the lesson is reduced.

After completing the description in the first cell or making comparisons in the first column, the teacher moves on to a second, a third, and so on until all of the information in the matrix has been examined.

In looking again at Kim's and Tony's lessons, we see that the processing is smooth, promoting high levels of success and interaction. Both teachers followed the rule of thumb, "Make it easy on yourself." They first asked the students to make observations (in Kim's case) or comparisons (in Tony's). Teachers sometimes feel that they should have to work harder at the initial question, but this isn't the case. Simple, straightforward questions or statements are very effective. To illustrate, let's look again at some of the dialogue from Kim's lesson:

Kim: Let's start with food since we're all familiar with it. Look carefully at the part that tells what toads eat. What do you notice here? . . . Serena?

Serena: Well, they eat earthworms.

Kim: And what else? . . . Dominique?

Dominique: Spiders.

David: Also grasshoppers.

Kim: Yes, very good, everyone. . . Now look at the frogs. Let's do the same with them. What can you tell me about what they eat? Judy?

Judy: They eat insects.

Bill: Also earthworms.

We see from the dialogue that Kim began the lesson in a comfortable, open-ended way with the students, which allowed them to get started successfully and build lesson momentum.

In contrast, Tony started his lesson by having the students work in groups, beginning by directing them, "Now, here's your assignment. I want you to look for patterns among the columns of the chart." He then went on to give them some guidance by modeling, "Let's look at a sample. Everyone take a look at the first column for a minute and see if you find some things that the four groups have in common, or something that two or three of the groups have in common." Common to both lessons was that they started out in a straightforward yet open-ended way.

Becoming more open-ended requires some adjustment on the part of many teachers, because it isn't a natural inclination and few have been taught this method. However, once the adjustment has been made, teachers find it to be a viable alternative to the more traditional one-question, specific-answer dialogue that is typical of most classrooms.

Recording Information

As students conduct their analysis, the teacher typically writes information on the board, overhead, or chart paper. This provides a public record of the process and reference points for students. Tony recorded both the comparisons the students made in groups and the summarizing generalizations, while Kim recorded only the summary statements. However, both teachers made a record of the information. Without some sort of public record, students can easily lose some of the most important points in the analysis, and the understanding that results is less complete. The process of recording information typically continues in Phases 2, 3, and 4.

Phase 2: Explain Similarities and Differences

If a model has a phase more exciting than any of the others, it is Phase 2 in the Integrative Model. This is the point where the students are immersed in the processes of higher-order and critical thinking, and once they warm to the task, their analyses can become quite sophisticated. While the questioning process in Phase 2 is more demanding than it was in the first phase, with practice teachers can become skilled to the point that their questioning is almost automatic.

As Kim's students were processing information in Phase 1, we saw that making comparisons was a natural outgrowth of the observations they made. Moving from making comparisons to forming explanations has a similar—although not quite as automatic—relationship. To illustrate this process, let's refer again to Kim's lesson:

Kim: Look at both the frog and the toad. How would you compare what they eat? Is there any kind of pattern there?

Tim: They both eat insects.

Leroy: They both eat earthworms too.

Kristy: . . . The food for each seems to be almost the same.

Kim: Why do you suppose that the food seems to be the same?

Asking students at this point to explain why a certain similarity (or difference) exists marks the shift from Phase 1 to Phase 2. The shift is virtually automatic, and the questioning sequence remains smooth. However, the thinking on the part of the students is significantly advanced. In Phase 1, students are merely asked to make an observation or identify a similarity or difference, while in Phase 2 they are asked to explain why it exists—a higher level of reasoning.

The transition to Phase 2 in Tony Horton's lesson was a bit more formal, primarily because he had his students work in pairs during Phase 1. Let's look again at a portion of the dialogue:

Tony: Good work. . . . Now, let's look a little more closely at the information. Why do you suppose that the Italians, Chinese, and Puerto Ricans tended to come from the lower socioeconomic classes, while the Cubans did not? . . . Anyone?

Antonio: . . . I think it's because of why they came. . . . The Italians, Chinese, and Puerto Ricans came so they could have a better life, but the Cubans were escaping from Fidel Castro's revolution.

Kevin: They wanted a better life too.

Antonio: Well, that's true, but the reasons were different. The others wanted to make a better living, and in Cuba it was politics mostly.

This type of analysis is what we're looking for in students. Students had identified a difference between the Cubans and the other three immigrant groups, and Tony capitalized on this observation, asking them to explain that difference. Antonio offered an explanation, which resulted in some additional student-student interaction. This process of developing understanding is consistent with constructivist views of effective instruction. As with Phase 1, the process continues until the opportunities for forming explanations have been exhausted.

We have presented the previous illustrations for the sake of clarity and brevity. Obviously, a large variety of possibilities exists in each case. With practice, these possibilities will be easily recognized. However, not every comparison is automatically explainable. Let's examine this issue now.

Explainable Comparisons

While Phases 1 and 2 are closely related and the move from one to the other should be smooth and comfortable, teacher judgment is required to effectively manage the transition. For example, consider again the topic dealing with frogs and toads. Suppose the teacher asks, "Look at the frog and toad in the left column. How would you compare them?" (a question in Phase 1).

A student might then respond, "The toad has rough skin with bumps on it, while the frog's skin is smooth." This type of comparison is essentially "unexplainable." The difference is characteristic of their physiology, and no data exist on the chart, nor in all probability in students' backgrounds, that could be used to help form the explanation. Asking students to explain why the toad's skin is bumpy and the frog's smooth is sort of like asking, "Why does gravity make objects fall to the earth?" It is one of the characteristics of gravity that we merely describe; it doesn't have an explanation.

As a contrasting example, Tony's students noted in their comparisons that the Chinese seemed to assimilate less rapidly than did the other immigrant groups. This is an eminently explainable comparison. The students explained the slower assimilation for the Chinese by suggesting that difference in culture was a cause, and they could find information in the matrix to support the explanation.

The teacher's task in guiding students' analysis is to recognize comparisons that can be appropriately explained and ask students to provide the explanation, while at the same time leaving unexplainable ones as simple comparisons. As with many aspects of the Integrative Model, recognizing explainable comparisons is not difficult and only requires a little getting used to. The exercises at the end of the chapter offer some practice with this process.

Promoting Critical Thinking: Documenting Assertions

In Chapter 2 we said that providing evidence is an important element of critical thinking. Phase 2 of the Integrative Model provides an excellent opportunity for students to practice this ability. To illustrate, let's look again at some dialogue from Kim's lesson:

Kim: Why do you suppose that the food seems to be the same? Fernando? (A question in phase 2)

Fernando: . . . The frog and toad live in about the same places.

Kim: How did you decide that?

Fernando: . . . It says on the chart that the frog lives on land, in water, and in trees, and it says that the toad lives on land and in the water.

Kim: Yes, excellent, Fernando. . . . Remember how we have talked about justifying our thinking in some of our work in math? This is exactly the same thing. Fernando provided evidence for his conclusion that their environments are about the same by pointing out where they live on the chart. This is the kind of thinking we're after.

Kim's question, "How did you decide that?" asked Fernando for evidence when he concluded that the animals' environments were about the same. Teachers can ask students for evidence when they ask questions such as, "How do you know?" "Why do you say that?" "What evidence do we have for that conclusion?" or a similar question. The exact wording of the question isn't important as long as it asks students to provide evidence for their conclusions.

While asking students for evidence is rare in classroom dialogue (Boyer, 1983), it isn't difficult once teachers get used to it, and students quickly "warm to the task" and begin to provide evidence without being prompted by their teachers. To illustrate, let's review part of Tony's lesson:

Tony: Let's look again at some of the comparisons we've made. We wrote that the Chinese assimilated less rapidly than did the other groups. Why do you suppose that was the case?"

Christine: They were more different culturally than the others were.

Tony: What information do we have on our chart that tells us they were more different culturally?

Christine: Their religion for one thing. The Italians, Puerto Ricans, and Cubans were mostly Catholic, which a lot of people in the United States are, but the Chinese were Confus . . . Confushist . . . whatever that religion is.

Estella: Also, it says in the chart that the Chinese learned English slower than the others.

Here we see that Estella—without prompting from Tony—referred to the matrix for some additional information offered as evidence in support of the cultural-differences contention.

Once students get used to the process of providing evidence, teachers can then capitalize on these opportunities to promote sophisticated critical-thinking discussions, such as quality of evidence. For instance, Tony could ask the class to examine Estella's comment with questions such as, "Is learning English less quickly really evidence for cultural differences?" "Why is it, or why is it not 'good' evidence?" "What would be better evidence of cultural differences?"

When questions such as these are discussed and analyzed, students obtain valuable experience in the processes of critical thinking.

We should also note that while we have presented the discussion of providing evidence in the context of Phase 2, it is every bit as appropriate in Phase 1, if the opportunity arises. Opportunities tend to appear more readily in Phase 2, and for this reason we have presented it here.

Phase 3: Hypothesize Outcomes for Different Conditions

Phase 3 marks an additional step in the development of students' ability to process information. As with the transition from Phase 1 to Phase 2, Phase 3 often evolves directly from Phase 2. Let's look again at Tony's lesson:

Estella: . . . it says in the chart that the Chinese learned English slower than the others. (Evidence for a response in Phase 1)

Tony: And why might that have been? (A question marking the transition to Phase 2)

Estella: Their language is different. There are letters for each of the languages in the chart, and the Italians, Puerto Ricans, and Cubans use the same letters as English, but the Chinese letters are really different. (An explanation—a response in Phase 2)

Tony: Suppose they weren't different, meaning they used the same letters as we do. How do you suppose that would have affected how fast they assimilated?

Tony's last question called for a hypothesis on the part of the students. His question asked the students to consider the outcome if conditions were changed—a hypothetical situation in which Chinese used the same letters as do the Italians, Puerto Ricans, and Cubans.

Though the dialogue we just read illustrates how Phase 3 can naturally evolve from Phase 2, this isn't a requirement. To illustrate, let's look again at Kim's lesson:

Kim: Look again at the toad and frog in the first column of the chart. In what ways are they different? (A question in Phase 1)

Fred: It says the toad is clumsy, but it doesn't say anything about the frog. (A response in Phase 1)

Kim: Suppose the toad wasn't clumsy. . . . How might that affect the food toads eat or where they live? . . . Anyone?"

Here Kim asked a question calling for an hypothesis (Phase 3) that followed directly from a comparison (Phase 1). The fact that Kim didn't ask the students to explain why the toad is clumsy, which would have been a question in Phase 2, is a matter of teacher judgment. It is part of the decision-making process that makes teaching—at least in part—an art. She might have felt that the toad's clumsiness was an unexplainable comparison, or she might have had another reason for choosing not to ask for an explanation.

As with Phases 1 and 2, the process of hypothesizing continues until opportunities for analysis have been exhausted.

Phase 4: Generalize to Form Broad Relationships

The lesson is summarized and comes to closure when students derive one or more generalizations that serve to summarize the content. To illustrate this process, let's look again at Kim's lesson:

Kim: Now, let's summarize what we've found here, and let's think about animals in general. . . . I want you to try and extend beyond the toad and frog, and I'll help you if you need it. . . . For instance, what can we say about the characteristics of animals that look a lot alike?

Adella: . . . They have mostly the same characteristics.

Kim: So, how should we write that? Help me out. . . . I'll get us started. (She then wrote, "Animals that look alike . . ." on the chalkboard.)

Carol: . . . Will have similar characteristics.

Kim: Okay. . . . What else? (after writing, "Animals that look alike have similar characteristics," on the chalkboard.)

Tony: They also eat the same kind of food.

Kim: Good. So, . . . tell me what to write. . . . Animals that look alike . . .

Nancy: And have the same characteristics.

Tonya: And have the same characteristics eat the same kind of food.

Kim then wrote the statement on the board, asked the students for additional summarizing statements, which resulted in the following list:

Animals that look alike have similar characteristics.

Animals that look alike and have similar characteristics eat the same kind of food.

Animals that are similar live in similar habitats.

Kim then asked the students for some additional examples such as deer and elk, different birds, and predators, such as lions and leopards, plus some exceptions to the patterns, and she then closed the lesson.

We can see from this dialogue that students won't automatically be good at making summarizing statements, and the teacher may initially have to do a considerable amount of prompting, as Kim did in her lesson. With practice, however, students' ability to summarize quickly develops.

In comparison, Tony Horton's students were older than Kim's and they had more experience with summarizing information, so Tony didn't have to prompt and guide his students as much as Kim did in summarizing the lesson.

Modifications of the Integrative Model

Developmental Considerations

You have now seen how the phases of the Integrative Model are implemented and how they can be applied in a learning activity. We want to turn now to some additional developmental considerations in using the model.

Displaying Information

The first relates to the way information is presented in the matrix. Tony's matrix—in a lesson designed for 8th graders—had the information presented in words. Kim, in comparison, used both words and pictures in her lesson designed for 4th graders. A primary teacher, or a teacher whose students lack language skills, might choose to present the information exclusively in pictures. As an example, consider the information in Figure 5.5.

A matrix such as this can be effectively used as a basis for guiding young children's analysis of data. As an illustration of its use, let's look at some abbreviated dialogue taken from a lesson focusing on this matrix:

T: How are the foods we eat in the summer different from the foods we eat in the winter? (Phase 1)

S: Foods with ice in summer.

S: Hot drinks in winter.

T: Why do you think we have hot drinks in the winter? (Phase 2)

S: It's cold outside.

Summer

Special Things To Do

Food

Clothing

FIGURE 5.5   Matrix Containing Information about Winter and Summer

T: How do we know it's cold outside?

S: ". . ."

T: Do you see anything on the chart that tells us that it's cold outside in the winter?

S: They're wearing coats (pointing to the chart).

T: What else?

S: No leaves on the trees.

T: Suppose we lived in the south, where it's warm all year 'round. How might the foods we eat in winter be different from what we see on the chart? (A question in Phase 3)

S: Our drinks might not be as hot.

T: What have we learned here about our foods? (A question asking for a summary)

S: We eat different foods.

T: How are they different?

S: We eat warm foods when it's cold outside.

T: And why do we do that?

S: Hot foods help keep us warm.

Special things to do and clothing were analyzed and summarized in the same way. As students developed their skills with the process, the teacher was able to move away from the traditional teacher-student-teacher-student form of interaction and toward a more teacher-student-student-student discussion, some of which we saw in Kim's and Tony's lessons.

In some cases teachers may choose to develop a matrix together with actual objects or people. For example, a teacher wanting to develop a lesson on community helpers could ask an actual fire fighter and a member of the police to come into the class as guests. After these guests visit the classroom, the teacher and students could list information they had learned, which in turn could be used as the basis for the analysis.

Any medium appropriate for the developmental level of the students can be effectively used for Integrative lessons. For example, consider again the example with the different types of popular music. The teacher in this lesson would not focus on pictures or on words, but would instead play excerpts and display music from each of the musical forms. Just as the type of example must be appropriate when teaching a specific concept or generalization, the medium for presenting the data must be congruent with your goals when doing a lesson with the Integrative Model.

Children's Language Abilities
The second developmental factor relates to students' ability to process the information and articulate their conclusions. With young children, Phase 1 may initially be emphasized more strongly than the other phases, since it focuses on observation and comparison. However, as

they acquire experience, even young children quickly learn to form explanations and even respond to hypothetical questions. Much of the value in using the model is the opportunity it provides for children to practice their developing language and thinking abilities.

Increasing Efficiency: Reducing Preparation Time

Anyone familiar with classrooms knows that teachers' jobs are enormously complex and demanding. Many teachers spend a considerable amount of after-school time scoring papers, planning, and talking to parents. Anything that can be done to help them reduce the time they spend planning new lessons—providing they can still meet their goals—is beneficial. In this section we want to examine and illustrate some options that will allow teachers to reduce their planning time and yet still help students acquire deep understanding of content and higher-order- and critical-thinking abilities.

Using Existing Materials

To this point in our discussion we have focused on data displayed in matrices, and these data served as the basis for analysis. Earlier in the chapter, we briefly discussed the efforts you must make at first to prepare the data displays and suggested that once the matrix is initially prepared, any additional preparation is minimal.

The planning process can often be further reduced, however. Tables, charts, graphs, and maps in textbooks and other resources are already-existing sources of information that provide opportunities for analysis. All the teacher has to do is capitalize on these representations and use them to simultaneously promote higher-order thinking and deep understanding of the topics that the students are learning.

To do this you must be able to recognize existing materials that can be used to help you reach your goals. Virtually any chart, graph, or map that contains raw data can be used for analysis with the Integrative Model. Let's look at some examples. Table 5.4 contains information in a chart taken from a typical chemistry book.

TABLE 5.4   Example of Chart Found in Text

IONIC RADII*

	IA	IIA	IIIA	VIA	VIIA
	$Li+$	Be^2+		O^2-	$F-$
	0.60	0.31		1.40	1.36
	$NA+$	Mg^2+	Al^3+	S^2-	$Cl-$
	0.95	0.65	0.50	1.84	1.81
	$K+$	Ca^2+	Ga^3+	Se^2-	$Br-$
	1.33	0.99	0.62	1.98	1.95
	$Rb+$	Sr^2+	In^3+	Te^2-	$I-$
	1.48	1.13	0.81	2.21	2.16
	$Cs+$	Ba^2+	Tl^3+		
	1.69	1.35	0.95		

*Radii given in angstrom units.

A chart such as this would be found in the text, and the teacher would need do nothing more than direct students to the page on which it is found. At that point, the analysis process could proceed in the following way:

Phase 1

T: What kind of pattern do you see in the Group IA ions?

S: The ionic radii get bigger as we move down the column.

T: How about the other groups?

S: They all get bigger as they move down the columns.

T: How would you compare the radii in each column to each other?

S: They get smaller for the positive ions and then get bigger for the negative ions.

T: What do you mean?

S: Magnesium (Mg) is smaller than sodium (Na), and aluminum is smaller yet, but sulfur and chlorine are bigger.

Phase 2

T: Why do you suppose magnesium is smaller than sodium?

S: Magnesium loses two electrons, so its ionic radius will decrease more than sodium's, which loses only one electron.

T: Then why isn't the ionic radius for chlorine bigger than the radius for sulfur?

S: Chlorine only adds one electron, so its ionic radius won't increase as much as sulfur's will.

Phase 3

T: Suppose that sulfur was somehow involved in a reaction in which it actually lost electrons rather than gained them. How would its ionic radius be affected?

S: Its ionic radius would maybe be smaller than aluminum's, rather than larger.

T: Can we be sure?

S: No; it may not follow that pattern. We would need more information to be sure.

Phase 4

T: What kinds of generalizations can we make about ionic radii?

S: As elements lose electrons their ionic radii get smaller, and the more electrons they lose the smaller they get.

S: Ionic radii with positive charges tend to be smaller than those with negative charges in comparable rows.

We have abbreviated this lesson for the sake of clarity; it wouldn't go as smoothly as it appears in the illustration, and teachers would probably have to prompt students to recognize some of the patterns. However, since most of the information needed to make the conclusions is available in the chart, students only need some guidance to get them started.

We also see from the dialogue that the chart—which already exists in the text—can be used for a great deal of higher-order thinking. In fact, a number of patterns, explanations, hypotheses, and generalizations could be added to those in the illustration. In this case, using the Integrative Model required no additional preparation at all. The teacher only needs to recognize opportunities to capitalize on already-existing data.

As an additional example, consider the maps Figures 5.6a and 5.6b. Let's look again at a sample lesson based on the maps:

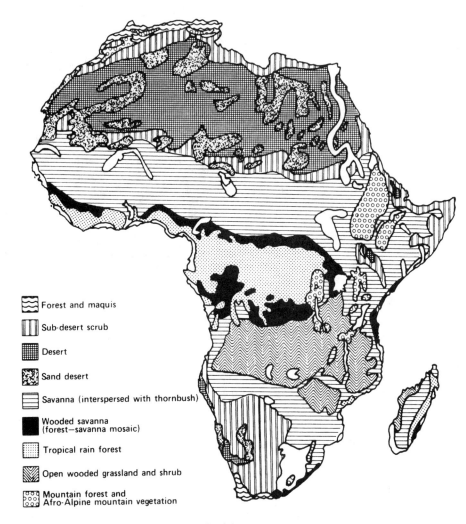

FIGURE 5.6a   Vegetation Zones of Africa

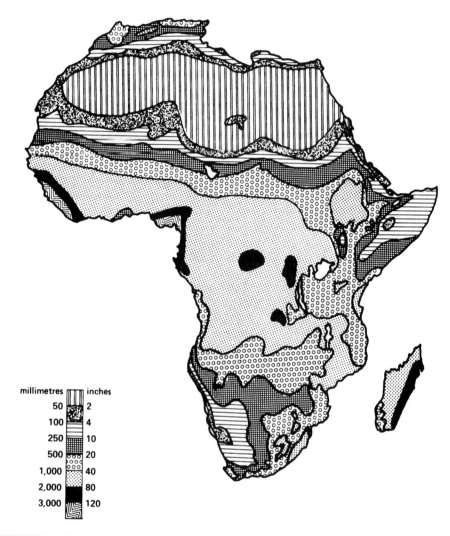

FIGURE 5.6b   Average Annual Precipitation for Africa

Phase 1:

T: Look at the northern parts of the two maps. How do they compare?

S: The northern part of the first one is mostly desert.

T: And the second one?

S: Very little rain, two inches a year.

T: How about other parts of the map?

S: There is tropical rainforest around the area near the equator, and there is a lot of rain in that area.

Phase 2:

T: Why is much of the northern part of the continent desert?

S: It gets very little rain.

T: Why do you think the rainfall is so sparse?

S: Maybe it has to do with the direction of the wind. The prevailing winds come from huge land areas, so they don't have much rain in them.

T: What else might impact the amount of rain a region gets? What do you see on the map?

S: Maybe the direction of the ocean currents has something to do with it.

Phase 3:

T: Suppose the winds over northern Africa came primarily from the west. How would the climate of that part of the continent be affected?

S: Maybe it wouldn't be a desert.

T: Can you look at any part of the map for some evidence that supports that idea?

S: We see that the winds are from the west over the central portion of the continent.

Phase 4:

T: What kinds of summary statements can we make based on the map?

S: The ocean currents and wind direction have an important impact on the amount of rain a region gets.

This dialogue only gives us a sample of the possibilities. Much more analysis of the maps could have occurred and the process could have been significantly expanded by adding a map showing physiographic regions on the continent. The students could then consider altitude, latitude, wind direction, and ocean currents as factors impacting climate. Significantly, this could all be done with little teacher preparation; all the teacher needs is to be clear about her goals and seize upon opportunities as they arise. As teachers become accustomed to the process, they will see more and more opportunities for using the charts, maps, and other instructional aids in their textbooks as a basis for promoting a great deal of analysis by the students.

Developing Matrices During Class Discussions

Teachers can also use information gathered in class discussions to capture data essentially "on the spot," which can then be used to further analyze the topic being studied. Let's look at an English class that is discussing *Romeo and Juliet:*

T: Let's think about some of the things we've found from the play. Let's just list anything you can think of based on your reading.

S: The Montagues and Capulets were feuding.

S: Escalus, the Prince, threatened the Montagues and Capulets with death if they didn't stop feuding.

S: Some of the people seemed to be sort of hung up on sex.

T: Why do you say that? Can you give us an example?

S: Sampson and Gregory were always fantasizing about women.

S: And the nurse and Mercutio seemed to be focused on sex.

T: Okay, what else?

S: Tybalt killed Mercutio, and then Romeo killed Tybalt.

S: Romeo and Juliet killed themselves.

T: Let's focus on the characters a little more. What kind of a young man was Romeo?

S: Well, he was actually a kid.

S: He was sort of innocent and naive.

As the students made their comments, the teacher listed them on large pieces of chart paper, which she rolled up and stored after the discussion. She also prompted them for additional information, such as the question, "What kind of a young man was Romeo?" and she added some information of her own about the themes of the play. She then stored the chart paper, telling the students that they would return to the information after they had read some additional plays. She then repeated the process with *Hamlet* and *Julius Caesar.*

After the students had read and reported on all three plays, the teacher displayed all of the information, and began a more extensive analysis of the plays by comparing them to each other. The information on the chart paper appeared as shown in Table 5.5.

In this case the teacher used the information students gathered from their reading as the matrix, and her preparation time was minimal.

This type of analysis does not have to be the focus of an entire lesson. For example, the illustration with the chemistry chart could be embedded within an overall topic of atomic structure, and the entire sequence may take only a few minutes. The same could be the case with maps.

As we can see, charts, maps, and even graphs can be very conducive to use with Integrative-Model activities, and the Integrative Model has wide applicability to many grade levels and content areas. We hope that this discussion has increased your awareness of the possibilities.

Making the Integrative Model More Student Centered

To this point the descriptions of the Integrative Model have focused on teacher-led activities. The teacher has directed the discussions, and the processing has been strongly teacher directed.

TABLE 5.5   Matrix with Information about Shakespearean Tragedies

	Plot	Key Characters	Themes
R O M E O & J U L I E T	Montagues and Capulets feud Escalus, the Prince, threatens Montagues and Capulets with death Sampson and Gregory fantasize about women The nurse and Mercutio focus on sex Romeo and Juliet fall in love Tybalt kills Mercutio Romeo kills Tybalt Juliet takes a potion Romeo kills himself Juliet kills herself Montagues and Capulets end feud	Romeo: romantic love struck guileless young unthinking innocent Juliet: romantic love struck guileless young innocent	Symbolism of "star-crossed lovers" Love amidst hate Innocence amid mature bawdry Conflicted loyalty to self and family
H A M L E T	King Hamlet dies Claudius marries Gertrude Hamlet regrets and resents Claudius's and Gertrude's marriage Hamlet seeks revenge on Claudius Hamlet mistreats Ophelia Laertes wounds Hamlet in a duel Hamlet wounds Laertes in a duel Hamlet kills Claudius Gertrude dies of poison meant for Hamlet Laertes dies Hamlet dies	Hamlet: sentimental dreamer witty sensitive loyal weak intelligent romantic indecisive ambitious Claudius: strong hypocritical skillfully political deceitful adroit	Ingenuousness and deceit Moral ambiguity The search for natural justice Loyalty and revenge Private and public conflict Internal conflict Courage and cowardliness Purging of evil Restoration of morality
J U L I U S C A E S A R	Caesar defeats Pompey Caesar becomes dictator Caesar pardons Brutus Caesar pardons Cassius Romans fear Caesar's growing power and ambition Conspiracy against Caesar develops Cassius influences Brutus Brutus feels he must stop Caesar Brutus kills Caesar Antony incites citizens Rome is in chaos The armies of Brutus and Cassius engage the armies of Antony and Octavius Cassius is stabbed by his servant and dies Brutus falls on sword and dies	Caesar: great soldier great politician brilliant scholar arrogant ambitious Brutus: quiet idealistic Caesar's friend feared Caesar's ambition Cassius: thin quick-tempered practical grudge against Caesar	Power Ambition Jealousy Revenge Idealism

As students gain experience, however, teachers can make the processing more student directed. For instance, instead of first asking students to look for patterns in the information (Phase 1) followed by questions that call for explanations (Phase 2), the teacher could begin the process by having the students work in teams and ask each team to generate a series of questions they would like answered based on the information in the chart. Through this process, students are learning to ask their own questions in Phase 2 rather than needing the teacher ask them.

As the students learn to ask questions, they get valuable practice in the process of inquiry. One of the weaknesses in activities that are strongly teacher directed is that students don't learn to generate their own questions, and learning to generate questions is an important element of the inquiry process.

This is developmentally quite advanced; initially students won't know how to respond. However, as they acquire experience—seeing the teacher model questions in Phase 2—and as they practice, students will learn to look for differences in parts of the matrix, chart, map, or graph, and ask why those differences exist. This marks a quantum leap forward in students' processing abilities and self-directed learning abilities.

Assessing Integrative-Model Activities

Of the models discussed so far, the content and thinking outcomes for the Integrative Model are the most complex. As a result, a variety of options exists in preparing items to measure student growth. Keep in mind as you read this section that the information is intended to be illustrative rather than exhaustive. Our goal in presenting these examples is to stimulate your own thinking about assessment.

Measuring Content Outcomes

In the planning section of the chapter we found that the Integrative Model, rather than teaching a single, precise concept or generalization, is designed to teach organized bodies of knowledge, which are combinations of facts, concepts, and generalizations and the relationships among them. During the assessment phase of the model, teachers attempt to measure students' understanding of those relationships.

To illustrate this process, let's look at some sample paper-and-pencil items. For example, consider how Kim Soo might measure her students' understanding of the generalizations they derived in her lesson. Look at the following item:

Think about the conclusion made about the frog and the toad, and their habits. Based on that conclusion, which of the following pairs of animals would likely have the most similar habits?

a. a deer and a bear
b. a deer and an elk
c. a deer and a rabbit
d. a rabbit and a bear

This item is designed to measure students' ability to apply the generalization, "Animals with similar characteristics have similar habits," to animals other than toads and frogs.

The item has the potential weakness, however, of measuring the students' knowledge of the animals, rather than their understanding of the generalization. For example, if students do not know what an elk is or how it appears, the item would be invalid. To eliminate this possibility, the teacher might prepare an item such as the following:

> Look at each of the following descriptions of animals. Then based on the descriptions, decide which two will have the most similar habits.
>
> The lemu is a swift-running, four-legged animal. It stands about four feet high and weighs over 200 pounds. It has long legs, hooves, and big horns on his head. The lemu has fairly sharp teeth in the front of its mouth and large flat ones in the back.
>
> The habax is a muscular, four-legged animal. It has a bulky, strong body covered with thick fur. Its teeth are sharp and two of them are a bit longer than the others. The habax is about three feet high and weighs about 280 pounds.
>
> The crandle is a short animal with a long tail. It has four short legs that are attached to the sides of its body. The crandle can move swiftly for a short distance. It can see in almost all directions with its eyes on the top of its head. The crandle's teeth are sharp and stick out a little bit even when its mouth is closed.
>
> The viben is a beautiful animal. It stands tall and gracefully on its four slim legs. The small hooves allow the viben to move swiftly if necessary. It is about five feet tall at the shoulder and weighs over 300 pounds. It is covered with short, light brown hair all over its body.

In this item, the characteristics of the animals are described and students would make their interpretation on the basis of these descriptions. The need for prior knowledge of any particular animal would be minimized. Notice, also, that any reference to food or habitat is avoided in the description. If they were included, the validity of the measurement would be reduced in that the item is designed to determine students' understanding of the relationship between characteristics and habits, such as where they live and what they eat.

An additional value in using the second item would be the potential it has for further discussion. Based on the descriptions, students could infer the habitat of each animal, the type of food they would eat, and other habits such as how they would protect themselves. In this way, a content measure has the potential for further developing thinking skills.

Measuring Higher-Order and Critical Thinking

Student thinking can be measured at several levels. In the first, students can be referred to the chart used in the lesson and be asked to form conclusions not developed in class. For instance, referring again to Kim's lesson, consider the following item:

> Look again at the chart involving frogs and toads. Based on the chart, which of the following would be the best conclusion?
>
> a. You would be more likely to be harmed by a frog than by a toad because a frog is poisonous and a toad is not.

b. A frog would be more likely to survive in a strange place because its habitat is more varied than that of a toad.

c. A toad would win a race with a frog because it can run faster.

d. Toads get bigger than frogs because the food they eat is different.

In this item, each of the choices but (b) is directly contradicted by information in the chart. An item such as this would be a good beginning point in helping students develop their abilities to critically assess information. However, the process can be advanced considerably by changing the level of sophistication. For example, consider the following item:

Look again at the information in the chart. Based on this information, which is the best conclusion?

a. A frog is more adaptable than is a toad.

b. A toad's diet is more varied than that of a frog.

c. A toad would probably win a race with a frog.

d. You would be in more danger holding a frog than you would be holding a toad.

In this item, the data in the chart support choice (a) more than any of the other choices, but more interpretation is required by students in this case than with the previous item.

As we saw from the illustrations, the first level of measuring thinking skills involves asking students to extend their thinking using familiar data, as was the case with the frogs and the toads. At the succeeding levels, the teacher could prepare items similar to the illustrations presented in this section, but students would have less prior experience with the content. In these cases, students would be presented with a chart not covered in a lesson, and would then be asked to form or identify conclusions based on the information.

Look again at Table 5.2. The following are sample items designed to measure specific higher-order thinking abilities. For example, consider the following item designed to measure students' ability to form explanatory inferences:

Of the following, the conclusion most supported by the data in the chart is:

a. The Chinese came primarily because of adventure while the Puerto Ricans came because of undesirable conditions at home.

b. While the Chinese and Italians came because of agricultural problems at home, the Puerto Ricans came primarily because of population pressures.

c. All three groups came partially because America seemed to offer more opportunities than their homelands.

d. All three groups came because of industrial problems in their homelands.

As a final example, consider an item designed to measure students' ability to identify irrelevant information, again in a multiple-choice format.

Look at the chart. Based on the information in it, which of the following is least relevant to the issue of assimilation?

a. The Italians were Catholics while the Chinese were Confucians.
b. The Italians learned English more quickly than did the Chinese.
c. The Chinese were found mostly in the western United States.
d. The second generation of Italians tended to intermarry with other Americans.

Each sample item so far has been written in a multiple-choice format. Short-essay formats can also be used equally or even more effectively. For instance, consider the following item designed to measure students' ability to assess hypotheses:

Let's think about some immigrant groups. Consider immigrants to the United States coming from Pakistan, Greece, and Kenya. Based on the information in the chart, which of the three would probably assimilate most rapidly, and which would probably assimilate least rapidly? Defend your answer based on the information in the chart (Table 5.2), and your understanding of the immigrant groups.

This item measures several outcomes:

- The students' knowledge of the immigrant groups and their cultures.
- Their ability to apply generalizations about assimilation to new immigrant groups.
- Their ability to make and defend an argument with evidence.
- The ability to write.

All of these are appropriate outcomes if the teacher has helped students develop these skills and abilities, and the assessment is consistent with the teacher's goals.

Measuring higher-order and critical thinking requires careful planning and judgment by the teacher. For instance, if items are based on a chart used in the lesson and the information related to the item has been discussed, it then measures knowledge and not thinking. This is appropriate if the teacher's goal is to measure knowledge; our concern is that the teacher is clear about what he or she is trying to accomplish and consciously moves toward that goal.

A solution to the inseparability of content and thinking skills is to develop items based on content not covered in the lesson. This also requires caution to be sure that all of the information needed to form the conclusions is included in the chart and that students understand the chart's content. Otherwise, the item measures students' knowledge of the content or their reading comprehension.

We do not want to suggest, however, that measuring thinking is impossible. With care and practice, you will develop the ability to write items that will not only measure student understanding and thinking, but will also serve as a means to promote further student thinking.

Please turn now to the following exercises, designed to reinforce your understanding of the content in the chapter.

Summary

The Integrative Model is an inductive-teaching model conceptually grounded in a constructivist view of learning. The model, which can be conducted in either small-group or whole-group settings, is designed to teach relationships among facts, concepts, principles, and generalizations, which are combined into organized bodies of knowledge. Information is organized into data displays that commonly appear as matrices, charts, tables, maps, or graphs. The students' analyses begin with observations and the search for patterns in the information, followed by explaining similarities and differences, hypothesizing outcomes for different conditions, and ending with summarizing and generalizing. The students' analysis is guided by the teachers' directed questions, which simultaneously emphasize deep understanding of content and higher-order and critical thinking.

Important Concepts

Organized Bodies of Knowledge (p. 149)

Exercises

Look at the following dialogue, which is based on the matrix containing information about Shakespeare's *Romeo and Juliet*, *Hamlet*, and *Julius Caesar*, which appeared earlier in Table 5.5. Classify each teacher question as Phase 1, Phase 2, Phase 3, Phase 4, or JT—a question that asks students to justify their thinking.

1. ___   *T*: Look at the "Events" for the three plays. What similarities do you see in the events?
   S: People die or are killed in each of the plays.

2. ___   *T*: What else?
   S: There are conflicts or fighting in each.

3. ___   *T*: For instance?
   S: For *Romeo and Juliet* it says that the Montagues and Capulets were feuding, for *Hamlet* it says that Hamlet was seeking revenge on Claudius, and in *Julius Caesar* it says that the armies of Brutus and Cassius fought with the armies of Antony and Octavius.

4. ___   *T*: We know that each of the three plays are tragedies. Suppose one or more of them were comedies instead. Do you think the patterns in the events would be different, and if so, how?
   S: I wouldn't expect to see so much conflict and death.

5. ___   *T*: What makes you say that?
   S: Conflict and death aren't all that happy, so they don't fit with comedies.

6. ___   *T*: Let's look at the second column. What similarities or differences do you see there?
   S: The characters in *Hamlet* and *Julius Caesar* appear to be less likable than the characters in *Romeo and Juliet*.

7. ___   *T*: What makes you say that?
   S: It says that Romeo and Juliet are innocent and guileless, but in *Hamlet* it says that Claudius is deceitful and hypocritical, and in *Julius Caesar* it says that Caesar is arrogant and that Cassius is quick-tempered.

8. ___ *T*: Look at the themes for *Julius Caesar*. We see ambition, jealousy, and revenge as themes, which appear somewhat negative, but we also see idealism as well. Why do you suppose idealism appears as a theme?

   S: Brutus was idealistic. He did what he did because he thought it was in the best interests of Rome and the people.

9. ___ *T*: Let's describe some general patterns in Shakespeare's tragedies if we can.

   S: The themes are complex and they vary a lot.

10. ___ *T*: What else?

    S: The characters aren't all good or all bad; they have some characteristics of both.

    S: There's a great deal of conflict between people in the plays.

    S: The characters all have conflicts within themselves too.

11. ___ *T*: Can you give us an example of what you mean?

    S: Hamlet is described as sentimental and sensitive, and at the same time he's ambitious.

    S: Brutus is caught between his feeling of loyalty to Caesar and his fear of Caesar's ambition.

12. Look again at the matrix containing the information about the solar system. Write a minimum of two questions in each of the phases, and provide what would be an acceptable answer to the questions.

Discussion Questions

1. We said that the Inductive Model is designed to teach concepts, generalizations, principles, and academic rules, and the Integrative Model is designed to teach organized bodies of knowledge. Prepare a list of topics that you have taught or you have seen taught in schools, and identify which of the two models is more appropriate for each of the topics. Are there topics that are inappropriate for either model? What are the characteristics of those topics that makes them inappropriate?

2. Prepare a matrix of the inductive and deductive thinking skills. On what dimensions would they be compared? Prepare another matrix on the Inductive Model, the Concept-Attainment Model, and the Integrative Model. Use the matrix as a basis of discussion to help form a schema for the models as discussed in Chapter 1.

3. Phase 4 is similar to closure for the Inductive and Concept Attainment Models. How is Phase 4 similar and different from its counterparts in the other two models?

4. We discussed prompting and repetition as questioning skills used with the Inductive Model. How might they be employed with the Integrative Model?

5. We said that the Integrative Model belongs in the inductive class of models, and we also said that forming explanations and hypotheses is a deductive process. Is there an inconsistency in these ideas? If not, why?

6. Consider using the Integrative Model in content areas such as art, music, physical education, and technology. Discuss how lessons could be designed to promote thinking in those areas.

7. Discuss how data might be gathered and displayed in ways other than using matrices, charts, maps, or other written materials. Provide an example in a content area of your choice.

Chapter *6*

The Direct-Instruction Model

The Direct-Instruction Model is a widely applicable strategy that can be used to teach both concepts and skills. Based on the effective-teaching research, this model places the teacher at the center of instruction. When direct instruction is used, the teacher assumes major responsibility for structuring the content or skill, explaining it to students, providing them with opportunities to practice, and giving feedback. Direct instruction derives from literally hundreds of studies that have attempted to identify links between teacher actions and student learning (Brophy and Good, 1986; Rosenshine and Stevens, 1986). The Direct-Instruction Model described in this chapter translates this research into a classroom-based teaching strategy.

When you have completed your study of this chapter, you should be able to meet the following objectives:

- Identify topics most effectively taught with the Direct-Instruction Model.
- Describe how examples can be used to illustrate ideas within the Direct-Instruction Model.
- Plan for the Direct-Instruction Model.
- Implement the Direct-Instruction Model, including all four phases in the lessons.
- Evaluate different forms of content acquisition in the Direct-Instruction Model.

To begin our discussion, let's look at two teachers using the Direct-Instruction Model in their classrooms.

Tim Hardaway looked up from his planning book and stared out the window. "I wonder if they are ready," he thought. "We've been working on addition for weeks now and they understand the process and most even know their math facts, but is this going to be tough? I wonder if they are ready for addition with two-digit numbers. I have to make sure that we review place value before we begin. I hope it works."

The next Monday Tim began his math class by saying, "Class, please put away your reading books and take out your math sticks. Today we are going to learn a new way to add. This new way to add will help us solve problems like this." With that, he put the following overhead on the board.

> *Sonya and Willy were brother and sister. They were saving special soda pop cans to get a free soccer ball. Sonya had 13 cans and Willy had 14. How many did they have together?*

After pausing for a while to give students an opportunity to read, Tim proceeded. "Problems like this are important in math because they help us in our everyday lives. When we're done with today's lesson, you'll be able to solve problems like this. We'll return to this problem in a minute, but before we do, we need to review some information we've already learned. To do that we will be using our math sticks to help us learn this new way. Before we do that, though, let's review what we have been working on. Everyone take out your sticks and do this problem."

Tim then put another problem on the board. Tim circulated around the room as students did the problem, using their unit sticks.

$$\begin{array}{r} 5 \\ +4 \\ \hline \end{array}$$

"Great! We really know how to do that. Now, I want you to try a slightly harder one. Do this one on your sticks," he said as he wrote the following problem on the board.

$$\begin{array}{r} 6 \\ +7 \\ \hline \end{array}$$

Again, Tim circulated around the room, helping students and answering questions that they had.

"Who would like to come to the flannel board to show us how they did this problem? Antonio? Good! Come on up here and use the same color sticks as you used at your desk."

Antonio walked up to the front of the room and started arranging the flannel sticks on the board.

"Antonio, talk out loud while you're doing it so everyone can understand."

"Well, you take six unit sticks and you add them to seven unit sticks and you get . . . thirteen unit sticks. That's the answer."

"Excellent Antonio. Does everyone see how he did that? Now, Antonio, do you remember what we can do when we have ten unit sticks? How can we make the problem simpler?"

"We can trade ten units for one ten stick."

"Okay, go ahead and do that. Class, if you haven't already done that, do that at your desk."

Tim paused for a second while the class rearranged their counting sticks so that they had one ten stick and three unit sticks.

"Does everyone see how Antonio did that? He traded ten of his unit sticks for one of his ten sticks and still got thirteen. Good thinking, Antonio.

"Now, class, we are ready to learn something new. Today we're going to learn how to add numbers that have tens in them. We already know how to add smaller numbers, and we know how to convert lots of units to tens so this shouldn't be too difficult if we all work hard. When we add numbers with tens and units we just have to remember to add the units with units and the tens with tens. Let's begin by looking at a problem."

With that, he returned the previous question to the overhead.

Sonya and Willy were brother and sister. They were saving special soda pop cans to get a free soccer ball. Sonya had 13 cans and Willy had 14. How many did they have together?

"Everyone look at the overhead. Good. Now what does the problem ask us? Shalinda?"

"How many they have together?" Shalinda asked hesitantly.

"Good. And what do we do, class, when we want to know how much two things are together? Everyone."

"Add!" the class responded in unison.

"Excellent," Tim replied. "Now let's put the problem on the board. What is one number that we add? Carlos?"

"Thirteen."

"Good, Carlos. And what's the other number we add, Cheryl?"

"Fourteen."

"Fine, so let's put the problem on the board like this," Tim continued, writing the following on the board:

$$\begin{array}{r} 14 \\ +13 \\ \hline \end{array}$$

"Now, I'd like everyone to show me how to make fourteen at your desk using both ten and unit sticks."

Tim paused as they class worked at their desks.

"Does everyone's set-up look like this?" Tim asked as he did the same at the flannel board.

"Now I'd like you to do the same with thirteen. Everyone do that at your desk," Tim added and then paused for them to work.

"Here's what my thirteen looks like. Is that right? Good. Now we're ready to add them. When I add three and four, what do I get? Hmm, let me think about that. . . . Three and four are seven. Let's put a seven up on the board," Tim said as he walked to the board and added a seven.

$$\begin{array}{r} 14 \\ +13 \\ \hline 7 \end{array}$$

"Now, we still have to add the tens. What do we get when we add two tens? Hmm, that should be easy. One ten and one ten is two tens. Class, look where I have to put the two up here. It is under the tens column because the two means two tens." With that he wrote the following on the board:

$$\begin{array}{r} 14 \\ +13 \\ \hline 27 \end{array}$$

"So how many cans did Sonya and Willy have together? Alesha?"

"Twenty-seven?"

"Good, Alesha. They had twenty-seven all together. Let's try another one."

Let's leave Tim and his first grade math class and visit Karen Hendricks, a middle school science teacher, who is beginning a unit on plants.

"Class, that was the bell so I need to have everyone's eyes up here," Karen announced loudly as she scanned the room for silence.

"Thank you. Billy, . . . thank you. Sandra, we're waiting."

After a short pause Karen continued, "Class, as you'll recall, we've been studying different kinds of plants for the past several weeks. We talked about one-celled plants, algae, mosses, and ferns and last week we talked about gymnosperms. Who can remember some plants that are gymnosperms? Becky?"

"Pine trees and that funny tree from China—Gingko."

"Good, Becky. Last week we also learned about angiosperms or flowering plant. Who can remember some examples of angiosperms? Wade?"

"Umm, roses and uhh . . . maple trees."

"Good, Wade. Today, class, we are going to learn about two kinds of angiosperms—monocotyledons and dicotyledons, or monocots and dicots for short. These are important members of the plant family because most of the food we eat comes from them. When we're all finished you will be able to tell the difference between monocots and dicots and explain how they're related to angiosperms. Look up here on the overhead and you'll see these terms defined.

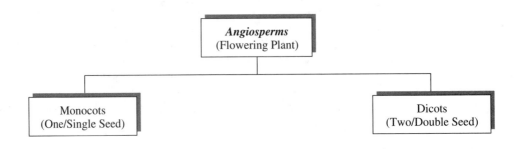

"Now first, I'd like to focus on monocots. Look up here (holding up a grass plant). This is a monocot that I found on the playground. Monocots are flowering plants that produce seeds with a single cotyledon. That's why we call them monocots—because *mono-* means one. If you look at the overhead you will see a cross section of a corn seed. Note that it has a unitary construction—it isn't in halves, and there is only one leaf coming out of the seed. Corn and this grass plant are examples of monocots. The second type of angiosperm we are going to learn about today is dicots or dicotyledons. Who knows what *di-* means? Maria?"

". . . If the other word meant one, . . . it must mean two," Maria replied.

"Excellent, Maria. So dicots have two seed leaves. Look at this cross-section of a bean plant. Can you see the two halves of the seed and the two seed leaves coming out? Good. Now, besides the seeds, there is a second difference between monocots and dicots. Look at the leaves of this grass plant and this bean plant and see if you can tell us about the other difference. Clarice?"

". . . Well, the grass leaves are long and thin and the bean leaves are kind of round."

"Good, Clarice. Now what about the leaf veins? Take a closer look. Alfredo, what do you see?" Karen asked.

". . . The veins in the grass plant are long and narrow; the veins in the bean plant go all over and are hooked to each other."

"Good, Alfredo. So a second difference is in the shape of the leaves and the veins in the leaves. Let's add these ideas to our diagram."

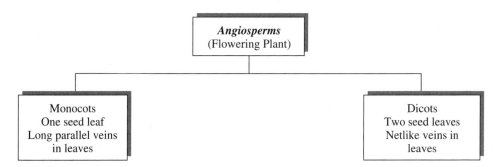

"Let's try another plant and see if these characteristics make sense," Karen continued, taking out a green onion and holding it in front of the class. "What do we have here and why?"

The class continued, with Karen presenting pictures and overheads of rice, corn, daffodil, rose, and sunflower plants. In each instance they talked about the plant structure and analyzed the seeds, when available.

Finally, Karen brought the lesson to a close by saying, "Class, let's summarize what we learned today. . . . Cheryl, what is one thing you learned today?"

". . . About angiosperms and how they have two families," Cheryl replied, pointing to the board.

"Good, what else? . . . Kenny?"

"We learned about monocots and dicots and how they're different," replied Kenny.

"Fine, and what is one difference between them? Trang?"

"Monocots have one seed leaf and they have long, parallel veins."

"Excellent, Trang. You were listening carefully. And what about dicots? Kaylynne?"

". . . Ummmm, dicots have two seed leaves and their leaves are rounder and have lots of veins that go every which way."

"Good, Kaylynne. Class, it seems like you are understanding the differences between these two types of plants. What I would like you to do now is work on this handout that has some additional examples of plants. Your job is to classify them as monocots or dicots, and then explain why."

After Karen passed the worksheet to the students she circulated around the class, answering questions. Toward the end of the class Karen began again, "Class, I have an assignment for each of you. I want you to go home tonight and look in your yards, or refrigerators, or even a park and find one more example of a monocot or dicot. Bring it in if you can, but don't pull up somebody's flowers. (Karen paused, as the class laughed and exchanged glances.) Make sure you write that assignment down and we'll discuss what you find first thing tomorrow morning."

Direct Instruction: An Overview

The **Direct-Instruction Model** *is a teacher-centered strategy that uses teacher explanation and modeling combined with student practice and feedback to teach concepts and skills.* It is teacher-centered in the sense that the teacher takes the responsibility for identifying the lesson goals, and then plays an active role in explaining the content or skills to the students. Students are then given several opportunities to practice the concept or skill being taught, and the teacher provides feedback. The process takes place in a highly structured learning activity.

The Direct-Instruction Model occurs in four phases. In the *introduction,* the teacher reviews prior learning with the students, shares learning goals, and provides a reason or rationale for the new content. During the *presentation* phase, the teacher explains the new concept or models the skill. In *guided practice,* the teacher provides students with opportunities to practice the new skill or categorize examples of the new concept. Finally, during *independent practice,* students are asked to practice the skill or concept on their own, which encourages both retention and transfer. These phases are summarized in Table 6.1.

The Direct-Instruction Model is a research-based instructional strategy that has wide applicability in a number of content areas. One of the distinguishing characteristics of the model is the pattern of interaction between the teacher and students. We examine this interaction in the next section.

Social Structure of the Model

The Direct-Instruction Model is teacher centered, meaning that the teacher plays a primary role in structuring content, explaining it, and using examples to increase student under-

TABLE 6.1   Phases in the Direct-Instruction Model

Phase	Purpose	Example
Introduction	Provides an overview of new content, explores connections with student's background knowledge, and helps students understand the value of the new content.	Karen reviewed gymnosperms and angiosperms. She expalined that monocots and dicots were important food sources.
Presentation	New content is explained and modeled by the teacher in an interactive format.	Karen displayed a hierarchy explaining monocots and dicots and provided examples of each.
Guided Practice	Students are provided with opportunities to try out the new content.	Karen had the students classify examples of monocots orally and on a worksheet.
Independent Practice	Retention and transfer are promoted by students practicing the concept or skill of their own.	Karen had the students find additional examples and bring them to class.

standing. However, we want to emphasize that "teacher centered" does not imply that the students are passive. Effective direct-instruction lessons actively involve students in learning through the use of teacher questioning, examples, practice, and feedback.

A central idea that guides interaction patterns in the Direct-Instruction Model is the idea of transfer of responsibility. In the first part of the lesson, the teacher assumes major responsibility for explaining and describing content. As the lesson progresses and students begin to understand the content or skill, they assume more responsibility for solving problems and analyzing examples.

The patterns of teacher and student interaction correspond to this transfer of responsibility. Initially, teachers do most of the talking as they take responsibility for presenting the content. As the lesson progresses, the teacher talks less and more questioning than explaining is used. As students become more proficient and confident, they talk more and assume more responsibility for explaining and describing their answers. These gradual transitions—both in terms of responsibility and speech—are characteristic of successful direct-instruction lessons. Let's look now at the research that supports the model.

Direct Instruction: Theoretical Perspectives

The structure of the Direct-Instruction Model is based on research from three areas. In one, researchers looked at classrooms of effective teachers and tried to discover what these teachers did to promote learning. This is the teacher-effectiveness research we discussed in Chapters 1 and 2. Many of the elements of the effectiveness research are incorporated into the Direct-Instruction Model.

The Direct-Instruction Model is also based on a second line of research that emphasizes the role of observation in learning complex behaviors and skills. Based on the work of Albert Bandura (1989, 1986), this research demonstrates the powerful role that modeling can play in learning new skills. A third research foundation for the Direct-Instruction

Model views learning as a social process. Based on the work of Lev Vygotsky (1978), a Russian psychologist, this line of research explores how social interactions between people facilitate learning. We discuss these three perspectives in the sections that follow.

Teacher-Effectiveness Research

We examined the teacher-effectiveness research in Chapters 1 and 2. There we found that teachers do indeed make a difference in terms of student learning; effective teachers helped their students learn significantly more—as measured by standardized tests—than did their less effective counterparts. The research also helped identify a number of specific behaviors that effective teachers demonstrated more frequently than their less effective peers. These behaviors included the efficient use of time, skilled questioning and management strategies, and the use of students' background knowledge to promote success.

As researchers analyzed their findings, they identified a general pattern or approach to instruction that produced improved learning. Experts used a variety of labels for this approach, and *direct instruction* (Rosenshine, 1979) was one of those labels.

Rosenshine (1979) described direct instruction as follows:

> *Direct instruction refers to academically focused, teacher-directed classrooms using sequenced and structured materials. It refers to teaching activities where goals are clear to students, time allocated for instruction is sufficient and continuous, coverage of content is extensive, the performance of students is monitored, . . . and feedback to students is immediate and academically oriented. In direct instruction the teacher controls instructional goals, chooses materials appropriate for the student's ability, and paces the instructional episode. Interaction is . . . structured, but not authoritarian. Learning takes place in a convivial academic atmosphere (p. 38).*

The research on this approach to teaching provides the major conceptual foundation for the Direct-Instruction Model described in this chapter.

Direct instruction incorporates six teaching functions. These teaching functions are effective across grade levels and a wide spectrum of content areas. They include:

- Reviewing the previous day's work.
- Presenting new material in clear and logical steps.
- Providing guided practice.
- Giving feedback with correctives.
- Providing independent practice.
- Reviewing to consolidate learning (Rosenshine and Stevens, 1986).

These teaching functions provide the structure for the Direct-Instruction Model.

Modeling: Learning by Observing Others

A second conceptual underpinning of the Direct-Instruction Model is the work on observational learning done by Albert Bandura (1986, 1989). The principle on which observational learning is based says that people tend to imitate behaviors they observe in others. We have all seen little children imitate others, and the tendency of teenagers to imitate the hair and fashion styles of rock and movie stars forms the basis for a multimillion dollar fashion industry.

Students also learn through observation in the classroom, and this observational learning often operates through modeling. **Observational learning** *includes changes in behavior, thinking, or emotions that result from observing the behavior of another person* (a model), and **modeling** *is the display of the behaviors.* In direct instruction, modeling provides a major way for teachers to help students learn complex skills. Tim Hardaway used modeling when he demonstrated adding at the flannel board. Tim also used modeling when he asked students to come to the board to demonstrate the skill.

Modeling of complex cognitive strategies is most effective when the thinking that is the basis for these strategies is made explicit by thinking out loud. **Think alouds** *are conscious attempts to verbalize internal cognitive strategies.* Tim Hardaway used think alouds in two ways. The first was when he thought out loud during his problem solving at the flannel board. The second time was when he encouraged students to think out loud while they were working at the flannel board. Both were attempts to make modeling more effective by sharing internal thought processes with other students.

Vygotsky: The Social Side of Skill Learning

The Direct-Instruction Model is a teacher-centered model that emphasizes the role of the teacher in structuring content and delivering it to students. However, part of the model's effectiveness lies in its ability to provide opportunities for both teachers and students to interact as new content is presented. Research on the social aspects of learning emphasizes the important role that this verbal interaction plays in helping students learn (Wertsch, 1991).

Much of this work is based on the writings of Lev Vygotsky (1978), a Russian psychologist who lived in the early part of this century. Unfortunately, Vygotsky died when he was thirty-eight and most of his work was not translated into English until recently. Vygotsky focused heavily on the social aspects of learning, believing that most human learning resulted from the interaction between people, both adult-child and child-child.

Two concepts from Vygotsky's work are relevant to the Direct-Instruction Model. One is the notion of scaffolding. **Scaffolding** *refers to instructional support that allows students to perform a skill.* Teachers provide instructional scaffolding in a number of ways, including breaking complex skills into subcomponents, adjusting the difficulty of questions, providing examples, and offering prompts and cues. Effective teachers help students achieve high levels of success, and instructional scaffolding explains how teachers adjust their instruction to help students succeed.

A second important concept from Vygotsky's work is called the zone of proximal development. The **zone of proximal development** *is the stage of learning in which a student cannot solve a problem or perform a skill alone, but can be successful with the help of a teacher.* The zone of proximal development can be thought of as instructional pay dirt; it is within that zone that teachers can be most effective in aiding student learning. Outside of the zone, students either don't need help (they have already mastered a new skill) or lack the prerequisite skills or background knowledge to benefit from instruction.

When the Direct-Instruction Model is being used, we attempt to implement lessons within students' zones of proximal development. For example, when Tim Hardaway first introduced adding two digit numbers, most of his students were not able to perform this skill by themselves. However, by the end of the lesson and with his help, most of Tim's students would be able to perform the skill on their own. Tim had successfully helped his students proceed through the zone of proximal development through his skilled instruction.

In summary, three lines of research provide the conceptual foundation for the Direct-Instruction Model.

- The effectiveness research analyzes the actions of effective teachers and summarizes these methods in terms of strategies that promote learning.
- Bandura's work on observational learning focuses on the importance of modeling in learning complex behaviors.
- Vygotsky's work stresses the importance of learning from others, but focuses more on the verbal interactions between adults and children.

Together, these three sources paint a picture of instruction in which the teacher assumes a central role in learning, actively guiding students in their understanding of new content. In the next section of this chapter we examine how the Direct-Instruction Model begins with the process of planning.

Planning Lessons with the Direct-Instruction Model

Planning for the Direct-Instruction Model is a three-step process that begins by specifying goals, continues by identifying prerequisite knowledge, and concludes when sample problems are selected or prepared. We describe each of these steps in the sections that follow.

Specifying Goals

The Direct-Instruction Model is designed to teach specific concepts and skills, and one of the model's strengths is its ability to focus students' attention on specific content. In order for the model to work effectively, the teacher must identify specific topics and create or find examples that will make them understandable.

Concepts

Concepts form a major content focus of the Direct-Instruction Model. As we saw in Chapter 3, students learn concepts, interrelationships with other concepts, and their characteristics by examining positive and negative examples.

Karen Hendricks taught two interrelated concepts—*monocots* and *dicots*—in her middle school science class. She first reviewed the superordinate concept, *angiosperm,* and then related dicots and monocots to it. In teaching monocots and dicots, Karen used real plants and pictures displayed on overheads as examples.

In this lesson Karen actually taught two concepts at one time, and one served as a nonexample for the other. There are a number of teaching situations where presenting two related concepts is not only time efficient but also effective in terms of learning (Tennyson and Cocchiarella, 1986). Some other pairs might include *antonym* and *synonym* or *simile* and *metaphor* in language arts, *longitude* and *latitude* in geography, and *acid* and *base* in science. In each case teaching the two items simultaneously helps students see the relationship between interrelated and sometimes confused concepts. In instances where there is no closely related coordinate concept, an array of negative examples can be used to help clarify the boundaries of the concept.

Skills

To begin this section we'd like to pose this problem:

$$987$$
$$-788$$

The answer to this problem is easy for most of us, but now let us change the focus of the problem. How would you go about teaching this problem to a second grader who understands simple subtraction but has not been introduced to the idea of regrouping (e.g., 7 − 8 cannot be done, so we need to borrow to make the 7 a 17, etc.)? You need to explain the process so that the child understands what he or she is doing and why, and also get him or her to the point that he or she can do this automatically, not only on quizzes and assignments but also at the grocery store and the bank. This type of content involves skill learning. The Direct-Instruction Model provides one alternative to teach skills such as these.

Skills *are cognitive operations with three essential characteristics:*

- They have a specific set of identifiable operations or procedures.
- They can be illustrated with a large and varied number of examples.
- They are developed through practice (Doyle, 1983).

These characteristics are interrelated; the operations are illustrated through examples or sample problems, which provide practice for students.

Skills can be found across the curriculum and at virtually every grade level. For example, the language arts curriculum contains writing skills, including general organizational strategies, as well as specific skills such as capitalization and punctuation. As we saw in our introductory case study, the area of math is replete with skills, ranging from basics such as addition and subtraction to those more complex like factoring and solving quadratic equations. Science and social studies also contain many skill areas. For example, students are asked to read maps and read and display information in charts and graphs in social studies, and science students measure and operate scientific equipment, form and test hypotheses, and conduct experiments.

We can think of skills as being generalized abilities. For example, math skills like adding and subtracting allow us to perform these operations with concrete objects like apples and cookies as well as abstract topics in finance or science. As another example, once people learn to capitalize and punctuate, they can use these writing skills to communicate in a variety of situations.

We have two long-range goals when we teach skills—automaticity and transfer. As we saw in Chapter 2, **automaticity** *results from overlearning a skill to the point that it can be performed with little conscious effort.* Driving a car and word processing are two skills that are learned to the point of automaticity. For example, once automaticity is achieved, we spend virtually no effort thinking about what keys we will press when we type. Rather, our effort is directed at composing the document we're preparing. Similarly, in order to solve word problems in math, automaticity in basic operations—such as addition and multiplication—is important because it allows us to focus most of our attention on the solution to the problem, rather than spending mental energy on the operations.

Teachers promote automaticity by providing practice opportunities to the point of overlearning. This practice can occur during guided practice, during independent practice in which students try the skill out on their own, or through reviews that help reinforce the skill.

A second goal of skills instruction is transfer. **Transfer** *occurs when a skill or knowledge learned in one setting can be applied in a different setting.* For example, transfer occurs when students apply algebra in solving physics problems, or when students use math skills to determine which of two products is a better buy.

Teachers teach for transfer in at least three ways. The first is by ensuring that students understand the skill at a conceptual level. Tim Hardaway used his counting sticks to help reach this goal. A second way to promote transfer is by providing a variety of examples in which the skill is required. Third, students can be given a chance to practice the skill independently on practical problems. Once the content goal for a lesson is identified, the teacher is then ready to examine prerequisite knowledge.

Identifying Prerequisite Knowledge

The Direct-Instruction Model focuses on the teaching and learning of specific concepts or skills. However, research on learning emphasizes the importance of student background knowledge for new learning (Eggen and Kauchak, 1994). Background knowledge provides "hooks" for new learning. In planning for direct-instruction lessons, teachers need to plan for how the concept or skill will be introduced and connected to what students already know.

Planning for accessing prerequisite knowledge is slightly different for teaching a concept compared to a skill. For concepts, the task usually involves identifying a superordinate concept to which the concept can be linked. Karen used the superordinate concept *angiosperm,* because she had taught the concept and it was meaningful to students. Though the goal in a direct instruction may be to understand a specific concept (or concepts), such as *monocot* and *dicot* in Karen's lesson, a broader goal is for students to understand how the concept relates to other facts, concepts, generalizations, and principles.

Identifying prerequisites for a skills-oriented lesson is slightly more complicated, because it involves identifying subskills that lay the foundation for the new skill. **Task analysis**, *or the process of breaking a skill into its component subparts,* can be helpful here. Tim Hardaway did this when he determined that students first needed to understand place value before they could learn to do two-column addition.

Consider a second example from the area of writing or language arts. Our ultimate goal is to teach students to write well. We first need to establish what knowledge or skills are required to accomplish this goal. Among them are punctuating sentences correctly, understanding what a sentence is, knowing the difference between sentence fragments and complete sentences, and being able to use the specific symbols that are used with each sentence type. Once learned, these prerequisite skills provide a foundation that allows students to focus on the skill at hand.

Selecting Examples and Problems

The final phase in planning for direct instruction lessons is selecting examples or problems. A major strength of the model is that it provides the opportunities for practice for students. When learning a concept, students can relate the definition to actual examples and can categorize the examples themselves. In learning a skill, sample problems both help students understand the procedures and give them a chance to practice the skill on their own. In both instances—concept and skill learning—selecting concrete examples and problems is essential to the success of the lesson.

When teaching concepts with the Direct-Instruction Model, the teacher has two tasks—selecting and sequencing the examples. Examples are selected based on the extent to which they illustrate the concept's essential characteristics. In Karen Hendricks's lesson these characteristics included the number of seed leaves and the type of venation. Karen used a combination of real examples and overheads to help illustrate these characteristics.

After selecting examples, the next task is to sequence them. Usually, the clearest and most obvious ones are presented first to help students grasp the concept as quickly as possible. For example, when teaching a simple concept, such as *mammal,* we would first use obvious examples like dog, cat, cow, or zebra rather than whale, seal, or bat. Once the basic concept is grasped, additional examples can be used to enrich students' concepts.

The extent to which examples illustrate the essential characteristics is a second way to think about sequencing. Again in a lesson on mammals, dog and cat are good examples because they illustrate characteristics such as being furry, warm-blooded, and milk producers. Further, most students have had direct experiences with these mammals, which makes them more meaningful.

In selecting and sequencing examples and problems for skill acquisition, consideration of student success is important. One reason for using the Direct-Instruction Model is to help students acquire proficiency with the skill as quickly and painlessly as possible. This suggests that problems should be selected and sequenced so that students can develop the skill and confidence through successful practice.

Tim Hardaway helped accomplish this goal by providing the easiest problems first. He first used problems that involved single-digit addition without regrouping, then moved to single-digit addition with regrouping, proceeded to double-digit addition without regrouping, and finally arrived at double-digit addition with regrouping. By moving from simple to complex, Tim provided instructional scaffolding that ensured high success rates and minimized frustration and confusion.

Having specified goals, identified prerequisite knowledge and skills, and selected and sequenced examples and problems, the teacher is ready to put these planning steps into action. In the next section we discuss the steps in implementing the Direct-Instruction Model.

Implementing Lessons Using the Direct-Instruction Model

Implementing lessons using the Direct-Instruction Model typically occurs in four phases. In the first, new content is introduced and linked to students' background knowledge, which is followed in the second phase by describing and explaining the new content and using concrete examples to make the topic meaningful. The second phase is followed by guided practice in which students experiment with the new content, either applying it to additional examples or trying it out on new problems. In the fourth phase students practice on their own, which promotes automaticity and transfer. We examine these stages in the sections that follow.

Introduction

The introductory phase of a direct-instruction lesson performs several functions. First, it draws students into the lesson; without student attention the teacher's best efforts are wasted. In addition, the introduction provides an overview of the content to follow, allowing students to see where the lesson is going, and how it relates to content already learned. The introduction also provides opportunities for the teacher to motivate students and to explain how the new content will be beneficial to them in the future. Let's examine each of these functions.

Introductory Focus
In Chapter 2 we defined introductory focus as ". . . teacher actions at the beginning of a lesson designed to attract students' attention and pull them into the lesson." It is important to draw students into any lesson and to focus their attention on the learning task. However, research indicates that teachers often neglect this essential attention-getting function; in one study of skills instruction researchers found that only 5 percent of the teachers made a conscious attempt to draw students into the lesson (Anderson, Brubaker, Alleman-Brooks, and Duffy, 1984).

Madeline Hunter (1984) called this part of the lesson *anticipatory set*, and emphasized the need for teachers to attract and maintain student attention at the beginning of a lesson. Tim Hardaway provided introductory focus by presenting his students with the word problem that he returned to later in the lesson, and Karen Hendricks used the transparency showing the relationship of dicots and monocots to angiosperms as her introductory focus.

Lesson Overview
A second function of the introduction is to provide students with an orientation to the lesson's content. The lesson overview often includes objectives, a brief summary of the new content, and the procedures in the lesson (Murphy, Weil, and McGreal, 1986). Tim Hardaway presented a sample problem on the overhead and explained that students would be able to do these when the lesson was completed as his lesson overview, and Karen Hendricks structured her lesson with the transparency by explaining that students would be able to differentiate between monocots and dicots when the lesson was over.

Motivating Students
Motivation is a third function performed by the introduction. In an attempt to motivate students the teacher explains how and why the new content should be studied. Tim Hardaway attempted to motivate his students by emphasizing that the new math skill would help the students solve common, everyday problems. Karen Hendricks addressed motivation when she explained how monocots and dicots formed an important food source. The motivational component builds on introductory focus by helping to sustain attention.

Presentation

During the presentation phase of a direct-instruction lesson, the teacher explains the concept or explains and models the skill being taught. Sometimes called the development phase (Murphy et al., 1986) or input and modeling (Hunter, 1984), it is during this phase that the teacher uses demonstrations and modeling to help make the topic meaningful to students.

While this phase of the model appears simple and straightforward, research indicates that implementing it is difficult for teachers. One of the problems is being able to think like a student and conceptualize the new content in a way that is simple and makes sense to students. Teachers describe the problem in this way:

> *I've never thought through (how to teach a cognitive skill). The most difficult thing is to think it through. . . . Figuring out how to model (the skill) is a hard thing for me. . . . I have to really sit down and write it out. I mean, I am still doing that pretty much, like every day with that group (Duffy and Roehler, 1985, p. 6).*

One explanation for this problem relates to internalization and automaticity. The concepts and skills that we teach often become so automatic for us that we perform them automatically and nearly unconsciously. As a result, we have problems when we try to verbalize—or even model—them for our students. For example, stop for a second and think about how you would explain and model tying a shoelace for a youngster. Our explanation might be somewhat vague, such as, "Well, first you do this, and then you put one lace over the other . . . ," and our modeling might be rushed and confusing. The difficulty you experience is similar to the one teachers encounter when they try to explain skills that are very familiar to them.

In reaction to this problem teachers often rush through this phase of the model, providing too little explanation and modeling, asking students to try the skill before they are ready (Good and Grouws, 1979; Good, Grouws and Ebmeier, 1983). A partial solution to this problem is to use task analysis to break complex skills into more specific parts.

The most productive presentations are clear, interactive, and contain enough examples and modeling to develop student comprehension. Both Tim Hardaway and Karen Hendricks effectively implemented this phase in their teaching. For example, Tim modeled problem-solving processes himself, and then he asked Antonio to demonstrate and explain how he solved his problem. Also, both Tim and Antonio *talked* while they were involved in problem solving, allowing others to share in their thinking.

Karen used several examples to make her presentation effective. As she introduced monocots and dicots, she shared examples of each with students, and as she discussed the concepts' essential characteristics, she related them to both examples and overheads. She also wrote the characteristics and important information on the board. Both Tim Hardaway and Karen Hendricks actively involved students through questioning during the presentation phases of their lessons.

Guided Practice

During guided practice, students try out the new content as the teacher carefully monitors their progress and provides feedback. During the guided practice phase of a direct-instruction lesson, both teacher and student roles change. The teacher moves from information giver and model to coach, and the students move from receiving information to testing their understanding with examples and problems provided by the teacher.

During the early phases of guided practice the teacher provides instructional scaffolding to ensure that students experience success when they try new skills. Gradually, teachers reduce the number of these prompts and transfer more responsibility to students.

The kind and amount of teacher talk characterizes this phase. Initially, the teacher gives cues and prompts that provide instructional scaffolding. Later, as students assume more responsibility for explaining problems and classifying examples, teachers' talk will be more probing, designed to raise the level of student thinking and application.

Guided practice occurred in Tim's lesson when he assisted his students in solving problems using their counting sticks and the flannel board. Karen provided guided practice when she presented pictures and overheads of plants like rice and corn and asked students to classify them and explain their answers.

During guided practice teachers must decide when to make the transition to independent practice—when students try out the new skill on their own. Effective independent practice requires that students have enough expertise to be successful with little teacher assistance.

There are several ways to gauge whether students are ready for this transition. One is student success rates; when 80 to 90 percent of students' responses during guided practice are correct, the class is probably ready for independent practice. A second gauge is the quality of student answers. Confident and quick answers signal that students are ready; hesitant or partially correct answers suggest the need for more practice under the guidance of the teacher.

A high level of interaction between teacher and student is essential during this phase of the model. Teachers need to ask clarifying and probing questions to determine whether the students actually understand the new content or are following a set of memorized procedures. Research indicates that more effective teachers ask three times as many questions during this phase of direct instruction than their less effective counterparts (Evertson, Anderson, Anderson, and Brophy, 1980). Teacher-student interaction also provides teachers with access to student thinking, allowing them to understand and "debug" student errors and misconceptions.

To this point the topic has been introduced, explained, and modeled, and students have had a chance to practice with the teacher's guidance. They should now be ready for independent practice.

Independent Practice

Independent practice is the final phase of the Direct-Instruction Model. During this phase students practice the new skill or concept on their own, developing both automaticity and transfer.

Ideally, independent practice occurs in two stages. During the first, students practice in class under the supportive umbrella of the teacher. Later, students work on their own in a homework assignment.

Independent practice in the classroom is important because it allows the teacher to monitor learning progress and to provide assistance if needed. Student success rates and the problems the students encounter both help the teacher in diagnosing learner problems. If few students are having problems, the teacher can work with individuals. If a number of students are having the same problems, it may be necessary to pull the class back together and reteach the parts of the topic that students don't understand (Brophy and Good, 1986).

The students began independent practice in Karen Hendricks's lesson when she passed out a worksheet and had each student classify additional examples of monocots and dicots. We left Tim Hardaway's lesson before it progressed to independent practice.

This concludes our discussion of the general procedures in implementing the Direct-Instruction Model. In the next section, we discuss adapting the model to teach principles, generalizations, and academic rules.

The Direct-Instruction Model: Variations

To this point in the chapter we have described the Direct-Instruction Model as a strategy for teaching concepts and skills. However, the model can also be used to teach generalizations, principles and academic rules.

In Chapter 3, we said that generalizations, principles and rules are similar in that each is a relationship between concepts that describes trends or patterns in the world. Some examples include:

- People immigrate for economic reasons. (A generalization)
- A diet high in saturated fat raises a person's cholesterol level. (A generalization)
- The greater the unbalanced force on an object, the greater the object's acceleration. (A principle)
- A pronoun must agree with its antecedent in number and gender. (An academic rule)
- In rounding off a number, if the last digit is 5 or more, you round up, and if it is 4 or less, you round down. (An academic rule)

Generalizations, principles, and rules are similar to concepts in that they can be illustrated with examples, and high-quality examples are the key to successful learning in all cases. In this section we discuss using the Direct-Instruction Model to teach these forms of content.

Planning

Planning to teach generalizations, principles, and rules with the Direct-Instruction Model is similar to the planning process necessary to teach concepts. Goals need to be clearly identified, prerequisite knowledge determined, and examples constructed or selected and sequenced. As with teaching concepts, a clear idea of teaching goals and a thorough understanding of the abstraction are essential.

Implementation

As in the planning stage, implementation of the Direct-Instruction Model to teach generalizations, principles and rules is similar to using the model to teach concepts. During the introductory phase the teacher provides an overview of new content, establishes links with students' background knowledge, and helps students understand the value of the new content. During the presentation phase, the teacher describes the topic, explains the concepts embedded in the abstraction, and uses examples to help students understand the relationships described in it. Guided practice allows students to experiment with the topic, and independent practice provides additional examples to develop automaticity and transfer. Look for these phases in the following case study:

> Tamra Evans, a high school social studies teacher, wanted to teach her students the generalization "If demand stays constant, price is inversely related to supply."
>
> She began her lesson by stating, "We have been studying the economics of different countries for several lessons, so let's review what we've done so far. What do we mean by economics? . . . Jerry?"
>
> "Economics sort of deals with money," he responded.
>
> "Good, and what particular aspects of money? Tim?"
>
> ". . . Well, it tells how money is made and how it is spread around," Tim answered.
>
> "Excellent Tim," Tamra smiled. "Now everyone, today we're going to deal with a particular law in economics. This law states that 'When demand stays constant, price and supply are inversely related.'" As she stated the generalization, she wrote it on the chalkboard.
>
> "This law is important," she continued, "because it will help us understand why the prices of things we buy in stores go up or down. Supply, as we'll see in today's lesson, is a major factor influencing price. Now, . . . how do supply, demand, and price relate to the larger topic of economics? . . . Cheryl?"
>
> ". . . I think . . . price relates to money and . . . how someone would make money," Cheryl answered hesitantly.
>
> "Yes! Very good, Cheryl. Now let's look at the terms supply, demand, price and inversely. What does the word inversely mean? . . . Mike?"
>
> ". . . It means something like when one thing gets bigger, another gets smaller," Mike responded.
>
> Tamra continued the discussion of each term until she was satisfied that students understood each. At that point she continued with the lesson by saying, "Let's look at the overhead. The paragraph on it illustrates the generalization." With that she showed the students the following example:
>
> > *As I drove into a city of approximately a half million people in August of 1992, I filled my car with gas at an independent station for 94.9 cents per gallon. In March of 1993, I made a trip into the same city. I looked at a pump that said $1.249 for unleaded. When I asked the attendant about the big price jump he explained that a strike at local refineries had made gas hard to get.*
>
> After allowing the students time to read the anecdote she asked, "How does the example relate to our generalization? . . . Judy?"
>
> ". . . The strike would mean that the supply was reduced, I guess."
>
> "Yes, good, you've identified a key variable in the example, Judy. What else? . . . David?"
>
> "The price shot way up," David answered quickly.

"And what do we call that kind of relationship?"

". . . Oh. That's what inverse means," David answered after thinking a moment.

"And the amount people wanted to buy stayed about the same," Anna volunteered.

"Very well done," Tamra smiled. "We see how the example illustrates that the price and supply are inversely related if the demand stays the same."

"Now look at another example and tell me if it illustrates the law," she went on. She then showed students the following example:

Jimmy decided to put up a lemonade stand. He charged four cents a cup, and people were buying lemonade at the corner of his father's lot faster than he could make it. Jimmy decided, "I'll bet they'll still buy my lemonade if I charge five cents a glass." So he did.

Two days later Joey, who saw how well Jimmy was making out, decided to open up his own lemonade stand across the street from Jimmy's. He charged three cents a glass, and soon most of the people who had been stopping at Jimmy's stand were going to Joey's instead. Jimmy then lowered his price to three cents a glass, and both boys sold lemonade.

"Does this example illustrate the principle we've been discussing?" Tamra wondered. ". . . How is the demand affected by Joey opening his stand? . . . Jason?"

"I guess it isn't. It should be about the same."

"Very good, Jason. There is no reason to think that Joey's stand would have any effect on the amount people wanted to buy."

"Yes, Kristy," Tamra smiled in response to Kristy's waving hand.

"I've got it," Kristy said excitedly. "Since the demand was the same and Joey's stand increased the supply, the price had to go down, which is an inverse relationship."

"Excellent analysis, Kristy. So does the example illustrate the principle?"

"Yes," Kristy replied confidently.

"Let me show you one more," Tamra said, and she displayed the following example on the screen:

In the 1980s, with the boom in computer technology, many universities dramatically expanded their computer science preparation programs and a campaign was on to try and maintain a lead over other industrialized countries, such as Germany and Japan. At that time, Ph.D.s in computer science could virtually name their salaries at most universities.

As the 1980s moved into the 1990s, many students still took majors in computer science, but with businesses restructuring and "downsizing," the emphasis on computer science was reduced somewhat.

In the mid 1990s, many computer scientists have been unable to get jobs, and those that are employed receive lower comparative salaries than those trained ten years earlier.

"Does this example illustrate the law we're discussing?" Tamra queried. "Karen?"

". . . I'm . . . I'm not sure," Karen answered.

"Let's look carefully," Tamra suggested. "What has happened to the price?"

". . . Their salaries were lower," Karen tentatively suggested.

"Yes they were. That's good, Karen. Now, how about the supply? . . . Jan?"

"It doesn't look to me as if it's changed that much."

"Aha! But the demand has gone down!" John added, with a look of insight on his face. "The example doesn't illustrate the idea we're discussing, because our generalization says the demand stays constant."

"Bravo, everyone!" Tamra praised. "That is an excellent analysis. Since you've done so well, think now and see if you can create some more examples that illustrate the generalization."

The students, with Tamra's help, then generated some additional examples, which they analyzed as they had the first three.

She then continued, "Class, I have some additional cases that I'd like you to do now. In each case if the generalization is illustrated, explain *how* it's illustrated by identifying each part—supply, demand, and price—in the generalization, and if it doesn't illustrate it, explain why. I'd like you to start on these with the time remaining, and I'll come around to see if you have any questions. Whatever you don't finish, take home for homework and we'll discuss them tomorrow."

As we can see, using the Direct-Instruction Model to teach generalizations, principles, and rules is very similar to procedures used in teaching concepts. In the introductory phase, the teacher still outlines the lesson and attempts to explain how the new content relates the students' lives. During the presentation phase, the teacher describes the generalization and makes sure that concepts contained within it are understood by students. The teacher then uses case studies to illustrate the generalization and to help students see how it relates to the real world. During independent practice, students analyze additional examples as both an in-class assignment and homework.

In summary, the Direct-Instruction Model provides an effective and time-efficient way to teach generalizations, principles, and rules. As with concept teaching, the essential ingredients for successful lessons are the liberal use of examples and teacher-student and student-student interaction that involves learners in making sense of these examples.

Assessing Student Understanding

The assessment of content outcomes in a direct-instruction lesson is similar to the process with the Inductive Model and the Concept-Attainment Model. This process was discussed in detail in Chapter 3 and reinforced in Chapter 4. You may want to review those sections at this time.

To further reinforce the evaluation process, let's look again at Karen Hendricks's lesson. She has several options to choose from in assessing her students. For example, she could do one or more of the following:

1. Have the students define monocots and dicots.
2. Give them pictures of monocots and dicots and ask them to identify each.

3. Give them actual examples of monocots and dicots and ask them to classify and explain their classifications.
4. Have them bring in their own examples of monocots and dicots and explain the examples in each case.

We can readily see that having the students define these concepts is a very superficial measure of their understanding of the concept unless it is used in conjunction with other measures. However, each of the others would be a valid indicator of students' understanding, with the demands on the students being progressively greater in each case.

An efficient measure of concept learning in general is to have students classify examples and nonexamples of the concept. For example, in a lesson on adjectives the teacher could present students with an item such as the following:

Circle each of the following words that could be adjectives.

a. pretty
b. go
c. ball
d. early
e. big
f. crazily
g. event

An item such as this is easy to prepare and score. However, this efficiency comes at a price. In the real world we want students to be able to write using adjectives appropriately. A much more valid item would require students to write a paragraph and identify the adjectives within it. Authentic assessments such as these attempt to place students in more realistic and life-like settings to make the assessment process as similar as possible to real-life situations.

However, scoring such an item is very time consuming. A reasonable compromise could be to present the students with an already-prepared passage and have them identify the adjectives within it. While not as effective as having them write their own, it could be scored efficiently. Obviously, several other measurement procedures could also be effectively used. We have presented the previous example for sake of reinforcement and understanding, and we do not intend to suggest that it is the only appropriate format.

Determining the appropriate compromise between the validity of the assessment and the demand on the teacher is a matter of professional judgment. Only the teacher can make that decision.

Summary

The Direct-Instruction Model is a strongly teacher-directed strategy that can be used to teach concepts and skills. Derived from the teacher-effectiveness research, observational learning theory, and the work of Lev Vygotsky, the model exists in four sequential phases—introduction, presentation, guided practice, and independent practice. The use of well-thought-out examples and problems is the key to the success of learning activities in which the model is used.

Though strongly teacher directed, effective use of the Direct-Instruction Model requires high levels of interaction between teacher and students. The patterns in this interaction shift as a lesson develops. Initially, the teacher presents information and closely guides the students as they work with examples and problems. Later, the students work more and more independently until they are able to analyze examples and solve problems without the teacher's help.

While the model is designed specifically to teach skills and concepts, it can be easily modified to teach principles, generalizations, and academic rules as well.

Important Concepts

Automaticity (p. 191)	Skills (p. 191)
Direct-Instruction Model (p. 186)	Task analysis (p. 192)
Modeling (p. 189)	Think alouds (p. 189)
Observational learning (p. 189)	Transfer (p. 192)
Scaffolding (p. 189)	Zone of proximal development (p. 189)

Exercises

1. Consider the following list of goals. Identify those most appropriately reached using the Direct-Instruction Model. The goals are as follows:
   a. To understand "prime number."
   b. To simplify arithmetic expressions following the rule: multiply and divide left to right and then add and subtract left to right.
   c. To understand "square."
   d. To understand "major scale."
   e. To understand "For nonmixing substances, less dense materials float on more dense materials."
   f. To understand "gerund."
   g. To identify the relationships between the economy and geography of the North and South prior to the Civil War and how these factors impacted the outcome of the war.

2. Select a topic in your teaching area. Then prepare a set of examples that could be used to effectively teach the topic.

3. Read the following description of a teacher using the Direct-Instruction Model and then answer the questions that follow.

   Kathe Lake began her language arts class saying, "Today, class, we're going to talk about a different kind of word pair. Who remembers what other word pairs we've been studying? John?"

   "Yesterday we were talking about synonyms," answered John.

   "Good, and who knows what a synonym is? . . . Mary?"

   "Synonyms are word pairs that mean the same thing, like big and large."

   "Very good, Mary. How about another example? . . . Toni?"

". . . Fast and speedy."

"Super! And one more? Bob?"

"How about skinny and thin?"

"Yes, very good example, Bob. Well, today we're going to study a different kind of word pair called antonyms. When we are finished with the lesson today, you will be able to give me some examples of antonyms. Also, when I give you a word you will be able to give me an antonym for it."

She then wrote the following on the board.

Synonyms	Antonyms
(Same Meaning)	(Opposite Meaning)

"Antonyms are word pairs that have opposite meaning. What do we mean by word pairs?" Kathe asked.

Susan hesitated and then said, "I think pair means two."

"Good, Susan," Kathe nodded with a smile. "So word pair means two words. Now, what does opposite mean?"

"It sort of means different or not the same, I think," Joe volunteered.

"That's very close, Joe," said Kathe. She continued, "Let me give you an example. Big and small have opposite meanings and they're two words, so they're antonyms. Opposite means having a different or almost a reversed meaning like big and small."

With that, she wrote big and small under the term *antonym.*

"Another example of antonyms is up and down. They are antonyms because they're pairs of words whose meanings are opposite. So let's put them up here under the antonym column. Let me try another one. Are happy and glad antonyms? Andy?"

"No," replied Andy.

"Why not?" Kathe asked.

"Because the words don't have opposite meanings. They mean the same thing."

"So what are they, Andy?"

"Synonyms."

"Fine, Andy. Let's put them under the synonym column. Now let's try another one. Are cold and hot antonyms? Ted?"

". . . Yes, because they're a word pair, and the words have opposite meanings."

"So, let's put them over here on the board. And what about alive and dead? Pat?"

"Those are antonyms, too, because they mean the opposite."

"Fine. Now I want to see if you can give me some examples of antonyms. Think real hard. Anyone? Lynne?"

"How about in and out?"

"Good. Anyone else? Alta?"

"How about high and low?"

"And why are those antonyms?" asked Kathe.

"Because they are word pairs that have opposite meanings."

"Real fine. Now one last test. Remember we had the word pair happy and glad and you said that they weren't antonyms? Can anyone make antonyms from these words? Jim?"

"How about happy and sad?"

"Good. Sam, do you have another one?"

"Glad and upset."

"Those are both excellent antonyms. I think you've all done a good job today in learning about this new kind of word pair. Now someone tell me what we learned today. Susan?"

". . . Well, we learned about antonyms."

"Good. Go on," Kathe smiled.

"Antonyms mean the opposite."

"Yes, excellent! And one more thing. Brad?"

"They're word pairs."

"Exactly. Very good, Brad."

She then closed the lesson by saying, "Remember, word pairs that mean the same are . . . class?"

"Synonyms!" they responded in unison.

"Fine, and word pairs that are opposite are . . . ?"

"Antonyms!" the class answered.

"Excellent. Now I have some exercises that I would like you to do individually." She then distributed a worksheet to the students and circulated as they began working on it.

a. Identify each of the phases of the Direct-Instruction Model in Kathe Lake's lesson.

b. Consider assessing the abstraction Kathe Lake taught. Prepare a test item that could be used to evaluate the concepts.

c. While Kathe's instruction technically followed the Direct-Instruction Model, we might criticize it on one important basis. Offer that criticism. (Hint: Think about the reference to the work of Brown, Collins, and Duguid [1989], which was first presented in Chapter 3.)

Discussion Questions

1. Compare the Direct-Instruction Model to the Inductive and Concept-Attainment Models. What are the similarities and differences? What are advantages and disadvantages of each?

2. How does the Direct-Instruction Model differ from typical lecture? What are its advantages and disadvantages compared to the lecture method?

3. In the exercises we encouraged an analysis of content that would be effectively taught with the Direct-Instruction Model. Consider now other circumstances that might make a direct-instruction lesson more effective than an Inductive-Model lesson. How do the type of students being taught and goals of the lesson affect this decision?

4. Consider content goals again. How do these goals affect the decision to select the Inductive or Direct-Instruction Model? Discuss this question in terms of the abstraction of the concept or generalization, how "vague" the topic is, and the background of the students.

5. What alternative does the teacher have if he or she reaches the end of a direct-instruction lesson and the students still do not understand the abstraction? How would this compare to an inductive lesson?

6. Compare the amount of teacher talk and student talk in direct instruction compared to an inductive lesson. What conditions could cause these amounts to vary?

7. It could be argued that the emphasis in thinking skills with the Direct-Instruction Model is less than with the Inductive Model. Consider again Karen Hendricks's lesson. How did she promote thinking skills on the part of her students while using the Direct-Instruction Model?

Chapter 7

Teaching Organized Bodies of Knowledge: The Lecture-Discussion Model

As we saw in Chapter 6, the Direct-Instruction Model is designed to teach skills, concepts, principles, and rules, with emphasis on active teaching and high levels of student involvement.

However, as we found in Chapter 5, teachers have many goals that are not the learning of skills, concepts, generalizations, principles, and rules. Goals such as understanding the Revolutionary War in social studies or the respiratory system in health are broader, organized bodies of information, and the Direct-Instruction Model is less effective for reaching these goals. A model is needed that helps students understand both the individual concepts, generalizations, principles, and rules, and the interconnections among them.

In this chapter we discuss the Lecture-Discussion Model, a model designed to help students learn organized bodies of information. The Lecture-Discussion Model takes the strengths of lectures—clear presentation of ideas and economy of effort—and combines them with an interactive format that encourages students to actively construct their own understanding.

When you have completed your study of this chapter you will be able to accomplish the following objectives:

- Describe the theoretical framework of the Lecture-Discussion Model.
- Use the Lecture-Discussion Model to plan for teaching organized bodies of information.
- Construct different kinds of advance organizers.
- Implement lecture-discussion lessons that include all steps.
- Assess content acquisition in lecture-discussion lessons.

Let's begin our study of the Lecture-Discussion Model by looking at a teacher using this model to teach a lesson from a unit on behaviorism in a high school psychology class.

Lorie Martello began her class by saying, "Class, today we are going to continue our discussion of operant conditioning by looking at different reinforcement schedules. I have a problem I'd like you to think about. There was a woman with a dog named Paxie. She wanted to train Paxie to get the newspaper from the lawn and put it on the porch every morning to keep it from getting wet and soggy. Now, she knew that some mornings she wouldn't be home to reward Paxie, but she wanted Paxie to get the paper anyway. What could she do to train her dog? . . . Stop and think about the situation for a moment."

Lorie paused briefly and then continued, "Let's keep the problem in mind and we'll return to it in a moment. For right now, let's review some points that we made yesterday. Who can give us an example of operant conditioning and explain why it's a form of behavioral learning? . . . Bill?"

". . . I . . . I think it's because in operant conditioning we focus on behaviors and rewards that we can see."

"Good, Bill. Now who can describe how it differs from classical conditioning? . . . Jack?"

". . . Well, in classical conditioning the response that the . . . the . . . whoever makes is out of their control, like the dog salivating. In operant conditioning the response is voluntary."

"Can you give us an example of that?" Lorie probed.

". . . Well, my mother always thanks my dad when he helps pick up the kitchen and living room, so he does it more now," Sherry responded hesitantly.

"Also, in classical conditioning the behavior follows the stimulus that influences it, and in operant conditioning the behavior comes before the stimulus, like in . . . reinforcement or punishment," Hakeem volunteered.

"Very good! Now today we're going to focus on one aspect of operant conditioning, which is the system of reinforcers that can be provided for desired behaviors." With that she displayed the following statement on the overhead.

Reinforcement schedules are applications of operant conditioning in which the frequency of rewards is specified. When we reinforce behaviors we can reinforce every time, not at all, or somewhere in between. The somewhere in between can be based on number of responses or time. When we periodically compliment a brother or sister for helping us clean up around the house, we are using a reinforcement schedule.

She then put the following outline on the board.

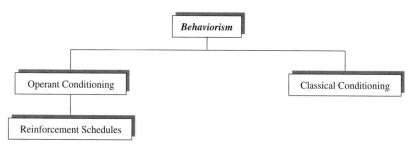

"Before we go on I'd like to talk a little about this statement. If it makes sense to us, it will help us understand the material that follows. The first concept we should focus on is reinforcement. Remember we said that reinforcement is an increase in behavior resulting from some desired consequence, such as a compliment for a person or a doggy treat for a dog.

"Now, we can decide to reinforce a behavior every time it occurs or only part of the time. That's what we mean by frequency or interval. So, if we're trying to train a dog to shake hands, we can reward it every time it does this or every other time or even some sort of random pattern. That's what we mean by frequency.

"Another way to reinforce is by time. Let's say we want to train a dog to stay on the porch. We could reward it every 15 seconds, every 30 seconds, or every minute it stays on the porch. That's what we mean by interval.

"Now, let's focus on this outline. What can you conclude based on it? . . . Jim?"

". . . Well, apparently reinforcement schedules only go with operant conditioning," Jim responded, "because we only see them under it and not under classical conditioning."

"Excellent, Jim. That's exactly right. Now look at the statement on the overhead again. It talks about rewards for desired behavior. This means that the reward comes after the organism has responded, so it's an operant kind of conditioning. Now, let's go on and focus on the rewards. What does the statement suggest about reinforcement schedules? . . . Juan?"

". . . They describe how often the person, or I guess even animals, get rewarded."

"Good, Juan, and what would continuous reinforcement mean? . . . Sandy?"

". . . I guess when they get a reward every time they did what you wanted," Sandy replied after thinking a moment.

"Excellent, Sandy. Now give us an example of that, . . . Susan."

". . . I guess it would be like every time Paxie brought the paper, he would get a doggy biscuit."

"Fine, Susan, and so now you can draw in your notes this outline."

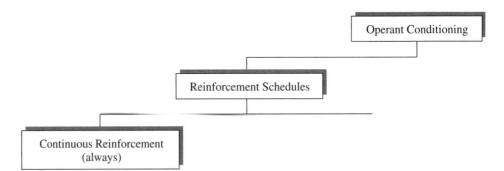

"And what do we have at the other end of the continuum? What happens when a behavior is never reinforced? Shanelle?"

". . . The dog or person or whatever would stop the behavior after a while."

"Excellent, Shanelle. That's called extinction. Let's put that up on our outline too."

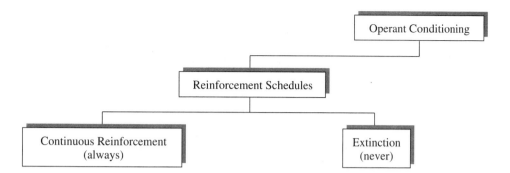

"How do continuous reinforcement and extinction compare?" Lorie continued.

"They're . . . like opposite of each other," Judy volunteered. "At one end you get reinforced for everything, and at the other, you don't get reinforced for anything."

"Let's look again at our statement," Lorie went on. "It said that a reinforcement schedule is the frequency or interval of rewards. How do the two items on our outline relate to the statement? . . . Nikki?"

". . . In the first case the frequency is high and in the second, it's low . . . actually doesn't exist," Nikki responded.

"Excellent, Nikki. So we see that both are forms of reinforcement schedules because they both describe a frequency of rewards. Now let's add intermittent reinforcement to our outline and define it as a schedule in which behavior is reinforced some of the time."

After writing the definition on the board, she continued, "There are two main kinds of intermittent-reinforcement schedules that depend on how the reinforcer is delivered. They are called ratio or interval schedules. Let's talk about ratio schedules first. In a ratio schedule the organism has to produce a certain number of responses before it is reinforced. It's like piecework in a factory. Who knows how that works? . . . Gerry?"

". . . Well, my dad works in a factory that has piecework, and he gets paid based on how many cars they make in a day."

"Good, Gerry. That would be an example of a ratio schedule. Who can give us an example from the Skinner box that we saw in the lab? . . . Latinda?"

". . . It would be like having a cat get rewarded for some number of times it pressed the bar."

"Fine, Latinda. Now let's compare intermittent and continuous reinforcement. Kathy?"

"I think it's kind of simple," Kathy answered. "Every behavior is rewarded with continuous reinforcement, but only some are with intermittent reinforcement."

"Good, Kathy. And, class, how does this type of reinforcement influence behavior? Kwan?

" . . . "

"Let's compare it to continuous," Lorie prompted. "Do you think the rate of response would be greater or less?"

". . . Greater."

"Why?"

". . . Because the rat would have to press faster or more times to get the reward and wouldn't take as much time off to eat it."

"Good answer, Kwan. And what would happen if we stopped reinforcing with an intermittent schedule? Would the behavior stop quicker or slower than with continuous reinforcement and why? . . . Dan?"

". . . I think . . . faster because the behavior isn't as firmly established."

"Sarah? You have your hand up."

"I think slower because the cat is used to not being reinforced."

"Interesting. We have two different predictions. What about our work with classical conditioning? Does that help us out any?"

The lesson continued as the students discussed the question of whether or not a continuous or an intermittent schedule would result in the most enduring behaviors. Lorie then moved to the topics of variable- and fixed-ratio schedules and a discussion of fixed- and variable-interval schedules. The period ended with Lorie using the following outline to review the major concepts discussed during the period.

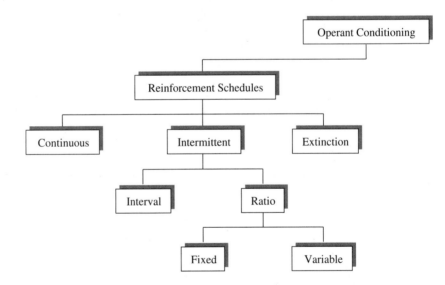

The Lecture-Discussion Model: An Overview

In the lesson we just saw, Lorie Martello used the Lecture-Discussion Model to help her students understand the connections among ideas within the topic of behaviorism. In implementing the model she first provided an overview that would serve as a framework for new information. She then introduced new concepts and helped the students link them to each other and to the content they already understood. Throughout the lesson, Lorie used questioning extensively to monitor the students' understanding and to prevent them from learning the concepts as isolated ideas. Finally, she further integrated the topics with a careful review and closure. These stages of the Lecture-Discussion Model are summarized in Table 7.1

TABLE 7.1   Structure of the Lecture Discussion Model

Stage	Function
Introduction	The purpose of the lesson is described, objectives are shared and an overview helps students see the organization of the lesson.
Presentation	Major ideas are defined and explained.
Comprehension Monitoring	The teacher determines whether or not students understand concepts and ideas.
Integration	Interconnections between important ideas are explored.
Review and closure	The lesson is carefully summarized.

The Lecture-Discussion Model: Theoretical Perspectives

The effectiveness of the Lecture-Discussion model comes from three sources. First, it is intended to utilize what students already know by building on their existing background. Second, based on the work of David Ausubel (1963, 1968), teachers using the model present information in a systematic way, which helps students construct their understanding of the topic. Finally, it uses teacher questioning to actively involve students in the learning process. We examine each of these underpinnings in the sections that follow.

Schema Theory: Building on Students' Background Knowledge

Schema theory *is a theoretical view of knowledge construction that says that the information people store in memory consists of networks of organized and interconnected ideas, relationships, and procedures* (Good and Brophy, 1994). *The interconnected ideas, relationships, and procedures are called* **schemata** (singular form is schema) (Anderson, 1990). For example, let's take the schema for the process of learning. This schema has information in it about learning in general and other more specific information about learning in school. It helps us understand how to dress, when to go to school, what to do when we get there, and how to act toward the teacher and the other students. Within it, even more specific procedures for specific learning situations such as lecture, discussion, or group work are embedded.

The beginnings of schema theory have been traced to the eighteenth century when the philosopher Kant described the mind as actively using schemata to guide perception and categorize information (Rumelhart, 1980). Contemporary interest in the concept of schemata goes back to the 1920s and the work of the psychologist F.C. Bartlett (1932). Bartlett was interested in the processes involved in remembering information from written passages. To examine these processes, he asked subjects to read passages about Indian folklore and to recall information from them at different times. His results were unexpected. First, he found that even with immediate recall, individuals remembered different parts of the stories. Also, because they interpreted the stories from their own frames of reference, they changed the facts to make them fit these reference frames. As time went on, subjects' distortions of the stories increased, but the distortions invariably were linked in such a way that the information was meaningful to the subjects themselves.

From the results, Bartlett concluded that there exists a strong drive in people to make sense of what they encounter. (This is related to the need for structure we discussed in Chapter 3.) In addition, he accounted for the personal and idiosyncratic nature of the distortions through the idea of individual schemata; each person was making sense of the passages based on the way his or her prior experiences were mentally organized. Let's see how this works. Read the following passage and answer the questions that follow.

> In 1367 Marain and the settlements ended a seven-year war with the Langurians and Pitoks. As a result of this war Languria was driven out of East Bacol. Marain would now rule Laman and other lands that had belonged to Languria. This brought peace to the Bacolian settlements. The settlers no longer had to fear attacks from Laman. The Bacolians were happy to be part of Marain in 1367. Yet a dozen years later, these same people would be fighting the Marish for independence, or freedom from United Marain's rule (Beck and McKeown, 1993, p. 2).

What is happening here? How much sense does the passage make? Let's try another passage.

> In 1763 Britain and the colonies ended a seven-year war with the French and Indians. As a result of this war France was driven out of North America. Britain would now rule Canada and other lands that had belonged to France. This brought peace to the American colonies. The colonists no longer had to fear attacks from Canada. The Americans were happy to be a part of Britain in 1763. Yet a dozen years later, these same people would be fighting the British for independence, or freedom from Great Britain's rule (Beck and McKeown, 1993, p. 2).

If you're like most other readers, the second passage made more sense than the first, even though both were similar in their length, structure, and amount of detail. The second was more meaningful because you were able to use your background knowledge or schema about the Revolutionary War to help integrate the separate facts.

A parallel situation exists in every classroom. As students enter classes with widely varying beliefs, attitudes, and background knowledge, they bring with them diverse schemata. They read the same account of the Vietnam War and some go away convinced of the need at that time for a strong stand against communism, while others interpret the passage as an example of a super power trying to exercise control over a basically internal struggle.

From these examples we can see that schemata have three major characteristics (Rumelhart and Ortony, 1977). First, each contains material determined by the person's past experiences. What do you know about soccer? What happens at dog shows? Your response to these questions provides some indication of the quality of your schemata for the topics and your past experiences with them. Second, each schema is embedded in other larger schemata and has other schemata embedded within it, such as schemata for learning in school embedded in larger schemata for learning in general. This embeddedness allows us to link schemata together to help us make sense of the world.

Third, schemata are active. They are constantly being evaluated based on their ability to explain the way the world works. When they make sense, they don't need to change; when they don't, we are motivated to adjust them (Eggen and Kauchak, 1994). For example, when we blow between two pieces of paper held parallel to each other, we expect the bottoms to fly apart. Instead they come together. For most people, this event can't be explained with existing schemata, and we are motivated to understand why. With additional experience we adapt our schemata to accommodate the principle, "Increasing the speed of air (or other fluids) over a surface decreases the force on that surface." This makes our entire schemata richer and more powerful, because we can now explain events such as how airplanes can fly, why tornados are so destructive, how atomizers work, why shower curtains wrap around our legs, and many others.

The process of learning can be thought of as the development of schemata that allow individuals to understand and function in their world. We can view teaching as a deliberate attempt to influence the content and structure of student schemata. In doing so we must keep in mind that students' preexisting schemata can either be liabilities or assets; they can either assist or hinder the new learning.

Let's see how Lorie Martello applied schema theory in her lesson on reinforcement schedules. She was attempting to aid the students in their development of organized schemata about operant conditioning by systematically introducing the subordinate concepts related to reinforcement schedules and displaying them in a hierarchy. She began by having them compare operant and classical conditioning to take advantage of a larger schema into which the present one would fit. Seeing reinforcement schedules under operant conditioning helped students avoid confusing operant and classical conditioning. Further, she called for and got examples of classical and operant conditioning to ensure that the background of the learners was developed enough to allow the lesson to move toward a discussion of reinforcement schedules.

As she introduced new concepts, she used the outline and examples to help students link them to their developing schemata. She also compared each concept to the others to be sure that they were connected.

Meaningful Verbal Learning: The Work of David Ausubel

One of the most influential people in bringing the ideas behind schema theory to classrooms was a psychologist named David Ausubel. Beginning with studies done in the early 1960s and captured in his book *The Psychology of Meaningful Verbal Learning* (1963), Ausubel stressed the importance of cognitive structures on learning.

Ausubel placed heavy emphasis on **meaningful verbal learning**, that is, *the acquisition of ideas that are linked to other ideas*. In contrast, **rote learning** *emphasizes the memorization of specific items of information rather than exploring relationships within the material*. Meaningful learning occurs when the ideas in a new schema are connected not only to each other but also to previously established schemata.

One other characteristic of Ausubel's theory should be stressed. Though he favored teacher-centered, deductively sequenced teaching sessions, he was adamantly opposed to passive learning on the part of students. An important task for the teacher is to involve the students in finding relationships between old and new content and among the different parts of the new topic.

One of the most prominent ideas to have emerged from Ausubel's work is the concept of *advance organizers*. Let's look at this concept now.

Advance Organizers

Advance organizers *are verbal statements at the beginning of a lesson that preview and structure the new material and link it to the students' existing schemata.* In this sense, advance organizers are like cognitive road maps; they allow students to see where they have been and where they are going.

Effective advance organizers:

- are presented prior to learning a larger body of information.
- are written in paragraph form.
- are written in concrete fashion.
- are designed to include an example that helps learners identify the relationship between the ideas in the organizer and the information to follow (Corkill, 1992).

To illustrate how advance organizers work, let's look at two that have been used at different levels of school. The first is from an elementary social studies lesson on governments.

The organization of a government is like a family. Different people in the government have different responsibilities and roles. When all the people work together, both families and governments operate efficiently.

The second involves college students studying linguistics.

We all use language every day. And yet, unless we are writing papers for a course or completing an assignment in English class, we generally give language very little thought. There are people who study language, much as there are scholars who study other important areas of life. These students of language analyze our language in ways that are far more complex than the sentence diagramming most of us have done. Not only do they study how the written language works, they also examine how it is generated. These language scholars also study spoken language—how it is learned, how people use it to share meaning with other people, and what the various parts of the spoken language are. In addition, the study of language relates what is known about spoken and written language.

Another point of interest in the study of language comes from comparing different languages (e.g., English and Spanish). Just as sociologists compare life in different cultures and anthropologists study the origin of cultures, the scholars of language compare different languages in terms of how they evolved and how they are now written and spoken. The scholars you will read about believe that the study of language can shed light on how people think and how human ideas have evolved. As is the case in any field such as law, education, or science, there are some basic conventions or rules that all who study language agree on. The chapter you are about to read explains the study of language and the rules followed by people in this profession (Dinnel and Glover, 1985, p. 521).

Both of these advance organizers attempted to provide a framework for new content. The second one is obviously longer and more detailed because it was designed for college students.

Differences between these advance organizers illustrate one other important feature: they must be tailored to the learner to be effective (Ausubel, 1978). The exact form that an advance organizer takes depends on: (1) the type of content; (2) the age of the learner; and (3) how familiar the students are with the learning material. Ways of constructing advance organizers based on these principles are discussed in the planning section of this chapter.

Active Learner Involvement

A third principle that increases the effectiveness of the Lecture-Discussion Model is its involvement of students through teacher questioning. As the name implies, lecture-discussions are based on the strengths of lectures, but build on these strengths by adding some of the positive features of discussions. In this section we'll examine the strengths and weaknesses of lectures and see how the Lecture-Discussion Model accommodates some of the weaknesses of lectures.

Lectures: Teacher Monologues

A **lecture** *is a form of instruction in which students passively receive information delivered in a (presumably) organized way by teachers.* Lectures have been a mainstay of instruction over the years, and they continue to be one of the most widely used instructional strategies in classrooms (Cuban, 1984). The popularity of lectures can be traced to three factors (Eggen and Kauchak, 1994):

- Lectures are economical in terms of planning; energy can be devoted to organizing content.
- Lectures are flexible; they can be applied to most, if not all, content areas.
- Lectures are relatively simple to implement; at their most basic level they involve presentation of content.

Despite these advantages, lectures have two important problems, which make them ineffective for many students. First, they promote passive learning, encouraging students to merely listen and absorb information, but not necessarily interrelate ideas. Lectures are usually monologues in which the teacher talks and students listen.

Research on young (Berk, 1994) and poorly motivated students (Brophy, 1986) indicates that passive listening is one of the most ineffective ways to transmit information. Watch a class of six or seven year olds during any kind of presentation where they're expected to be passive. At first they sit quietly, but soon they start to fidget and look around. If the monologue continues, they not only tune out, but start talking and poking each other, seeking some type of activity.

Older, poorly motivated students are often less disruptive during lectures than younger students, but little more learning takes place. Because they've learned that fidgeting and talking can get them into trouble, they may feign interest by propping their heads on their hands and attempting to make eye contact. Harder cases give up completely and work on homework for other classes, read, or put their heads down on their desks. Unfortunately, we've seen a number of teachers continue to lecture in spite of these nonverbal signals indicating that few are listening or learning.

The second problem with lectures is that they do not allow teachers to assess students' understanding or learning progress. During interactive lessons, teachers informally assess student understanding by asking questions. Because communication is one way in lectures, teachers have no way of making these assessments.

The ineffectiveness of lecture as a teaching method is well documented. In seven comparisons of lecture to discussion, discussion was superior in all seven on measures of retention and higher-order thinking. In addition, discussion was superior in seven of nine studies on measures of student attitude and motivation (McKeachie and Kulik, 1975). The fact that lectures require the students to be passive is the major reason for these differences.

The Lecture-Discussion Model is designed to overcome these deficiencies by requiring the active involvement of learners. This involvement requires them to build on their existing schemata and integrate new knowledge with old. Through questioning, teachers not only encourage student involvement but also monitor learning progress, allowing teachers to adapt their presentations if necessary. We turn now to planning for lecture-discussion lessons.

Planning for Lecture-Discussion Lessons

In the previous sections we discussed schema theory and the implications of this theory for teaching. In addition, we discussed the work of David Ausubel in the area of meaningful verbal learning and the need for active student involvement in learning activities.

In this section we discuss the planning for individual lessons, incorporating the content of that lesson into existing schemata. In addition, we discuss how to construct advance organizers, structure content, and plan for the use of questioning during the lesson.

Identifying Goals

In beginning the planning for lecture-discussion lessons, as with any lesson, the teacher first considers goals. The Lecture-Discussion Model is similar to the Integrative Model, because both are designed to teach organized bodies of knowledge, but it differs from the Integrative Model in that the process is more expository and deductive rather than inductive.

The model can be effectively used in classrooms in two ways. First, it can be used to organize content for an entire course, a unit within a course, or a single lesson. Teachers can use it to help them decide on the scope and sequence of the content, and it can guide the students in their progress throughout the material.

Second, the model can be used to help students make information they've already learned more meaningful. To illustrate this process let's consider again Lorie Martello's lesson. Using the model, she helped students understand the interconnections between the concepts of operant and classical conditioning, continuous reinforcement, extinction, and intermittent reinforcement.

Lorie was both clear and organized in her planning. She first planned to make sure that individual concepts were clear, and then planned to help students see the relationships among the concepts that would help them form valid understandings (schemata).

The same process would apply in other classrooms. To see how this might look in a geography class, look at Figure 7.1.

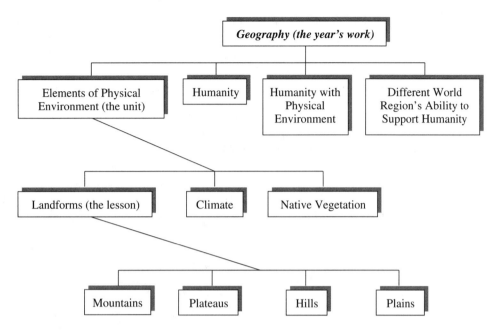

FIGURE 7.1 **Organization of Content in Geography**

From the diagram we see the model's two functions illustrated. First, the Lecture-Discussion Model was used as a guide for long-range planning for the year's work on geography and a smaller unit on elements of the physical environment. Second, it was used to relate concepts in a single lesson focusing on landforms. The focus of the lesson was to understand the characteristics of the different landforms and form an overall structure of these landforms. The model was used both to organize content and to teach specific topics.

Diagnosing Students' Backgrounds

In planning for a lecture-discussion lesson it is essential to consider what students already know. Their backgrounds provide the foundation for new learning and provide links or hooks to which new knowledge is connected.

Pretesting the students is an obvious way to assess their background knowledge. However, preparing frequent pretests is demanding and time consuming, and most teachers look for simpler and more efficient ways of learning about the students' backgrounds.

A second way of informally assessing students is to ask them to list, group, and label ideas related to a concept (Taba, 1966, 1967). Using this strategy the teacher would first ask, "What comes to mind when I say the word . . . ? Let's write down everything we can think of when we see the word." The concept would be the focus of an upcoming unit or lesson (e.g., landforms, reptiles, novels, etc.). The responses the students make give the teacher some insight into their understanding of the topic.

The process can be extended by asking the students to group the ideas they've listed and attach a label to the categories. Again, quality of classifications gives the teacher some information about the students' background knowledge.

A slightly more complicated process for assessing students' backgrounds asks students to first define as many of the terms on the board that they can (Champagne, Klopfer, Solomon, and Cahn, 1980). Then, students are asked to explain the relationships among the terms. The combination of the two tasks provides a fairly accurate description of their backgrounds. While conducting the exercise in writing is demanding because the teacher must collect the papers and give the students some form of feedback, having the students first complete it and then report orally would be reasonably efficient.

Perhaps the simplest way to informally assess the students' backgrounds is by reviewing the background material. (Remember that in Chapter 2 we identified review as one of the essential teaching skills.) The process takes little time and if the teacher gets responses from a variety of students, it is a reasonably accurate assessment of their backgrounds. This is the process Lorie Martello used in her lesson. As another example, a teacher in the lesson on landforms might list the concepts on the board and ask the students to give examples, if possible, or describe them in their own words.

One disadvantage of these informal assessments is that the more knowledgeable and outspoken students may dominate, giving the teacher a false impression of the overall knowledge of the class. The teacher must be careful to get responses from enough students to be as sure as possible that the information he or she is getting is representative of the class as a whole.

The results of such diagnoses help teachers decide which topics must receive the most time and effort, how rapidly the material can be covered, and how the content must be structured to make it as meaningful as possible. These are the topics of the next sections.

Structuring Content

After goals for the unit or lesson have been identified and the students' backgrounds have been assessed, the next planning step is to structure the content so that it is as meaningful as possible for the students.

One effective way to structure content is to use hierarchies. A number of topics are hierarchical, and for those that aren't, a hierarchical form of structuring can often be imposed. Also, preparing hierarchies is fairly simple, and the relationships in them are clear. For these reasons we will examine hierachies first; for example, a lesson on mammals could be structured according to taxonomic description. The structure of such a lesson might appear as shown in Figure 7.2.

The real number system is also hierarchically structured, as illustrated in Figure 7.3.

In many cases where the material doesn't have a natural structure, the teacher can easily impose structure on it. For example, a social studies topic on community helpers might be structured as Figure 7.4 shows.

Structuring the content in this way allows students to see the relationship of community helpers to each other as well as their relationship to the general idea of community helpers. Here we see that a hierarchical structure was imposed on the topic.

Another way of imposing a hierarchy on the content is through the use of interrelated generalizations. An example would be to structure a lesson around generalizations such as, "America has expanded because of natural resources, form of government, and a unique

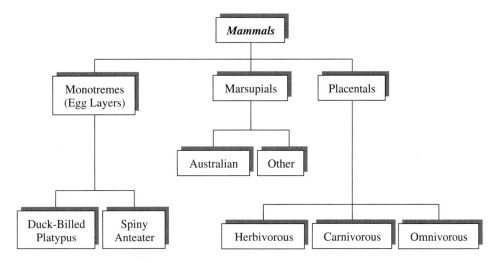

FIGURE 7.2   Hierarchy for Organizing Information on Mammals

mixture of people." The structure that evolved from this generalization might appear as shown in Figure 7.5.

Again, with this form of structure, the generalization is broken down into narrower topics, and these are either illustrated with examples or further broken down into subordinate concepts.

An extended analogy is a third way of using hierarchies. For example, the structure for a lesson using the solar system as an analogy for the structure of an atom might appear as shown in Figure 7.6.

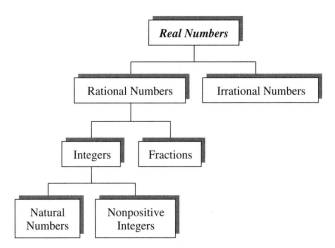

FIGURE 7.3   Hierarchy for Organizing the Real Number System

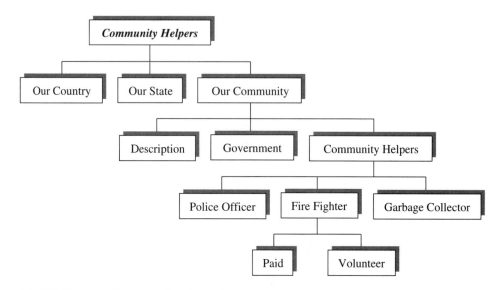

FIGURE 7.4   Hierarchy for Organizing Community Helpers

We discuss the use of analogies in more detail when we discuss the construction of advance organizers.

In each of the above cases, hierarchies have been used to impose a form of structure on the content. Structure can be imposed in a variety of other ways as well. Outlines, models, graphs, maps, and matrices all impose structure on content. For example, the outlines that we have included at the beginning of each chapter of this book are attempts to structure the content of each chapter to make it as meaningful as possible for you. Figure 2.3

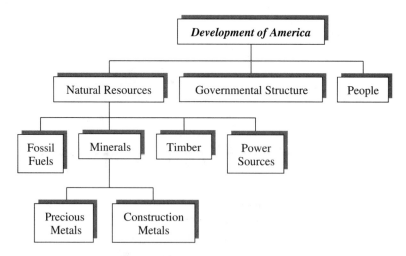

FIGURE 7.5   Hierarchy for Organizing Generalizations

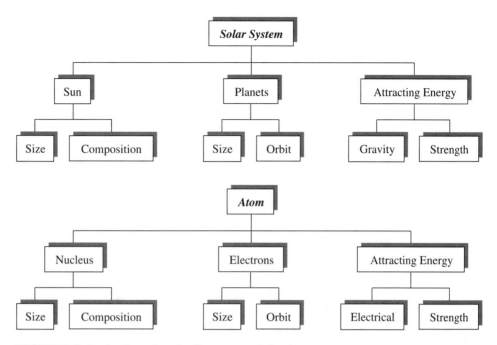

FIGURE 7.6   Analogy for the Structure of the Atom

on page 47 is a hierarchy for types of conclusions that is an attempt to make the information meaningful by providing both a verbal and visual form of structure. The matrices you saw in Chapter 5 are all forms of structuring content.

In many cases teachers will combine different forms of structure to help organize their lessons. For instance, a teacher doing a unit on the Civil War might use a hierarchy to structure the content for the unit. The hierarchy would include elements such as causes of the war, significant battles and events during the war, outcomes from the war, and how the war still affects us today. A lesson or lessons on the causes of the war would probably include a map showing the northern and southern colonies together with a matrix or outline examining the geography and economics of the North and the South. Significant battles and events could be structured with a matrix, and outcomes might be structured with a matrix, outline, or some other organizer. There is no single best way to structure the content, and the form used is a matter of professional judgment. The key in structuring the content is to make the relationships as clear as possible, which in turn makes the topic meaningful for the students.

In all cases, when teachers are structuring their material, they must keep the students' backgrounds in mind. For example, if "modern capitalist democratic countries" are part of the content, and the students don't understand terms such as capitalist and democratic, the teacher's planning must include ways of illustrating these concepts. Otherwise, the entire lesson or even unit will be less meaningful to the students.

Preparing Advance Organizers

An additional way to promote learning in lecture-discussions is through advance organizers. We have already discussed the concept of advance organizers as they relate to Ausubel's theory of meaningful verbal learning. We now want to describe advance organizers in a bit more detail and apply their use to classrooms.

As we saw earlier in the chapter, an advance organizer is a statement preceding a lesson that is designed to preview the material and link it to content that learners already understand. It is more general and abstract than the content to be structured and subsumes the material that follows. For example, Lorie Martello's advance organizer was:

> Reinforcement schedules are applications of operant conditioning in which the frequency of rewards is specified. When we reinforce behaviors, we can reinforce every time, not at all, or somewhere in between. The somewhere in between can be based on number of responses or time. When we periodically compliment a brother or sister for helping us clean up around the house, we are using a reinforcement schedule.

Notice that this organizer was presented at the beginning of the lesson, it was more general than the content that followed, it was written in paragraph form, and it contained a concrete example—complimenting a brother or sister—that helped the students identify the relationship between the ideas in the organizer and the information in the lesson. These are the characteristics of effective organizers that Corkill (1992) identified.

Implementing Lecture-Discussion Lessons

Having identified goals, diagnosed students' background knowledge, structured content, and prepared an advance organizer, the teacher is prepared to implement the lesson.

As described in the introduction to this chapter, the Lecture-Discussion Model has five steps:

1. Introduction
2. Presentation
3. Comprehension Monitoring
4. Integration
5. Review and Closure

We discuss implementation of each of these individual steps in the sections that follow.

Introduction

The introduction phase of a lecture-discussion lesson includes three elements, which are:

- Introductory Focus
- Stating Lesson Objectives
- Overview

These elements are outlined in Table 7.2.

TABLE 7.2   Components of the Introduction to Lecture-Discussion Lessons

Component	Function
Introductory focus	Draws students into the lesson
Stating Lesson Objectives	Identifies important learning goals
Overview	Provides overview of topic and shows how major concepts are interrelated

Introductory Focus

When we begin lessons or make transitions from one lesson to another, we often incorrectly assume that students have the ability or inclination to focus their attention on the topic at hand. In one study of elementary classrooms, researchers found that only 5% of the teachers being observed made an explicit effort to draw students into the lesson (Anderson, Brubaker, Alleman-Brooks, and Duffy, 1985).

To draw students into a lesson, teachers use the essential teaching skill **introductory focus**, which we defined in Chapter 2 *as the set of teacher actions at the beginning of lessons that attracts students' attention and pulls them into the lesson.* Also called anticipatory set (Hunter, 1984), introductory focus alerts students that a transition is taking place and provides something tangible and interesting about which to think. Lorie Martello did this when she posed the problem about training her dog to get the newspaper. Other forms of introductory focus are summarized in Table 7.3.

What is common to each of these strategies is that the teacher makes a conscious attempt at the beginning of the lesson to attract and maintain students' attention.

While introductory focus is important for any teaching strategy, it is particularly important when the Lecture-Discussion Model is used because, unlike the Inductive, Concept-Attainment, and Integrative Models, the learning activity begins with the teacher presenting information. If the students are not focused on the topic at the beginning of the lesson, the information that follows will be much less meaningful.

TABLE 7.3   Types of Introductory Focus

Type of Introductory Focus	Example
Discrepant (Counterintuitive Events)	An ice cube is placed in a glass of water and floats, and a second cube is dropped in pure alcohol (which students often believe is water) and it sinks
Personalization	A lesson on genetics begins with the teacher identifying a student with blue eyes and "guessing" the eye color of the parents.
Examples	A lesson on adverbs begins with an overhead with sentences containing colorful adverbs
Demonstration	A teacher begins a lesson on electromagnetism by showing how a magnet can penetrate certain substances (e.g., paper) and not others (e.g., a sheet of metal).

Objectives

As we saw with the Direct-Instruction Model, objectives help students identify the important points in a lesson—what they should know and be able to do when the lesson is over. Sharing objectives is especially important because the content taught with the Lecture-Discussion Model focuses on organized bodies of knowledge, which by their nature are less precise than concepts, generalizations, principles, and rules. Research indicates that objectives help learners focus on important ideas that are part of large bodies of information (Klauer, 1984).

Overview

The overview in a lecture-discussion lesson takes two forms. The lesson structure—hierarchy, model, outline, matrix, etc.—provides a means for identifying the relationships among the major ideas; the advance organizer provides a link between old and new content.

A common mistake teachers make is to present the lesson structure and advance organizer and then ignore it as the lesson develops. If our goal is to have students understand relationships among ideas, they must be reminded of these relationships throughout the lesson. Putting the hierarchy, model, etc., and advance organizer on an overhead or on the board at the beginning of the lesson and periodically referring to them can help meet this goal. Lorie displayed her hierarchy and advance organizer at the beginning of the lesson and kept them in front of the students throughout.

Presentation

After the introduction, the lesson proceeds with the teacher using the advance organizer and hierarchy or other form of structure as reference points. Lorie displayed her advance organizer and the first part of her hierarchy and then carefully described the content, dividing behaviorism into operant and classical conditioning. She then moved to reinforcement schedules as a part of operant conditioning and divided reinforcement schedules into continuous reinforcement, intermittent reinforcement, and extinction. As she made her presentation, she added the concepts to the hierarchy that she used to structure her content. All of her descriptions followed the hierarchy and each concept was linked to her advance organizer.

The value of this presentation format relates to schema theory and the relationships among ideas. Broader concepts are used as the foundations for new concepts, and as students learn the new concepts, they are connected to the broad ones; they are not learned in isolation. Knowledge is cumulative and the outcome is an interconnected set of ideas.

How long should this presenting of information last before the teacher uses questions to check the students' comprehension? Experience suggests that it should be short—literally a few minutes.

Teachers continually overestimate the listening capacities of their students. Before a recent Superbowl football game advertisers were concerned whether ninety-second commercials would be too long to hold viewers' attention. Ninety seconds! Compare this with the length of some lectures. Research indicates that retention rates drop sharply after the beginning of a lecture (Gage and Berliner, 1992). Student inattention and information overload are likely explanations. (Remember in Chapter 2 where we said that the capacity of working memory is limited? It's easy to overload learners' working memories, and when this happens, information is lost rather than encoded into long-term memory.) Comprehension monitoring through teacher questioning is one way to prevent or minimize this problem.

Comprehension Monitoring

Comprehension monitoring *is the process of informally assessing student understanding in lecture-discussion lessons,* and it is usually accomplished through teacher questioning. It is critical because it promotes student involvement and gives the students feedback about their understanding.

How often should comprehension monitoring occur? While technically the answer depends on the difficulty of the content and the development of the students, it rarely can be done too frequently. First, it's easy for lecture-discussion lessons to disintegrate into teacher monologues. Second, it's difficult for students to be too involved in a lesson, and third, students need constant feedback and teachers need to continually assess their students' understanding.

To see how quickly Lorie moved to the comprehension-monitoring phase of the lesson, let's look again at her initial presentation.

> The first concept we should focus on is reinforcement. Remember we said that reinforcement is an increase in behavior resulting from some desired consequence, such as a compliment for a person or a doggy treat for a dog.
>
> Now, we can decide to reinforce a behavior every time it occurs or only part of the time. That's what we mean by frequency or interval. So, if we're trying to train a dog to shake hands, we can reward it every time it does this or every other time or even some sort of random pattern. That's what we mean by frequency.
>
> Another way to reinforce is by time. Let's say we want to train a dog to stay on the porch. We could reward it every 15 seconds, every 30 seconds, or every minute it stays on the porch. That's what we mean by interval.
>
> Now, let's focus on this outline. What can you conclude based on the outline? . . . Jim?

In an actual classroom, her description would have taken no more than a couple of minutes. This is, indeed, a very short presentation time compared to some of the teacher monologues that we've all experienced.

The importance of the comprehension-monitoring phase is based on schema theory. Since learners bring with them diverse schemata, and all new learning will be interpreted in the context of prior understanding, the students will interpret the information teachers present in a variety of ways. If their interpretations are invalid, their entire new schemata will be distorted. To determine whether or not the students are interpreting the information accurately, teachers must check the students' understanding of the information.

Integration

Questions perform another important function when the Lecture-Discussion Model is used. Remember that the model is designed to teach interrelationships in organized bodies of knowledge. The way teachers accomplish this goal is to first present information in a systematic way and then check the students' comprehension of the information.

Simple monitoring of comprehension isn't enough, however; integration is required. **Integration** *is the process of linking new information to prior learning and linking different parts of new learning to each other.* If new knowledge isn't integrated with old, and the parts of the new information aren't integrated with each other, the goal of understanding interrelationships won't be reached.

As with monitoring comprehension, teachers use questioning to encourage integration. Questions can encourage vertical integration by asking students to link superordinate with subordinate concepts, such as Lorie asking students to explain why operant conditioning is a form of behaviorism. (Her vertical integration would have been more complete if she had also asked why classical conditioning was a form of behaviorism.)

Questions can also encourage horizontal integration—most commonly by asking students to describe the similarities and differences among coordinate ideas, or by simply asking students to describe how different ideas relate to each other. (Remember also from Chapter 2 that we found identifying similarities and differences to be an important higher-order thinking skill.) Identifying differences helps specify what makes each idea distinct, such as knowing that the behavior is involuntary in a classical conditioning example but is voluntary in the case of operant conditioning. Identifying similarities helps specify important relationships, such as both classical and operant conditioning illustrating a relationship between behavior and the influence of the environment.

Lorie encouraged horizontal integration in two important places. In addition to having the students compare classical and operant conditioning, later in the lesson she had them describe the similarities and differences among the reinforcement schedules.

We saw the process of integration at two different points in Lorie's lesson. In classrooms it should take place whenever new ideas are introduced. As teachers get comfortable with the model, knowing when to check for comprehension and promote integration by asking for similarities and differences will become nearly automatic.

Review and Closure

Review and closure are essential for any lesson, as we saw in Chapter 2. They are particularly important when the Lecture-Discussion Model is used because review and closure further promote integration. Review summarizes the topic, emphasizes important points, and provides a link to new learning. Although it is appropriate at any point in a learning activity, it is most commonly used at the beginnings and ends of lessons. Lorie reviewed at the beginning of her lesson to remind students of the larger topic of behaviorism and to ensure that new information was embedded in that content.

As we saw in Chapter 2, closure is a form of review that occurs at the end of a lesson; it summarizes, structures, and completes the topic. Lorie brought her lesson to closure when she used her outline to provide an overview of the major concepts studied.

Variations of the Model

In the preceding sections we described the primary purpose of the Lecture-Discussion Model as helping learners form schemata by finding relationships between old and new

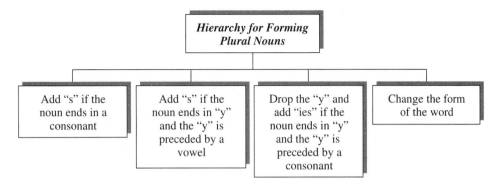

FIGURE 7.7   **Hierarchy for Rules in Forming Singular and Plural Possessives**

learning and among the different parts of an organized body of knowledge—such as rein-forcement schedules in Lorie Martello's lesson. Within this general framework, however, the model can be used to organize content in a number of ways. One of these is the use of "mini" hierarchies to supplement other models. For example, think about Jim Rooney's lesson on the rules for forming singular and plural possessives in Chapter 3. At some point in the lesson a hierarchy identifying the relationships among the different parts of the rules would make the material more meaningful for the students. The hierarchy might appear as shown in Figure 7.7.

Using this hierarchy would help the students see the relationships among the different parts of the rule. It gives a visual illustration of when the apostrophe appears before the *s*, when it is used after the *s*, and why no apostrophe is used in some cases.

As another example, consider a teacher discussing the topic of closure in mathematics. (An operation is considered to be closed if the outcome of the operation produces a num-ber that belongs to the same set as the numbers combined in the operation.) A discussion of the topic could be supplemented with a brief hierarchy such as the one shown in Figure 7.8.

This outline is also interesting in that it implies a pattern; the number of closed oper-ations increases as we go from counting to rational numbers. The students could then be encouraged to hypothesize on the basis of the pattern and test their hypotheses with other

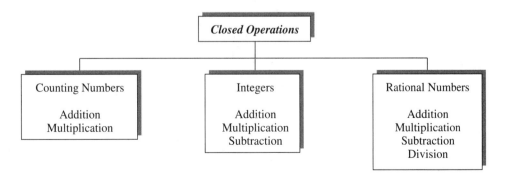

FIGURE 7.8   **Hierarchy for Representing Closure in Mathematical Operations**

numbers and sets. In this way the hierarchy, in addition to helping make the concepts more meaningful, could provide an avenue for promoting higher-order and critical thinking.

As teachers use hierarchies to supplement lessons, they uncover other opportunities to enhance their students' learning. We are presenting these examples in the hope that they might further stimulate your thinking about the uses of the Lecture-Discussion Model.

A second option that takes advantage of the organizing powers of the Lecture-Discussion Model uses hierarchies in conjunction with matrices. (Remember some of the matrices we saw in Chapter 5.)

As an example, consider the outline in Figure 7.9 used with a unit of study on the novel

The advantage of an outline such as this is that it shows at a glance the superordinate, coordinate, and subordinate relationships contained in the material. However, diagrams can become cluttered, and when they do, the information in them is harder to use. In this case a matrix, such as the one shown in Figure 7.10, could be used as a supplement. Matrices illustrating salient aspects of closely related concepts can do much to help students organize similarities and differences in their minds.

The use of a data-retrieval chart as a supplement to a hierarchy has two advantages. One is that a chart allows the teacher to include and organize data for a lesson, and second, it helps promote thorough integration. The structural outline graphically illustrates how the concepts are differentiated; the chart, in turn, ensures their integration through an analysis of the data in it.

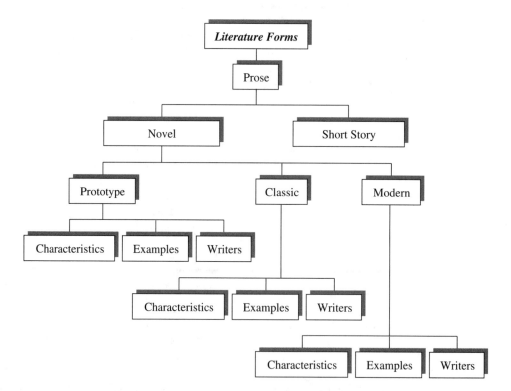

FIGURE 7.9   Hierarchy for Organizing Information on the Novel

TYPES OF NOVELS

	Characteristics	Examples	Writers
Prototypes			
Classic			
Modern			

FIGURE 7.10   Matrix Used as a Supplement for Organizing Content

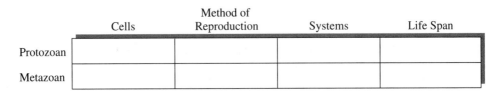

	Cells	Method of Reproduction	Systems	Life Span
Protozoan				
Metazoan				

FIGURE 7.11   Matrix Used to Organize Information on Protozoans and Metazoans

As another example of a chart used to organize content for a lecture-discussion lesson, look at Figure 7.11.

Here protozoans (one-celled animals) and metazoans (many-celled animals) are compared. A chart such as this could be used to supplement the hierarchy shown in Figure 7.12.

Matrices have the additional advantage of being easy to use; information in them can be conveniently organized and stored in the individual cells. This allows the teacher to present

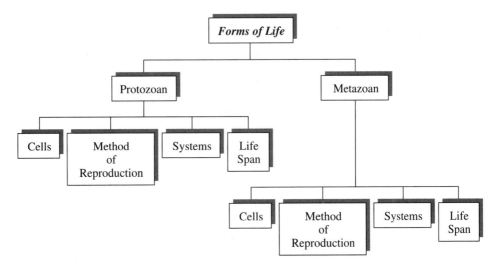

FIGURE 7.12   Hierarchy Used to Organize Information on Protozoans and Metazoans

data rather than processed conclusions to students, which gives them more opportunities to practice higher-order and critical thinking.

We have shown how hierarchies can be used in conjunction with matrices to help organize information for students. Maps, graphs, models, and outlines could be used equally effectively. Remember that all are means toward ends—that students understand organized bodies of information. If combining different ways of structuring information helps meet the goal of understanding, they are all effective. How you use them is a matter of your own judgment.

This completes our discussion of implementing lecture-discussion lessons. In the next section we examine the process of assessing student understanding when the Lecture-Discussion Model is used.

Assessing Student Understanding in Lecture-Discussion Lessons

The Lecture-Discussion Model as described to this point in the chapter is designed to teach relationships in organized bodies of knowledge. This is similar to the goals for the Integrative Model, but different from those for the Inductive, Concept-Attainment, and Direct-Instruction Models, which are designed to teach specific topics in the form of concepts, generalizations, principles, academic rules, and skills.

As described in the previous sections, the Lecture-Discussion Model can be used to teach relationships among concepts, generalizations, principles, and rules. Assessing understanding of these specific forms of content has been discussed in earlier chapters, so we won't examine it further here. Instead, we want to focus on the decisions teachers must make in assessing students' understanding of relationships among different topics.

The ability to relate different topics depends on an understanding of the topics themselves, so assessment should involve both the specific topics and the relationships among them. As an example, consider the following item, which could be used to assess Lorie's students' understanding of reinforcement schedules.

Read the following anecdote and answer the questions that follow:

Mrs. Cortez collects homework on Mondays, Wednesdays, and Fridays, while Mrs. Amato collects it periodically but doesn't announce when she will collect it. (She averages three days a week on different days.) Both teachers score and return the homework each day after giving it.

1. Identify the type of reinforcement schedule each teacher is using.
2. Explain why it is that type in each case.
3. Based on our understanding of reinforcement schedules, which teacher is likely to be most effective in promoting the students' efforts on homework?

This item accomplishes at least three goals:

- It measures the students' understanding of the concepts of fixed-interval and variable-interval schedules of reinforcement.
- It measures their understanding of the differences between the two concepts.
- It shows the students how the topics they're studying can be applied to the real world.

In addition, being able to explain why the first was fixed-interval and the second was variable-interval requires higher-order thinking. Ideally, assessments should accomplish all of these goals.

As another example of asking students to apply information to a new situation, consider the following item:

> *Describe how the staging for the Greek play, Oedipus Rex, would be different if it were done in an Elizabethan theater.*

In order to answer this question correctly, the students must know the characteristics of Elizabethan theater and apply them to a Greek play. This information provides the teacher with a measure of the extent to which the schema for theater had been integrated in the students' schemata.

Another way of measuring students' understanding of subordinate, coordinate, and superordinate relationships is to provide them with a list of concepts and ask them to arrange the concepts hierarchically. As an example, consider a lesson on vertebrates in a high school biology class. The teacher would provide the students with a list of concepts related to vertebrates and ask the students to organize them hierarchically.

Reptiles	Birds	Vertebrates
Fish	Warm-blooded	Mammals
Snakes	Monotremes	Placentals
Frogs	Salamanders	Cold-blooded
Marsupials	Turtles	Lizards
Amphibians		

The hierarchy might then appear as shown in Figure 7.13.

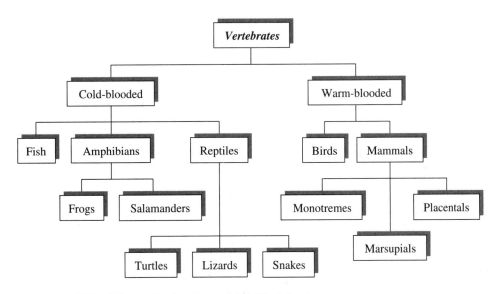

FIGURE 7.13 Hierarchy for Organizing Vertebrates

Note that this item is similar to the diagnostic exercise described in the planning section. The difference between the two is that this item would be used after the concepts had been covered, and it is explicitly designed to measure relationships between concepts.

The examples we've given are obviously only a few of the ways that learners' understanding of relationships among ideas can be assessed; many more exist. Our reasons for offering them are to emphasize that instruction using the Lecture-Discussion Model focuses on relationships in organized bodies of knowledge and not on memorized information. With effort and that focus in mind you will continually improve your assessments and with them the quality of your students' learning.

Summary

The Lecture-Discussion Model is a teacher-directed model designed to help learners understand relationships in organized bodies of knowledge. Grounded in schema theory and David Ausubel's concept of meaningful verbal learning, the model is designed to help learners link new and prior learning and relate the different parts of new learning to each other. The model is designed to overcome some of the most important weaknesses of the lecture method by strongly emphasizing learner involvement in the learning process.

Planning for lecture-discussion lessons involves identifying goals, diagnosing students' backgrounds, structuring content, and preparing advance organizers. Lessons are implemented in three cyclical phases: presentation (of content), monitoring the students' comprehension, and integration of ideas (both new with old and new with each other).

Assessment when the Lecture-Discussion Model is used should focus on students' understanding of relationships among the topics they study and application of those topics to new situations.

Important Concepts

Advance organizers (p. 214)
Comprehension monitoring (p. 225)
Integration (p. 226)
Introductory focus (p. 223)
Lecture (p. 215)

Meaningful verbal learning (p. 213)
Rote learning (p. 213)
Schema theory (p. 211)
Schemata (p. 211)

Exercises

1. Read the case study below and answer the questions that follow.

Iris Brown was teaching his English class about parts of speech. He wanted them to understand the function of different parts of speech in the total communication process. He also wanted them to understand the relationship between the different parts of speech. He began his class with a review of previously discussed material.

"Who can remember how we started our unit on communication and parts of speech?" Iris asked.

". . . We said communication is . . . the . . . two-way sending back and forth of information that usually is done with language, . . . and we said that the parts of speech and the way we punctuate are . . . parts of . . . the whole process," Steve said haltingly.

"Good, Steve. What did we say about parts of speech yesterday?" Iris continued.

After thinking for a few seconds, Quiana replied, "We said that parts of speech are like building blocks in a house. The parts of speech are sort of like the . . . like the building blocks of the way we communicate and the way the blocks are put together determines the form of the message and what it means."

"We also said words could be divided into naming words, action words, describing words, and other words," Evelyn added.

"That's good," Iris smiled. "Now how did we describe these groups?"

The lesson continued with a discussion of each of these parts of speech.

a. Describe the scope of the teacher's planning for the lesson.

b. Identify and describe the two advance organizers in the case study.

c. Diagram the organization of the material illustrated in the anecdote.

2. The following is a description of a college class involved in a discussion of teaching models. This is the last day of a three-day presentation.

a. Identify the advance organizers in the lesson (some may be from previous lessons).

b. Draw a hierarchy of the content contained in the lesson.

c. Identify in the lesson where integration took place.

1. Ms. Peebles, the instructor, began her Friday class with a review of her Monday and Wednesday classes.

2. "How did we begin the Monday session?" she asked.

3. "Well," Ron began, "you said a teaching model is like a conceptual blueprint in that both are used to achieve some purpose. A blueprint is used as a guide for an engineering objective, while a teaching model is a guide to achieving content and process objectives.

4. Arlene added, "You noted that models can be grouped according to whether they emphasize cognitive, affective, psychomotor, or a special kind of cognitive goal called information processing."

5. "You said that our emphasis in this class would be on information processing," Mary added.

6. "Wednesday you began to deal with the information-processing family," Bob interjected.

7. "And you said you wanted to deal with each of the models separately so that they would remain clear and distinct in our minds," Martha added.

8. George then said, "You began the lesson on information-processing models by stating that they are designed to help students handle stimuli and input from the environment and transform it into more meaningful output."

9. "You then went on to say that the models are grouped according to whether they are primarily deductive, primarily inductive, or inquiry," Kay noted.

10. "You further broke the inductive models into the Integrative Model, the Inductive Model, and the Concept-Attainment Model, and the deductive models into Direct-Instruction which teaches concepts and skills, and the Lecture-Discussion Model," Russ added.

11. "You also noted that while the Lecture-Discussion Model is primarily expository and deductive and the Integrative Model is inductive, they aren't as unrelated as you would expect; both can be used to process large amounts of information, but the way in which this is done differs."

12. "We also added that the Integrative Model is much more process oriented than the Lecture-Discussion Model," Carol commented.

13. "You also suggested," Linda noted, "that Ausubel sees the nervous system as an information-processing mechanism analogous to a discipline that organizes concepts hierarchically."

14. "Excellent," commented Ms. Peebles. "You seem to have formed stable concepts of the ideas that we've discussed so far. Today, I want to consider a new model. This information-processing model is the Inquiry Model which is designed to help students develop their ability to form causal explanations for events that occur in people's environments."

15. "This model combines both inductive and deductive modes of thinking. The first part of the model involves identification of some kind of a problem, and the second part of the model involves gathering information to explain the problem."

16. Wayne interjected, "We have noted that there are primarily three forms of knowledge we try to teach: concepts, generalizations, and facts. Which of these is the Inquiry Model designed to teach?"

17. "That's a good question," Ms. Peebles noted. "But before I answer that I'd like to show you some examples of the Inquiry Model and see if you can answer that question yourself." The class then proceeded to analyze the examples presented and ultimately came up with the answer to Wayne's question. (We will examine the Inquiry Model in Chapter 8.)

Discussion Questions

1. How are schemata acquired? Give at least three examples from common experience.

2. Though schema theory was described as the theoretical background for the Lecture-Discussion Model, it could be described as a framework for the other models presented to this point as well. Why then would it have been described specifically as the theoretical foundation for this chapter?

3. The Inductive Model was described as being based on constructivist views of learning. In what ways could lecture-discussion lessons be constructivist? Offer two specific ways.

4. What are the particular strengths of the Lecture-Discussion Model? What are its primary weaknesses?

5. What conditions might influence the effectiveness of advance organizers? Are they more effective with younger students or older? Are they more effective with new material or old? Are they more effective with abstract or concrete material?

6. Consider advance organizers in a broad sense. What kinds of aids and/or teacher behaviors can serve as organizers for students? What might be a metaphor for advance organizers in the affective domain? In the psychomotor domain?

7. The Integrative and Lecture-Discussion Models appear to be quite different, but in reality they are similar in several ways. Identify at least three of them.

8. Identify at least three similarities and at least two differences between the Lecture-Discussion Model and the Direct-Instruction Model.

9. How do you think David Ausubel would react to the Inductive Model? The Integrative Model? The Direct-Instruction Model?

Chapter 8

Developing Thinking
Skills through Inquiry

The process of inquiry sounds somewhat erudite and remote, but in fact it is very much a part of our everyday lives. The investigation of disease and other health-related matters, and conclusions suggesting that smoking, high cholesterol foods, and lack of exercise are detrimental to health are all results of inquiry processes. These conclusions originate in studies that ask questions such as, "Why does one sample of people have a higher incidence of heart disease than another?"

In other cases, government fact-finding missions, congressional investigations, or probes into alleged wrongdoing are all questions of inquiry. The research studies cited in earlier chapters of this text are all based on inquiry problems, which have attempted to answer questions such as, "Why do students in one kind of classroom learn more than those in another?"

Inquiry also occurs on a more personal level. An owner, checking his or her auto's gas mileage when running the air conditioner compared to not running it, is involved in inquiry.

Involving students in inquiry problems is one the most effective ways to help them develop their higher-order- and critical-thinking skills. The inquiry models in this chapter are designed to give students systematic practice with these processes.

When you have completed your study of this chapter you should be able to meet the following objectives:

- Identify the phases of the inquiry process.
- Identify goals appropriate for the inquiry process.
- Design inquiry lessons including all of their characteristics.
- Describe the differences between general inquiry and Suchman inquiry.
- Describe appropriate data-gathering questions for Suchman Inquiry.
- Plan inquiry lessons including each of the elements of the inquiry process.
- Implement inquiry lessons in classrooms.
- Prepare assessments that validly measure learners' understanding of the inquiry process.

To begin our discussion, let's take a look at a home economics teacher using the inquiry process with her students.

Karen Hill, a junior high home economics teacher, was beginning a unit on baking breads and other types of baked goods. As she was discussing general baking procedures at the beginning of a lesson on bread making, she began to explain that it is very important to knead the dough thoroughly.

Partway through her explanation, José raised his hand and asked, "Why do you have to knead it so long?"

"That's a good question, José. Why do you think so? . . . Anyone?"

". . . Maybe it's to mix the ingredients together well," Jill offered.

Ed added, "Yeah. If the stuff isn't mixed well enough, it might affect the way the yeast works. If you don't knead the dough enough, it won't raise."

Seizing on the chance to expand her goals for the lesson, Karen wrote the students' ideas on the board, and then said, "What Jill and Ed have collectively offered is a tentative answer to José's question. When people offer tentative answers to questions or tentative solutions to problems, we can call these proposals *hypotheses*. So, they suggested that thorough mixing affects the yeast, which affects how well the bread will raise. Now," she continued. "Does anybody have an idea of how we could check to see if this idea is correct?"

". . . We could take a batch of dough and separate it into about . . . maybe. . . three parts, . . . and then knead them for different amounts of time," Chris suggested tentatively after thinking for several seconds.

"Excellent thinking, Chris," Karen smiled. "What do you say, everyone? Should we try it?"

Amid, "Neat," "OK," "Why not?" and a number of nods at a unique idea, Karen went on, "How long should we knead each? The book recommends about ten minutes."

". . . How about five minutes for one, ten for the second one, and fifteen for the third?" Naomi suggested.

"Then we'll bake them all the same way," Natasha put in.

"To be sure that we're getting a good test of Jill's hypothesis," Karen continued, "what else do we need to take into account?"

". . . Well, we'd have to have the same dough," Jeremy suggested, "and we'd have to have the same amount of dough, wouldn't we?"

"And we'd have to knead them the same way," Andrea added, beginning to see the point in the activity. "If people's kneading was different, it could affect the mixing, and that's what we're trying to test, isn't it?"

"Very good thinking, Andrea," Karen nodded. "Anything else, anyone?"

". . . I think one more thing," Mandy added. "You said that the ovens in here are different. We'll need to bake them all in the same oven, won't we, or won't that throw us off?"

"That's excellent thinking, everyone. . . . Now, let's think back for a minute. . . . We talked about having the same dough, kneading each batch the same way, and baking them all in the same oven. . . . Why do we want to do that?"

". . . Well, if we had . . . different dough, and they came out different, . . . we wouldn't know if it was the amount of time we kneaded them or if it was the dough, would we?" Tollitha offered uncertainly.

"Excellent thinking, Tollitha. What we're doing there is keeping each of those constant, and the only thing we're changing is the amount of time we knead each piece of dough. When we keep them the same, we say that we've controlled those variables. . . . So, let's review for a minute and identify the variables we're controlling. . . . Someone?"

". . . Type of dough," Adam offered.

"Good, . . . what else?"

"The way we do the kneading."

"Excellent. . . . What else?"

"The oven."

"Good everyone. That's some excellent thinking."

The students then followed the dough they had made, separating a piece of dough into three equal parts, carefully kneading each piece in the same way, and baking them in the same oven, but kneading one part for five minutes, the second for ten minutes, and the third for fifteen minutes. They then checked to see if there were differences in the way the different pieces had raised. They discussed their results and related them to the hypothesis. They found that the pieces they kneaded for both ten and fifteen minutes seemed to have raised higher than the piece kneaded for only five minutes. There was a considerable amount of uncertainty about what those results actually meant, but they tentatively concluded that bread must be kneaded an adequate amount, but kneading beyond that amount didn't matter. Karen reminded them that they had only studied three pieces, so that generalizing must be done with caution, and the discussion then ended.

The Inquiry Model: An Overview

To begin our discussion of Inquiry Models, let's compare Karen Hill's instruction to those we've seen in other chapters of the book. An important difference sets her lesson apart from most of the others we've seen. In the other models (with the exception of the Concept-Attainment Model), a specific content goal served as the focus for the lesson—a concept, generalization, principle, or rule in the case of the Inductive Model, a concept or skill in the case of the Direct-Instruction Model, and an organized body of knowledge in the case of the Integrative and Lecture-Discussion Models. In contrast, Karen's goal was primarily the development of higher-order- and critical-thinking skills, and the development of these skills served as the focus for her lesson. (The Concept-Attainment Model is similar in that the development of higher-order and critical thinking is the primary goal when the model is used.)

Inquiry *at the most fundamental level can be viewed as a process for answering questions and solving problems based on facts and observations.* One of our goals in including a discussion of inquiry in this text is to increase your awareness of the powerful role this process plays in our lives.

Instructionally, the **General Inquiry Model** *is a teaching strategy designed to teach students how to investigate problems and questions with facts. The Inquiry Model is implemented in five steps, which are:*

1. *Identifying a question or problem*
2. *Making hypotheses*
3. *Gathering data*
4. *Assessing hypotheses*
5. *Generalizing*

When teachers use the Inquiry Model, they guide students through these five steps as the students work toward a solution to the problem. For example, a problem/question was identified in Karen's class when José asked about the length of time the dough had to be kneaded. This was followed by Jill's and Ed's suggestion that the kneading affected the way the dough would raise—the process of making an hypothesis. The class then discussed ways of controlling their investigation so that the information they got would be valid. They then baked the pieces and observed the results. This was all part of data gathering. Finally, the students discussed the results and concluded that an optimum amount of kneading was necessary, which partially supported their hypothesis. This discussion and their tentative conclusion were part of the assessing hypothesis phase. They then ended the lesson with generalization—also tentative—relating the optimum amount of kneading to the amount the bread raised.

We discuss two inquiry models in this chapter. The first is a strategy that teaches students to investigate questions and problems as they arise naturally. This was the case in Karen's lesson when the question about mixing bread dough came up. The second, based on original work by Richard Suchman (1966a) teaches inquiry skills by simulating data gathering through student questioning. Both models have the development of higher-order and critical thinking as their goal, but they differ in the way they're implemented.

Social Structure of the Model

As with the other models discussed in the text, the Inquiry Model requires a classroom environment in which the students feel free to take personal risks and feel free to offer their conclusions, conjectures, and evidence without fear of criticism or embarrassment. As with the Inductive, Concept-Attainment, and Integrative Models, this atmosphere is particularly important because the success of the lessons depends on the students' thinking. If students are fearful or unwilling to participate, much of the effectiveness of the process is lost. The teacher has a critical role in developing this atmosphere.

The Teacher's Role

In using the Inquiry Model, both Karen's and the students' roles were quite different from the roles they would play in "traditional" instruction. First, she became a facilitator of the process rather than merely lecturing and presenting information to the students. For example, she could have answered José's question directly and then moved along with the lesson. Her choice to respond the way she did was related to her goals—both long range and immediate. The development of higher-order and critical thinking was a theme for her in all of her instruction, so she chose to seize the opportunity to develop these skills whenever opportunities arose. A teacher with different goals may have chosen to respond to José directly.

Doyle (1983), in a review of research investigating the type of tasks students are asked to perform in school, makes a persuasive argument that students learn by doing. If they spend their time passively learning facts, they not only develop misconceptions about how and where knowledge originates, but also fail to develop the skills necessary to generate their own knowledge. In contrast, if they experience processes such as inquiry, in time they develop important life skills, such as the inclination to make conclusions based on evidence, to consider others' points of view, to reserve judgment, and to maintain a healthy skepticism. Obviously, these inclinations don't develop quickly, but with time and effort on the part of the teacher, significant progress can be made. It is the teacher who determines whether or not the students are given these opportunities. Let's turn now to some considerations a teacher must make in planning for inquiry activities in the classroom.

Planning for Inquiry Activities

Using the Inquiry Model is different from using the models we've discussed so far in three important ways. First, the Inquiry Model is used when teachers' goals are primarily higher-order and critical thinking rather than understanding some content topic. (Understanding content is important, as always, because content understanding and thinking are inseparable, but the emphasis is on thinking when the Inquiry Model is used.)

Second, since inquiry problems, hypotheses, and the data used to test them ideally come from the students, teachers must plan carefully, so they can provide enough guidance to keep the process moving, but not so much guidance that they intrude on the students' experience. This requires skill and experience.

Third, most inquiry lessons are ongoing; that is, they will require more than a single class period, and the teacher must also take this factor into account when planning. We turn now to planning for inquiry lessons.

Identifying Goals

As with all the models described in this text, the planning process begins with the careful consideration of goals. We have also suggested that content goals and goals for teaching thinking are inextricably interrelated. The emphasis placed on content compared to thinking varies among the models, but in all cases both kinds of goals co-exist. The inquiry models described in this chapter follow this pattern.

Content Goals

When the Inquiry Model is used, content primarily serves as the context for practicing higher-order and critical thinking. However, the Inquiry Model also helps students reach an important content goal, which is finding relationships between different ideas. In Karen's lesson, for example, students looked for a relationship between the amount of time bread was kneaded and the amount it raised. Most content areas have topics that contain cause and effect relationships. Table 8.1 includes some examples.

As a result of inquiry lessons, students construct generalizations such as, "The higher the level of aerobic exercise, the greater the cardiovascular fitness," or "Many wars are the result of economic problems." Some of the generalizations are more valid than others. As students' thinking improves, they develop their ability to assess the generalizations based on facts and observations. This illustrates the inextricable relationship between content and thinking.

Higher-Order and Critical Thinking

A teacher conducting inquiry lessons has as a primary goal the development of students' abilities to recognize problems, suggest tentative answers, identify and gather relevant facts, and critically assess tentative solutions. These are the skills of inquiry, and the development of these skills is an explicit process goal when inquiry models are used.

While students are the primary investigators in an inquiry lesson, a teacher must carefully plan in order to facilitate the process. To conduct inquiry lessons, students need a problem or question to examine and must have access to data that allow investigation of the problem. Both of these require planning.

Identifying Problems

Once the teacher has identified a relationship that can be investigated, the next task is to prepare a question or problem involving the relationship. For instance, a problem in an English

TABLE 8.1 Relationships in Different Content Areas

Content Area	Relationship
English/Language Arts	Author's lives compared to the content of their writing
Science	Plant growth related to the amount of sunlight, water, or type of soil
Social Studies	Wars related to economics, political problems, repression, or religion
Building Technology	Type of building material compared to durability
Health	Type of exercise related to level of fitness

discussion could be, "What factors in Poe's life may have impacted the style of his writing?" In a science class a problem could be, "What factors affect plant growth?" Ideally, these problems grow spontaneously out of class discussions, as occurred in Karen's lesson, but they often have to be planned by the teacher in advance.

With preplanning, the teacher can guide a class toward inquiry problems. For example, as students discuss different American authors, the teacher could introduce facts about one or two authors' lives. As these authors' works are discussed, the teacher could then raise a question, such as, "What impact do you think authors' lives in general have on their work?" Study of additional authors, their works, and their lives could then serve as the data-gathering phase for the inquiry problem.

As another example, the science teacher could embed an inquiry lesson on plant growth in a larger unit on plants in general. As the unit develops, the teacher could relate the investigation of plant growth to characteristics of different plants, plant growth and the environment, and plant nutrition.

Planning for Data Gathering

Once the teacher has planned for identifying problems, he or she must consider how the students will gather information to be used in assessing hypotheses. As with the process of identifying problems, in order for an inquiry lesson to succeed, the teacher usually must plan in advance for gathering data. Otherwise, valuable class time can be wasted and students may be confused. While procedures for gathering the data should come from students to the extent possible, the teacher must guide and facilitate the process. This requires planning.

The available data-gathering options are as broad and diverse as the subject areas themselves. Table 8.2 presents examples of problems and potential data-gathering procedures.

Primary and Secondary Data Sources

For advanced learners and for goals that focus on critical thinking, the distinction between primary and secondary sources of data can be important. **Primary data sources** *are indi-*

TABLE 8.2   Problems and Procedures for Gathering Data

Questions/Problems	Possible Data Sources
How are authors' works related to their personal lives? (English)	Author biographies and samples of their works
How is the road system in a city related to the city's traffic patterns? (Social Studies)	Observations of traffic flow at different times of the day City traffic reports
How is the type of shingle related to its durability? (Industrial Technology)	Shingles subjected to different kinds of wear
What factors impact the growth rate of cities? (Social Studies)	Geographical information, census data, and historical events
What factors influence the frequency of a simple pendulum? (Science/Math)	Pendulums of different weights and lengths

viduals' direct observations of the events being studied. Karen's students' observations of the baked bread, the observations of the pendulum swinging under different conditions, or interviews with people are primary sources. **Secondary data sources** *are other individuals' interpretations of primary sources.* Textbooks, encyclopedias, biographies, and other reference books are all secondary sources.

Because secondary sources have been screened through the perceptions and potential biases of others, primary sources are preferred, if available. In some cases, such as Karen's lesson or the lesson on pendulums or plant growth, using primary sources is quite easy. Karen could have referred the class to reference books on baking, but the students would have had less opportunity to practice thinking skills—controlling variables and experimenting. In her case, using primary sources provided a much better learning experience. In other cases, such as the lesson on authors and their works, using primary sources is nearly impossible, and secondary sources are almost a must. On the other hand, an analysis of secondary sources for potential bias is, in itself, a valuable critical-thinking skill. Therefore, both primary and secondary sources can be effectively used to promote higher-order and critical thinking.

Grouping Students

In planning for data gathering, teachers should also consider whether to gather information as a whole class, in small groups, or individually. For example, in the investigation of American authors, students could gather information individually or in small groups. The activity with plant growth could probably be conducted as a large group, with individuals assigned to measure, water, and care for the plants. The pendulum investigation would probably be most effectively conducted in pairs. One arrangement is not necessarily better than another, but the teacher should made a conscious decision about grouping in advance, or the actual process of gathering data can be disorganized and confusing.

Time

Based on our discussion so far, we see that inquiry lessons usually take more than a single class period to complete. Because of the time required, teachers must consider how the lesson will be integrated with other activities. For example, the English teacher might pose the question about authors' lives and their works. Discussion would then result in one or more hypotheses, such as "Authors' personal lifestyles are reflected in their works," or "Authors' works reflect their personal beliefs and needs." Individuals or teams of students could then be assigned to gather personal information about different authors and report this information to the class. As the students complete their assignments, class time could be spent in discussing different authors' works, or some other aspect of the curriculum, such as writing, or even grammar. As the students report, the class would revisit the problem, discuss the hypotheses, and form tentative conclusions about their validity. These discussions might take only a few minutes or they may take an entire class period.

In the science example, the teacher could guide the students through a process where plants are grown under different sets of conditions and their growth monitored over a period of weeks. Again, while this is occurring, the teacher could continue with other topics in the unit or even move on to other topics, returning to plant growth when data become available.

Having determined how students will be guided into identifying meaningful problems, how data will be gathered, and how the lesson will be integrated within the regular curriculum, the teacher is ready to implement inquiry lessons.

Implementing Inquiry Lessons

As described in the introductory section of this chapter, inquiry lessons begin with a question or problem, which is followed by a tentative answer or solution (hypothesis). Data are gathered to help determine the validity of the hypothesis, and once an assessment has been made, generalizations are constructed. We discuss implementing these steps in the sections that follow.

Presenting the Question or Problem

The inquiry investigation begins when a question or problem is identified. As we saw in Karen Hill's lesson, the question can grow naturally out of a class discussion, or as we discussed in the last section, the teacher can plan for and guide the students into identifying the question/problem.

To ensure that the problem is clear, the teacher should write it on the board or display it on an overhead and check to be sure that the students understand the language and concepts in it. Asking students to explain the problem in their own words or relate it to prior discussions can help determine whether the problem is clear. An even better indicator of whether a problem is clear to students is by asking them to form hypotheses that answer the question or solve the problem.

Forming Hypotheses

Once a question or problem has been clarified, the class is ready to try to answer or solve it. In providing a tentative answer, students are involved in the process of hypothesizing. An **hypothesis** *is a tentative answer to a question or solution to a problem that can be verified with data.* Often an hypothesis is a tentative generalization; for young children, it can be presented as a "hunch" or "educated guess."

To facilitate the process, you may ask the students to brainstorm possible hypotheses. Initially, all ideas should be accepted and listed. Then, students can be asked to determine whether each is relevant to the question or problem. (The ability to identify relevant and irrelevant information is part of the critical-thinking process.)

After students have developed a list of hypotheses, the hypotheses should be prioritized for the purposes of investigation. For example, suppose that a science class is investigating the problem, "What factors determine the frequency of a simple pendulum?" Students suggest hypotheses, such as:

"The shorter the pendulum the greater the frequency";
"The heavier the weight, the greater the frequency"; and
"The greater the initial angle, the greater the frequency."

The students need to be clear as to which hypothesis they are investigating in order to know which variables they must control and how they will gather the data. After having investigated the first hypothesis, they can move to the second, and then the third. (If the problem should only generate one hypothesis, prioritizing the hypotheses isn't an issue, and the lesson moves to the process of gathering data.) Once hypotheses have been stated and prioritized, the class is ready to gather data.

Data Gathering

However generated, hypotheses are used to guide the data-gathering process. The complexity of the process depends on the problem. For example, in the investigation of plant growth, students could plant seeds, such as beans or radishes, systematically vary the growing conditions, and measure the growth. To investigate the first hypothesis in the pendulum problem, students would systematically vary the pendulum length, keeping the weight and angle constant, and measure the number of swings in a specified amount of time for each length. To investigate the second, they would systematically vary the weight and keep the length and angle constant, and for the third they would vary the angle, keeping the length and weight constant.

For the lesson on authors' lives compared to their works, gathering data would be more complex and demanding, thus requiring older and more advanced learners. They would have to go to libraries to get biographical information about the authors, study a variety of sources to get insight into the authors' needs and attitudes, and carefully study the authors' works. In this case, the teacher would probably have to provide considerable assistance in gathering the information.

On the other hand, while demanding, the experience would help students develop skills far beyond the inquiry problem. For example, they would learn library research techniques, critical assessment of secondary sources, how to decide what information is important and what should be neglected, and would develop tolerance for ambiguity when information in different sources is inconsistent. These are valuable experiences for students.

Displaying Data

The process of gathering data seems simple and straightforward, and, conceptually, it is fairly straightforward. However, some techniques are far better than others, and even when good data-gathering techniques are used, results will be inconsistent. The best way to develop data-gathering skills is to involve students in the process, display their results, and discuss the techniques that were used. With experience, their abilities to gather the most valid and reliable data possible will improve. A variety of displays, such as tables, matrices, or graphs can be used. Table 8.3 shows a display of data gathered for the pendulum problem.

The pendulum problem is somewhat unique in that very consistent data can be gathered with very simple equipment. However, even then a discussion of data-gathering technique is worthwhile. For instance, we see that the students made three trials for each length and averaged the number of swings. The teacher could ask them to consider what they might do if two of the trials were identical and a third was very different (suggesting human error in the third trial), why they chose a fifteen-second time trial, two paper clips,

TABLE 8.3 Data Gathered for the Pendulum Problem

Weight—two large paper clips
Time—15 seconds
Angle—45°

Length	Average number of swings for three trials
30 cm	12
40 cm	11
50 cm	10
60 cm	9
70 cm	8.5
80 cm	8
90 cm	7.5
100 cm	7

a 45° angle, and variations in length of ten centimeters (probably arbitrary). The teacher might also ask if varying the length by the same amount (ten centimeters in this case) each time is necessary. The class could also be asked what improvements might be made in the data-gathering technique.

In the lesson on authors and their works, the data might be displayed in a matrix similar to those we saw in Chapter 5 when we discussed the Integrative Model. A skeleton of the matrix could appear as follows:

Author	Personal Characteristics	Experiences	Samples from Works
Poe			
Faulkner			
Hemingway			
Fitzgerald			

As with the pendulum problem a discussion of why some information was included and other information was neglected, and why the matrix was organized the way it was could be conducted. This process is valuable and helps students understand the kinds of decisions journalists, authors, and historians, among others, make when they study.

Data Analysis

In this phase of the lesson, students are responsible for assessing their hypotheses on the basis of the data. In some instances the analysis is simple; for example, a casual glance at the table comparing lengths of pendulums to the number of swings indicates that frequency decreases as length increases. Assessment of the other hypotheses in the case of the pendulum problem and in the case of plant growth would also be easy.

In other cases, such as the problem with authors, the process will be much more complex. Distinct patterns, such as the relationship between frequency and length of a pendulum won't exist. Trends that do exist will be much more problematic and arguable. Seeing that the data are inconsistent is, in itself, a valuable experience for students. Little in life is clear and unambiguous, and the more experience students have in dealing with ambiguity—which requires tentative rather than firm conclusions—the better prepared they are for "the real world." The discussion of the data as they relate to the hypothesis is the most valuable part of the inquiry process.

An important factor in the assessment of hypotheses is the notion of "right" and "wrong." If data do not support an hypothesis, the tendency is to describe the hypothesis as wrong, with the implication that whoever proposed it made a mistake. This is an inappropriate view of the inquiry process. Hypotheses provide focus for the investigation, and they are always presented as tentative. At the time an hypothesis is proposed, it is the most appropriate conclusion based on the information available. New data may require that the hypothesis be rejected, but viewing or describing an hypothesis as either right or wrong gives students a distorted view of the inquiry process.

Generalizing

Closure occurs in an inquiry lesson when students tentatively generalize—if possible—about the results on the basis of the data. For example, in investigating the relationship between the frequency of a pendulum and its weight, if the data indicate that weight doesn't impact the frequency, the students would reject the hypothesis, "The heavier the pendulum, the greater its frequency," and would conclude, "The weight of a pendulum doesn't affect its frequency." (The hypothesis "The heavier the pendulum, the lower its frequency" would, of course, also be rejected.) Since the data are consistent, generalizing would be straightforward.

In other cases, such as the problem with authors and their works, the data will be much less consistent, accepting or rejecting the hypothesis will be less certain, and generalizing will need to be more tentative. In fact, generalizing may then lead to additional questions, setting the stage for new inquiry problems. This is the process that goes on continually in science and the world at large. The examples that we cited in the introduction to the chapter are all cases in point. In learning to generalize tentatively, students learn an important lesson about living. They begin to realize that the tidy, structured answers for which we all strive often do not exist. In time, they develop tolerance for ambiguity, which is a powerful aid in helping them understand and cope with life.

Spontaneous Inquiry

So far we have focused on carefully planned and systematic approaches to inquiry lessons. However, one of the greatest benefits of studying inquiry is an increased awareness that inquiry activities can begin from questions that occur spontaneously. This was the case in Karen Hill's lesson at the beginning of the chapter. The investigation in that case developed "on the spot." A question came from the class, and Karen was alert and sensitive enough to capitalize on the opportunity when it occurred. A full-scale inquiry lesson was the result.

Other opportunities abound if teachers are aware of the possibilities. In some ways it's like learning a new word. Once learned, it begins to "appear" in everything we read. One of our goals in writing this chapter is for you to increase your awareness so that you will seize these opportunities when they present themselves.

Opportunities commonly occur when students encounter situations that have no clear answers. For instance, consider the following simple science demonstration where students see an inverted cup of water covered by a card, and the card stays on the cup, preventing the water from spilling, as shown in Figure 8.1. We have seen this lesson being taught to elementary students and have heard students ask questions such as:

"What if the cup wasn't completely full?"
"What if the cup only had a small amount of water in it?"
"What if the cup were turned 90 degrees?"
"What if we used a liquid other than water?"

Each of these is a question that could be a starting point for an inquiry mini-lesson. Students could be asked to conjecture answers to the questions and explain their beliefs; then, each could be systematically investigated. For example, the class could vary the amount of water to see if this variable makes a difference (it doesn't). Finding that the card stayed against the cup in each case, the class would eliminate amount of water as a variable causing the card to stay against the cup and would then pursue others.

Spontaneous inquiry lessons have several advantages. First, motivation is high. Students can see that the investigation results directly from a question they (rather than the teacher) ask. Often students can suggest clever ways to investigate a problem, and a classroom climate of teamwork and cooperation develops. Second, the spirit of inquiry is captured, yet very little time and effort are required from the teacher except to guide students toward thinking about the question and how it could be investigated rather than instantly responding with a definitive answer.

Another advantage of inquiry lessons that occur spontaneously is that students see how the process relates to the subjects they study. The distinction between teacher- and student-generated questions is a subtle but powerful one. When students only pursue questions generated by others, they learn that knowledge is external and impersonal rather than

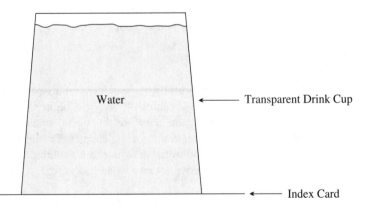

FIGURE 8.1   Simple Science Demonstration

TABLE 8.4   A Comparison of Inquiry and Concept Attainment Processes

Inquiry	Concept Attainment
1. Problem or question	Problem: What is the concept?
2. Hypothesizing	Hypothesizing: The name of the concept could be . . .
3. Data gathering	Data gathering: Students are presented with positive and negative examples
4. Analysis of hypotheses	Analysis of hypotheses: Hypotheses not supported by the examples are rejected
5. Generalizing	Generalizing: The concept is defined

functional and integrated. Our view, which is corroborated by others (Goodlad, 1984), is that content is too often presented as preestablished truths to be memorized and repeated. Students are seldom asked to investigate or generate their own problems. The use of spontaneously generated student investigations can do much to help them understand how knowledge is produced and the relationship of that knowledge to themselves.

Inquiry and Concept Attainment

When we discussed the Concept-Attainment Model in Chapter 4, we suggested that it also could be used to help students understand the process of inquiry and the scientific method. Based on the first positive and negative example, students hypothesize possible labels for the concept, and these hypotheses are analyzed based on additional examples. The examples and nonexamples then serve as the data used to analyze the hypotheses. Table 8.4 provides a comparison of inquiry and concept-attainment activities.

Concept attainment can be an effective tool to introduce students to the processes of inquiry. It doesn't take a great deal of time to complete a lesson, and the teacher needs only to prepare examples and nonexamples. It doesn't give students a totally valid notion of the process of inquiry, since the teacher provides them with all of the data—the examples and nonexamples. However, it can be an effective way to help students develop an idea of what inquiry is all about before they conduct full-blown inquiry investigations on their own.

This concludes our discussion of the General Inquiry Model. We turn now to a discussion of the Suchman Inquiry Model, a creative and clever way of conducting inquiry investigations in single class periods.

Suchman Inquiry: Student Questioning in Inquiry Lessons

In the first part of the chapter, we described the general process of inquiry and how it could be applied in classrooms. From our discussion of the Inquiry Model we can see that time and available resources can be problems in trying to conduct inquiry lessons. Certain problems or topics often require more time, equipment, and effort than are available.

In response to these problems, Richard Suchman (1966a, 1966b) developed a modification of inquiry that utilized student questions as alternatives to expensive and unwieldy data-gathering procedures. Research conducted on the Suchman Inquiry Model showed that students learned content as well as a control group and improved in their inquiry skills. In a controlled experiment with 196 fifth and sixth graders, Suchman (1966a) found that students exposed to inquiry classes learned as much content as a control group that was taught through traditional lecture. More importantly, the inquiry group produced 50 percent more questions on a posttest task and researchers judged the questions to be of higher quality than those generated by the control group. Further, students in the inquiry group were more motivated to learn.

Suchman Inquiry *is a form of inquiry in which data are gathered in a simulated setting through a process of student questioning.* Suchman Inquiry has two advantages over the General Inquiry Model. First, an investigation can usually be completed in a single class period. This brevity allows students to experience the complete inquiry cycle relatively quickly, and with practice they become quite good at it. Second, Suchman Inquiry can be effectively used in virtually all curriculum areas. As we have seen from the examples in the first part of the chapter, General Inquiry is easier to use in science than in areas such as English or social studies. However, experiencing the thought processes involved in inquiry is valuable for all areas of the curriculum.

The major difference between Suchman Inquiry and General Inquiry is in the data-gathering process. Suchman developed an innovative way of having students gather data by asking questions. Let's look at a classroom illustration.

Chris Florio, a biology teacher, is doing a unit on prey-predator relationships in the balance of nature. She completes her beginning-of-class routines and then says, "We've been studying prey-predator relationships and the balance of nature for the last three days, and today I want to extend our discussion and see if we can apply our background in solving a problem. So, the goal for today's lesson is to examine and solve the following problem. . . . Everybody ready? . . . Good, . . . let's go."

She then displayed the following information to her class on an overhead.

In the mountains of the Southwest a number of years ago, deer were plentiful, although the population would fluctuate somewhat. There were also wolves in the mountains. Some people from a small town witnessed a wolf pack pull down two of the smaller deer in the herd and were horrified. As a result, the people launched a campaign to eliminate the wolves. To the dismay of the people, the years following the elimination of the wolves showed a marked decrease in the population of the deer. Why, when the wolf is the deer's natural predator, should this have happened?

Chris then went on, "You all remember how we do these lessons. We have a problem here, and we are trying to solve it. Does anyone want to offer a tentative solution?"

After several seconds of hesitation, Damon offered, "After the wolves were killed off, it was easier for other predators such as cougars, coyotes, and eagles to prey on the deer, so their population went down."

"Okay, that's a good thought, Damon," Chris smiled. "That's our first hypothesis. . . . We'll probably have others, or we may need to revise that one. I want to emphasize that we can offer alternate hypotheses at any time. . . . Any others? . . . Okay, that's fine. Let's go ahead," she said as she wrote Damon's idea on the board.

"Now, let's imagine that we're field biologists, and we're out in the woods and mountains trying to look for some evidence that will help us make some decisions about our hypothesis. That means that we're observing to see what we can find.

"Imagining that we're out there is important, because it will give us a feel for the way the process works. As you know, we will actually be in our classroom, and the way we'll make our observations is for you to ask me questions, and your questions, together with my responses, will give you your data. Now, what do we know about the questions you'll ask? . . . Someone?"

". . . You must be able to answer them 'yes' or 'no,'" Miguel responded.

"Good. And why is that?"

". . . If you had to say more than yes or no, then it wouldn't be like we were making observations."

"Yes, good thinking, Miguel. That's exactly the reason. . . . Now, we need to go a little farther. Not only must the question be answerable yes or no, but what else? . . . Someone? . . . Go ahead, Tanya."

". . . Sometimes even if you can answer yes or no, the answer might be more than an observation."

"Can you think of an example of that?"

". . . Well, if we asked something like . . . 'Is the number of predators that can prey on deer related to the explanation?'"

"Excellent example, Tanya. That question requires a conclusion; in other words, it goes beyond observation, so we would need to reword it to make it observable. . . . Someone try and reword that question so that it is an observation."

". . . Maybe something like . . . 'Have cougars been seen killing deer?'"

"What do you think everyone? . . . Is that an appropriate question for a Suchman-Inquiry activity?"

The class discussed the question briefly and concluded that the question was acceptable.

Chris then went on with the lesson, saying, "Now that we've reviewed how we operate in the lesson, let's go back to our hypothesis and begin gathering some data to try and determine whether we can accept it, if we must reject it, or if we can modify it. . . . Remember, we're imagining that we're out in the field trying to gather evidence, and we're trying to think like field biologists. . . . OK, . . . Look again at the hypothesis, and let's go."

After studying the statement on the board and thinking for several seconds, Steve began, "Have other animals been seen killing deer?"

Chris responded, "Yes, they have, Steve," as she wrote Steve's question on the board and put a *Y* in parentheses beside it.

"Different animals?" Steve continued.

"Yes," Chris nodded, again writing the question on the board and putting a *Y* by it.

"I have an idea!" Pam exclaimed.

"Fine, Pam," Chris smiled, "but if you would please hold onto your idea until Steve has had a chance to finish his line of thinking."

Steve went on, "Does prey-predator balance have anything to do with the problem?"

"That's an excellent thought, Steve. We want to try and answer that. Now, if you were out in the woods looking for evidence, what would you look for to try and answer the question?" Chris nodded encouragingly.

". . . Let me think about it," Steve said tentatively.

Steve then appeared to be finished for the moment, so Chris returned to Pam.

"Jim and I have another idea," Pam suggested.

"OK," Chris smiled. "Go ahead."

"After the deers' predator was eliminated, the population got so big that their habitat couldn't support them, and they starved off, and the population went down," Pam said.

"OK," Chris waved. "What do we have here?"

"Another hypothesis," several people in the class said in unison.

"Good, exactly. . . . We said that we'd most likely have some additional hypotheses, so let's write this one down too, and then we'll try to gather some data for either one of the two that we have so far. Go ahead, anyone."

". . . Were more cougars seen in the deers' habitat after the wolves were eliminated?" Leroy queried after thinking for a few seconds.

"No," Chris shook her head as she wrote the question on the board and put an *N* by it in parentheses.

"How about coyotes?" Leroy continued.

"No again," Chris replied, again writing the question on the board.

She then interjected, "To which hypothesis are Leroy's questions most closely related? . . . Think about it for a moment."

". . . I think the first one," Dawn offered after studying the information on the board.

"Go ahead," Chris waved.

"Well, Leroy was asking questions about cougars and coyotes, which are other predators, and the hypothesis says that when the wolves were killed off, other predators took over."

"What do the rest of you think?" Chris asked.

The class generally agreed that the data were most relevant to the first hypothesis, and Chris then said, "Do the data seem to generally support the hypothesis, or do they detract from the hypothesis?"

Felicia volunteered, "I think detract."

"Why, Felicia?" Chris queried.

". . . The hypothesis says that other predators got the deer after the wolves were gone, . . . but there were no more cougars in the area after the wolves," she said, pointing to the question about cougars on the board, "And there were no more coyotes either, the way it looks."

"What does that tell us?" Chris probed.

"The hypothesis is wrong," Michele answered.

"Woops, let's be careful here," Chris cautioned. "How do we think about hypotheses?"

". . . We don't use the idea of right and wrong," Heather answered. "Besides, we have only two questions that relate to the hypothesis, so we can't be sure."

"Excellent thinking, Heather. That's exactly how we want to operate. . . . Now, what do we think about the data?"

". . . The evidence we have looks like it detracts from the hypothesis," Deborah put it.

"What do the rest of you think?"

The class agreed that the data seemed to detract from the first hypothesis, and Chris again emphasized that their conclusions must be tentative at this point. She then encouraged the class to move forward with the lesson.

"Hey, I have an idea," Carla waved after several seconds. ". . . Let me see how I want to word this. . . . Were a lot of trees found . . . no, were a lot of trees with the bark chewed off found in the deers' habitat after the wolves were eliminated?"

"Yes," Chris nodded, smiling at Carla's efforts, and again recording the question on the board.

"Were deer bodies found in the region after the wolves were eliminated?" Harold continued.

"Yes," Chris answered, again recording the question.

"Before the wolves were eliminated?" Harold went on.

"Yes," Chris answered.

"More after?" Steve added.

"Yes," Chris nodded.

"Were the carcasses skinny?" Jama continued.

"Yes."

"Were the carcasses deformed, like maybe from disease?" Ed asked.

"Some were," Chris answered.

"Are the winters in the region cold?" Susan asked.

"Yes," Chris responded.

"Is there a lot of snow?"

"Yes, again."

Chris waited a few seconds for additional questions, and then interjected, "Let's look at the hypotheses again and see what the data have to say about them."

After peering intently at the hypotheses, Bill raised his hand and said tentatively, "I think we need to change the second hypothesis a little."

"Go ahead, Bill," Chris encouraged.

Bill began, "We found that some of the deer must have starved because skinny carcasses were found and the trees were stripped of their bark, but we also found that some of the carcasses were diseased, so maybe disease caused some deaths. . . . I think the hypothesis should say that after the wolves were eliminated, the population expanded so their habitat couldn't support them and they became susceptible to both starvation and disease. Wolves take the weakest members, so they actually help the herds to stay healthy."

"Think about that, everyone. What does our evidence say about Bill's suggestion?"

The class discussed Bill's suggested modification and additional data-gathering questions to investigate the suggestion that wolves only take the weakest members of a population. They then discussed the hypothesis, tentatively concluding that it seemed to be valid.

Chris then continued, "What does this tentatively tell us about prey-predator relationships? Go ahead, Alicia."

"I think it must be something like . . . to keep an animal group like the deer healthy, they have to have some predators to keep their numbers right."

"Can anyone add anything to what Alicia has said?"

"The prey and predators have to sort of be in balance. Not too many predators and not too many prey," Dawn put in.

"Very good description, both of you," Chris waved. "You've described the prey-predator relationship in general, and it holds for most animal populations."

The class then discussed for a few minutes what happens when the balance is disrupted and they related it back to what happened to the deer in the problem they were studying. Chris then ended the lesson for the day.

The case study you just read illustrates a teacher using the Suchman Inquiry Model to teach a lesson on ecology. Let's turn now to a description of the model and see how it relates to inquiry in general.

Suchman Inquiry: An Overview

Suchman Inquiry is a specialized form of inquiry, so it follows the same steps as does General Inquiry. Table 8.5 gives a comparison of the two forms of inquiry using Karen Hill's and Chris Florio's lessons as examples.

From Table 8.5 we see that the processes—with the exception of the way data are gathered—are similar for each. The difference is that actual data in the form of primary or

TABLE 8.5   A Comparison of General Inquiry and Suchman Inquiry

Inquiry Phase	Karen's Lesson	Chris's Lesson
Problem	Why must bread be kneaded for so long?	Why when the wolves were eliminated did the deer population go down?
Hypothesizing	Ingredients must be mixed so the bread will raise	Other predators were allowed to deplete the population.
		The deer's habitat couldn't support them, so they starved and became diseased.
Data Gathering	Baking bread samples that had been mixed for different amounts of time	Questions about the cougar and coyote population.
		Questions about barkless trees and deer carcasses.
Assessing Hypotheses	Comparing the amount each sample raised.	Using the answers to the questions to determine which hypothesis was more valid.
Generalizing	Generalizations about the optimum amount of mixing for producing the best bread.	Generalizations about prey-predator relationships and the balance of nature.

secondary sources are used for General Inquiry, while data are gathered in a simulated form when Suchman Inquiry is used.

Social Structure of the Model

The classroom environment required for Suchman Inquiry to be successful is similar to that required for each of the other models. An atmosphere of emotional safety is critical, so students will feel free to offer their thoughts without threat. A safe climate is particularly critical when Suchman-Inquiry lessons are conducted because questions must come from students to keep the lesson moving. In contrast with the Inductive Model, in which the teacher can direct open-ended questions to particular students, if students are unwilling to participate in Suchman-Inquiry lessons, the teacher has fewer available techniques on which to rely.

Second, not only is collaboration appropriate in Suchman-Inquiry lessons, it is actively encouraged. If two or more students can collaborate in their thinking and develop a line of questioning on the basis of it, the results are often better than if students work alone. Suchman (1966a, 1966b) strongly encouraged collaboration in his original development of the model.

The Teacher's Role

The teacher's role during Suchman-Inquiry lessons is similar to the teacher's role for all of the models in that the teacher is responsible for guiding the students' learning. If, for example, students are unable to offer hypotheses or ask questions to gather data, teachers must be able to intervene to get or keep the lesson moving.

In Suchman-Inquiry lessons, teachers have a second role that is subtle and quite sophisticated. They must monitor the questions students ask to prevent the process from disintegrating into a guessing game. This requires adhering to the two primary rules—questions must be answerable by yes or no, and they must be worded in such a way that they could be answered with observations.

The second rule is the one that requires the most careful monitoring; for example, consider the following two questions:

- Were more cougars found in the deer's habitat after the wolves were eliminated?
- Is the number of predators that can prey on deer related to the explanation?

The first question could be answered on the basis of observation, while the second requires an inference or conclusion. If the teacher answers questions, such as the second one, the students are robbed of much of the critical-thinking process, which is the primary goal of Suchman-Inquiry lessons. The subtle and sophisticated part of the process is that the acceptability of the question won't be cut and dried; that is, some questions won't be clearly answerable with observation or clearly require a conclusion, and the teacher will have to judge the question "on the spot." This takes a bit of practice. We will discuss the teacher's role in more detail in the following sections. We turn now to a description of planning for Suchman-Inquiry lessons.

Planning Suchman-Inquiry Lessons

Identifying Goals

Content Goals. As with the General Inquiry Model, planning for Suchman Inquiry first involves identifying appropriate goals. Since the lesson begins with a problem, the content outcomes of Suchman activities are solutions to the problem and the generalizations that are based on the solution. In Chris's case, the solution suggested that starvation and disease caused the decline in the deer population, and the students then generalized about prey-predatory relationships and the balance of nature.

As another example of topics suitable for Suchman Inquiry, an English class might be asked to explain why a particular writer's style changed abruptly in the middle of his career, or a social studies class might be asked to explain why a political candidate was elected when all of the polls indicated that her opponent would win. Each of these examples requires an explanation from students, which would be followed by—tentative—generalizations.

The Development of Thinking.   Again, as with General Inquiry, the development of higher-order and critical thinking is the primary goal when Suchman Inquiry is used. The emphasis on thinking was clear in Chris's lesson. Her primary goal was the assessing of hypotheses based on evidence. This is a skill that improves with practice and epitomizes the goals of the Suchman Model.

Consider Chris's lesson once more. The first hypothesis suggested that other predators reduced the population when the wolves were eliminated, but the fact that the cougar population had not increased detracted from the hypothesis. Learning to relate facts, such as the cougar population stability, to the hypotheses—other predators reduced the deer population—requires practice. With ongoing practice, students develop the inclination to assess conclusions based on evidence and not whim, authority, or emotion. This is a powerful life skill, and one that schools should view as basic to all learning.

Preparing a Problem

After identifying goals for Suchman-Inquiry activities, the teacher's next task is to develop a problem that will be the focus of the activity. When first introduced to any form of inquiry, teachers often wonder how it can be integrated with the regular curriculum. This can be difficult because teachers feel responsible for delivering units of content to students based on district- or state-mandated curricula. (As we saw in Chapter 3, this is changing, and emphasis is now being placed on presenting fewer topics in more depth [Brophy, 1992].) This means the problems must be based on topics in the regular curriculum.

As examples of this process, consider the following topics:

- A social studies teacher wants to teach a unit on major transportation centers in the United States. The unit would include factors that contribute to the growth of the cities.
- An English teacher wants the class to read *The Oxbow Incident* and to understand the human dynamics in the story. The study would include such issues as mob behavior and violence, and how these themes are blended into the plot of a novel.

- A teacher of physical science wants students to understand density, buoyancy, and Archimedes' Principle.
- Psychology students are involved in an investigation of motivation, self-concept, sibling rivalry, and related concepts.

Examples such as these could be cited for nearly every discipline. Let's see what they have in common.

Consider first the social studies example. In a traditional approach the teacher might list and describe factors associated with the growth of cities. This description might be followed by selecting several large cities and determining to what extent the factors exist in each.

However, as an alternative, the teacher could introduce the unit in the following way. An outline map showing the location of two fictitious cities might be presented, and the teacher might say,

> *Look carefully at the map. These two cities are both at the mouths of rivers and are both on the coast of this country. Yet one of these two cities (Metropolis) has grown and thrived while the other (Podunk) has remained insignificant as a population center. Why do you suppose this might be the case?*

This is an example of a problem that could be used to start a Suchman-Inquiry activity. The students would then be asked to offer some tentative explanations for the difference (hypotheses), and gather data to assess the hypotheses. The explanation would be the basis for generalizing about the growth of cities.

In the case of *The Oxbow Incident*, the teacher might introduce the unit by saying,

> *Three innocent men ride into a Western town, are taken captive, and are tried and hanged for a crime they didn't commit. Why did this happen?*

Again, through their inquiry, students would be led to the content goal while at the same time practicing their thinking skills.

In the psychology example, the teacher might ask the class to explain why one brother in a family becomes a scholar and honor student while the other becomes a delinquent. In designing problems, the teacher should keep two factors in mind.

Learner Backgrounds. The first factor teachers should consider is learner background. Research literature is consistent in suggesting that all new learning is based on prior understanding (Bransford, 1993; Good and Brophy, 1994; Resnick and Klopfer, 1989). For example, Chris's lesson could not have succeeded if her students had not known that deer are browsers and that cougars and coyotes sometimes feed on deer. They also needed to understand the effects of overcrowding in a population. In planning, the teacher designs the problem so that students have to "reach" to solve it, but the problems can't be so far beyond their understanding that they're simply bewildered.

Structuring Problems.   Experience indicates that the way problems are structured contributes a great deal to the success of a lesson. The most successful problems have at least three important characteristics:

- They appear discrepant or counterintuitive.
- They are specific.
- They involve a comparison.

Let's look at these characteristics.

Student motivation can be increased if problems are structured to make them appear discrepant. For instance, we are more likely to expect brothers from a family to be similar than vastly different. Major differences in attitude and behavior are somewhat discrepant. Major differences in the growth rates of cities having similar geographic conditions are also discrepant, as are hanging innocent men for no apparent reason. Presenting a discrepancy is intended to arouse students' curiosity and create added interest in the problem.

Problems can be structured to increase their discrepant characteristics. For example, in a lesson on the effect of altitude on boiling temperature, rather than merely asking why it takes longer to hard-boil an egg in the mountains, the teacher might present the following problem.

Two groups of girls were camping at different locations and began preparing their evening meals. Sondra's group built a fire, prepared a stew of meat and vegetables, and put it on to cook. Gloria's group did the same. In a short while, Sondra's group tested their stew and found it ready to eat. Gloria's group also tested their stew and found the potatoes and carrots still uncooked. Why should there be a difference?

An event or problem presented in this way arouses students' curiosity to a greater extent than merely asking why it takes longer to boil an egg in the mountains. Presenting the topic as a problem takes little more effort than merely asking the question. All it requires is some awareness and imagination on the part of the teacher.

As one more example, a teacher whose goal is promoting good health habits might pose the following problem:

Pat and Jean are sisters. Pat is a bright girl with a lot of energy who is rarely ill and almost never misses school. On the other hand Jean, who is also bright, is often ill and misses a considerable amount of school. Why should there be so much difference in the health of two girls from the same family?

This example is similar to the previous one in that it is developed in a way that does not seem intuitively sensible. The solution to the problem would relate to Pat having better health habits than does Jean.

The second characteristic—specificity—allows the students to understand the problem, increases the chance that all students perceive the problem the same way, and makes it easier to hypothesize and begin gathering data. For instance, it is easier to begin gathering data about two girls in a family than it is to begin analyzing health habits in the general population; focusing on two cities makes the problem more concrete and specific than focusing on the growth rate of cities in general; and examining the experiences of two groups of girls on camping trips is easier than considering the general relationship between altitude and boiling point.

In addition to being discrepant and specific, the most effective inquiry problems involve a comparison. In looking at each of the examples, we see a comparison in each case. In Chris's lesson, the deer populations were compared before and after the wolves were eliminated. Two cities and two brothers were compared in the social studies and psychology examples, as were two sisters in the health lesson. The only case not involving a comparison was the example with *The Oxbow Incident*.

In general, problems that are discrepant, specific, and involve a comparison aid in the effectiveness of inquiry lessons because they provide a productive starting point for inquiry. The major purpose of the problem is to present a simulated portion of the real world for analysis. Films, audiotapes, demonstrations, graphs, tables, maps, and case studies can all be used to start inquiry activities, and if properly planned, all can provide enough information to initiate the data-gathering process.

Designing Problems for Young Students.   With younger students inquiry problems must be as concrete as possible to be effective. For instance, a first grade teacher, in planning a Suchman-Inquiry lesson, planted two plants. After a period of time she brought the plants to class and displayed them for the children. One obviously had grown much higher and looked much healthier than the other. The problem was to try and explain why the plants should look so different. Her activity with the children was quite successful, largely because they could see the actual plants. With older students, drawings or a even a verbal description would probably have been adequate, but with the younger children the actual plants were necessary.

In summary, the characteristics of an effective inquiry problem can be outlined as follows:

1. The problem must be appropriately matched with the developmental level of the students.
2. Curiosity and motivation are enhanced if the problem is prepared to appear discrepant.
3. Effective problems are stated specifically.
4. Effective problems usually involve a comparison.

Having identified goals and prepared a problem, we are now ready to implement the lesson.

Implementing Suchman-Inquiry Lessons

Presenting the Problem

After class routines are completed, the teacher introduces the problem. While the problem can be presented in a variety of ways, a description such as the one Chris Florio used in her lesson is effective. She said,

We've been studying prey-predator relationships and the balance of nature for the last three days, and today I want to extend our discussion and have us see if we can apply our background in solving a problem. So, the goal for today's lesson is to examine and solve the following problem. . . . Everybody ready? Good, . . . let's go.

The goal at this point is to be sure that the problem is clear, and the students are able to begin working on it. The problem should probably be displayed on an overhead or written on the board to provide a reference point for the students during the lesson.

Forming Hypotheses

After the problem is presented, students are encouraged to hypothesize possible solutions to it. This was the case in Chris's lesson when Damon offered,

After the wolves were killed off, it was easier for other predators such as cougars, coyotes, and eagles to prey on the deer so their population went down.

While Chris's lesson followed the suggested sequence for inquiry activities, in some cases, and particularly until the students understand the process, they are often inclined to begin the activity by asking questions (gathering data). Beginning with data gathering is not as "pure" philosophically, but the goal of inquiry is the development of thinking skills, and this goal can be accomplished either way. If students are inclined to begin with data gathering, our suggestion is that you allow them to do so for a few minutes, and then encourage them to try and form an hypothesis on the basis of the gathered information. Another possibility is that as illustrated by Chris's comment, "I want to emphasize that we can offer alternate hypotheses at any time," they may want to offer alternate hypotheses as well. Chris's students turned to data gathering after the first hypothesis was presented, but they could have offered additional hypotheses before they began gathering data.

We should offer one caution at this point, however. The number of hypotheses should be small enough so that students can see to which hypothesis their data relate. One of the goals in any inquiry process is to gather evidence to test a particular hypothesis, not randomly gather information and hope to draw some conclusion from it. One of the elements of inquiry is the assessment of hypotheses with data; therefore, an hypothesis must exist before this can take place.

Keeping Hypotheses General.   Just as stating problems in a particular way helps make the learning activity more effective, encouraging students to form hypotheses in a certain way makes the learning activity work more smoothly. This suggestion is to guide the students into wording the hypothesis in the form of a general rather than a specific statement.

To illustrate what we mean, let's look at the following problem and two possible hypotheses:

Jim, in comparing his car's gas mileage with that of his neighbor Judy's car, finds that he gets five fewer miles to the gallon than Judy does on her car, even though their cars are approximately the same size. Why might this be the case?

An hypothesis related to this problem might be:

Jim's car has mechanical problems, and as a result, his gas mileage is lower.

A second hypothesis could be:

Judy's car has radial tires and Jim's doesn't, so she gets better mileage.

The first hypothesis is more effective, and if students should offer one such as the second, you might guide them into an alternative or even offer one based on their thinking, such as illustrated in the following dialogue:

T: So what might an hypothesis be?

S: Judy's car has radial tires and Jim's doesn't, so she gets better mileage.

T: So, are you suggesting that perhaps Judy has better equipment on her car than does Jim?

While we might criticize the teacher for "leading" the student in this way, the first hypothesis is much more effective than the second for data gathering. We'll see why in the next section.

Gathering Data

As we saw in our discussion of General Inquiry, assessing hypotheses with "real" data, such as an on-site visit to a city, observing an animal population, or studying a variety of written references, can be a difficult and time-consuming process, which may discourage the use of inquiry in learning activities. In addition, because inquiry lessons can take several days, or even weeks, students may lose sight of the goals in the process.

To overcome these difficulties—as we saw in Chris's lesson—Suchman devised a clever way of gathering data so that inquiry lessons could be completed in single class periods. Since lessons can be completed fairly quickly, inquiry can become an integral part of instruction rather than an activity that occurs once or twice a year (or less).

Keeping Chris's lesson in mind, let's review the two important rules for gathering data in Suchman-Inquiry activities.

- Students gather data by asking questions that are answerable by yes or no. This places the responsibility for forming the explanation on the students and promotes the development of higher-order and critical thinking.
- The question must be worded so that the answer could be obtained through observation alone.

To illustrate the rules, let's look again at the problem with Jim and Judy and their cars' economy.

Jim, in comparing his car's gas mileage with that of his neighbor Judy's car, finds that he gets five fewer miles to the gallon than Judy does on her car, even though their cars are approximately the same size. Why might this be the case?

Now, let's look again at the first hypothesis:

Jim's car has mechanical problems, and as a result, his gas mileage is lower.

Adhering to the first rule is quite simple. If a question isn't answerable by yes or no, students are asked to rephrase it.

The second rule is more subtle and requires more judgment from the teacher. For example, in investigating the hypothesis suggesting that Jim's car has mechanical problems, a student might ask:

Does Jim's car have mechanical problems?

While answerable by yes or no, the question requires a conclusion from the teacher, which takes the responsibility for assessing the hypothesis away from the students. Further, allowing such a question would reduce the learning activity to a simple guessing game—the students would "guess" at an hypothesis, and then, for all intents and purposes, ask if it was valid.

Now, let's consider the following questions related to the "mechanical problems" hypothesis:

Is Judy's car newer than Jim's?
Has Judy's car been tuned up more recently than Jim's?
Does Jim use his car to commute to work?
Does Judy use her car to commute to work?
Do Jim and Judy work near each other?

The answers to each of these questions could be gotten from observation alone, and the answers would help assess the hypothesis (and others). For example, if Jim's and Judy's cars are the same age, and have been tuned up at about the same time, the data would detract from the hypothesis.

Another tacit hypothesis is being examined with the questions. For example, if Jim uses his car for commuting, and Judy doesn't, or if he has to drive in more stop-and-go traffic, all relate to an hypothesis about driving conditions, which could be stated as:

Jim's gas mileage is lower because his driving conditions are more difficult than Judy's.

Let's return now to the suggestion we made in the last section about stating hypotheses in general rather than specific terms. For instance, the second hypothesis said,

Judy's car has radial tires and Jim's doesn't, so she gets better mileage.

The students could then ask, "Does Jim's car have radial tires?" and "Does Judy's car have radial tires?" These questions adhere to the rules but they do little to promote the process of assessing hypotheses with conclusions; in effect, because the hypothesis is a specific statement, the activity is again essentially a guessing game.

In contrast, if the hypothesis is, "Judy's car has better equipment than Jim's," the questions about radial tires require the students to make conclusions, and they have more of an opportunity to practice thinking. This is the reason we suggested that hypotheses be in the form of general rather than specific statements.

Rephrasing Questions.   Let's look once more at some dialogue from Chris's lesson.

Steve: Does prey-predator balance have anything to do with the problem?"

Chris: That's an excellent thought, Steve. We want to try and answer that. Now, if you were out in the woods looking for evidence, what would you look for to try and answer the question?"

Steve's question was answerable by yes or no, but the answer wasn't based on observation alone, so Chris asked Steve to rephrase it. It is important to note that Chris encouraged Steve's thinking in asking him to rephrase the question rather than merely saying that the question wasn't acceptable and leaving it at that. When students are first introduced to the process, they may need some guidance in rewording questions to get them into acceptable form, but with practice they quickly understand.

Let's look at some other possible questions related to Chris's lesson:

"Were the deer starving?"
"Was the fertility of the deer affected?"

Neither of the answers to these questions are based on observation alone—we don't observe starving or fertility, for example, so each would need to be reworded. In reference to the first question, the teacher might say something such as,

The question of starvation is a very good thought. Now, what would we look for that would allow us to determine whether or not we might make some conclusion about starvation?

A similar statement could be made for the question about fertility.

As an additional example of the data-gathering process, let's look again at the problem with the two cities:

Look carefully at the map. These two cities are both at the mouths of rivers and are both on the coast of this country. Yet one of these two cities (Metropolis) has grown and thrived while the other (Podunk) has remained insignificant as a population center. Why do you suppose this might be the case?

Consider the following questions:

1. Is there a large mountain range around Metropolis?
2. Is there a large mountain range around Podunk?
3. Is the highest peak of the mountains around Metropolis more than 5,000 feet in elevation?
4. Is the highest peak of the mountains around Podunk more than 5,000 feet in elevation?

The first two questions suggest that the student is attempting to see whether either of the cities is isolated by mountains, which could affect growth. (If the third and fourth questions are asked before the first two, the teacher may want to suggest that whether there are mountains around the cities hasn't been established, and perhaps students should gather this information.)

Contrast the first four questions with the following:

5. Are the mountains in the area a factor in the cities' different growth rates?
6. Are the mountains related to the growth rate?
7. Are the mountains in the area significant to the growth of the cities?
8. How big are the mountains around Podunk?

Questions 5, 6, and 7 are answerable by yes or no, but the information cannot be obtained through observation alone. Question 8 would be unacceptable because it requires something other than a yes/no answer.

Consider another second set of questions designed to test the hypothesis:

The river near Metropolis has a greater capability than the river near Podunk for carrying goods and people to and from the interior and, therefore, Metropolis grew more than Podunk.

Now consider the following questions:

1. Is Podunk on the mouth of a large river?
2. Are the rivers near the cities significant to their growth?
3. Is Metropolis on the mouth of a large river?
4. Is access to the country's interior a factor?
5. Is the river near Podunk capable of carrying ocean liners?
6. Is it important to know about the rivers?
7. Is the river near Metropolis capable of carrying ocean liners?

Questions 1, 3, 5, and 7 are acceptable, while 2, 4, and 6 are not. Again, students who ask unacceptable questions should be asked to rephrase them, and their thinking should be encouraged. The teacher should be sensitive to the possibility of discouraging students who ask "unacceptable questions." Often, a compliment about the thought or the opportunity to ask the rephrased question is all that is needed to prevent students from becoming discouraged.

Assessing Hypotheses

To illustrate the process of assessing hypotheses, let's look again at some dialogue from Chris's lesson.

Leroy: . . . Were more cougars seen in the deer's habitat after the wolves were eliminated?

Chris: No.

Leroy: How about coyotes?

Chris: No again.

Chris: To which hypothesis are Leroy's questions most closely related? . . . Think about it for a moment.

Dawn: I think the first one.

Chris: Go ahead.

Dawn: Well, Leroy was asking questions about cougars and coyotes, which are other predators, and the hypothesis says that when the wolves were killed off, other predators took over.

Chris: Do the data seem to generally support the hypothesis, or do they detract from the hypothesis?

Felicia: I think detract.

Chris: Why, Felicia?

Felicia: The hypothesis says that other predators got the deer after the wolves were gone, . . . but there were no more cougars in the area after the wolves. And there were no more coyotes either, the way it looks.

Chris: What does that tell us?

Michele: The hypothesis is wrong.

Chris: Woops, let's be careful here. How do we think about hypotheses?

Heather: . . . We don't use the idea of right and wrong. Besides we have only two questions that relate to the hypothesis, so we can't be sure.

Chris: Excellent thinking, Heather. That's exactly how we want to operate. . . . Now, what do we think about the data?

Deborah: The evidence we have looks like it detracts from the hypothesis.

Chris was very effective in leading the students' assessment of the hypothesis, and she was also effective in encouraging the students to remain tentative in their conclusions. As a lesson develops, the teacher simply judges when to suggest that the students evaluate an hypothesis based on the data. When it appeared to Chris that enough data existed so that an assessment could be made, she guided the students in that direction. After they decided that the data detracted from the hypothesis, they "stored" that information for the time being and went on with the process of gathering data. Let's look again at some dialogue.

Chris: Let's look at the hypotheses again and see what the data have to say about them.

Bill: I think we need to change the second hypothesis a little.

Chris: Go ahead, Bill.

Bill: We found that some of the deer must have starved because skinny carcasses were found and the trees were stripped of their bark, but we also found that some of the carcasses were diseased, so maybe disease caused some deaths. . . . I think the hypothesis should say that after the wolves were eliminated, the population expanded so their habitat couldn't support them and they became susceptible to both starvation and disease. Wolves take the weakest members, so they actually help the herds to stay healthy.

Chris: Think about that everyone. What does our evidence say about Bill's suggestion?

Here we see how assessing hypotheses can result in modifying rather than eliminating them outright. This illustrates the cyclical nature of forming hypotheses, gathering data, and modifying hypotheses or creating new ones. This process is represented pictorially in Figure 8.2.

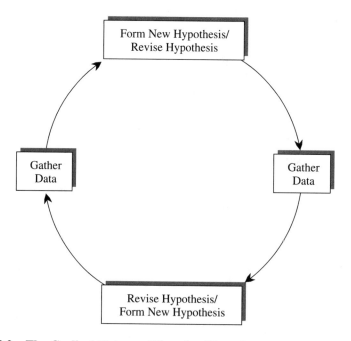

FIGURE 8.2   The Cyclical Nature of Forming Hypotheses and Gathering Data

Closure

An intrinsic feature of the process of assessing hypotheses is that it ultimately leads to closure. A Suchman-Inquiry lesson arrives at closure when an explanation is developed that best accounts for the data. (In the real world, situations exist where one explanation that is clearly better than all others cannot be found. As students become sophisticated with the inquiry process, they may progress to this point in their solution to problems. In that case, closure would occur when more than one explanation remained at the end of the lesson.)

To see how Chris guided her class to closure, let's look again at some of the dialogue in the lesson.

Chris: What does this [the problem with the deer population] tentatively tell us about prey-predator relationships? . . . Go ahead, Alicia.

Alicia: . . . I think it must be something like . . . to keep an animal group . . . like the deer healthy they have to have some predators to keep their numbers right.

Chris: Can anyone add anything to what Alicia has said?

Dawn: . . . The prey and predators have to sort of be in balance. Not too many predators and not too many prey.

Chris: Very good description, both of you. You've described the prey-predator relationship in general, and it holds for most animal populations.

From the dialogue we see how Chris's students summarized their conclusion and formed a generalization—although it wasn't worded like a typical generalization—about prey-predator relationships. The class then went on to discuss what happened when the relationship is thrown out of balance.

While advocates of inquiry might consider teacher confirmation of an explanation as a detraction from the spirit of independent inquiry, teachers may have to make decisions based on the students' reaction to the lesson. It is preferable for students to have a positive, effective experience with the inquiry process, leaving them eager to pursue inquiry again, rather than having them leave an inquiry session unsettled and frustrated. If the teacher must confirm students' explanations in order for this to happen, then so be it. As students gain experience and confidence in their ability to form and analyze explanations, they become more willing to accept their own conclusions and will have moved an additional step toward becoming truly independent inquirers.

Implementing Suchman-Inquiry Lessons: Developmental Considerations

When first using Suchman-Inquiry activities, teachers often experience difficulties and complain, "My students can't do this." Of course not: if they were good at being self-directed learners, we wouldn't have to teach them these abilities. Both kinds of inquiry activities described in this chapter need a lot of teacher support when first introduced. As students gain experience, their abilities quickly develop, but the teacher must get through the initial difficulties.

In a sense, it's analogous to learning a new game. We have to understand "how the game is played" and "how to play the game." This is not a play on words. The first type of knowledge relates to the rules and goals of the game—how the game operates. The second relates to strategies for winning.

To get students started, teachers might choose a sample lesson on a simple topic. For example, the teacher might begin an inquiry lesson with a problem such as:

- Why is watching TV Billy's favorite leisure time activity while reading is Joe's?
- Why does Nikki like one TV show, and Megan like another?
- Why does one group of students like a particular rock star and another group prefer a different star?

Because the students will be very familiar with the topic, they can focus their energy on "how to play the game." Then, as they become more experienced the teacher can focus on more substantive problems.

In beginning lessons as well as those more advanced, modeling can be very helpful. The teacher can model by "thinking out loud" while illustrating an aspect of the process or can encourage students to think aloud as they explain their own ideas.

As a final note on developmental aspects of using inquiry, some teachers express concern over the ability of young children to participate in inquiry. Our experience has been that children as young as kindergarten can profit from General Inquiry activities if they deal with comprehensible content areas that are properly structured by the teacher.

Assessing Student Understanding in Inquiry Lessons

To this point in the chapter we have discussed planning and implementing both General Inquiry and Suchman Inquiry. We now want to examine the process of assessing student understanding when these models are used.

Assessing Content Acquisition and Process Skills

As with the other models we've discussed, content and higher-order and critical thinking are so interrelated that it is difficult to assess one without the other. Because of this relationship, all assessments must be described as having an emphasis rather than being a separate assessment.

The assessment phase of any lesson is an important one because it provides the teacher with information about an individual's progress, something that can be masked in the group inquiry process. We want students to participate equally, but in reality they won't, so we must get assessment information from individual students.

One of the most important aspects of assessment in inquiry lessons is determining whether students can form hypotheses and relate data to explanations. Case studies provide one way of accomplishing this. When case studies are used, students are given a problem and are asked to provide relevant hypotheses, data-gathering questions, and observations or data from the problem itself.

As an example, consider the following item.

For the following situation, develop an hypothesis for Joe's behavior, write two data-gathering questions that could be used to test this hypothesis, and list three observations that can be made from reading the passage.

> *Two boys had been good friends throughout their childhood. One day the boys were diving from a tree into a swimming hole. As Lionel crawled out to the end of the tree branch and prepared to dive, Joe shook the branch and Lionel fell to the ground, suffering a permanent injury to his hip. Why did this happen?*

A. Hypothesis:
B. Data-gathering questions:
C. Observations:

The following might be responses to the questions.

A. Hypothesis: Joe was jealous of Lionel's athletic ability.
B. Data-gathering questions:
   1. Is Joe the smaller of the two boys?
   2. Are Lionel and Joe on an athletic team together?
C. Observations:
   1. The boys were good friends.
   2. The boys went swimming together.
   3. Joe shook the branch.

(This problem was adapted from John Knowles' novel, *A Separate Peace*.)

An alternate way of measuring students' inquiry skills is to provide them with the script from an inquiry session together with a possible explanation and ask them to determine the relationship of data to that explanation. As an example of this format, consider the following example based on the social studies problem concerning the two cities.

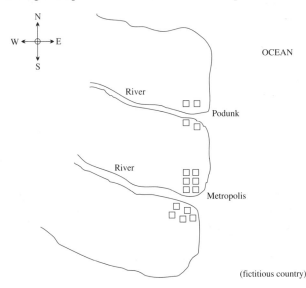

(fictitious country)

Both cities are on the coast and exist at the mouth of rivers. However, Metropolis is large and a busy transportation center while Podunk is small and insignificant.

The following is a proposed explanation for why there should be so much difference in size and significance:

While both Podunk and Metropolis are on the coast and are at the mouths of rivers, the entrance to Podunk's harbor is quite small, and the prevailing winds and tricky currents made entrance dangerous in the early years when sailing ships were used. Further, the coast range of mountains isolated Podunk by land but became foothills by the time they reached Metropolis, leaving it freely accessible to overland shipping.

The following data were gathered in the form of questions with the responding answer in parentheses. In the blank by each question write Support (S), Not Support (NS), or Unrelated (U) if the data support the explanation, do not support the explanation, or aren't related to the explanation, respectively.

a. Does the current along the coast run from north to south? (Yes)
b. Is Metropolis's harbor larger than Podunk's? (Yes)
c. Are Metropolis and Podunk over one-hundred miles apart? (Yes)
d. Did approximately as many ships run aground near Metropolis as near Podunk in the sailing days? (Yes)
e. Is the river near Metropolis capable of carrying heavier ships than the river near Podunk? (Yes)
f. Are the mountains around Podunk more rugged than the mountains around Metropolis? (Yes)
g. Are Metropolis and Podunk both in the meteorological belt of the prevailing westerly winds? (Yes)
h. Are the local winds more variable around Podunk than they are around Metropolis? (Yes)

As an additional measure of students' inquiry skills, the teacher may also choose to expand the measurement process by asking students to rewrite the explanation (hypothesis) in keeping with the additional data.

With any type of format for measuring higher-order and critical thinking, the teacher should be certain that the situation used in the measurement is one not previously presented. Otherwise, students may be merely recalling previous information.

The preceding discussion centered primarily on measurement of the higher-order- and critical-thinking aspects of inquiry. The teacher can, of course, assess the acquisition of content in the same way that content is measured in lessons where the other models are used.

Summary

Inquiry is a process of solving problems based on evidence. The inquiry process typically begins with a problem or question. Tentative solutions or answers (hypotheses) to the problem or question are offered, and data are then gathered, which allows an assessment of these solutions and answers. The hypotheses are then assessed based on the available data, and generalizations are made about the conclusions.

The inquiry process, while seemingly remote and academic, is very much a part of our everyday lives. Simple activities, such as deciding which of two items is a better buy or better meets our needs involves inquiry. Most of the findings related to health and quality of life are based on the process of inquiry.

Suchman Inquiry is similar to General Inquiry except in the way data are gathered. To overcome difficulties with time and available resources, Suchman devised a way of having learners gather data by asking questions instead of making actual observations in a natural setting. In addition, Suchman's procedures make inquiry more accessible to all content areas, whereas General Inquiry is most commonly seen in the sciences.

Important Concepts

General Inquiry Model (p. 239)   Primary Data Sources (p. 242)
Hypothesis (p. 244)   Secondary Data Sources (p. 243)
Inquiry (p. 239)   Suchman Inquiry (p. 250)

Exercises

1. Look at the following content objectives. Identify those that are not appropriate for Suchman Inquiry and explain why they are inappropriate.
   a. A social studies teacher wants students to know the time span of the Civil War.
   b. A science teacher wants students to know the difference between the processes of observation and inference.
   c. A humanities teacher wants students to know why the work of Van Gogh changed in emphasis over the period of his productive life.
   d. A math teacher wants students to understand the closure property.
   e. A science teacher wants students to know why dew forms.

2. Select from the following list one or more objectives appropriate to your teaching area. Describe a problem that would allow the objective to be met using a Suchman-Inquiry activity.
   a. A music teacher wants students to understand the reasons why some sounds are considered music and others are considered noise.
   b. A teacher of literature wants to study the nature of traditions and has chosen the story "The Lottery" as a vehicle for study.
   c. A social studies teacher wants students to know factors affecting the decision to drop the first atomic bomb on Hiroshima.
   d. A social studies teacher wants students to understand the factors involved in the astounding victory of Truman over Dewey in 1948.
   e. A science teacher wants students to understand that objects will float on a fluid if they are less dense than the fluid.
   f. An art teacher wants students to understand the factors that will affect the price of a commercial painting.

3. Read the following problems prepared for Suchman-Inquiry activities. After reading each, decide which one is most appropriate according to the characteristics described in the previous chapter.

a. Two countries have a common border. Their natural resources are similar, both possessing considerable wealth in minerals and timber. They are of approximately the same size. Country A is a thriving dynamic society with a sound economy, while Country B is struggling for its economic existence and is on the brink of bankruptcy. Why should there be such a difference between the two?

b. Animals have many different ways of protecting themselves. Some animals are small and can hide, others have long legs so they can run. Still others have a form of protection called protective coloration. What do we mean by protective coloration?

c. Students in classes are asked to write themes. Some get high scores while others are low. Why should we see such a difference?

4. Read the following teaching episode, which describes a teacher using the Inquiry Model, and answer the questions that follow.

Renee Stanley was beginning a unit on the newspaper in her high school journalism class. She wanted students to understand factors that shaped the form that newspapers took and the role that newspapers played in the total context of journalism. She began her lesson by saying, "Class, today we are going to begin our unit on the newspaper. As an introductory activity, I'd like us to take a look at some newspapers that I've saved from the past week and see what we can discover." With that, she placed newspapers from each day of the previous week on a table in front of the class and put a little sign on each indicating the day of the week.

"Class, what do you notice about these newspapers? Jill?"

"The ones toward the end of the week are fatter than the ones toward the beginning."

"OK. Anything else, Tod?"

"Sunday looks to be the fattest and seems to have the most color photographs."

"Does everyone agree? Any other observations? Mary?"

"There seem to be more inserts in Wednesday and Thursday's papers."

"Those are all good observations, class. Now I'd like us to go one step farther with one of those, which is the size of the newspaper. I'd like us to investigate factors that influence the size and composition of our daily newspaper."

Saying that, she then proceeded to write the following on the board:

"What factors influence the size and composition of the daily newspaper?"

She continued, "Any ideas, class? How about you, Rob, do you have an hypothesis?"

"It might be feature articles, like things to do on the weekend or travel stuff. Maybe that's what makes some newspapers fatter than others."

"OK, let's put that on the board under hypotheses. Any other ideas, Sally?"

"It could also be advertising. People have more time to shop for things on the weekend."

"All right, let's put advertising up there, too. Any others, Dave?"

"Another factor could also be sports. There are more sports events on weekends, so that might be one reason why Sunday is so fat."

"That's a good idea, too. Let's stop there in terms of working on hypotheses, and let's spend a moment trying to figure out how we could gather some data related to our hypotheses. Any ideas, Susan?"

"I'm not sure if this will work, but we could count the number of pages that have these different topics on them."

"Interesting idea. Jim, did you have a comment?"

"What about pages that have more than one thing on them? What would we do there?"

The class continued to discuss the procedures they would use to analyze the newspapers and finally arrived at the following table:

National and International News, Local News
No. of Pages
Features
Sports
Advertising
Percent of Total

Renee then assigned students to seven groups, with each group responsible for analyzing a newspaper from a given day of the week. As each group completed its task, it put its information in the form of a table on the board to share with others. When all of the groups were finished, Renee continued.

"Well, class, what do we have here? That sure is an awful lot of data. To make our job a little bit easier I think we ought to analyze the data systematically. Let's take our hypotheses one by one and see what we find out. Can we look at the 'features' hypothesis first? What patterns do you see? Jackie?"

"It looks like in terms of pages there are the most feature articles on Sunday."

"Does everyone agree? Why do you think we see that pattern, Sam?"

"I think it's because people have more leisure time on Sunday to read feature stuff."

"Everyone agree? Joe, did you have an idea?"

"Look at the percentage column for features on Sunday. It's no higher than any of the others. I can't figure that out."

"Any ideas, class? I see that the bell is going to ring in a few minutes. Let's save the information on the board and continue our discussion tomorrow, beginning with Joe's question."

Answer the following questions based on the information in the scenario.

a. Was Renee's inquiry lesson spontaneous or preplanned?
b. Were the data sources that students used to investigate their problem primary or secondary? Explain.
c. Identify in the teaching lesson where each of these phases occurred.
    1. Question or problem definition
    2. Hypothesis generation
    3. Data gathering
    4. Investigation of hypotheses through data analysis
    5. Generalizing

5. David Smith wanted to measure his students' process inquiry skills so he prepared a case study for students. The case study was composed of (a) a problem, (b) hypotheses suggested as an explanation for the problem, and (c) data gathered to test the hypotheses. He then prepared several questions for his students. Your task is to analyze the quality and appropriateness of David's questions. The case study appeared as follows:

There is a country that is shaped as it appears on the map. This country is unusual in that most of the population lives on the eastern coast. Why did this unequal distribution of population occur?
    The following hypotheses were included with the case study.

1. There are more natural seaports on the east coast that promote shipping to that area, thus leading to a buildup in population.

2. A mountain range exists on the west coast, preventing the area from being developed.

3. A railroad extended from the country to the north down the east coast, promoting immigration and commerce between the two countries and leading to a buildup in the population in the east.

The data relating to the problem are as follows:

a. The number of seaports on the east and west coasts are approximately the same.
b. The country is flat throughout its area.
c. The climate conditions in all parts of the country are similar.
d. The ocean currents along the east coast run from south to north.
f. Railroads run north and south in the country on both coasts.
g. The first railroad was built on the east coast.
h. A mountain range runs from north to south in the country above the country in question, about 200 mi. inland from the coast.

David then prepared the three questions that follow. Your task as a reader is to analyze each question and determine whether each is appropriate for measuring the process abilities of David's students.

Question a. Which of the following factors can influence the location of cities?

1. Rail line
2. Currents
3. Mountains
4. Harbors

Question b. On the basis of the data, decide which of the three hypotheses can be accepted and which must be rejected, and explain the basis for the decision.

Question c. On the basis of the data, revise the hypotheses to form a final explanation for the problem.

6. Consider the problem cited earlier that described two girls from the same family named Pat and Jean. Pat was rarely ill but Jean often was. The question was why should there be such a difference between the two girls? From the list that follows, identify the questions that *do not* satisfy the rules of the Suchman-Inquiry Model and would consequently need to be rephrased.
a. How old are the girls?
b. Is Jean heavier than Pat?
c. Are their cleanliness habits a factor in the difference in their health?
d. Does Pat take vitamins every day?
e. Does Jean get enough exercise?
f. Does Pat eat from the four basic food groups every day? Does Jean?

7. Read the following anecdote and answer the questions that follow.

Two teachers, Susan and Bill, were sitting in the lounge one day discussing an incident between two other teachers.

"I've never seen Joan flare up that way," Susan said to Bill. "Why do you suppose she jumped all over Mary?"

"I don't know for sure," Bill responded. "But I think she's having some trouble at home. I notice that she's edgy when she first comes in in the morning but settles down as the day goes on. Also, she made some snide remark about her husband yesterday morning."

"Yes, I heard that, too," Susan nodded. "But I think it was all in fun. Also, she commented only last week how happy she was and how well things were going both at home and at school. I really don't think her home life would cause her to jump on Mary that way."

Joe had also been in the lounge, had seen the incident, and had been listening to Susan and Bill talking. "I think," he said, "that she's simply exhausted and her nerves are on edge. She's taking two classes at the university in addition to teaching, she's the annual and school paper advisor, and now that it's spring she's trying to help with the girls' tennis team. It's just too much."

"That's probably it," Susan agreed.

"She commented that she's averaged five hours of sleep since she started with the coaching. That's been three weeks, and she's probably exhausted."

"Also, her husband sells," Bill added, "and they do an awful lot of entertaining of prospective buyers."

a. Identify the inquiry problem/question in the anecdote.

b. Identify two hypotheses that were offered to answer the question.

c. Identify at least four comments in the anecdote that could be called items of data. (Some of the items are inferential, and therefore not as valid as observations, but include them anyway.)

d. For each item of data, identify to which hypothesis it relates, and whether it supports the hypothesis or detracts from it.

Discussion Questions

1. Identify at least two areas of the curriculum that are well suited to inquiry activities. Identify at least two areas of the curriculum in which it is difficult to implement inquiry activities. Explain why you offered the choices you did.

2. Are inquiry activities more effectively taught at the beginning or end of a unit? Why?

3. From a developmental perspective, what would be an optimal sequence for introducing the General Inquiry Model, Suchman Inquiry, and Concept Attainment I, II, and III?

4. What are the advantages and disadvantages of asking students to independently pursue a research topic using the General Inquiry Model? If you did this, what would have to precede individual inquiry?

5. List as many primary data sources as you can in your area of the curriculum. Do the same with secondary data sources. Compare your answers with others in your class.

6. The Suchman-Inquiry Model has been erroneously compared to a game of twenty questions. In reality, it is very different. Identify the key characteristics that make it different.

7. How are the planning processes for the General Inquiry Model similar to those in Suchman Inquiry? How are they different?

8. Using concept learning as a perspective, what can the teacher do to improve the quality of questions in Suchman Inquiry?

Chapter *9*

The Cooperative-Learning Model

Cooperative learning *is a cluster of instructional strategies that involve students working collaboratively to reach common goals.* Cooperative learning evolved in an effort to increase student participation, provide students with leadership and group decision-making experiences, and give students the chance to interact and learn with students from different cultural, SES, and ability backgrounds. In this chapter you will study the philosophy and research that support cooperative learning, and you will learn how to implement three specific cooperative-learning strategies in your classroom.

When you've completed your study of this chapter, you should be able to meet the following objectives:

- Describe how cooperative learning differs from traditional, competitive learning strategies.
- Explain why cooperative learning is effective based on two different theoretical views.
- Identify the elements common to all cooperative-learning models.
- Plan, implement, and evaluate lessons using the STAD Cooperative-Learning Model.

- Plan, implement, and evaluate lessons using the Jigsaw II Cooperative-Learning Model.
- Plan, implement, and evaluate lessons using the Group-Investigation Cooperative-Learning Model.

To begin our discussion of cooperative learning, let's look at three teachers using the strategy in their classrooms.

Isabelle Ortega walks around her fourth-grade classroom as groups of students take turns quizzing each other on the week's spelling words. Isabelle implemented the group work when she noticed that her spelling grades were bimodal; some of the students were doing well, but others seemed to be "tuned out."

As an experiment, she formed learning teams. Students took turns quizzing each other on the spelling words and providing feedback. At the end of each week Isabelle gave the class a quiz and graded individual students based on the amount they had improved from previous weeks.

Jim Felton grinned as he saw the assortment of cereal boxes on the front table in his classroom. He finally found a topic that not only interested his middle school students but also one on which they were "experts." Jim's health class had been studying nutrition and the class had been discussing breakfasts. Some students claimed that cereal provided a balanced meal; others argued that most cereals were loaded with sugar, salt, and fat. Then the topic of school lunches came up. Some students defended the school lunches, but the "brown baggers" claimed the meals were high in fat and calories. Jim decided to do something to capitalize on this interest and energy.

He divided his students into teams, each team focusing on a different aspect of nutrition. One group focused on cereals, another on soft drinks, a third on school lunches. Each group used sources such as cereal boxes, magazine articles, and the school dietitian to gather data on its topic. The groups then presented their findings, and the class discussed them.

Jesse Kantor watched as her Biology I students silently studied the chapter on amphibians. The students had study guides that helped them focus on different aspects of amphibian anatomy. Some studied the digestive system, others the circulatory, and still others the nervous system. The next day the "experts" on each system would get together to pool their knowledge and compare notes. The third day these "experts" would take turns teaching their topics to other members of their group. This would be followed by a quiz that would assess students' knowledge of all of the topics.

How are these teaching episodes similar? How are they different? What characteristics do they share and how do these characteristics promote learning? What roles do teachers and students play in this process?

In this chapter, we look at three cooperative-learning strategies. We begin by examining their similarities and then look at ways in which cooperative learning can be adapted to meet specific learning goals.

Cooperative Learning: An Overview

As we saw in our introduction to the chapter, cooperative learning is a group of teaching strategies that puts students in both learning and teaching roles. In addition, cooperative learning requires that students learn to work collaboratively toward common goals, which develops human-relations skills similar to those useful in the world outside of school. In the chapter we'll look at three cooperative-learning models—Student Teams Achievement Division (STAD), Jigsaw II, and Group Investigation—all of which have three essential components:

- Group goals
- Individual accountability
- Equal opportunity for success (Slavin, 1995)

Let's examine each of these more closely.

Group Goals

Cooperative learning gets its name from the fact that students are placed in learning situations in which they work together to reach common goals. These group goals have advantages for both learning and motivation.

Classrooms typically operate under one of three goal structures (Slavin, 1989). In competitive classrooms an individual's goal-directed efforts can frustrate other students. This occurs when teachers grade "on the curve" and students compete with each other for grades; one student's success means another's failure. In individualistic classrooms, each student's efforts have no consequences for others. Individualistic learning occurs when each student works alone. In cooperative classrooms individuals' efforts contribute to others' goal attainment. This is similar to the group reward structure that occurs on soccer or basketball teams in which individuals of unequal ability work together for team goals. Though individual effort is important, the gauge of this effort is the team's performance. **Group goals** *are incentives within cooperative learning that help create a team spirit and encourage students to help each other.* Contrast this group goal orientation with what typically occurs in classrooms.

> The teacher is in front of the class; he or she asks the students questions. Following each question a number of hands go up. Some students are anxiously stretching their hands in the hopes of being called. Others, of course, do not have their hands up and try not to have their eyes meet those of the teacher in hopes they will not be called. The teacher calls on Juan. Peter, who sits next to Juan, knows the right answer. As Juan begins to hesitate, Peter becomes glad and stretches his hand higher. Peter knows that if Juan misses, the teacher may call on him. In fact, the only way in which Peter can obtain a reward in this situation is if Juan fails. It is only natural in this competitive class structure for students to begin to take pleasure in the failure of others. Their own rewards are contingent on the failure of others (S. Kagan, 1986, p. 250).

Cooperative learning tries to avoid these problems by placing students in learning situations where group goals reward cooperation.

Individual Accountability

Though group goals are emphasized, individual learning is still important in the Cooperative-Learning Model. **Individual accountability** *requires that each member of a cooperative-learning group demonstrates mastery of the concepts and skills being taught.* Isabelle held her students accountable by giving each student a spelling quiz at the end of the week but individual reports, papers, or projects could be used as well. The teacher communicates the expectation for individual accountability by emphasizing that all students must understand the content and by requiring that each student demonstrate that understanding.

Equal Opportunity for Success

Group goals build group cohesiveness; individual accountability ensures that each team member learns the content. Equal opportunity for success is a third cooperative-learning element that can increase student motivation. This element is particularly important in heterogeneous classes in which background knowledge and skill levels vary. **Equal opportunity for success** *means that all students, regardless of ability or background, can expect to be recognized for their efforts.*

To promote success, cooperative-learning strategies focus on individual effort and improvement. When teams are used, as in Isabelle's class, team progress is based on individual improvement points. Individuals earn improvement points by earning quiz scores that are higher than their overall averages. The averages are called base scores, which take into account the students' beginning level of achievement. Individual improvement points then contribute to the team's overall performance. Using this system, students who begin at a lower level of achievement can actually make a greater contribution to group goals than a higher-achieving student. Having students compete only against their past performances not only promotes individual motivation but also reduces competition between students. We will discuss implementing improvement point scoring in a later section.

Social Structure of Cooperative Learning

Cooperative-learning models require different classroom roles for both teachers and students than are found in traditional classrooms. In traditional classrooms teachers are the centers of activity and typically use whole-group instruction to disseminate information or explain skills. Also, in these classrooms students are often passive, spending much of their time listening or taking notes. Research indicates that passive students learn less than those who are more active (Eggen and Kauchak, 1994; Wittrock, 1986).

The Teacher's Role
In cooperative-learning activities, teachers often use whole-group instruction to introduce and explain basic concepts and skills, but after this presentation the teacher facilitates

group learning. This begins with the organization of groups, continues with building a sense of teamwork, and includes monitoring the students to ensure that all students are learning.

The Students' Roles

Student roles also change. Cooperative learning requires that students are active and responsible for their own learning. This goal is accomplished by having students act as both teachers and learners. In addition, students also learn to explain, compromise, negotiate, and motivate as they participate as group members. Growth in these social-interaction skills may be some of the most important outcomes of cooperative-learning activities.

Cooperative Learning: Why It Works

Cooperative learning has been thoroughly researched, and the results generally indicate that it is effective (Slavin, 1995). It has been used to reach academic goals ranging from basic skills to higher-order and critical thinking. It has also been used to improve students' interaction skills and to help different racial and ethnic groups learn to work together. Research indicates that it also can help increase the acceptance of students with exceptionalities who are in the regular classroom (Slavin, 1995). How does it accomplish all of these goals?

The success of cooperative learning can be explained from at least three different points of view (Slavin, 1989). Each of these theoretical positions offers a different perspective on what cooperative learning is and how it promotes student growth.

Behaviorist Perspectives

From a behaviorist view, cooperative learning works because of the way it motivates students. Cooperative learning places students in learning situations in which group rewards are given based on group members' performances. This is similar to the group contingencies used in behavior modification in which the whole class is rewarded for the collective efforts of individual members. Cooperative learning works because students are rewarded for working together.

Social Explanations

Other researchers focus on the social aspects of cooperative learning, emphasizing the power of social cohesiveness to build and sustain individual efforts (Sharon and Sharon, 1988). The social cohesion perspective argues that if a learning task is challenging and interesting, the process of working together as a group can be intrinsically motivating. In essence, it's more rewarding to work together than alone. To be successful, this option often requires team-building activities before cooperative-learning activities are conducted and processing and group self-evaluation during and after group work. This process can be long and demanding, but advocates claim that the social and interpersonal benefits are equal to or greater than the cognitive ones (Johnson and Johnson, 1991). Students not only learn more effectively but also learn how to cooperate with others. The importance of growth in these interpersonal skills is hard to overemphasize.

Cognitive Perspectives on Cooperative Learning

A third group of researchers stresses the cognitive benefits of cooperative learning. Cognitive perspectives emphasize the kinds of processing that occur in cooperative-learning groups. Within this perspective, experts stress either student development, cognitive elaboration, or practice with feedback.

Student Development

From a developmental perspective, cooperative learning works because students have opportunities to interact with and learn from other students. Developmentally, one of the most effective ways to encourage conceptual growth is to expose students to higher or more complex ways of thinking (Eggen and Kauchak, 1994). For example, if some students in a science class are having problems controlling variables in science experiments, one way to increase comprehension is to pair them with students who already understand this process. As students work together, less advanced students learn from their more advanced peers, and the understandings of more advanced students are increased as they try to explain abstract ideas to their teammates. Cooperative learning promotes this learning through the give-and-take that occurs in the groups.

Cognitive Elaboration

Cooperative learning is also effective in encouraging cognitive elaboration. Research indicates that elaboration—the process of forming links between ideas that are stored in memory—is one of the most effective ways of promoting learning and long-term retention (Eggen and Kauchak, 1994; Wittrock, 1986). Teachers use elaboration to promote learning by encouraging students to search for and form connections between new content and concepts they already understand. In cooperative-learning activities, one of the most effective ways to encourage elaboration is to ask students to explain material to someone else. Research on this process indicates that students who explain and elaborate learn more than students who just listen to explanations, who in turn learn more than students who learn alone (Slavin, 1989).

Applications of the concept of elaboration can be found throughout education. Teachers often ask students to paraphrase ideas, putting them into their own words. A number of study strategies recommend that students summarize, outline, and draw pictorial representations of the connections between ideas, each of which uses the process of elaboration (Eggen and Kauchak, 1994). Reciprocal teaching uses the processes of summarizing, clarifying, predicting, and asking content-related questions to encourage elaboration (Brown and Palincsar, 1985). Cooperative learning encourages elaboration by requiring students to talk about new ideas with other students in their group.

Practice and Feedback

A final explanation for the effectiveness of cooperative-learning activities relates to the practice and feedback that students receive in the groups. In contrast with whole-group instruction, the feedback in small groups can be individualized and matched to students' present understanding. Student explanations are sometimes more effective than those from adults, because they are offered in terms to which other students can relate.

The perspective people find most satisfying is not important; evidence consistently indicates that cooperative learning can be used to reach a variety of goals. However, as with any model, successful implementation requires careful planning. Let's look at planning for Student Teams Achievement Divisions, the first of the models we discuss in this chapter.

STAD: Student Teams Achievement Divisions

Anya Lozano is beginning a unit on fractions with her fifth graders. She realizes that some of the content is review, so she gives a pretest to help her determine how much her students already know.

As she hands out the pretest, she begins by saying, "Class, this week we're starting a new unit in math on fractions and I'm passing out this pretest to help me find out how much you remember from last year." As she walks from aisle to aisle she hears comments like, "I hate fractions!" and "Not fractions again." Though students often don't care for math, she was surprised at how negative they were. She decided to talk to her friend, co-teacher, and mentor, Kay Reilly, at lunch.

"What do you do when the kids hate the stuff that you have to teach?" she asked as she rifled through her lunch bag trying to decide where to begin.

"Hate is a pretty strong word," Kay grinned. "What could prompt those feelings in our fifth graders?"

"Fractions!" Anya responded. "When I gave them a pretest today I was surprised at the faces and groans I got. Not all of them, granted, but more than usual. . . . I'm not looking forward to this unit."

"Well, be careful about jumping to conclusions, and think for a minute. What are kids usually telling us when they say they hate something?" Kay countered.

". . . Good question," Anya nodded after thinking for a few seconds. ". . . Usually it's something like 'I really dislike this stuff and am going to make it miserable for you if you try and teach it to me.'"

"Oh good, Anya, very analytical and perceptive," Kay replied dryly. "But, seriously, usually when they say they hate something it means they don't understand it or they're afraid of it. They may have had a bad experience last year with fractions and are just afraid of having the same thing happen again."

". . . Could be . . . actually, you're probably right," Anya acknowledged. "The ones who were complaining the loudest were the ones who are a little shaky in math anyway. Makes sense . . . but now what? What do I do now? Help, help!"

"Well, here's what you might try. I've been doing it for a while now, and it takes some work, but it's starting to pay off. . . . Do you have the pretests graded yet? . . . Good. Let me explain what I'm doing."

The next day Anya began her math class in the same way she had planned—by passing out squares of paper and having students divide the squares into halves, thirds, and fourths. Using the chalkboard, overhead, and the papers, she guided her students toward a concept of fractions, and the process of adding fractions with like denominators.

When the students seemed to understand the concept and processes, Anya continued, "You've all been working hard and it looks like you remember a lot about fractions. Now to give you some practice with the ideas we've been discussing, we're going to try something different. Rather than work on our practice sheets alone, like we usually do, we're going to work on them in groups. In a minute I'll tell you how we're going to do this and what group you're in."

She continued, "One of the first things I want you to do when you get in your group is get to know each other and decide on a team name. Your team is important because you will work together for the whole unit. Everyone look up here for a moment. I'm passing out this worksheet that I want everyone to do. It's important for everyone to do their own work and work hard on the work sheet because I'll be giving you a quiz in a week, and your team's score will depend on how well all of the team members do—not just some. Any questions? . . . Hakeem?"

"But how do we know the teams are fair?" Hakeem asked. "Maybe some teams are smarter than others."

"Good question, Hakeem. We'll make sure the teams are fair in two ways. First, everyone took a pretest and I put people on different teams on the basis of their scores. Second, the teams aren't competing with each other. You can all do very well. All teams can win, and no teams have to lose. That's the beauty of what we're going to do."

She went on, "The way we all win is for team members to improve on their understanding. If we improve, we win, and if we all improve, we all win. I'll explain how this works after the first quiz. For now, let's get into our groups and get started. Listen carefully when I call your name. Team one, over here in this corner. Alysia, Manuel. . . ."

After students moved to their groups, Anya spent the next half hour explaining to them how cooperative learning works and modeling for them effective small-group behaviors.

When Kay Reilly first explained cooperative learning to Anya, she stressed the importance of teacher work and attention at this point. "Good cooperative-learning groups don't just happen, they need to be developed," Kay stressed. At first Anya was a little skeptical, but she listened anyway and as she listened she became convinced.

As Anya worked with her students in these groups, she was grateful for Kay's advice. Some of the students argued and others had trouble sharing materials, but after some work in these areas Anya finally had the groups working together.

As students talked in their groups Anya circulated around the room to be sure all the groups were functioning as smoothly as possible. In a few groups she had to stop some students from dominating the activity while in others she had to clarify procedures and expectations. Once the groups were working satisfactorily, Anya quietly circulated among them thinking to herself, "Maybe this will work."

Each math class that week followed a similar format. Anya began by introducing the concept or skill, then modeled different computational and problem-solving processes for the students, and finally had the students work in their groups to practice. While they worked, Anya continued to circulate around the room, monitoring their work and offering suggestions.

On the fourth day of group work, she interrupted the students to announce, "Class, can I have your attention for a minute? I just wanted to share with you an idea that the Eagle team is trying out. They weren't as confident about the topic today, so they started out by doing the first three problems together. When they thought they all understood what they were doing, they went back to doing them on their own and checking them with each other. This is an idea you might want to try out in your group; however you want to do these problems is fine with me. The important thing is that everyone should thoroughly understand how to do the problems when you're finished."

Anya checked students' papers each night to monitor her class's learning progress. She was pleasantly surprised by the work students were handing in—especially some of students who had been low achievers. After five days of group work, Anya decided they were ready for a quiz. She gave the quiz and scored the papers over the weekend. She was pleased and somewhat surprised with the results. The general level of understanding on the quiz was high and, more importantly, she didn't have the usual few scores that were well below those of the rest of the class. Most of them seemed to understand fractions!

Student Teams Achievement Divisions (STAD) *is a form of cooperative learning that uses multi-ability learning teams to teach specific forms of content—facts, concepts, generalizations, principles, academic rules, and skills.* Developed by Robert Slavin (1986, 1995), it is one of the most popular cooperative-learning strategies in use in the schools today.

STAD is closely related to the Direct-Instruction Model, which we discussed in Chapter 6. There we saw that direct instruction followed four steps, which are:

- Introduction
- Presentation
- Guided Practice
- Independent Practice

When STAD is used, the introduction, presentation, and guided practice phases are (or can be) identical to those in direct instruction, or the presentation phase could be done using the Inductive Model. The key difference is in the independent practice phase. When STAD is used, independent practice isn't independent; rather, it is done in cooperative-learning groups. We'll discuss organizing these groups in the sections that follow.

Planning Lessons with the STAD Model

Planning for using the STAD Cooperative-Learning Model is a five-step process that includes the following:

- Planning for instruction
- Organizing groups

- Planning team-building activities
- Planning for team study
- Calculating base scores

Planning for Instruction

Since instruction using STAD is conducted using either the Inductive Model or the Direct-Instruction Model, planning for instruction using STAD is identical to planning using either of those models. Table 9.1 reviews planning for instruction using those models.

As with either the Inductive Model or the Direct-Instruction Model, having clear goals in mind and preparing high-quality examples is critical when STAD is used.

Organizing Groups

To effectively implement any kind of cooperative learning, teams must be organized in advance. The goal is to create teams of four or five members that have approximately equal ranges of ability and are mixed by gender and ethnicity (Slavin, 1995). Slavin suggests that four is an ideally sized group, but groups of five can also be effective.

One way to form cooperative-learning groups that are similar in range of ability is to rank the students, divide them into quartiles and place one student from each quartile into each group. Students can be ranked according to a pretest, as Anya did, or grades or scores from previous units, or some combination can be used. Forming groups based on the rankings are illustrated in Table 9.2, with a sample class of 25 students.

A common way of grouping the students is to take the highest achievers from the first two quartiles and pair them with the lowest achievers from the third and fourth quartiles. For example, the first group would then include Natacha, Tolitha, Stephan, and Mary, and the second group would be Lucinda, Marvin, Howard, and David. The sixth group, having five members because of the number of people in the class, would then be Juan, Leroy, Julia, Gerald, and Cynthia.

After initially forming the groups, the teacher should check their makeup to see if they are balanced by gender and ethnicity. For example, the first group has three girls and a boy, while the second has three boys and a girl. The teacher might arbitrarily switch two of the students to balance the groups. This is a matter of judgment.

Other ways of forming groups are also acceptable as long as they meet the goal of having the groups balanced by range of achievement, gender, and ethnicity.

TABLE 9.1   Planning for Instruction Using the Inductive Model and the Direct-Instruction Model

Model	Content Taught	Planning Steps
Inductive Model	Concepts Principles Generalizations Academic rules	Identify topic Specify objective Prepare examples
Direct-Instruction Model	Skills Concepts	Identify topic Specify objective Select problems and examples

TABLE 9.2   Grouping Students Based on Rankings

1	Natacha	13	Julia
2	Lucinda	14	Gerald
3	Vicki	15	Henrietta
4	Jerome	16	Lawsekia
5	Steve	17	Andrea
6	Juan	18	Howard
		19	Stephan
7	Tolitha	20	Cynthia
8	Marvin	21	Kevin
9	Enrico	22	Kathe
10	Sara	23	Ron
11	Eugene	24	David
12	Leroy	25	Mary

Planning Team-Building Activities

Research indicates that merely placing students together in groups doesn't ensure trust and cooperation (Scruggs and Richter, 1988). An important planning task is to design group-building activities that help students learn to accept and trust each other. The purpose of team-building exercises is to help students get acquainted, develop a team identity, and help individuals get to know each other as partners and helpmates. Anya began by having each of her teams select a name for their group. Some additional examples of team-building exercises are found in Table 9.3.

A variety of other team-building activities could be used as well. Some teachers identify specific behaviors that they expect from students, such as, "using quiet voices," "making supporting statements," and "listening while a teammate is talking," and then giving groups tokens as rewards for displaying the behaviors. Others argue that a system of rewards detracts from self-regulation and shouldn't be used. The issue is a matter of teacher judgment. The goal is to promote teamwork and cooperation, and reaching the goal requires planning.

Planning for Team Study

The success of STAD learning teams depends on having high-quality materials that guide the interactions within the groups. As teachers plan their lessons, they need to ask themselves, "What specific concepts or skills are students learning, and how can I design materials that

TABLE 9.3   Team-Building Activities

Activity	Description
Favorites	Team members interview each other about their favorites—food, music, hobby, sport, etc.
Biographies	Students interview each other and find out about each other's backgrounds.
Occupations	Students talk about what they might want to be later on in life.
Most Interesting Topics	Students interview each other about different topics in the class that interest them.

will allow them to learn effectively in their groups?" This is where clearly specified objectives are important. They ensure that the instruction and team study are aligned with the objectives.

A variety of team study materials can be used. In math, as in Anya's case, they might be problems to be solved. In language arts they could be paragraphs to be punctuated or corrected grammatically. In geography the exercises might require students to identify cities closest to given longitude and latitude coordinates.

It is important that the team study materials require convergent answers; that is, answers that are clearly correct or incorrect, such as the solutions to problems with fractions, or paragraphs that are punctuated properly. If the content doesn't lend itself to convergent answers, STAD isn't the most effective model to use.

Calculating Base Scores

In an earlier section we said that one of the characteristics of the cooperative-learning models described in this chapter is the concept of equal opportunity for success, which means that all students, regardless of past achievement, can expect to succeed if they genuinely try.

Equal opportunity for success is accomplished by awarding students improvement points if their score on a test or quiz is higher than their base score. A student's base score is the student's average on past tests and quizzes, or it could be determined based on a previous year's or term's grade. Table 9.4 illustrates a sample calculation of base scores from grades.

The teacher should determine each student's base score prior to introducing the students to STAD.

Improvement Points.   Improvement points are awarded based on how students perform on a test or quiz compared to their base scores. A sample system for awarding improvement points is illustrated in Table 9.5.

The system you see illustrated is arbitrary, and it can be adapted to meet the needs of specific classes. For example, you may choose to award some improvement points for any score that is no more than five points below the base score. On the other hand, you may require an improvement of twelve, fifteen, or even more in order to be awarded thirty improvement points. You can also change the system as student confidence and skills increase. You may want to begin by rewarding virtually any effort—particularly with chronic low achievers—and then raise the standards as the students' achievement increases. Whatever system you use for determining the base scores, you need to have considered and planned for it in advance.

Before closing this section we want to emphasize one point. Note that students can receive the maximum of thirty points if they get a perfect paper, regardless of their base

TABLE 9.4   Calculating Base Scores from Grades

A	90
A–/B+	85
B	80
B–/C+	75
C	70
C–/D+	65
D	60
F	55

Adapted from Kagan, 1992; Slavin, 1995

TABLE 9.5   Awarding Improvement Points

Improvement Points	Score on Test or Quiz
0	Below base score
10	One to five points above base score
20	Six to ten points above base score
30	More than ten points above base score, or
	Perfect paper (regardless of base score)

scores. This is important for high-achieving students. For example, if a student has a 95 average, it is impossible to improve by more than five points, so the student's incentive to improve would be reduced if the perfect-score provision didn't exist.

Implementing Lessons Using the STAD Cooperative-Learning Model

Having planned for instruction, identified group membership, planned for team building and team study, and calculated the students' base scores, you are ready to implement STAD with your students.

Implementing STAD cooperative-learning lessons is much like implementing lessons with the Direct-Instruction Model. The lesson is introduced, the content is explained, and students are involved in guided practice. Then, team study takes the place of independent practice. However, STAD differs from the simple Direct-Instruction Model in that some instruction is often required to ensure a smooth transition from whole-group to team study, and testing, improvement points, and team recognition are integral parts of STAD. These phases are outlined in Table 9.6.

Phase 1: Instruction
When STAD is used, the instruction is identical to the instruction used in the Direct-Instruction Model. The lesson is introduced by specifying the goals, presenting, explaining, and modeling the skills or applications of concepts, principles, generalizations, and rules, and providing for guided practice. Anya's instruction illustrated this process. She

TABLE 9.6   Phases in Implementing STAD

Phase	Purpose
Instruction	Introduce lesson
	Explain and model content
	Provide guided practice
Transition to teams	Move students from whole group to learning teams
Team study and monitoring	Ensure that groups are functioning effectively
Testing	Provide feedback about learning
	Provide basis for awarding improvement points
Recognition of achievement	Increase motivation

carefully explained and illustrated fractions with her manipulatives and had the students practice under her guidance. When she felt the students had an acceptable grasp on the concept of fractions and the procedures for adding them, she moved to team study.

Phase 2: Transition to Teams

Obstacles to smoothly functioning cooperative lessons are often logistical. Research indicates that whole-group instruction is easier to manage than small-group work for at least two reasons (Good and Brophy, 1994). First, in large-group work the teacher is able to "steer the lesson," speeding up and slowing down based on the students' progress, and second, large groups allow the teacher to monitor and deal with learning or management problems. When first introducing small-group work, the teacher needs to be carefully organized, trying to anticipate logistical problems in advance.

When first introducing team study, teachers should thoroughly explain how cooperative learning works and the specific procedures to be followed. Let's see how Anya helped her students make the transition to teams.

"OK everyone, I think we have a pretty good idea of what fractions mean and how we add them together when the denominators are the same. Now we're ready to practice. The way we're going to do that is by assigning each of you to a team, and having each team practice the new content. Because this is a little new, I'm going to show you how it works before I ask you to do it.

"In a few minutes I'm going to break you into the groups that you'll be working with for this unit. Before that, I want to show you how one group should work. Tanya, Mariko, Willy, can you come up here and sit at these desks? . . . Thanks! Class, this is what your group will look like—it will have four members, and for sake of this illustration, I will be the fourth member. After we break into groups I'll give each group four worksheets, just like I'm doing here."

Anya then took a few seconds to give the materials to the group at the front of the room and took one herself.

She then continued, "Now, Tanya and Willy are a pair, and Mariko and I are a pair. Each person does the problem and checks with his or her partner. For example, Tanya does the problem and then checks the answer with Willy, and Mariko and I do the problem and we check with each other. If Tanya and Willy agree on the answer and believe that they both understand it, they move to the next problem. Mariko and I do the same. If Tanya and Willy disagree, they ask Mariko and me, and we do the same with them. We all discuss the problem until we're all sure we understand it. OK, let's go ahead."

The four of them then worked the first problem and checked with their partners. (Anya intentionally got a wrong answer for sake of the illustration.)

"I didn't get that," she said loud enough for the class to hear. "Please explain that to me."

Anya then discussed ways of providing helpful feedback to each other, and she also modeled appropriate and inappropriate ways of interacting with partners.

"What happens if we all disagree?" Leanne asked, after seeing the process modeled.

"Good question, Leanne. If all four of you have thoroughly discussed the problem and cannot come to an understanding, then you may ask me, . . . but remember," she emphasized, "you may only ask me after all four of you have carefully discussed the problem."

Anya then assigned the rest of the class to their groups and had them begin.

When introducing students to cooperative learning, the initial directions need to be very detailed. In Anya's case, for example, we saw that she illustrated and modeled the process with one group before she had all the students begin team study.

Some teachers even prearrange the desks in the room, suggesting that pairs sit side-by-side facing their teammates who are also side-by-side. This prevents the disturbance of moving desks around.

Teachers have also found it useful to place the following information on a poster, discuss it with the class, and leave it displayed for reference:

- Group memberships for different teams
- Location in the room for different teams
- Procedures for obtaining and turning in materials
- Time frames

By spending extra time on logistics at the beginning of cooperative-learning lessons, the teacher is laying the foundation for smoothly functioning groups later on.

Phase 3: Team Study and Monitoring

As students work in their groups, teachers need to carefully monitor their work to ensure that they are functioning smoothly, but they need to be careful about intervening too soon. One of the goals of cooperative learning is to teach students to work together, and like many types of learning, this process isn't always smooth; more often it is characterized by fits and starts and uneven progress. Early intervention may actually be counterproductive, as students often need time and freedom to work through group problems. However, if students aren't working together, one is dominating a group or someone isn't participating, intervention may be necessary. Again, when to intervene is a matter of professional judgment.

What can be more helpful than individual intervention is calling attention to particularly productive groups. Let's see how Anya did this.

"Class, can I have your attention, please, just for a second? I know you're all working hard but I just wanted to share an idea with you. The Cheetah team came up with a great idea to work through their problems. They got a box of the blocks, the ones we used earlier, and every time one of the members is having trouble with one of the problems, they use the blocks to explain the answer. I heard one of the group members say, 'Sure you can do this. Just try it again.' That is very helpful and supportive and that's the way we want to treat our teammates."

Group interventions that focus on positive practice help students understand different roles in the groups and provide positive models for the other students.

Phase 4: Testing

Testing serves several functions in the STAD Cooperative-Learning Model. From a traditional assessment point of view, it provides both the teacher and students with feedback about learning progress. From a motivational perspective it can provide incentives for work and effort. The key to the first function—evaluation and feedback—is a well-designed test that accurately assesses important concepts and skills. Here, again, clear objectives are critical because they specify important learning outcomes.

Recognizing Achievement

Results from tests and quizzes can also serve as strong motivators when integrated into a scoring system based on improvement points. The basic idea behind an improvement scoring system is that individuals compete only against their own past performance to earn points. When they match past performances, they are given a small number of improvement points; when they exceed their past performance, the improvement points increase in proportion.

Team Scoring. Team scoring is based on the improvement of individual team members. As an example, let's look again at the group composed of Natacha, Tolitha, Stephan, and Mary. Suppose that their averages and quiz scores are as follows:

Name	Average	Quiz Score
Natacha	95	96
Tolitha	88	90
Stephan	75	84
Mary	69	80

Based on the system illustrated in the section on planning for improvement points, Natacha would receive ten improvement points and Tolitha would also get ten since their scores were in the range of one to five points higher than their base score (average). In comparison Stephan would receive twenty improvement points since his quiz score was nine points above his base score, and Mary would receive thirty points, because her score was more than ten points above her base. Mary, the student in the group with the history of lowest achievement, actually got the most improvement points. This is how the equal opportunity for success provision is accomplished when STAD is used.

While the use of reinforcers, such as improvement points, is somewhat controversial, research indicates that the system has a positive effect on motivation (Slavin, 1995). The extent to which teachers use the system in their classes is a matter of professional judgment.

Team Awards. Team scores are determined by averaging the improvement points for the team, and the awards are then given. The following is an example of a reward system.

Criterion	*Award*
(Average Improvement)	
10	WINNERS
15	STARS
20	ALL STARS
25	MAJOR LEAGUERS

Group awards can take a variety of forms; teachers can judge the exact form based on what is attractive to the students. For example, *Winners* might be asked to stand and be recognized in class, *Stars* could get a certificate of congratulations, *All Stars* a more elaborate certificate, and *Major Leaguers* a group photo on a "hall of fame" section of the bulletin board. Other options could include buttons to wear around school, letters to parents, special privileges, and leadership roles.

Students should be reminded that neither teams nor individuals are competing with each other; individuals only compete with their past performances. If individuals improve, all teams can potentially become Major Leaguers. Teams can be changed periodically, such as after four or five weeks, to allow students to work with other classmates and to give students on low-scoring teams a chance for increased success.

Assessing Learning Using STAD

Assessment of STAD lessons occurs on two levels. The first relates to the content goals of the lesson and are similar to assessing understanding when the Inductive Model or the Direct-Instruction Model is used. Assessments should be aligned with objectives, instruction, and team study activities. For example, Anya had as her content objectives:

- Identifying the numerator and denominator in a fraction.
- Adding fractions with like denominators.

Assessment would measure individual students' attainment of these objectives.

Using Improvement Points in Grading
While somewhat controversial, some teachers develop grading systems that reflect improvement. For instance, if a student averages 15 or more improvement points on tests and quizzes, his or her grade might be raised from a B– to a B, or from a B to a B+. The decision is a matter of professional judgment. Many teachers feel that seeing improvement reflected in their grades is an added incentive for students.

Assessing Group Work and Cooperation
At a second, more complex level, assessment of STAD activities attempts to answer questions such as, "Are students getting better at working together as a team?" Here, the best source of information comes from observing students as they work together in groups. Some questions to ask as you are doing this include:

- Are all members contributing?
- Are some members dominating?

- Do males and females contribute equally?
- Are members from different racial and ethnic groups being included?
- Is the group interaction positive and supportive?

By continually attending to these questions, teachers can help individuals and groups learn to cooperate and work together.

As teachers assess cooperation using these criteria, they can provide feedback to the class, using smoothly functioning groups as models. This may be as simple as noting, "I really like the way this group is taking turns giving feedback," or may involve role-playing, where students publicly work out problems that individual groups are having. The goal of this process is to help students become aware of their interactions in the groups and the influence these interactions are having on their own and others' learning.

This completes our discussion of Student Teams Achievement Divisions. We turn now to another cooperative-learning model, Jigsaw II.

Jigsaw II

Kevin Davis looked out his classroom window on a blustery spring Friday and let out an audible "Hmmmm." The year had gone well so far for his world geography class but he wasn't quite sure where to go from there. The next section of the text was Central America and Kevin had had problems with it last year. Maybe it was the timing—spring fever—and perhaps students were just getting tired of their intellectual journey around the world. Maybe, though, he thought, it was the way he taught it last year—minilectures supplemented with small-group discussions. He had tried this strategy on Thursday when he presented an overview of the new unit, but the students didn't seem excited about the content. Kevin knew he had to try something new, if only for change and energy.

He spent part of that weekend glancing at notes and books from workshops and graduate classes that he had kept. One idea that kept popping up was student involvement—how to get students actively involved in their own learning. As he thought about this idea he kept flashing on cooperative learning. He had tried learning teams in another class where there were a number of important names and dates that students had to master, but he didn't feel that would be appropriate here. What he really wanted students to remember was the "big picture" in terms of the Central American countries, not a lot of facts about each. He decided to try something different.

Monday morning he arrived early, sat down at his computer, and prepared several handouts. As he duplicated them, he finalized plans for introducing the new activity and organizing the groups. He hoped he was ready.

"Class," Kevin began as the students settled in after the tardy bell, "we're going to try something different for our next unit. I've decided to make you folks the experts on this content and have you teach each other."

He paused to survey the class to gauge its initial reaction. From their puzzled looks Kevin could tell they were curious. So far so good.

"To do this," he continued, "I've placed each of you in teams of four. I've tried to divide these teams so that all of the teams are about equal. We'll be working in these teams for the next couple of weeks. Your job on these teams is to do two things. First, each of you needs to become an expert on one part of each chapter. Can everyone take out their texts and turn to Chapter 17? That's on page 346. I'll show you what I mean."

He paused as students turned to the correct page, and then went on, "You'll notice in the introduction to the chapter on Costa Rica that it is divided into four sections—the physical geography of the country, its history, its culture, and its economy. We talked about these areas on Thursday. I'm going to ask each of you to become an expert in one of these areas and then teach that content to your other group members. To help you become 'experts,' I have a summary sheet for each of these topics to help you in your note taking. Let's see what one of these looks like."

With that, he walked over to the overhead and displayed the transparency shown in Table 9.7 for the class.

"We'll call this our 'expert sheet'; each of you will have one of these when you read the chapter, and it will help you in your note taking. We'll take the rest of today and all of tomorrow to work on this. At the beginning of class on Wednesday, the experts on each topic will get together to review their notes and make sure everyone has the essential information. On Thursday the experts in each group will take turns teaching their topics to each other. For example, if Miguel has history he'll teach the other members what he learned about the history of Costa Rica; then, if Yolanda has culture she'll learn about history from Miguel and then teach him about the culture of Costa Rica. On Friday we'll take the first part of the class to review and put all this information together, and then we'll take a quiz on this chapter. The quiz will have an even number of questions on each of the topics, so you'll get some questions on the topic that you've studied extensively and some on the other areas. That means you need to learn everything—not just your topic. We'll record team scores and keep a running tally from chapter to chapter. I'll talk more about this later. . . . Any questions? . . . Good."

"Then, let me quickly review our procedures. We'll break into groups in a minute. When you get into your groups, I have an activity that will help you get to know each other a little better. Then you, as a group, decide who's going to be the expert in each of the four areas. If you don't get your first pick this time, you will the next. We'll rotate these around. All right everyone, look up here for your group assignment. Note that the assignment also tells where in the room your group should meet. Let's go!"

TABLE 9.7   Jigsaw II Expert Sheet

Physical Geography

1. Climate
   a. Seasons
   b. Temperatures
   c. Rainfall
2. Topography
   a. Mountains
   b. Water
   c. Land
   d. Prominent features

The students quickly moved into their groups, and Kevin called for their attention. He then had them do a "team-building activity" for ten minutes. Finally, he announced, "I think you've done a good job with the activity, and we'll do more team building as we continue with the unit. . . . Now, I want the room quiet while each of you reads your section of the chapter and takes notes. We'll finish this on Tuesday and move into our expert groups on Wednesday. I'll be around to help you. Thursday is expert teaching day. You'll each teach the other members of your group and learn from them about their topic. Make sure you take good notes to study from for the test on Friday. . . . Questions? . . . Good. . . . Look up at the board. I've written the schedule for the week there as a reminder."

Structure of the Jigsaw II Model

Like other cooperative-learning strategies, Jigsaw II derives its effectiveness from the active involvement of students as they work in small groups. **Jigsaw II** *is a form of cooperative learning in which individual students become experts on subsections of a topic and teach that subsection to others.*

Jigsaw II differs from STAD in that it uses a concept called task specialization. **Task specialization** *requires that different students assume specialized roles in reaching the goals of a learning activity.* In the case of Jigsaw II, students become experts on a particular portion of a learning task and use their expertise to teach other students. Kevin Davis had his students focus on different aspects of a country's geography as they learned about Central American countries. Then, when they worked as a team, each member contributed a different piece in the knowledge puzzle—thus, the name Jigsaw. One key to the success of Jigsaw II is the interdependence it fosters in team members; students must depend on each other to learn the content.

Jigsaw II was developed by Robert Slavin (1986) as an adaptation of the original Jigsaw strategy. The original Jigsaw, developed by Aronson and his associates (1978) to encourage interdependence among team members, used customized learning materials designed especially for the Jigsaw strategy. These materials were designed so that the expert was the only one who saw the materials for a particular section. Consequently, students *had* to depend on each other to learn the information in each others' sections.

There were two drawbacks to the original Jigsaw that Jigsaw II overcomes. The biggest problem was the need for special learning materials, which had to be prepared in advance, making the teacher's planning too demanding. The second drawback was the fact that the "nonexperts" didn't have access to all of the materials. If students didn't learn well from the "expert" presentations, they had nothing to fall back on. Jigsaw II, which uses existing text materials, intends to eliminate both of these problems.

Jigsaw II is designed to increase understanding of preexisting written materials such as student textbooks, but it can be used to provide background information to supplement other strategies (Kagan, 1992). For example, it could be used to provide background information on controversial issues in social studies. Before a discussion on nuclear energy, for example, some students might study the history, others the technology, and still others the ecological perspectives. Prior to the discussion, each group of students could share expertise on their topics.

As another example, in a unit on poetry, different students might learn about rhyme, meter, symbolism, and authors' lives. Then, in analyses of different poems, each student or group of students would contribute a perspective on the work.

Planning for the Jigsaw II Model

Planning for Jigsaw II lessons is similar to planning for STAD. Objectives need to be specified, learning materials need to be prepared, and students need to be assigned to teams. In addition, materials to assess learning progress also need to be constructed.

However, because Jigsaw II relies on individual study, planning for whole-group instruction is not required. These steps are summarized in Figure 9.1. In the following sections we'll examine how planning activities can be adapted to meet the special goals of the Jigsaw II Model.

Specifying Objectives

As opposed to STAD, which focuses on learning specific facts, concepts, or skills, Jigsaw II is designed to teach mastery of organized bodies of knowledge. These could be chapters in a text, story, biography, or history of events. The goal for Jigsaw II lessons is to help students understand a topic using available materials, such as books, videotapes, and videodiscs.

Designing Learning Materials

The major tasks during this part of the planning process are the gathering of materials and the construction of expert sheets that guide students' study and teaching efforts. Resource materials can come from a number of sources: present texts, previously used texts, library books, encyclopedias, magazines, and nonprint sources such as videotapes and videodiscs.

In addition to resource materials, teachers also need to plan for the study sheets that help students focus on important information and issues. These can include questions, outlines, matrices, charts, and hierarchies. Kevin used outlines that divided key topics into subcategories. Research indicates that well-organized expert sheets help guide student thinking and result in effective presentations (Eggen and Kauchak, 1994).

Form Student Teams

In forming student teams, the same considerations that existed for STAD apply here. As with STAD, groups should be balanced in terms of achievement, gender, and cultural background.

1. Specify Objectives

2. Design Learning Materials

3. Form Student Teams

4. Design Evaluation Instruments

FIGURE 9.1   Planning for Jigsaw II

Once groups are formed, it is important that members get to know each other and that group identity and cohesion develop. The same strategies described earlier for STAD can also be used here.

Assigning Experts.   An additional factor in forming teams exists with Jigsaw II that didn't exist with STAD. Since each member of a team is required to develop expertise with respect to part of the topic, it is important that the expert teams also be mixed according to achievement. Kevin allowed the students to decide and assured them that if they didn't get their first pick this time, they would get it next time.

Students will be more committed to a topic of their choice than to one that is assigned. On the other hand, if the lowest achievers for each group all happened to be responsible for the cultures of the countries, for example, the quality of learning for that segment of the topic would probably suffer. In a mixed-ability group, by contrast, since all members of an expert group are responsible for understanding that aspect of the topic, the lower achievers in the group would learn from the higher achievers, and they would then be in a better position to teach the members of their team.

Designing Assessments

As we've seen, cooperative learning is most effective when all students are held account-able for learning and when hard-working individuals and teams are rewarded for their efforts. Effective assessments can help accomplish both of these goals.

In designing assessments, a table or planning matrix is helpful to ensure that all top-ics receive equal weight on the quiz or test and that the items are at an appropriate level of difficulty. A sample for Kevin's class is shown in Figure 9.2.

Implementing Lessons Using Jigsaw II

Jigsaw II is a five-phase strategy that begins with information gathering, proceeds through a process of disseminating information within groups, and culminates in assessment and recognition (Slavin, 1995). The specific phases in implementing lessons are presented and described in Table 9.8.

Topic	Items		
	Knowledge	Comprehension	Application
Physical Geography			
History			
Culture			
Economy			

FIGURE 9.2   Planning for Assessment Matrix

TABLE 9.8   Phases in Implementing Jigsaw II

Phase	Description
Information Gathering	Students are assigned to groups Student "experts" are assigned topics "Experts" locate and study essential information
Expert Meetings	Experts meet to compare notes and refine presentations
Team Reports	Experts teach topic to other team members
Test	Students take individual quiz on all topics
Recognition	Individual and group performances are recognized

Information Gathering

In the first phase of Jigsaw II, students are assigned to groups and given topics about which they are to develop expertise. Since Jigsaw II uses preexisting materials such as chapters from books, the only logistical task is being certain that the learning materials—textbooks, videotapes, etc.—are available for the students, and that the sheets guiding the experts' study are available. The first time you use Jigsaw II you may have to walk students through one of the expert sheets to help them understand how they can be used to structure and guide their efforts.

The actual study time can be done either in class or as a homework assignment. When first introducing Jigsaw II, it is helpful to do the first few sessions as in-class activities. This provides the teacher with opportunities to monitor the activity and offer suggestions to the groups.

Expert Meetings

After students have had time to study their individual topics, expert meetings allow "experts" opportunities to compare notes and clarify areas of misunderstanding. A discussion leader should be assigned to moderate the session and make sure everyone is actively involved. This role can be rotated so that everyone gets an opportunity to lead and participate. The expert sheets passed out earlier help provide structure for this discussion.

Team Report

During team report meetings experts return to their groups and take turns teaching the group about their topic. This not only shares the experts' knowledge but also encourages experts to organize and summarize their information. Encouraging and helping experts organize their information and offering suggestions for presentations can help increase the effectiveness of the learning in these sessions.

Evaluation and Recognition

The process for evaluating individual student performance and recognizing group achievement can be similar to the process used for STAD. Individual students are held accountable for their understanding of the content, improvement points can be given for continually increasing achievement, and group recognition in the form of certificates, letters to parents, names and pictures on the bulletin board, and privileges can all be used.

Assessing Student Understanding with Jigsaw II

Assessing student understanding with Jigsaw II lessons occurs on three levels. First, we want to know if groups are functioning smoothly and whether students are growing in their ability to work together. Second, we want to know if students can investigate and organize topics and share this learning with others. Third, we want to know if individual students understand the content. Each of these is discussed in the following sections.

Assessing Group Processes

In assessing group processes, we want to know if students are learning to function as productive members of a group. This includes speaking, listening, sharing ideas, and helping the group move in a positive direction. The same kinds of questions asked about STAD lessons apply here. Some are:

- Are all members contributing?
- Are some members dominating?
- Do males and females contribute equally?
- Are members from different racial and ethnic groups being included?
- Is the group interaction positive and supportive?

To these we would add questions about whether experts are explaining content clearly. Again, this may need to be taught through modeling and role-playing.

Assessing the Development of Expertise

A second assessment question is whether or not students are growing as expert presenters and members of each team. Jigsaw II requires sophisticated learning skills such as note-taking and organization, and it requires the even more sophisticated ability of teaching content to others. These skills must be taught and monitored. One way to teach the skills is through think-alouds in which the teacher models the skill while talking out loud. As students practice in their groups, teachers should monitor their work and provide feedback.

Assessing Student Understanding of Content

In terms of content evaluation, the objectives and evaluation matrices (see Figure 9.2) that were used during the planning process help ensure that evaluation instruments are congruent with goals. One of the challenges of assessing Jigsaw II activities is to construct instruments that challenge experts, but don't overwhelm nonexperts. A combination of paper-and-pencil items together with actual work samples can often be combined into effective assessments.

This concludes our discussion of the Jigsaw II Cooperative-Learning Model. In the next section we describe Group Investigation, a Cooperative-Learning Model designed to help students learn to conduct research on specific topics.

Group Investigation

To this point we have described cooperative-learning strategies designed to help students learn facts, concepts, skills, and organized bodies of content. Cooperative learning can also be used to help students learn problem solving and higher-order and critical-thinking abilities. A cooperative-learning strategy called Group Investigation is designed to reach these goals. Let's see how one teacher implements the strategy in her classroom.

Kim Herron had been teaching junior high science for three years and was generally happy with her teaching. She felt that she gave the students a sound foundation for their work in high school and a general understanding of the role of science in their lives. She wasn't quite as happy with her progress in helping students "think," however. They seemed all too happy to memorize the material she gave them, rather than thinking on their own. Kim decided that this year would be different.

The school science fair was coming up in two months. She had encouraged her students to participate and most did, but the quality of the projects was uneven. Kim could tell which students had received help from their parents—which was fine—but what about the rest of the students? She decided to make Fridays in her class group-project day, and the focal point for the projects would be the science fair to be held in May.

As she sat down to plan for these Fridays, Kim asked herself, "Where do I start? What do they need to get started on their group projects?" After looking out the window, considerable doodling on her notepad, and occasional thumbing through old science-methods texts and teachers' editions, she decided on a two-pronged attack. First, they would need some information about good science projects—what they did, how they were implemented, and how they were reported.

"That shouldn't be too difficult," she thought. "I have got some winners from the last few years."

Then they would need some background knowledge on the topics they were studying. As she thought about this, she jotted down some possibilities and made a note to work on them.

On the next Friday she began her class by saying, "OK, listen everybody. . . . We're going to try something different in here today and for the remainder of the Fridays until the Science Fair, which is May 7. We're going to use Friday classes to work on our science projects and we're going to do this a little differently than we have in the past. First, I'll give you class time to work on the projects and I'll expect weekly progress reports on how you're doing. Second, I'd like you to do the projects in groups rather than individually. This will result in better-quality work, and I think you'll learn a lot from each other. To divide you into groups I'm going to ask each of you to write your name and some topics you're interested in studying on a piece of paper. I'll pull this information together and assign you to groups by next Friday. These groups won't be set in stone but this process will allow us to get started."

The next Friday she had the different groups listed on the bulletin board by topics and members. Students congregated around the board buzzing and talking as they entered the room. As Kim observed the excitement, she hoped that the group activity wouldn't interfere with learning.

"Oh well," she thought to herself as the bell rang, "here goes."

As the class quieted down, Kim walked to the front of the room, paused briefly, and began, "You've probably already seen your assignments as you came in the room. If you didn't, you can check up here (gesturing to the bulletin board) when we break into groups. For today, our first job will be to get to know the other members on our teams. To do that, I'd like each person to interview another team member, so when you first get into your groups select a partner. Then, ask your partner why he or she is interested in that topic. Also, see if you can find any other interesting information about your partner with respect to science. Remember, the interview must focus on your topic and science in general. One person should interview the other, and then switch. Each person will make a short introduction of that person to your group. Take notes so you can remember all the important points."

Kim paused and then said, "Before we break into groups let's quickly review to make sure we know what each person's responsibility will be. What's the first thing you'll do in your groups? Alysha?"

"Find a partner."

"Good, Alysha. Then what? . . . Anyone? . . . Selena?"

"Interview your partner?"

"Fine. And what questions will you ask? . . . Antonia?"

"The ones on the board."

"Good. And what will you do with the interview information? Juan?"

"Report back to the group," Juan replied.

"Excellent, everyone!" Kim exclaimed. "Now remember our goal here is to begin to get to know each other so we can work effectively in our teams."

"To avoid congestion let's have Group 1 over here at the front of the room, Group 2 over here, Group 3 back there, Group 4 over there, Group 5 in the corner, Group 6 over here, and Group 7 up here. If you don't know what group you're in, check the bulletin board. All set? . . . It's 1:20. I expect you to be done by 1:40. OK, let's go, move."

Kim watched as the students got into their groups. Surprisingly, it went smoother than she anticipated and the groups quickly settled into the rhythm of interviewing.

A hand went up. "What do we do if there isn't an even number of students?"

"Good question, Jianna. Class, if there is an odd number in your group due to absence or some other reason, do your interviews in threes."

The class settled again into a low hum as Kim moved around the room. Most of the groups were working well and the others seemed to need only a gentle reminder to get back on track.

At 1:30 Kim announced, "Everyone, you should be done with your interviews by now and should be sharing your findings with other members of the group. You have five more minutes and then we'll move on to another activity."

At 1:35 Kim brought the class together again and announced, "Good job everyone. We're now ready to begin our next task, which is to try and understand what a good project looks like. To help us, I've placed several award-winning projects around the room. I'd like the groups to examine each of the projects to try to figure out why they won awards. Take notes and talk about your ideas in your group and then we'll come back together as a class to discuss our findings. OK, questions? . . . Then let's move."

The class spent the remainder of the period examining the projects and discussing the criteria for good projects.

Near the end of the period Kim concluded the class by saying, "We've made good progress in trying to understand what makes a good project. Our job next Friday will be to lay the foundation for one of the components we talked about today—background information. I'd like you all to be thinking about the kind of information you will need to enable you to ask meaningful questions and make interesting hypotheses. I'll try to bring in some reference books for everyone to use and each of you needs to bring in at least one book on the topic you are studying by Friday. You can get these either at the school library or a public library. Any questions? . . . OK, then I'll see you on Monday— and don't forget your books on Friday."

During the next week Kim worked with the school librarian to build a collection of reference books on the different topics the students were studying. She also raided her own college textbook collection and asked her colleagues to do the same. By Friday she had over forty books on the different topics that students were investigating.

At the beginning of the period she called the class together and explained that their goals for the day were to look at the resources available to the groups and to begin a plan of action for their projects.

As students moved into their groups Kim again circulated around the room, talking to the groups and answering questions. She often sat down with a group and helped them structure the tasks so that members of the group could collaborate and help each other on the different tasks.

During the next few weeks, students worked on their projects in their groups. The general topic, like electricity or pollution, served as the framework for each group, while the specific projects directed the students' efforts during class. Some of the projects, like the one in electricity, were actually done in school, while others, like an investigation of factors affecting plant growth, were done at home.

During the fifth and sixth weeks students started analyzing their results and writing reports. Kim helped students by sharing exemplary reports with them and by working with students in their groups. Kim showed them how the computer in the back of the room could be used to describe and display data, and a number of groups used it to write up their projects.

For the next two weeks students organized poster board sessions where they presented their results to other students. As students circulated from project to project they evaluated each other's work with a form the class had discussed and prepared. At the end of each session Kim took fifteen minutes of class time to discuss the different projects, pointing out strengths in each. Using this feedback, students in the groups refined their presentations. The unit culminated in the Science Fair where students presented their projects to the whole school.

As Kim circulated up and down the aisles of the Science Fair, she was pleased with the comments she overheard from other people. The projects *were* of higher quality than in any previous year, but more importantly, Kim felt good about the confidence of the students' presentations. They weren't just going through the motions, they really *did* understand the ideas contained in their projects.

Group Investigation: An Overview

Group investigation *is a cooperative-learning strategy that places students in groups to investigate a given topic.* Like other cooperative-learning strategies, it uses student help and cooperation as a major learning vehicle. Unlike other strategies, its primary focus is the investigation of a specific subject or topic.

Group investigation traces its roots to several earlier educational thinkers. John Dewey (1916) viewed the classroom as a microcosm for society. Schools needed to help students learn to work together on meaningful projects so that they could do the same in society. The teacher's role in this process was to help students identify and solve problems that were meaningful to them. Group investigation can help reach this goal.

Herbert Thelen (1960) was another educator who influenced the development of the Group-Investigation Model. Thelen stressed the importance of active inquiry in student learning. He felt that learning was most effective when it involved the search for an answer to some question or problem. Like Dewey, Thelen felt that inquiry was most meaningful when pursued in a social context. Group investigation provides an opportunity for students to pursue meaningful questions in groups of their peers.

More recently, Sharon and Sharon (1988) have used group investigation to promote social cohesion between different groups. These researchers found that group investigation can be effective in helping students from diverse backgrounds learn to work together. Group investigation provides a context in which students learn about themselves and each other.

Teachers who use group investigation have at least three interrelated goals. First, group investigation helps students learn how to investigate topics systematically and analytically—a goal similar to those reached with the General and Suchman Inquiry Models. This results in the development of inquiry skills, and it helps reach a second goal, which is the deep understanding of content. Third, and perhaps most important, students learn how to work cooperatively toward the solution of a problem. This is a valuable life skill and unfortunately one that students don't often practice in our schools (Goodlad, 1984). Group investigation provides teachers with one instructional strategy to reach all three goals—inquiry, content learning, and learning to work cooperatively.

Planning for the Group-Investigation Model

Planning for group investigation involves five steps, two of which—specifying objectives and designing team-building activities—are similar to planning for the other cooperative-learning models. The steps are outlined in Figure 9.3.

Specifying Objectives
As we said earlier, group-investigation activities are designed to help students meet three interrelated goals—to develop inquiry skills, to develop cooperative-learning skills, and to

1. Specifying Objectives

2. Planning for Information Gathering

3. Forming Student Teams

4. Designing Team-Building Activities

5. Planning Whole-Group Activities

FIGURE 9.3   Planning for Group Investigation

acquire a deep understanding of content. Of the three, the third is least emphasized. If a deep understanding of content is the primary goal, other models are probably more effective. The Group-Investigation Model is most effective for helping students develop problem-solving skills and the ability to work together.

Planning for Information Gathering

Problem solving and inquiry don't exist in an information vacuum. Students need access to information that they can use to guide their efforts. Kim planned information gathering by collecting used college science texts and working with the school librarian to be sure that school resources were available. Other sources of information include:

- Textbooks from other classes or levels
- Books from the public library
- Encyclopedias and other reference books
- Videotapes, videodiscs, and CD-ROM discs
- Resource people (e.g., doctors, engineers, scientists)

To develop research skills, teachers may want to make this search for information part of the overall investigation; that is, rather than gathering the resources yourself, you may have students do it, so they learn how to access their own information.

Forming Student Teams

There are at least three factors to consider in forming teams for group investigation. Perhaps the most obvious is interest. Kim, for example, formed her teams based on the interest individuals expressed in different topics. Second, if possible, an equal number of high and low achievers should be on each team, and third, the teams should be balanced in gender and ethnicity. One of the benefits of all cooperative-learning strategies is that they help students with varying backgrounds learn to work together. Group investigation offers unique opportunities for promoting cooperation and teamwork, because it is less structured than other strategies, and consequently it requires higher levels of trust and cooperation. The first step in reaching these goals is forming teams whose members are diverse.

Designing Team-Building Activities

Group investigation requires a greater degree of cooperation than STAD or Jigsaw II; in them, student roles are clearly defined. When group investigation is used, students must work together in making decisions about their roles, which will be interdependent. This interdependence makes team-building activities very important.

Team-building activities can take a number of forms. In addition to the general team-building activities described in earlier sections of the chapter, teachers can use the content they're investigating as the focal point for student interviews. For example Kim had her students interview each other about topics they were interested in and why. This information then served as a springboard for their work.

Planning Whole-Group Activities

The final planning task is to design activities that will introduce the class to the goals for the group investigation. This is especially important when it is first used, because group investigations are not highly structured, so students must thoroughly understand the process if investigations are to proceed smoothly.

This introduction/orientation is designed to have students understand the goal of the activity and the kinds of products that are expected. Kim, for example, shared and discussed examples produced in previous years. In a sense, the process is like learning a concept, which we found in Chapter 3 is accomplished primarily through the use of examples.

The introduction is also designed to help students understand the procedures that they should follow in producing their product. An overview of the process on the first day and periodic review and additional reminders help students gradually become comfortable with the procedures. Also, putting key steps on overheads, charts, or the board can also help.

Implementing Group-Investigation Activities

As with planning, implementing group-investigation activities involves five steps or phases. These phases are outlined in Table 9.9 and are discussed in the sections that follow.

Phase One: Organizing Groups and Identifying Topics

The first phase of group-investigation lessons involves organizing students into groups and having them identify a topic. The order of these two tasks will vary with the topic and students. In some cases, the teacher may want to select topics first and then form groups based on student interest; this is what Kim did. She first asked students what topic they were interested in studying, and she formed the groups based on these topics. The alternative is

TABLE 9.9   Implementing Group-Investigation Activities

Phase One	Organizing groups and identifying topics
Phase Two	Group planning
Phase Three	Implementing investigations
Phase Four	Analyzing results and preparing reports
Phase Five	Presenting reports

to form groups and let the students in each group select the topic. This alternative gives students more experience in negotiating and compromising on the final choice.

Team-Building Activities.   Regardless of how topics are selected, it is important to conduct some team-building activities that develop a sense of group cohesion and solidarity. The Group-Investigation Model is a complex strategy, requiring levels of cooperation among members not found in other models. For groups to work effectively, members must have productive and cooperative working relationships. Kim planned for team building when she had students learn something about their teammates and report to the whole class. Many other team-building activities also exist, and teachers can select those that work the best with their students.

Phase Two: Group Planning

During group planning, students determine the scope of the investigation, assess resources, plan a course of action, and assign responsibilities to different members of the group. In some configurations group planning is easier than in others. If all members of the group are investigating the same topic, the primary task is deciding how to share background information. If pairs or groups of three are investigating subtopics related to the overall project, decisions must be made about coordinating their efforts, such as who will be responsible for background information, gathering data, analyzing the data, combining the different subprojects within the overall project, and writing the report. These tasks are not cleanly divided or clear-cut, and part of the learning process involves making decisions about how they will be handled.

In Kim's class, group planning took several forms. First, group members had to decide for which portion of the overall project each would be responsible, how they would pool their resources, and how to collaborate on gathering data and reporting the results. These deliberations and negotiations—"No, I don't want to do that, you do it." "OK, I'll do it if you'll do that, or let's both do it."—are some of the more valuable aspects of learning.

Phase Three: Implementing the Investigation

Groups are organized, topics for investigation have been identified, and the groups have a plan for accomplishing the task. The groups are now ready to implement their plans. This is usually the longest phase. Students need time to design data-gathering procedures, gather data, analyze and evaluate data, and reach conclusions.

Keeping all groups working productively during this phase of the activity can be difficult because some projects take longer than others. Progress reports help groups monitor their progress and help the teacher coordinate efforts among the groups.

Phase Four: Analyzing Results and Preparing a Report

As students gather information, it needs to be analyzed and evaluated. Teachers can help in this process in several says. One way is to continually focus each group's attention on the question or problem it is investigating. In a lengthy investigation, students can lose track of the central focus of their study. A second way to help students analyze results is to encourage them to talk about and share their findings with other group members. A third way is to encourage students to experiment with different ways of displaying data. The construction of charts, diagrams, and tables helps students understand and see relationships in their data. The students in Kim's class used the computer to help them here.

The actual form that the report takes is up to the teacher. Options include oral presentations, written reports, poster boards, and demonstrations. If oral presentations are used, they should be supplemented with a written report or some other physical product. The thinking that goes into writing or constructing a report helps students learn to clearly present their findings.

Phase Five: Presenting the Report

This phase of the project has two goals. The first is to disseminate information; the second is to help students learn to present information in clear and interesting ways. The format for these presentations can vary. Some options include:

- Whole-class presentations
- Presentations to segments of class
- Poster-board presentations
- Demonstrations
- Videotape presentation
- Learning stations or centers

The students' task in this phase of the model is to go beyond the information itself, consider the audience, and create a presentation that is informative and interesting. Again, this is a task that will be useful later in life and one that isn't often encountered in traditional classrooms.

Assessing Group-Investigation Activities

Assessment of a group-investigation activity should focus on each of the goals that can be met with the model. Let's look at them.

Assessing the Inquiry Process

One goal of group-investigation activities is for students to learn about the process of inquiry—its goals, how it proceeds, and its products. Students should be encouraged to reflect on the process and assess their own performance in each of the areas. A rating scale or checklist such as the one found in Figure 9.4 can be a valuable tool to guide self-assessment activities.

A rating scale can help students reflect on the processes they use and learn to be analytical in their thinking. It can also stimulate discussion between group members by providing a concrete frame of reference.

Assessing Group Work

A second goal to be assessed in group investigations is the efficiency of the group and the extent to which group members effectively work together. The teacher can aid in the process by providing helpful feedback as the investigation progresses. The teacher can also help by discussing the kinds of behaviors that help build effective groups. Rating scales can also help students learn to focus on critical skills. Figure 9.5 offers a sample.

	Needs Work	Fair	Good	Very Good	Excellent
Clearly Stated Problem	1	2	3	4	5
Clearly Stated Hypothesis(es)	1	2	3	4	5
Hypothesis Connected to Problem	1	2	3	4	5
Variables Controlled	1	2	3	4	5
Data Gathering Appropriate to Hypothesis	1	2	3	4	5
Data Analyzed Clearly	1	2	3	4	5
Conclusions Logically Connected to Hypotheses and Data	1	2	3	4	5
Inquiry Evaluation Instrument	1	2	3	4	5

FIGURE 9.4   Rating Scale for Assessing the Inquiry Process

Rating scales can be used as a basis for helping students understand how effective groups function, providing feedback to different groups, or making decisions about group composition and whether or not to intervene with some groups. At a minimum, they serve as a reminder to both teachers and students that an important goal of group investigation is to learn to work together.

Assessing Understanding of Content
Understanding of content is the third aspect of group investigation that needs to be assessed. The teacher wants to know if individual students understand their projects and

	Rarely				Always
Group members listened to each other.	1	2	3	4	5
Group members shared information and ideas.	1	2	3	4	5
Group members helped each other clarify ideas.	1	2	3	4	5
Group members asked thought-provoking questions.	1	2	3	4	5
Group members gave each other feedback.	1	2	3	4	5

FIGURE 9.5   Rating Scale for Assessing Group Effectiveness

the conceptual foundation on which they're based. The report itself, essay questions asking students to explain the project, oral presentations, and interviews can all help the teacher assess the students' understanding.

Summary

Cooperative learning is an approach to learning that involves students working together to reach a common goal. Several cooperative-learning strategies exist, and three of them were discussed in this chapter. Each is based on group goals, individual accountability, and equal opportunity for success as guiding principles. Having students learn to work together effectively is an overriding goal for all cooperative-learning strategies.

Student Teams Achievement Divisions (STAD) has teams of four or five work toward automaticity on facts, concepts, and skills. Closely related to the Direct-Instruction Model, STAD uses team study in place of independent practice. Students compete with their past performances to earn improvement points, which contribute to team awards.

Jigsaw II, designed to help students understand organized bodies of information, develops student experts who in turn teach their teammates. Team members develop deep understanding of content as all team members share their expertise. Improvement points and team awards—as used with STAD—can also be used with Jigsaw II to promote success and provide recognition for team accomplishment.

Group investigation, the most complex and ill-defined model of the three, has groups collaborate on inquiry problems. When group investigation is used, defining problems, stating hypotheses, gathering data, and assessing hypotheses are similar to the processes used with General and Suchman Inquiry. Group investigation differs from the other inquiry models in its emphasis on group work, collaboration, negotiation, and making written and oral reports that summarize the group's work.

Important Concepts

Cooperative learning (p. 277)   Individual accountability (p. 280)
Equal opportunity for success (p. 280)   Jigsaw II (p. 296)
Group goals (p. 279)   Student Teams Achievement Divisions (STAD) (p. 285)
Group investigation (p. 304)   Task specialization (p. 296)

Exercises

1. Examine the introductory cases at the beginning of the chapter involving Isabelle Ortega, Anya Lozano, and Kim Herron. Which cooperative-learning model was each using? Defend your answer with specific information from the cases.

2. Analyze the following list of goals and decide whether they are most appropriate for STAD, Jigsaw II, or group investigation.
   a. A third-grade teacher wanted his students to know their multiplication facts.

b. A junior high social studies teacher wanted to teach his students how to analyze social issues. Since it was an election year, he selected voting, and asked each group to design a research project around this topic.

c. An English teacher was comparing Faulkner, Fitzgerald, and Hemingway and wanted her students to understand similarities and differences between each of the writers.

d. A junior high science teacher was studying pollution. He assigned students to groups and asked each group to investigate either air, water, or solid-waste pollution in their geographic area.

e. A fourth-grade teacher wanted to develop her students' ability to research a topic. She selected the topic of pets and asked each group to design and implement a project on this subject.

f. A health teacher wanted his students to know and understand the four major food groups.

g. A social studies teacher wanted her students to know the names of the states as well as their capitals.

3. Analyze the STAD lesson involving Anya Lozano and identify in it where each of the following components of cooperative learning were found:
   a. Group goals
   b. Individual accountability
   c. Equal opportunity for success

4. A math teacher is preparing to assign students from her basic algebra class to STAD learning groups. Averages of the students' past quiz scores are as follows:

Juan	97	Juanita	81
Bettina	94	Henry	80
Sheri	93	Lisa	79
Akeem	90	Joan	77
Kim	87	Pat	75
Heather	84	Alonza	72
Peter	83	May	70
Marcia	82	Ted	69

   a. She wants to use teams of four. How might the teams be composed?
   b. What factors other than past quiz scores might the teacher consider?

5. In the introduction to the chapter, the effectiveness of cooperative learning was explained from several perspectives. Using information from the STAD lesson involving Anya Lozano, provide examples of how the following explanations were illustrated.
   a. Behaviorism
   b. Social explanations
   c. Developmental theory
   d. Cognitive elaboration

Discussion Questions

1. How are the following essential components of cooperative learning—group goals, individual accountability, and equal opportunity for success—contained in
   - STAD?
   - Jigsaw II?
   - Group investigation?

2. Identify at least three similarities among STAD, Jigsaw II, and group investigation. Identify at least two ways in which each differs from the other two.

3. Which of the three cooperative-learning models presented—STAD, Jigsaw II, or group investigation—is easiest to implement? Most difficult? Why? From a student development perspective, what might this suggest about the order in which they're used?

4. Researchers have found that cooperative learning is an effective way of breaking down barriers between different ethnic groups. Which of the following elements is most important for reaching this goal? Explain your answer.
   - Group goals
   - Individual accountability
   - Equal opportunity for success

5. How is the "cognitive elaboration" argument that supports cooperative learning similar to the developmental perspective? How is it different?

6. Which of the three cooperative-learning models is most widely applicable to different grade levels and across different content areas? Why? Which is least applicable? Explain your answer.

7. How is the form that assessment takes in each of the three cooperative-learning models similar? Different? How do these differences correspond to the different goals of each model?

8. To which of the other models in the book do each of the three cooperative-learning models most closely relate? Explain your answer.

Chapter 10

Adapting Instruction to Improve Effectiveness

I. Teaching Models: Adaptations
A. Examining Goals
B. Synthesizing the Models
C. Models and Goals: A Critical Connection

II. Teaching Expertise: Beyond Instructional Models

We've now finished the major portion of the book. In Chapter 1 we discussed the teacher-effectiveness research, expanded the discussion to emphasize teaching for understanding, and emphasized that differences in content and students require different teaching strategies. These factors led to a discussion of a "models" approach to instruction.

The teaching models in this book focused on information processing—the ways people gather and organize information to form patterns and explain and predict events in their experiences. Information processing developed in response to dissatisfaction with behaviorism as a basis for guiding instruction. Information processing assumes learners actively construct their own understanding rather than passively receiving that understanding from teachers or other authorities.

Chapter 2 introduced you to the essential teaching skills that form the foundation for teaching effectiveness. Higher-order and critical-thinking strategies build on this foundation, resulting in deep understanding of content.

Chapters 3 through 9 discussed and illustrated specific models, each designed to help students reach specific content goals while practicing higher-order and critical thinking. In the real world, however, teachers face many situations that require flexibility and adaptation in their instruction. This chapter is intended to illustrate that professional adaptability, which represents an even more advanced stage of teaching expertise.

When you've completed your study of this chapter, you should be able to meet the following objectives:

- Identify the model most effective for specific goals.
- Identify similarities and differences among the models.
- Identify elements of each of the models in a single teaching episode.
- Adapt elements of each model to reach particular goals.

To begin our discussion, let's look at a teacher adapting the models to best meet her students' needs.

Marita Eng is beginning a unit on sea animals with her fifth graders, and she plans to spend about a week and a half on it. She introduces the unit on a Monday by showing a large poster board with an outline on it that looks like the outline shown at the top of the following page.

She begins her first lesson of the unit by saying, "Everyone, this is what we'll be covering for the next few days. . . . Now let's look at the outline. What does it tell us? . . . Anyone?"

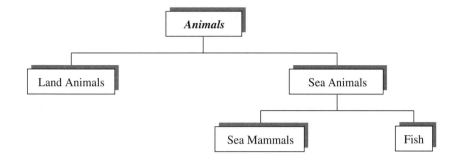

". . . It looks like . . . sea mammals and . . . fish are both . . . kinds of animals that live in the sea," Brad volunteered hesitantly.

"Good, Brad," Marita smiled. "Yes, when we see this kind of outline, it tells us, like we see up here," she nods, pointing to the outline, "that sea mammals and fish are both kinds of sea animals. . . . It also tells us that land animals and sea animals are both kinds of animals in general.

"Now," she continued, "today, we want to watch this video, and we all want to be very good observers. Then we're going to think some more as we make conclusions based on what we see. So, our goal for today is to learn to make good conclusions. Now, what makes a conclusion a good one? . . . Anyone?"

". . ."

"What did we say we were going to do first when we look at the video?"

"Be good observers," Cal volunteered.

"Good, exactly," Marita smiled. "So, how do our observations relate to our conclusions?"

". . . We use the observations to help us with our conclusions," Ken said after thinking about the question for a few seconds.

"Well done, Ken. That's right. We will base our conclusions on our observations. . . . That's our goal for today."

Marita then started the videotape, which showed a number of short scenes of whales and dolphins, such as a baby dolphin nursing from its mother, a baby whale being born, and a whale surfacing and "blowing" (exhaling). After a few minutes, she stopped the tape and asked her students to describe what they had seen.

"A little dolphin was feeding from its mother," Brenda volunteered.

"The animals come up to the top of the water every now and then," Andre added.

"Yes, and they blow water," Steve put in.

"What do you think that blowing water is?" Marita queried.

". . ."

Marita tilted her head back and blew a rush of air through her nose toward the ceiling.

"Breathing?" two of the children wondered simultaneously.

Marita smiled, "What do you think? . . . Does that make sense?"

". . . I don't think so," Andrew shook his head. "That would mean their noses are on the tops of their heads."

". . . Why not?" Janine shrugged after thinking about it. "It could be there. We breathe up when we lay on our backs."

Marita watched as the students debated for a few more minutes whether or not animals' noses could be on the tops of their heads. They finally agreed, in a few cases a bit reluctantly, that it probably was possible.

Wayne then interjected, "These animals look like fish but if they come up to breathe, and their babies are born like dogs and cats and stuff, they can't be fish."

"What must they be then?" Marita wondered.

". . . Mammals?" Letitia answered slowly, with a question in her voice.

"How do you know?" Marita probed.

". . . If they breathe air, . . . and they nurse their babies, . . . and they're born like dogs and . . . you know, . . . they must be mammals."

"That's excellent thinking," Marita waved and nodded. "Remember that we said we were going to practice making conclusions. What Letitia just did is an example of that. Very well done, everyone."

Marita then showed another part of the videotape, and more discussion followed. She continued this process until the end of the class.

She started her Tuesday class by saying, "Yesterday we were talking about sea mammals, one kind of sea animal. Let's look again at our outline," she continued, pointing to 'sea mammals' on the hierarchy.

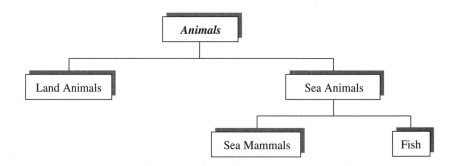

"What did we find out about them?"

The class spent several minutes listing some of the observations and conclusions that they had made the day before, and Marita concluded the review by saying, "Now, keep in mind what we know about sea mammals while we talk about another kind of sea animal, fish. . . . We all know some things about fish. For example, we know that fish are cold-blooded animals that breathe through gills and usually lay eggs to have babies," she noted, again pointing to the hierarchy.

She then motioned, "Let's look at the fish bowls," and she directed their attention to the two large fish tanks at the side of the room.

"Let's compare these fish to the mammals we talked about yesterday" she suggested. "How are they alike and how are they different?"

The students offered several observations, such as identifying the gills on some of the fish, and noting that they didn't go to the surface and "blow."

Marita continued the activity by showing some colored pictures of other fish. As the students examined the pictures, they discussed how the pictures were similar to the fish in the bowl and the whales and dolphins they had seen in the video. This continued until it was time to go to recess.

Marita began Wednesday's class by reviewing Monday's and Tuesday's activities. She began her review by asking about the differences between fish and sea mammals.

Sharon commented, "I think they're sort of hard to tell apart unless you're up close."

Maurice added, "Fish can stay under water the whole time, but mammals have to come up to the top to breathe."

Ray said, "They look quite a bit alike. They have fins on them . . . on their sides and tails."

Marita then asked, "Why do you suppose the sea mammals and fish look so much alike when they are actually very different?"

" . . . "

"Well, what do we know about where they live?"

"They both live in the water," Tim shrugged.

"Good, Tim," Marita smiled. "What else?"

" . . . "

"OK, let me show you a few more pictures. I want you to think about what they have in common."

She showed the students a picture of an African grassland with gazelles and antelope on it, a jungle picture with chimpanzees, and another with orangutans.

After the students looked back and forth from one picture to another, Juanita tentatively offered, "The animals in the same sort of place kind of look alike."

"What do you mean?" Marita queried.

"Like the antelope and the . . ."

"Gazelle," Marita offered.

"The gazelle, . . . and the antelope, . . ." Juanita went on, "well, they . . . look alike. . . . See they both have long legs and stuff. . . . and the whale and the fish in the water look alike too."

"What do the rest of you think?" Marita smiled.

"Yeah, the chimps and that other one look alike, too, kind of," Emilio added, pointing to the pictures with the chimpanzees and the orangutan, "and they both live in the jungle."

"Anyone else?" Marita encouraged.

The class agreed that what Juanita and Emilio suggested seemed to make sense, and Marita then asked, "What do we call 'where an animal lives'?"

". . . Their environment," Sandy offered after a couple of seconds.

"Good. Yes, it's called their environment," Marita responded, writing the term on the board. . . . "And here we have three different environments, the ocean, grasslands, and the jungle.

"Now," Marita said with emphasis, leaning forward. "Let's see if we can describe a relationship between animals and their environment. . . . Think about it for a few seconds, and someone give it a try."

". . . Animals in the same environment look alike," Tina offered.

"What do you think everyone? Do animals in the same environment look alike?"

Some of the class members agreed that they did and pointed to the examples that they had already discussed. Others disagreed and noted that a wide variety of animals live on the plains other than antelope and gazelles. The class discussed the issue and finally concluded that animals in particular environments had characteristics that allowed them to survive in those environments.

Marita then offered, "What we've been talking about is the ability of animals to *adapt* to their environments. Later we'll see that plants also adapt, but we'll wait to get into that."

Marita then asked the students to summarize what had gone on during the period, closing the lesson for the day.

To begin Thursday's lesson, Marita reviewed by having the students offer some additional examples of adaptation, and then continued by saying, "There are actually two kinds of fish, those with backbones like ours and those with softer backbones."

She went to her original outline and added these categories below "fish" so it appeared as follows:

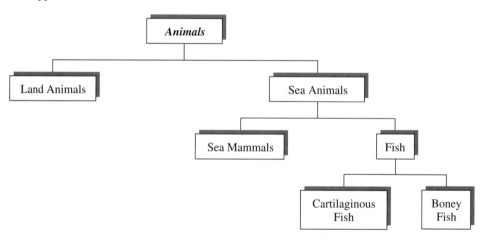

"We're going to change the routine a little today," Marita went on. "I have a chart here, and some materials, and we're going to gather some information about the two different kinds of fish."

She then displayed the following matrix for the students.

	Examples	Gill Opening	Covering	Teeth	Reproduction	Circulatory System
Boney Fish						
Cartilaginous Fish						

Marita then continued, "We're going to work together as groups today, and I've arranged for us to go to the media center where we'll have some books, videodiscs, and information on CD-ROM that you can look at to gather your information. Now to get us started, I want you to break up into teams of two with each group gathering information about a different part of the matrix. Work with your partner from your cooperative-learning groups."

Marita then assigned a pair to volunteer to find examples of boney fish, another pair to find information about the gill openings of boney fish, a third pair to find information about the covering of boney fish, and so on until all twelve cells of the matrix were covered by a pair. (Since she had 26 students in her class, two of the teams worked as trios.)

The class then went to the media center and spent the rest of Thursday's class gathering information. They finished on Friday, returned to the classroom, and reported their findings on a large piece of chart paper.

On Monday Marita spent several minutes reviewing what they had done the previous week. She then began discussing the information in the chart by asking the students for similarities and differences in boney and cartilaginous fish, asking them to explain their answers whenever possible. The discussion continued for the remainder of the class time.

On Tuesday, Marita again reviewed the work of the previous six days, then had the students examine the two fish bowls as they had the previous week.

"What do you notice?" she asked.

The students made several comments, and finally Joan asked, "Why are the fish in the bowl on the left moving around so slowly while the others are acting like they always do?"

"That's a good question, Joan," Marita answered. "Let's see if we can figure out why."

"The fish aren't in the bowls they're usually in and they can't adapt," Gerald said with a big smile. "See what I learned last week, Mrs. Eng?"

"Okay, Gerald," Marita smiled. "How could we find out if that's true?"

After several seconds, Gabriella suggested, "Put them back the way they were."

"Yeah," "Hey," "Neat idea," "OK," several of the students responded, so the class decided to follow Gabriella's suggestion.

While they waited to see what happened, the class discussed some of the possibilities. "What if the fish start behaving like they did before? What will that tell us?" Marita queried.

The students offered some possibilities, they discussed them, and Marita followed with other questions.

They turned back to the fish when Fran noted, "There's a film on one of the bowls."

"I know, I know," Javier jumped up excitedly. "We learned this week that fish are cold-blooded, and the water is cold so the fish don't move around as much."

This led to another investigation. The class measured the water temperature in the bowls and counted the number of times the gills moved in the different water temperatures. As the students gathered the information, Marita recorded it on the board, and they continued with this process for the rest of the period.

On Wednesday, Marita guided the students through a summary of the entire unit, again looking at sea mammals and fish (both boney and cartilaginous), the process of adaptation, and how the environment affects the behavior of animals. She asked the students to compare the behavior of the fish in the different water temperatures to their own behavior in the winter compared to the summer. This led to a discussion of different ways of dressing and a comparison of warm-blooded and cold-blooded animals.

Marita then reminded the students that they would continue with their discussion of adaptation beginning the next day.

In the case study we've just read, we see how a teacher has used all or part of several different models to reach her goals for a unit. In some cases, such as Sue Grant's lesson on Charles's Law in Chapter 3, or Tim Hardaway's lesson on the addition of two-digit numbers in Chapter 6, a single model is used exclusively—Sue using the Inductive Model and Tim using the Direct-Instruction Model. Often, however, teachers' goals are not as narrow and specific as Sue's and Tim's were, so effective teachers adapt the models, using portions of several of them to best help their students learn. This is a totally appropriate use of the models, and this is how Marita used them in her unit. Let's look at how she combined and adapted the models in the next section.

Teaching Models: Adaptations

Examining Goals

To begin our discussion, let's think about Marita's goals, which included the following:

* To know that mammals live in the sea
* To understand how animals adapt to their environments
* To understand the differences between boney and cartilaginous fish
* To develop higher-order and critical-thinking skills

In addition, student questions led to inquiry about the behavior of fish. Students formed hypotheses, gathered data, and made conclusions about the relationship between behavior and environment. We don't know for sure, but the inquiry appeared to be spontaneous, rather than a predetermined goal that Marita consciously considered in her planning. Because of her expertise, she was able to capitalize on students' questions and turn them into an excellent learning experience.

Let's turn now to some of the specific elements of Marita's teaching as she proceeded through her unit.

She began by presenting a hierarchy as a way of organizing the information for students. She then had the students briefly discuss what the hierarchy implied. The combination of the hierarchy and the discussion served as an advance organizer for the content that followed. While her "organizer" didn't have the characteristics of advance organizers that

Corkill (1992) identified, her adaptation nevertheless resulted in an effective organizer. In this sense her unit began as a form of the Lecture-Discussion Model. The content of her unit was an organized body of knowledge—knowledge about sea mammals, boney and cartilaginous fish, the concept of adaptation, and the impact of the environment on behavior.

In the first lesson of the unit, Marita showed the videotape of sea mammals, using the Inductive Model. The video provided the examples, she stopped the tape periodically to allow the students to make observations and conclusions, and she guided their discussion according to the structure of the Inductive Model. Through her guidance they arrived at the conclusion that mammals live in the sea as well as on land.

Let's look again at some of the discussion.

Brenda: A little dolphin was feeding from its mother.

Andre: The animals come up to the top of the water every now and then.

Steve: Yes, and they blow water.

Marita: What do you think that blowing water is?

Children: Breathing? (After Marita tilted her head back and blew a rush of air through her nose toward the ceiling.)

Marita: What do you think? . . . Does that make sense?

Andrew: I don't think so. That would mean their noses are on the tops of their heads.

Janine: Why not? It could be there. We breathe up when we lay on our backs.

Wayne: These animals look like fish but if they come up to breathe, and their babies are born like dogs and cats and stuff, they can't be fish. (Conclusion made after the students discussed whether it was possible for animals to have their noses on the tops of their heads.)

Marita: What must they be then?

Letitia: Mammals?

Marita: How do you know?

Letitia: If they breathe air, . . . and they nurse their babies, . . . and they're born like dogs and . . . you know, . . . they must be mammals.

Marita skillfully guided her students as they discussed the information they gathered from the video. She used constructivism as a view of learning to actively involve her students, and she conducted her instruction in the general context of the Lecture-Discussion Model. Her lesson was a skillful hybridization and adaptation of both models to help her reach her goals. The Lecture-Discussion Model provided structure as the overall approach to her unit because the unit content was an organized body of knowledge. The Inductive Model was effective for her first lesson because she was teaching a concept—the concept of sea mammal.

Marita began the second lesson of her unit on Tuesday with another "mini" lecture discussion and another adaptation of an advance organizer, which included the outline and the statement:

> We know that fish are cold-blooded animals that breathe through gills and usually lay eggs to have babies.

Having provided the organizer, she again turned to an inductive procedure as she had students compare fish to sea mammals, identifying their similarities and differences. This process continued into Wednesday, where she used the observations and conclusions that the students had made to lead them to the concept of adaptation. Much of her instruction on Tuesday and Wednesday utilized the Inductive Model.

On Thursday Marita turned to the Integrative Model and an adaptation of cooperative learning. She provided the skeleton of a matrix and asked student pairs to gather information to be placed in it. While she could have—and perhaps should have—asked the students to suggest the categories, such as skin covering, that the students would investigate with respect to boney and cartilaginous fish, she chose to select the categories herself; this was another example of a professional decision.

After the students had gathered their information, Marita used the Integrative Model to guide students' analysis. They looked for similarities and differences in boney and cartilaginous fish and formed explanations as they went along. Her analysis took her through Friday of the first week and Monday of the second week of her unit.

On Tuesday, Marita planned to return to the discussion of different kinds of fish, but a question arose from the students' observations. Let's look again at how the lesson proceeded.

Joan: Why are the fish in the bowl on the left moving around so slowly while the others are acting like they always do?

Marita: That's a good question, Joan. Let's see if we can figure out why.

Gerald: The fish aren't in the bowls they're usually in and they can't adapt. See what I learned last week, Mrs Eng?

Marita: OK, Gerald. How could we find out if that's true?

Gabriella: Put them back the way they were.

Joan's question provided the opportunity for an inquiry lesson. Marita alertly capitalized on the opportunity by asking the students to try and figure out how they could answer the question. Gerald offered an hypothesis, and Gabriella suggested a way that data could be gathered to investigate the hypothesis. The entire process began spontaneously with Joan's question.

As the students waited to see if the behavior of the fish changed, Fran noted, "There's a film on one of the bowls," which was followed by Javier's comment, "We learned this week that fish are cold-blooded, and the water is cold so the fish don't move around as much." Javier's point was essentially an alternative hypothesis, which led to a change in the investigation.

The students then investigated Javier's hypothesis by measuring the water temperature and studying the movements of the gills on each fish. While Marita might be criticized for not following up on the initial investigation with at least some discussion, she showed a great deal of expertise in adapting her instruction to the thinking of the students. This is consistent with the suggestions of constructivism; so while we discussed constructivism as the foundation of the Inductive Model, we see that it also serves as a framework for the other models as well.

Synthesizing the Models

From our analysis of the case study and our discussion, we see how effective teachers combine and adapt the models to help them accomplish different goals, and that many similarities exist in what appear to be very different models. Also, we see that models that seem to be grounded in different reference frames are highly compatible instructionally. For example, Marita had her students do a great deal of comparing, contrasting, and linking of new information to old. These processes, which appeared in the context of Inductive and Integrative lessons, are virtually the same as the process of integration within the Lecture-Discussion Model.

Also, while the Lecture-Discussion Model and the Inductive Model appear to be quite different, Marita found them to be very compatible. She established a conceptual framework with the Lecture-Discussion Model, and then taught specific concepts, such as sea mammals and adaptation using the Inductive Model. Combining and adapting teaching models in this way epitomizes effective teaching.

Models and Goals: A Critical Connection

From this discussion, we see that the key to teachers' decisions in using the models is a careful consideration of goals. Marita chose to begin her unit with the Lecture-Discussion Model because her unit goals focused on organized bodies of knowledge. She turned to the Inductive Model when her goals were for students to understand concepts, such as sea mammals and adaptation, and she moved to the Integrative Model when she wanted the students to understand differences between boney and cartilaginous fish. Notice that in the final example her goal was not to merely acquire a simple concept of boney and cartilaginous fish, but to understand organized bodies of information about each. She could have chosen the Lecture-Discussion Model for this portion of her unit, but chose the Integrative Model instead, because it gave her a greater opportunity to help her students practice higher-order and critical thinking—one of her goals for the unit.

When the inquiry question arose, Marita seized the opportunity to capitalize on an additional goal, one that hadn't been part of her original planning. Opportunities to capitalize on "incidental" goals often occur in classrooms. The fact that Marita was able to turn it into a learning experience for her students is a tribute to her expertise as a teacher.

We see that Marita didn't use the Direct-Instruction Model or the Concept-Attainment Model in her lesson. She made this decision because her lesson goals didn't call for teaching a skill, which could be effectively taught with the Direct-Instruction Model, and they didn't include reinforcing concepts that the students already partially understood—a goal that could be reached with the Concept-Attainment Model. In her unit, the goal of developing inquiry skills was more effectively reached with the Inquiry Model. This is the way the models should be used in helping teachers reach their goals; they select the most appropriate model for each situation.

Teaching Expertise: Beyond Instructional Models

In this final section of the book, we will attempt to place the models—as wholes or in parts—into perspective with teaching in general. In doing so, we will discuss some basic principles upon which the models rest. To put the models in perspective, we would like to return to a point that we made in Chapter 1. There we said,

> *. . . a teaching model is not a substitute for basic teaching skills. A model cannot take the place of fundamental qualities in a teacher, such as knowledge of subject matter, creativity, and sensitivity to people. It is, instead, a tool to help good teachers teach more effectively by making their teaching more systematic and efficient. Models provide sufficient flexibility to allow teachers to use their own creativity. . . . As with a blueprint, a teaching model is a design for teaching within which the teacher uses all the skill and insights at his or her command.*

The statement is a reminder that the models described in this book are not solutions for all of the problems a teacher may face in trying to help students learn, and they don't automatically work magic in the classroom. They must be used by intelligent and sensitive teachers with clear ideas of what they're trying to teach; they cannot be followed mechanically according to a prescriptive format. They can help a teacher improve learning experiences for students, but they cannot, by themselves, make a bad learning environment a good one.

The models we have discussed are effective because they are based on fundamental principles of teaching that extend beyond the models themselves. These principles have been illustrated throughout the text. For example, the use of examples is critical in order for the learner to learn any abstraction—concept, principle, generalization, or rule. We have tried to be consistent with this principle by illustrating each idea in the book with one or more examples. The case studies that we used to introduce each chapter serve that same purpose; they are examples that illustrate the concepts in the chapter. The concepts are sophisticated and abstract in many cases, but they are concepts nevertheless, so they require examples. In fact their complexity and abstractness makes the need for examples even greater than it is with more concrete and simpler concepts. The point here is that using examples, with or without the structured steps in a model, increases learning.

Another principle that underlies the models is the importance of clear goals and instructional alignment. Unless teachers are clear about what they are trying to accomplish, they have no way of selecting appropriate instructional strategies or determining whether or not they are reaching their goals. Teaching models have alignment built into them; each is designed to accomplish specific goals. However, Marita Eng's teaching reminds us that models don't substitute for basic teaching ability. Her goals for her unit were established in advance, but she capitalized on opportunities to involve her students in critical thinking and inquiry when possible. Her flexibility, both in using the models and in her overall approach to instruction, illustrates the models as tools to improve instruction, not remedies for instructional problems.

We have tried to demonstrate the relationship between planning, implementing, and assessing learning by presenting the discussions of each of the models in these three phases. In addition, we have tried to be consistent with this approach by using objectives to communicate our planning, by teaching to the objectives, and by measuring your attainment of the objectives for each section. In this sense we have made an effort to "practice what we preach."

We have made an effort to be consistent with what we're suggesting in one final way. We have encouraged teachers to adapt the models to their own particular needs, using parts of the models as they see fit. Our presentation of Marita Eng's unit illustrates this effort.

In addition to the specific techniques discussed in this text, there is another capability that we hope we've developed in the reader: the ability to recognize and seize opportunities to encourage students to practice higher-order and critical thinking. This means taking advantage of opportunities whenever they arise, as Marita did in her teaching. It is through this processing of information that students not only acquire deep understanding of the topics they study, but also develop the ability to add to and refine this understanding on their own. To illustrate this point, consider the following example.

A teacher is doing a lesson on ancient and extinct animals. In this lesson the teacher showed students pictures from a book and read the captions under the pictures. Two of the pictures are shown below.

BRONTOTHERE

BRONTOSAURUS

The teacher, in reading the descriptions to the children, noted that the name *brontothere* meant thunder beast and the name *brontosaurus* meant thunder lizard. The alert teacher then seized on the opportunity to involve the students in a simple thinking activity. She asked them to note what the two names had in common and to recall the meaning of these names. With some prompting, the students generalized from the prefix *bronto-* in each example to determine that it meant "thunder."

The important point here is that the teacher wasn't using one of the specific models per se, but she captured the essence of observing and generalizing in what amounted to a "mini" inductive lesson. This entire process probably took less than two minutes, but the students had an important learning experience. In this simple activity the students had a chance to practice higher-order thinking—specifically observing and generalizing about the prefix *bronto-*. If teachers capitalize on these opportunities when they arise, they can do much to develop both their students' thinking and the depth of understanding of the topics they study, even if they didn't use the models in structured lessons. Perhaps more importantly, in time students develop the ability to look for relationships on their own, making them more responsible for their own learning. This is the essence of the "self-regulation" that is so important in teaching and learning.

Obviously, it isn't particularly important that students know what *bronto-* means. However, the skill they acquire in analyzing words and relationships as well as the idea that the world makes sense may be the best of what they take away from schools.

As another example, let's look in on a first-grade teacher, Bette Washington, as she reads a story to her students.

> During the story, the word *dissolve* comes up.
>
> "What's dissolve, Mrs. Washington?" Calvin asks.
>
> After several futile attempts at explaining the concept, Mrs. Washington tries a different approach. (Think for a second how you would verbally explain this concept to a six-year-old.) She went to the front of the room, got a glass, poured water into it, and then poured a packet of sugar she had in her desk into the water.
>
> "What do you see here?" she asked as she stirred the sugar.
>
> "The sugar is gone," Andrew answered.
>
> "Good, Andrew," Mrs. Washington smiled. "Where did it go?"
>
> " . . . "
>
> "What are some possibilities?"
>
> "In the water," Karen answered with a shrug.
>
> "Any other possibilities?" Bette asked.
>
> ". . . Maybe the air?" Delmar suggested.
>
> "Which do you think is more likely?" Bette probed.
>
> After some discussion (and actual tasting of the water), the students concluded that the sugar must have gone into the water.
>
> She finally said, "That's dissolve everyone. We say that the sugar has dissolved in the water."

Bette Washington also displayed expertise and creativity in her teaching. She realized that for abstract concepts, such as dissolve, words are often insufficient; students understand best if they see a concrete, tangible example. Bette's creativity was in her ability to create an example "on the spot." Her expertise was displayed in the fact that she didn't merely show the students and tell them what they were supposed to see. She guided their understanding in a constructivist-oriented form of instruction.

As another example, consider a teacher of American literature who had students read biographical descriptions of authors followed by excerpts of their writing. Using selections from different time periods in our country's history, he then led a detailed discussion in which the authors from similar time periods, such as post–Civil War, were compared. This group was then compared to authors who wrote in the 1920s. In all cases the authors' works were related to their biographies. From this discussion students concluded that an artist's work is influenced by both biography and the context in which that biography occurred. The teacher accomplished this using no other materials than the textbook, and involved the students in a creative activity requiring all the higher-order and critical thinking of a highly organized Integrative Model lesson.

Teachers with the insights demonstrated in these examples illustrate the best the models have to offer in terms of developing students' higher-order and critical thinking and helping them acquire deep understanding of content. Whenever teachers ask students to observe, identify trends, and compare and predict, they are capturing the essence of the models whether or not they use all of the elements of a particular model. In doing so, they demonstrate expertise as teachers, and they contribute to increased student learning. We hope that your study of this text has contributed to that expertise.

Summary

Effective teachers consciously adapt and combine teaching models to best meet their instructional goals. While structured quite differently, the models can often be used effectively in combination, such as introducing a lesson or unit with the Lecture-Discussion Model, and then teaching specific topics within the lesson with the Inductive Model.

The choice of model depends on the teacher's goal. Goals involving concepts, principles, generalizations, and rules are effectively taught with the Inductive Model; goals involving organized bodies of knowledge can call for either the Integrative Model or the Lecture-Discussion Model; goals involving skills are efficiently taught with the Direct Instruction Model; and inquiry goals call for either General or Suchman Inquiry.

Expert teachers capitalize on opportunities to promote both thinking and deep understanding of content when they arise. In doing so they often teach "mini" lessons involving one or more of the models. A deep understanding of the models increases the likelihood that teachers will seize these opportunities.

Discussion Questions

1. Compare and contrast each of the models. Identify the similarities and differences in two or more of them.

2. Compare the theoretical foundations for each of the models. In what ways are these foundations similar and different?

3. Constructivism is receiving a great deal of attention in education. Which of the models—other than the Inductive Model, which is based directly on constructivism—are constructivist in their orientation? How can each of the models be made constructivist?

4. Which of the models are most effective for promoting higher-order and critical thinking? Which are least effective? Defend your answer with specific examples.

5. The Direct-Instruction Model has been criticized as being too behaviorist in its orientation. Is this criticism justified? Under what conditions might the criticism be justified? Under what conditions would the criticism lack justification?

6. Which models require the most sophisticated teaching skills? Which ones require the least sophisticated skills? Again, defend your response with specific examples.

Exercise Feedback

Chapter 2

1. Choice *a* is most valid. The two ideas that are being presented in this passage are technology and time. Choice *b* merely discusses technology in the United States, choice *c* doesn't take the level of technology into account, and choice *d* is essentially irrelevant. Choice *d* misses the point of the passage—the relationship between technology and time.

2. Choice *b* is most valid. In answering Item 1, you demonstrated critical-thinking behaviors: The statements already existed. You then assessed each with the specific information in the passage. Your choice as to which was most valid was the result of that assessment.

3. A precise answer cannot be given, but a reasonable approximation would be somewhere between 35,000 and 50,000.

4. Choice *c* is the most valid choice. You were making a specific conclusion (prediction) based on a general pattern.

5. Choice *a* is most valid. In order to make the prediction, you had to identify a pattern. The pattern shows generally high populations in the years 1930 and 1935, generally low population in 1940 and 1945, high again in 1950 and 1955, etc. The last information we have is for 1990. If the pattern continues, the population should have remained quite high for 1995, and should then be lower again in 2000.

Chapter 3

1. Teaching that isn't active tends to rely on materials such as worksheets and other seatwork assignments for delivery of instruction rather than having the teacher direct the learning activity. Seatwork and homework are effective for reinforcing students' learning, but they are ineffective as initial learning activities.

2. Judy Nelson's comment, "When we're done, we'll be so good at this that we'll be able to pinpoint any city in the world. Keep this in mind as we work today." was an attempt to establish positive expectations in her students.

3. a. Generalization
   b. Rule
   c. Generalization
   d. Principle

4. a. Immigration & economics
   b. Number & verb form
   c. Type of diet & cholesterol level
   d. Polarity & attraction

5. a. Brief case studies could be used to illustrate this generalization. An example might be the following:

Enrique Rodriguez came home exhausted from a long day in the fields. The third year of drought had nearly destroyed his small farm in northern Mexico, and now he could barely grow enough corn and beans to feed his family of five.
   "We must do something," his wife said with concern as they sat quietly one evening. "The children are hungry."
   "I will go to the city," Enrique finally said with determination. "I will get the papers and see if we can go north of the border to find better work."

Cases, such as the one we see, illustrate the relationship between immigration and economics and could be effectively used with the Inductive Model. An alternative would be to use historical data displayed in charts that showed how immigration was related to economics.
   b. Ideal examples would be sentences in the context of a reading passage. Some of the sentences would be written so that the subjects and verbs agree in number and others would have subjects and verbs that disagree. The teacher would then guide the students to identify the differences in the sentences.
   c. As with the generalization relating immigration and economics, brief cases describing people and their diets together with their cholesterol counts would be good choices for examples. In addition, charts or graphs showing this relationship could also be used.
   d. To illustrate this principle, the teacher could have students experiment with actual magnets, calling their attention to the fact that some ends are labeled *S* and some *N*.

6. A concept analysis might appear as follows:

Definition	A quadrilateral with opposite sides equal in length and all angles 90°
Characteristics	Opposite sides equal in length, 90° angles
Examples	
Superordinate Concept	Quadrilateral, parallelogram
Subordinate Concept	Square
Coordinate Concept	Rhombus

7. a. Jim Rooney's passage was a type of realia.
   b. Judy Nelson's beach ball was a model.
   c. Maps are also forms of models. We don't typically think of them that way, but they allow us to visualize what is too vast to be directly observed.
   d. Sue Grant's balloons were a form of realia.
   e. Sue Grant's drawings were models.
   f. Dawn Adams's sentences were a form of realia.

8. a. The question, "What do you notice about the two pieces of paper?" is the better choice because it's more open-ended and less convergent. It allows the teacher to call on several different students quite quickly, which promotes involvement and equitable distribution. The question also assures that the students will be able to answer successfully, and it allows the teacher to informally diagnose the students' background knowledge.

   A question that asks the students to compare the papers, such as, "Look at the two pieces of paper and tell us how they are alike or different," would also be a good question. It is open-ended and provides multiple opportunities for students to respond.

   b. The question, "How do the two papers compare now?" is the better choice. Through their observations students will quickly recognize that the number of small blocks is the same for the two, and the teacher can then quickly lead them to see that the same number are shaded.

9. a. The lesson introduction began at paragraph 1, where Tony told the students that he wanted them to observe and compare the words.

   The open-ended phase began at paragraph 2 when he wrote the words on the board and then asked the students to observe and describe them in paragraph 3. (Either 2 or 3 would be an appropriate answer.)

   The convergent phase began at about paragraph 19, when Tony asked the students to compare the first two columns to the last two columns. (To suggest that the convergent phase began at paragraph 21 instead, when Tony asked a more specific question, would also be appropriate.)

   Closure began at about paragraph 46 when Tony asked the students to relate the information they had found. He began guiding the students to the specific statement of the rule in paragraph 51.

   The application phase began at paragraph 54 when Tony asked the students to give him a word and add *-ing* to it.
   b. Tony's questions at paragraphs 3, 5, 7, 9, 13, 15, and 16 were all open-ended and called for observation and description. The question in paragraph 19 was also open-ended but in this case, a comparison. The questions in paragraphs 25 and 35—even though part of the convergent phase—were also open-ended.
   c. A prompting sequence began at paragraph 25 when Tony asked Roy to compare the sounds of the vowels and Roy didn't respond. It continued through Roy's response in paragraph 28. (Notice that once Tony was able to elicit an acceptable response from Roy, he turned his next question to another student. The teacher has the option of staying with the original student or turning to someone else at this point.)

   A second sequence began at paragraph 37 when Kareem was unable to respond.
   d. Tony asked a repetition question in paragraph 42.
   e. The two processes used most extensively were observing and comparing. The students also generalized when they formed the rule in a statement. They later applied the rule when they wrote their paragraphs.

10. a. The teacher used *one* example. The water and oil on the balance demonstrated that the water was more dense, and the oil on the water demonstrated that the oil floated. The two together provided one illustration of the relationship.

b. The examples were a form of realia.

c. The teacher would have to prompt the students to recognize that the volumes were the same, that the mass of the water was greater (because that side of the balance went down), and therefore, the water was more dense. The students would readily see that the oil floated on the water, and the teacher would then have to prompt them to state the principle.

d. The teacher could discuss oil spills and the cleanup of oil as one example of application.

Chapter 4

1. Goals *c* and *e* would *not* be appropriately taught with the Concept-Attainment Model. Let's look at the two goals.

(c) A teacher who wants students to know why two coffee cans roll down an incline at different rates has an objective that requires an explanation. Explanations include concepts but are broader than the concepts themselves. As such, they are not appropriately taught with the Concept-Attainment Model. The material could be taught using the Inquiry Model, which is described in Chapter 7.

(e) A literature teacher who wants his students to know the time period during which Poe wrote has an objective that calls for factual information; that is, "Poe wrote in the first half of the nineteenth century" is a fact. Facts are not taught as the content goal in a Concept-Attainment activity.

All of the other goals involve the learning of a concept and are appropriate for concept attainment.

2. Let's now consider sequences of examples for the concepts gerund, soft, and miscible fluids.

a. For the concept gerund, a sequence might be the following: (The positive examples are in italics. The sentences not italicized are the negative examples.)

Hunting is a popular sport in many parts of the country. Walking is a major part of hunting, and hunters get a lot of exercise.

Susan and Jimmy were hunting together. Suddenly, they saw another hunter chasing a deer out of the woods. Their hunting dog, Ginger, jumped out of their truck and also gave chase. *Running off the road isn't a good idea*, but this is what Jimmy did when he saw the bizarre events in front of him. Jimmy stared very disgustedly as he looked at his crumpled fender. He didn't know what to do.

Obviously, there are many ways that a sequence of examples could be prepared to allow attainment of the concept gerund. The prepared sequence illustrates only one possibility. The sequence does, however, illustrate how the sequence can be embedded in the context of a short passage instead of being presented as a list of unrelated sentences. The important point is that each of the yes examples contains a gerund, while none of the no examples contain a gerund.

b. A sequence of examples for the concept soft might be the following:

1. Piece of terry cloth Yes
2. Piece of sandpaper No
3. Chamois skin Yes
4. Diaper Yes
5. Drinking glass No

6. Sponge ball Yes
7. Toy car No
8. Wadded facial tissue Yes
9. Piece of chalk No

The positive examples could be indicated by smiling faces, plus signs, or the word yes. Note again that the yes and no examples do not always alternate. There is no rule that says every yes must be followed by a no or vice versa. As with the number of examples, the ordering of the examples depends on the judgment of the teacher.

c. An appropriate sequence to teach miscible fluids might appear as illustrated below. Notice that the actual fluids should be used if the examples are to be most effective. Using the actual fluids (a form of realia) would allow students to directly observe the characteristics of the concept. If a compromise is required, a combination of actual fluids for some examples and models for the other examples would be the next most effective. The least effective form of example would be the use of words alone. The following is a possible sequence:

1. Water and alcohol   Yes
2. Alcohol and cooking oil   No
3. Benzene and gasoline   Yes
4. Water and cooking oil   No
5. Benzene and alcohol   No
6. Water and hydrochloric acid   Yes
7. Oil and sulfuric acid   No
8. Water and motor oil   No
9. Benzene and toluene   Yes
10. Vinegar and water   Yes
11. Hydrogen and oxygen   Yes

In some cases—water, cooking oil, alcohol, gasoline, motor oil, and vinegar—the actual liquids are easy to obtain, and in these cases they should be used. For the others, models are a reasonable compromise. The model could represent the different sizes of the respective elements and could show the mixing process. While words are most commonly used in an instance such as this, a model would be vastly superior.

3. The examples and sequences will be highly individual depending on background knowledge and experience. Check with a fellow student or your instructor for feedback. Keep in mind as you design the sequence that all of the positive examples must illustrate the concept and none of the negative examples can illustrate it. Also, use your imagination and try to design the sequence cleverly to promote critical skills in the students.

4. a. The examples of the concept in the anecdote are:

German shepherd   Fox
Collie   Wolf
Beagle

The other examples cited in the anecdote, such as Siamese cat, were the nonexamples (negative examples). The negative examples further clarify the concept by showing what it is not, while the positive examples show the characteristics of the concept.

b. The characteristics cited in the anecdote are:

Four legs   Prominent teeth
Barks   Hair

Note that none of these attributes alone is sufficient to describe the concept; however, together they provide an adequate description for the purposes of the teacher's lesson.
c. The hypotheses that students offered were:

  1. "It's an animal."
  2. "It could be pet."
  3. "I think it's mammal."
  7. "I think it's dogs."
  12. "Maybe it's dog family."

d. Michele's sequence was presented as follows:

Yes 1. German shepherd   No   6. Siamese cat
No   2. Oak tree   Yes 7. Fox
Yes 3. Collie   No   8. Leopard
No   4. Magnolia tree   Yes 9. Wolf
Yes 5. Beagle

Consider now a second partial sequence.

Yes 1. German shepherd
No   2. Siamese cat
Yes 3. Wolf
No   4. Leopard

The sequence Michele used allowed students much more opportunity to practice their thinking skills than would the second, because the first few examples she used were more general and allowed for a variety of hypotheses. In the second sequence, "Siamese cat" as the first negative example would eliminate "animal" or "pet" as initial hypotheses, and "wolf" as the second positive example would probably cause the students to immediately identify the concept. The first sequence, in contrast, allowed many hypotheses which were successively narrowed until the concept was isolated.
e. Michele could have further enriched the concept by including other positive examples, such as "jackal" and "coyote," to broaden the concept for the students.
f. Michele presented examples two at a time rather than singly. This is not critical and demonstrates the flexibility in the procedure. The only argument against this practice is that it might increase the cognitive load on young or inexperienced students to the point where they have some difficulty processing the information.
g. There were several points (e.g., line numbers 9 and 10) in the lesson where students voluntarily made the logic behind their answers explicit. Michele made a conscious effort to encourage this when she asked Phyllis to explain her hypothesis in line 4.

Chapter 5

1. Phase 1   Asking for similarities is part of phase 1.

2. Phase 1   The teacher continues to ask for similarities.

3. JT   Providing an example based on the information in the matrix supplies evidence for the earlier statement.

4. Phase 3   The teacher asks students to consider different conditions and suggest the outcomes of those conditions, which is a call for hypothetical reasoning.

5. JT   In asking, "What makes you say that?" the teacher asks the student to justify their thinking.

6. Phase 1   By again asking for similarities or differences, the teacher returns to phase 1.

7. JT   Asking, "What makes you say that?" is another way of requiring students to justify their thinking.

8. Phase 2   "Why do you suppose idealism appears as a theme?"

9. Phase 4   Describing general patterns near the end of the lesson is a form of summarizing used to bring the lesson to closure.

10. Phase 4   The teacher continues to ask the students for summarizing statements.

11. JT   Again the teacher asks the student to justify her thinking by providing an example.

12. A variety of responses are possible. The following examples are offered as illustrations. They are not the only possible answers, nor are they necessarily the best possible answers.

Phase 1:

Look at the diameters of the planets. What do you notice here?

The diameters of Jupiter, Saturn, Uranus, and Neptune are dramatically bigger than those of the other planets.

How do the planets' densities compare to their diameters?

The planets with large diameters have low densities compared to the other planets.

Phase 2:

Why do you think the planets with large diameters have low densities?

They are composed of materials that aren't very dense, such as gases.

Why do you suppose that Mercury's temperature varies so much—from –300° to 800°?

It rotates very slowly on its axis, so one side faces the sun for a long time and gets very hot, while the other side faces away from the sun for a long time and stays very cold.

It is generally believed that the earth is the only planet in the solar system that supports life as we know it. Why might that be the case?

It is the only planet with water.

It is the only planet that has a livable average temperature—other than possibly Mars.

In spite of its large diameter, Saturn's gravity isn't much greater than the earth's. Why might that be the case?

The density of Saturn is very low, so its gravity would be lower than would be expected for its size.

Phase 3:

Suppose that Mercury rotated on its own axis much more rapidly than it presently does. How might that affect its ability to support life?

It still wouldn't support life. It has no atmosphere. It is close to the sun, so it would still be very hot. It has no water.

Suppose that Saturn was a solid planet like the earth. How would that effect its gravity?

Its gravity would be much greater than it is now.

Phase 4:

What kinds of general descriptions can we make about the planets in the solar system?

The planets with large diameters have generally low masses and densities, so their gravities are lower than would be expected for their large size.

The farther away the planets are from the sun, the colder they are.

The farther away planets are from the sun, the longer their years.

All the planets rotate on their own axes.

All the planets except Mercury and Venus have at least one moon.

Chapter 6

Exercises 1 and 2 do not have clear-cut answers, and the responses will be a matter of professional judgment. The feedback is presented not as the "correct" answer, but rather as information designed to further stimulate your consideration and analysis of the material in this section. Please read the feedback to Exercises 1 and 2 with this idea in mind.

1. Choices A—Prime number, C—Square, D—Major scale, and F—Gerund are all concepts and are appropriately taught with the Direct-Instruction Model. Choice B—To simplify arithmetic expressions following the rule: multiply and divide left to right and then add and subtract left to right—is a skill and is also appropriate for the Direct-Instruction Model. Choice E—To understand that for nonmixing substances, less dense materials float on more dense materials—is a principle, and the model can be modified to effectively teach it. Choice G—To identify the relationships between the economy and geography of the North and South prior to the Civil War and how these factors impacted the outcome of the war—is an organized body of knowledge. A model such as the Integrative Model discussed in Chapter 5 would be more appropriate for teaching it. The reason the Direct-Instruction Model would be less appropriate is that the content described in the goal cannot be illustrated with a variety of examples as can skills, concepts, generalizations, principles, and academic rules, and as a result, teaching the topic requires a different form of organization and presentation.

2. The responses to this item will vary widely. Select the topic and discuss the examples with your instructor or a colleague. The criteria for good examples are the same for the Direct-Instruction Model as they would be for the Inductive or Concept-Attainment Models.

3. a. The four phases of the Direct-Instruction Model appeared in the lesson in the following ways.

   - Introduction: The introduction to the lesson occurred when Kathe linked the concept antonym to the superordinate concept word pairs and to the coordinate concept synonyms, which they had previously learned. Note that the introduction didn't contain any motivational component.
   - Presentation: This phase of the lesson occurred when Kathe defined the concept and illustrated it with examples.
   - Guided Practice: Guided practice occurred when Kathe presented examples and nonexamples of the concept and asked students for their own examples.
   - Independent Practice: The final phase of the model consisted of the students working on exercises that contained additional examples of antonyms.

   b. The most effective form of assessment would be to have the students write a paragraph in which a specified number of antonyms would be embedded.

   c. The primary problem with the lesson was that the concept *antonyms* was presented out of context. A better way of presenting the examples would be to have them embedded in the context of a passage.

Chapter Seven

1. a. The Lecture-Discussion Model was used to plan in two ways. The first was to organize a unit of study on communication, and the second was to organize the lesson on parts of speech.

b. There were two advance organizers illustrated in the anecdote. The first advance organizer was used to organize the unit on communication and was a definition ("communication is the two-way transmission of information that typically takes place through language"). The second advance organizer was an analogy comparing parts of speech to building blocks and was used to organize the lesson on parts of speech.

c. The organization for the unit as well as the lesson can be diagrammed as follows:

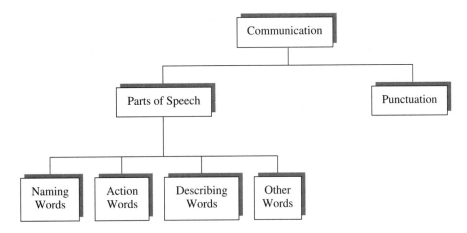

2. a. There were three advance organizers mentioned in the lesson. Line 3 contained an analogy, and lines 8 and 14 contained descriptions.

b. A hierarchical outline for the content presented would look like this.

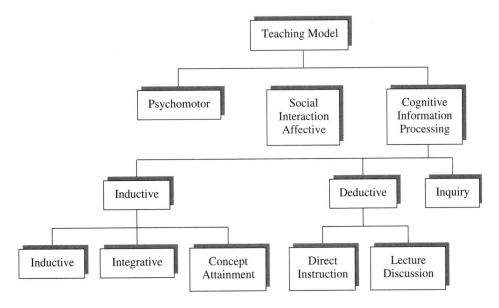

c. Integration took place in lines 11 and 12 where the Integrative and Lecture-Discussion Models were compared and contrasted.

Chapter 8

1. The following is a brief analysis of each objective:
   a. This objective involves teaching factual information and is not amenable to inquiry.
   b. The science teacher wanting students to know the difference between the processes of observation and inference actually wants his students to learn concepts. The concepts could be taught with a Concept-Attainment or an Inductive Model.
   c. A humanities teacher wanting his students to know why the work of Van Gogh changed in emphasis requires an explanation and is appropriate for inquiry.
   d. A math teacher wanting students to understand closure again has an objective that is essentially concept learning and therefore more appropriate to the models designed for this goal.
   e. This objective is appropriate for inquiry. However, merely asking students why dew forms would not narrow the phenomenon sufficiently to allow the student to deal with it, nor does it give them concrete information to work with. One of the functions of the event is to focus students' attention on a specific portion of the environment. A more appropriate stimulus event for Suchman Inquiry might be:

   Mr. Anderson went out of his house on Monday morning and found that the windshield of his car was wet. Before he left for work he wiped all of the windows of his car with a towel. Tuesday morning as Mr. Anderson prepared to go to work he noted that the car windows were all dry. Why should they be wet on Monday and dry on Tuesday?

   The students, in explaining this phenomenon, would actually be explaining the conditions under which dew forms. This description narrows the scope for students and allows them to focus directly on the problem.

2. a. An event that the teacher could present might appear as follows: He could play excerpts of sounds considered to be musical and excerpts of sounds considered to be noise. After playing the excerpts, the teacher might say something such as "Why was the first selection considered to be music and the second selection noise?"
   b. The teacher might begin the description of the event in either verbal or written form in this way:

   Mrs. Jones was a typical housewife in the town of Stevensville. She was married to a respected citizen, was the mother of three children, was active in civic groups, and she attended church regularly. However, on Saturday, June 17, the day of the annual community picnic, Mrs. Jones was taken aside and stoned to death by the rest of the people in the town. Mrs. Jones had done nothing to deserve this execution and yet it was performed by most of the townspeople in front of the rest of the citizens who did nothing to prevent it. Why would this happen?

   c. The teacher's description of the event might be as follows:

   Hiroshima, a city of approximately 250,000 people, was located at the end of the main island of the Japanese chain. Hiroshima was not the largest city, nor was it the city with the bulk of the military supplies on the Japanese mainland. It was not the main cultural center of Japan. Yet, this city was selected as the target for the dropping of the first atomic bomb in World War II. Why was Hiroshima selected as the first target when other places would seem to be more desirable?

   d. A description of the event could be:

   Prior to the 1948 presidential election that pitted Truman against Dewey, public polls favored Dewey by a wide margin. In fact, on the night of the election, one prominent newspaper's headlines reported a victory for Dewey. According to the preelection polls, Dewey was more popular, was felt to be better qualified for the presidency, and had powerful people on his side. Yet, when the final tally was taken, Truman had won a tremendous upset victory. How could this have happened?

e. One description of an event is the following:

The teacher places two beakers of colorless liquid (water and alcohol) on a demonstration table for the children to observe. The teacher then puts an ice cube into each of the containers of fluid. The ice cube floats on one of the fluids and sinks in the other. The two fluids appear to be the same, and the ice cubes are the same or nearly identical. The teacher would then ask why the object floats on one of the fluids and sinks in the other.

   f. In this case the teacher might show the students pictures of apparently similar paintings. They could be similar in style, coloring, and framing. The teacher might say something on the order of the following: "The painting on the right sold for five thousand dollars while the painting on the left sold for twenty-five dollars. When the paintings appear to be similar, why should the one be so much more valuable than the other?"

3. a. This event has all the characteristics required of an appropriate inquiry problem and is probably the best designed of the three. It poses a problem to be solved, provides students with starting points for data gathering, and yet is limited enough in scope to provide focus for the inquiry process.

   b. This problem is inappropriate in that it actually is designed to teach the concept *protective coloration* rather than an explanation. It also is general as opposed to being narrow in focus and shows no apparent discrepancy.

   c. This problem is essentially appropriate for an inquiry activity. It could be improved by making it appear more discrepant and narrower in focus. For instance, the event could be described as follows:

Jim and Susan are two students in Mr. Jones's tenth-grade English class. They each wrote an essay on the same topic, and the length of the essay was almost the same in each case. Both had typed their final products. However, Susan received an A, while Jim got a C. Why should there have been such a dramatic difference in their grades?

This event narrows the focus of the problem and increases its discrepant nature. In addition, the information provided would facilitate the data-gathering process and arouse the curiosity of students to seek an explanation for this discrepancy.

4. a. Ms. Stanley's actions in the lesson suggested that the lesson was preplanned rather than spontaneous. She had a content goal in mind (for students to understand factors that shaped the form that newspapers took) and came to class with the materials necessary for the activity.

   b. Students used primary data sources in pursuing their goals. An alternative secondary source would be to have students look up the information in a textbook.

   c. 1. Problem identification began when students compared the various newspapers. This phase of the model concluded when the teacher wrote "What factors influence the size and composition of the daily newspaper?" on the board.

     2. Hypothesis generation took place when students offered their ideas (sports, advertising) about factors affecting newspapers and when Ms. Stanley wrote these on the board.

     3. Data gathering occurred in small groups as each group analyzed its individual newspaper.

     4. The data analyses were just beginning as time ran out. This is a common problem for inquiry lessons, and teachers need to simply adjust to it.

After having examined the hypotheses, students would cautiously generalize to include other instances.

5. Question a would be inappropriate for measuring process skills because it primarily covers content that has already been discussed in class. Consequently, what is being measured here is recall of information rather than process skills. An important factor in measuring for process skills is uniqueness, i.e., students are asked to analyze a problem not previously discussed. If the problem is previously unfamiliar, students' ability to analyze is being measured. If the problem has been discussed, the problem measures recall or comprehension of content rather than process abilities.

Question b is appropriate and directly measures students' ability to relate explanations and data. The question could probably have been described more specifically to provide better directions to students. For example, the illustrated item with the two cities is clearer and more specific. Again, however, the reader is reminded that the explanation and the data regarding the cities must be unfamiliar to students or the teacher will be measuring recall of previously covered content.

Question c is also appropriate and measures students' ability to apply the information they've analyzed to develop a revised explanation. A combination of Questions b and c would be excellent for measuring students' process abilities.

6. The following questions would require rephrasing.

a. This question is not answerable yes or no and is therefore inappropriate.

c. This question is answerable yes or no but the answer to the question cannot be obtained through observation. To answer either yes or no to the question requires the teacher to make an inference and denies students practice in making inferences.

e. This question also cannot be answered through observation. The question could be rephrased in the following way: "Does Jean get over five hours of exercise a week?" or "Does Jean get more exercise than Pat?" Both questions are answerable through observation and would allow the inquirer to infer whether she got enough exercise.

7. a. The problem needing explanation was why Joan flared up at another teacher.

b.–d. The first hypothesis suggested to explain this phenomenon was that Joan was having marital problems. However, this hypothesis was not supported by the data, which indicated that Joan was happy both at home and at school. Having rejected this hypothesis, our inquirers then formed an hypothesis suggesting fatigue as a cause for Joan's behavior. Subsequent data seem to support this hypothesis but the reader should note that no formal closure was reached.

Chapter 9

1. Isabelle Ortega was using STAD. The content that she focused on was convergent, students practiced by giving the spelling words to each other, and were evaluated through a weekly quiz.

Jim Felton used Group Investigation to help his students learn about nutrition. To do this, he divided students into teams, made each team responsible for investigating different topics, and asked each team to report on its findings.

Jesse Kantor used Jigsaw II to help her students learn about amphibians. Different members of each team were responsible for different topics (e.g., circulatory system), these "experts" then taught other members of the team, and all members of the team were evaluated with a quiz covering all of the topics.

2. a. Knowledge of multiplication facts is convergent information best taught by the STAD model.

b. Analyzing social issues suggests that the teacher is interested in process in addition to content. Designing a research project on voting would best be taught using the Group-Investigation Model.

   c. This goal is content-oriented and involves learning large bodies of interconnected information rather than discrete bits of information. Consequently, this goal would best be taught through Jigsaw II.

   d. Studying pollution using group projects would best be taught through Group Investigation.

   e. Helping students learn to research a topic would best be taught through Group Investigation.

   f. Knowing and understanding the four major food groups suggests that the teacher not only wants his students to understand basic facts about nutrition but also the interconnections between the facts. This suggests Jigsaw II.

   g. Knowing the names of capitals of states involves the learning of facts. Facts are best taught through STAD.

3. a. The targeting of group goals was suggested when Anya said, ". . . we're going to work on them together in groups." Group goals were also suggested when she said, ". . . when we take the quiz each team will be scored on the basis of how much team members improved."

   b. Individual accountability was suggested by Anya saying, "your team's score will depend upon how well *all* the team members do—not just some."

   c. Equal opportunity for success was addressed when Anya discussed improvement points and explained, "So team members with lower scores in the beginning can actually score more points if they improve more than other team members."

4. a. One way to form teams is to divide students into quartiles and take the top and bottom students from the lowest and highest quartiles, and add them to the top and bottom students in the middle quartiles. Doing this, the first group would be composed of Juan, Ted, Kim, and Joan; the second group would have Bettina, May, Heather, and Lisa, etc.

   b. Other factors to consider include gender, ethnicity, and ability to work together in groups. For example, note that the second group formed was composed of all females. If one of the teacher's goals was to teach boys and girls to work together cooperatively, then a better gender mix would be desired.

5. a. A behavioral explanation of cooperative learning's effectiveness focuses on group rewards or contingencies. STAD does this by placing students on a team and rewarding individual members for the group's performance.

   b. Social explanations for cooperative learning's effectiveness focus on the intrinsic motivation of working together effectively in a group. Anya tried to ensure effective group functioning through monitoring and by highlighting the exemplary practices of smoothly functioning groups.

   c. Developmental theory explains cooperative learning's effectiveness through modeling and the interaction of less-advanced students with their more-advanced peers. Anya took advantage of this situation by encouraging members of the groups to explain their problem-solving strategies to each other.

   d. Cognitive-elaboration explanations also focus on the explanations they share with each other, but place more emphasis on the internal processes that take place within the explainer. By having to wrestle with ideas to place them in comprehensible form, students develop better understandings themselves. This commonly happens to teachers who find that the process of teaching a subject helps develop a deeper and richer understanding of the topic.

References

Anderson, J. (1990). *Cognitive Psychology and Its Implications* 3rd (Ed.) New York: Freeman.

Anderson, L., Brubaker, N., Alleman-Brooks, J., and Duffy, G. (1984). *Making Seatwork Work* (Research Series No. 142). East Lansing: Michigan State University, Institute for Research on Teaching.

Anderson, L., Brubaker, N., Alleman-Brooks, J., and Duffy, G. (1985). "A Qualitative Study of Seatwork in First-Grade Classrooms." *The Elementary School Journal* 86, 123–140.

Anderson, L., Evertson, C., and Brophy, J. (1979). "An Experimental Study of Effective Teaching in First Grade Reading Groups." *Elementary School Journal* 79, 193–223.

Anderson, R. (1959). "Learning in Discussions: A Resume/The Authoritarian-Democratic Studies." *Harvard Educational Review* 29, 201–216.

Aronson, E., Blaney, N., Stephan, C., Sikes, J., and Snapp, M. (1978). *The Jigsaw Classroom.* Beverly Hills, CA: Sage.

Atkinson, J. (1983). *Personality, Motivation and Action.* New York: Praeger.

Ausubel, D. (1963). *The Psychology of Meaningful Verbal Learning.* New York: Grune and Stratton.

Ausubel, D. (1968). *Educational Psychology: A Cognitive View.* New York: Holt, Rinehart and Winston.

Ausubel, D. (1978). "In Defense of Advance Organizers: A Reply to the Critics." *Review of Educational Research* 48, 251–257.

Babad, E., Bernieri, F., and Rosenthal, R. (1991). "Students as Judges of Teachers' Verbal and Nonverbal Behavior." *American Educational Research Journal* 28(1), 211–234.

Bandura, A. (1986). *Social Foundations of Thought and Action: A Social Cognitive Theory.* Englewood Cliffs, NJ: Prentice-Hall.

Bandura, A. (1989). "Social Cognitive Theory." In R. Vasta, (Ed.), *Annals of Child Development* Volume 6. (1–60). Greenwich, CT: JAI Press.

Bartlett, F. (1932). *Remembering.* London: Cambridge University Press.

Beck, I., and McKeown, M. (1993). *Why Textbooks Can Baffle Students. Learning* 1(1). University of Pittsburgh: Learning Research Development Center, 2–4.

Bennett, S. (1978). "Recent Research on Teaching: A Dream, a Belief, and a Model. *British Journal of Educational Psychology* 48, 27–147.

Berk, L. (1994). *Child Development* 3rd (Ed.) Boston: Allyn and Bacon.

Berliner, D. (1985, April). "Effective Teaching." Paper presented at the meeting of the Florida Educational Research and Development Council, Pensacola, Florida.

Berlyne, D. (1966). "Curiosity and Exploration." *Science* 153, 25–33.

Beyer, B. (1983). "Common Sense about Teaching Thinking Skills." *Educational Leadership* 41, 44–49.

Beyer, B. (1984). "Improving Thinking Skills—Practical Approaches." *Phi Delta Kappan* 65, 556–560.

Bloom, B. (1986). "Automaticity." *Educational Leadership* 43(5), 70–77.

Blumenfeld, P. (1992). "Classroom Learning and Motivation: Clarifying and Expanding Goal Theory." *Journal of Educational Psychology* 84(3), 272–281.

Blumenfeld, P., Pintrich, P., and Hamilton, V.L. (1987). "Teacher Talk and Students' Reasoning about Morals, Conventions, and Achievement." *Child Development* 58, 1389–1401.

Boyer, E. (1983). High School: A Report on Secondary Education in America. New York: Harper and Row.

Bransford, J. (1993). "Who Ya Gonna Call? Thoughts about Teaching Problem Solving." In P. Hallinger, K. Leatherwood, and J. Murphy, (Eds.), *Cognitive Perspectives on Educational Leadership.* (171–191). New York: Teachers College Press.

Bransford, J., Goldman, S., and Vye, N. (1991). "Making a Difference in People's Abilities to Think: Reflections on a Decade of Work and Some Hopes for the Future." In L. Okagaki and R. Sternberg, (Eds.), *Directors of Development.* (147–180). Hillsdale, NJ: Erlbaum.

Brooks, J., and Brooks, M. (1993). *In Search of Understanding: The Case for Constructivist Classrooms.* Alexandria, VA: Association for Supervision and Curriculum Development.

Brophy, J. (1986). "Research Linking Teacher Behavior to Student Achievement: Potential Implications for Instruction of Chapter 1 Students." In B. Williams, P. Richmond, and B. Mason, (Eds.), *Designs for Compensatory Education Conference Proceedings and Papers.* (IV-121–IV-179). Washington, DC: Research and Evaluation Associates.

Brophy, J. (1987). "On Motivating Students." In D. Berliner and B.B. Rosenshine, (Eds.), *Talks to Teachers.* (201–245). New York: Random House.

Brophy, J. (1992). "Probing the Subtleties of Subject-Matter Teaching." *Educational Leadership* 49, 4–8.

Brophy, J., and Evertson, C. (1974). *Texas Teacher Effectiveness Project: Final Report (Research Rep. No. 74-4).* Austin: University of Texas, Research and Development Center for Teacher Education.

Brophy, J., and Evertson, C. (1976). *Learning from Teaching: A Developmental Perspective.* Boston: Allyn and Bacon.

Brophy, J., and Good, T. (1986). "Teacher Behavior and Student Achievement. In M. Wittrock, (Ed.), *Handbook of Research on Teaching* 3rd (Ed.) (328–375). New York: Macmillan.

Brown, A. (1988). "Motivation to Learn and Understand: On Taking Charge of One's Own Learning." *Cognition and Instruction* 5, 311–321.

Brown, A., and Campione, J. (1990). "Interactive Learning Environments and the Teaching of Science and Mathematics." In M. Gardner, J. Greeno, F. Reif, A. Schoenfeld, A. diSessa, and E. Stage, (Eds.), *Toward a Scientific Practice of Science Education.* (111–139). Hillsdale, NJ: Erlbaum.

Brown, A., and Palincsar, A. (1985). *Reciprocal Teaching and Comprehension Strategies: A Natural History of One Program for Enhancing Learning.* (Tech. Rep. No. 334). Champaign-Urbana: University of Illinois Center for Reading.

Brown, J., Collins, A., and Duguid, P. (1989). "Situated Cognition and the Culture of Learning." *Educational Researcher* 18, 32–42.

Brown, S., Fauvel, J., and Finnegan, R., (Eds.) (1981). *Conceptions of Inquiry.* New York: Methuen.

Bruner, J., Goodnow, J., and Austin, G. (1956). *A Study of Thinking.* New York: John Wiley and Sons.

Carlsen, W. (1987, April). "Why Do You Ask? The Effects of Science Teacher Subject-Matter Knowledge on Teacher Questioning and Classroom Discourse." Paper presented at the annual meeting of the American Educational Research Association, Washington, DC.

Case, R. (1978). "Intellectual Development from Birth to Adulthood: A Neo-Piagetian Interpretation." In R. Siegler, (Ed.), *Children's Thinking: What Develops?* (37–71). Hillsdale, NJ: Erlbaum.

Champagne, A., Klopfor, L., Solomon, C., and Cahn, A. (1980). *Interactions of Students' Knowledge with Their Comprehension and Design of Science Experiments.* (Ed188–950). Pittsburgh: University of Pittsburgh, Learning Research and Development Center.

Chi, M., (1983). *Interactive Roles of Knowledge and Strategies in the Development of Organized Sorting and Recall.* Pittsburgh: University of Pittsburgh, Learning Research and Development Center.

Chi, M., and Glaser, R. (1983). *Problem-Solving Abilities.* Pittsburgh: University of Pittsburgh, Learning Research and Development Center.

Clark, C.M., and Peterson, P.L. (1986). Teachers' Thought Processes. In M.C. Wittrock, (Ed.), *Handbook of Research on Teaching*, 3rd (Ed.) New York: Macmillan.

Clark, W. (1942). *The Oxbow Incident*. New York: The Press of the Readers Club.

Clements, D., and Battista, M. (1990). "Constructivist Learning and Teaching." *Arithmetic Teacher* 38, 34–35.

Cohen, S. (1987). "Instructional Alignment: Searching for a Magic Bullet." *Educational Researcher* 16(8), 16–20.

Coker, H., Lorentz, C., and Coker, J. (1980, April). "Teacher Behavior and Student Outcomes in the Georgia Study." Paper presented at the annual meeting of the American Educational Research Association, Boston.

Coker, H., Medley, D., and Soar, R. (1980). "How Valid Are Expert Opinions about Effectiveness Teaching?" *Phi Delta Kappan* 62, 131–134, 149.

Coleman, J., Campbell, E., Hobson, D., McPartland, J., Mood, A., Weinfield, F., and York, R. (1966). *Equality of Educational Opportunity*. Washington, DC: U.S. Department of Health, Education and Welfare.

Collins, M. (1978). "Effects of Enthusiasm Training on Preservice Elementary Teachers." *Journal of Teacher Education* 29(1), 53–57.

Corkill, A. (1992). "Advance Organizers: Facilitators of Recall." *Educational Psychology Review* 4, 33–67.

Cornbleth, C. (1985). "Critical Thinking and Cognitive Processes." In W. Stanley, (Ed.), *Review of Research in Social Studies Education 1976–1983* (12–64). Washington DC: National Council for the Social Studies.

Corno, L., and Snow, R. (1986). "Adapting Teaching to Individual Differences among Learners." In M. Wittrock, (Ed.), *Third Handbook of Research on Teaching*. (570–604). New York: Macmillan.

Cronbach, L., and Snow, R. (Eds.) (1977). *Aptitudes and Instructional Methods*. New York: Irvington/Naiburg.

Crooks, T. (1988). "The Impact of Classroom Evaluation Practices on Students." *Review of Educational Research* 58, 438–481.

Cruickshank, D. (1985). "Applying Research on Teacher Clarity." *Journal of Teacher Education* 35(2), 44–48.

Cuban, L. (1984). *How Teachers Taught: Constancy and Change in American Classrooms: 1890–1980*. White Plains, NY: Longman.

Cushner, K., McClelland, A., and Safford, P. (1992). *Human Diversity in Education*. New York: McGraw-Hill.

Deci, E. (1981). *Psychology of Self-Determination*. Lexington, MA: Heath.

Dempster, F. (1991). "Synthesis of Research on Reviews and Tests." *Educational Leadership* 48(7), 71–76.

DeTure, L. (1985). *Acquisition of Wait Time: Training Techniques and Related Teaching Behaviors: Model-ing Protocols*. Cincinnati, OH: National Science Teachers Association.

Dewey, J. (1916). *Democracy in Education*. New York: Macmillan.

Dinnel, D., and Glover, J. (1985). "Advance Organizers: Encoding Manipulations." *Journal of Educational Psychology* 77, 514–521.

Doyle, W. (1983). "Academic Work." *Review of Educational Research* 53, 159–199.

Driver, R. (1983). *The Pupil as Scientist?* Milton Keynes, England: Open University Press.

Duffy, G., Roehler, L., Meloth, M., and Vavrus, L. (1985, April). "Conceptualizing Instructional Explanation." Paper presented at the annual meeting of the American Educational Research Association, Chicago.

Dunkin, M., and Biddle, B. (1974). *The Study of Teaching*. New York: Holt, Rinehart and Winston.

Eggen, P., Kauchak, D., and Kirk, S. (1978). "Hierarchical Cues and the Learning of Concepts from Prose Materials." *Journal of Experimental Education* 46, 7–10.

Eggen, P., and Kauchak, D. (1994). *Educational Psychology: Classroom Connections*. 2nd (Ed.) Columbus OH: Merrill.

Eggen, P., and McDonald, S. (1987, April). "Student Misconceptions of Physical Science Concepts: Implications for Science Instruction." Paper presented at the annual meeting of the National Association for Research in Science Teaching, Washington, DC.

Emmer, E., Evertson, C., and Brophy, J. (1979). "Stability of Teacher Effects in Junior High Classrooms." *American Educational Research Journal* 16, 71–75.

Evertson, C. (1987). "Managing Classrooms: A Framework for Teachers." In D. Berliner and B. Rosenshine, (Eds.), *Talks to Teachers* (54–74). New York: Random House.

Evertson, C., Anderson, C., Anderson, L., and Brophy, J. (1980). "Relationship between Classroom Behaviors and Student Outcomes in Junior High Mathematics and English Classes." *American Educational Research Journal* 17, 43–60.

Farnham-Diggory, S. (1972). *Cognitive Processes in Education: A Psychological Preparation for Teaching and Curriculum Development*. New York: Harper and Row.

Feldman, K. (1972). "The Effects of Number of Positive and Negative Instances and Concept Definition on the Learning of Mathematical Concepts." Paper presented at the meeting of the American Educational Research Association, in *Review of Educational Research* 50, 33–67.

Flavell, J. (1985). *Cognitive Development* 2nd (Ed.) Englewood Cliffs, NJ: Prentice-Hall, Inc.

Frayer, D. (1970). *Effect of Number of Instances and Emphasis of Relevant Attribute Values on Mastery of Geometric Concepts by Fourth and Sixth Grade Children.* (Technical Report 116) University of Wisconsin: Madison, Research and Development Center for Cognitive Learning.

Gage, N. (1985). *Hard Gains in the Soft Sciences.* Bloomington, IN: Phi Delta Kappa.

Gage, N., and Berliner, D. (1992). *Educational Psychology* 5th (Ed.) Boston: Houghton-Mifflin.

Gage, N., and Giaconia, R. (1981). "Teaching Practices and Student Achievement: Causal Connections." *New York University Education Quarterly* XII, 2–9.

Gagne, E., Yekovich, C., and Yekovich, F. (1993). *The Cognitive Psychology of School Learning* 2nd (Ed.) New York: HarperCollins.

Gall, M. (1984). "Synthesis of Research on Teachers' Questioning." *Educational Leadership* 42(3), 40–47.

Good, T. (1979). "Teacher Effectiveness in the Elementary School." *Journal of Teacher Education* 30(2), 52–64.

Good, T. (1983). "Research on Classroom Teaching." In L. Shulman and G. Sykes, (Eds.), *Handbook of Teaching and Policy.* (42–80). New York: Longman.

Good, T. (1987). "Teacher Expectations." In D. Berliner and B. Rosenshine, (Eds.), *Talks to Teachers.* (159–200). New York: Random House.

Good, T., and Brophy, J. (1986). "School Effects." In M. Wittrock, (Ed.), *Third Handbook of Research on Teaching.* (570–604). New York: Macmillan.

Good, T., and Brophy, J. (1994). *Looking in Classrooms* 6th (Ed.) New York: HarperCollins.

Good, T., and Grouws, D. (1979). "The Missouri Mathematics Effectiveness Project: An Experimental Study in Fourth Grade Classrooms." *Journal of Educational Psychology* 71, 355–362.

Good, T., Grouws, D., and Ebmeier, H. (1983). *Active Mathematics Teaching.* New York: Longman.

Goodlad, J. (1984). *A Place Called School.* New York: McGraw Hill.

Grossman, P., Wilson, S., and Shulman, L. (1989). "Teachers of Substance: Subject Matter Knowledge for Teaching." In M. Reynolds, (Ed.), *Knowledge Base for the Beginning Teacher.* (23–36). Elmsford, NY: Pergamon Press.

Harris, D., and Eggen, P. (1993, April). "The Impact of Experience on Conceptions of Expertise: A Comparison of the Thinking of Veteran, First-Year, and Preservice Teachers." Paper presented at the annual meeting of the American Educational Research Association, Atlanta.

Hunter, M. (1984). "Knowing, Teaching and Supervising." In P. Hosford, (Ed.), *Using What We Know about Teaching.* Alexandria, VA: Association for Supervision and Curriculum Development.

Jencks, C., Smith, M., Acland, H., Bane, M., Cohen, D., Gintis, H., Heyns, B., and Michelson, S. (1972). *Inequality: A Reassessment of the Effect of Family and Schooling in America.* New York: Basic Books.

Joyce, B., and Weil, M. (1972). *Models of Teaching.* Englewood Cliffs, NJ: Prentice-Hall.

Johnson, D., and Johnson, F. (1991). *Learning Together and Alone* 3rd (Ed.) Englewood Cliffs, NJ: Prentice-Hall.

Kagan, S. (1992). *Cooperative Learning.* San Juan Capistrano, CA: Resources for Teacher.

Kagan, D. (1992). "Professional Growth among Preservice and Beginning Teachers." *Review of Educational Research* 62, 129–169.

Kagan, J. (1972). "Motives and Development." *Journal of Personality and Social Psychology* 22, 51–66.

Kagan, S. (1986). "Cooperative Learning and Sociocultural Factors in Schooling." In *Beyond Language: Social and Cultural Factors in Schooling Language Minority Students.* (231–298). Los Angeles: California State University; Evaluation, Dissemination and Achievement Center.

Kauchak, D., and Eggen, P. (1993). *Learning and Teaching: Research Based Methods* 2nd (Ed.) Needham Heights, MA: Allyn and Bacon.

Keislar, E., and Shulman, L., (Eds.) (1966). *Learning by Discovery: A Critical Appraisal.* Chicago: Rand McNally.

Kerman, S. (1979). "Teacher Expectations and Student Achievement." *Phi Delta Kappan* 60, 70–72.

Klauer, K. (1984). "Intentional and Incidental Learning with Instructional Texts: A Meta-Analysis for 1970–1980." *American Educational Research Journal* 21, 323–339.

Klausmeier, H. (1985). *Educational Psychology* 5th (Ed.) New York: Harper and Row.

Langer, J., Bartolome, L., Vasquez, O., and Lucas, T. (1990). "Meaning Construction in School Literacy Tasks: A Study of Bilingual Students." *American Educational Research Journal* 27, 427–471.

Machado, L. (1980). *The Right to be Intelligent.* Oxford, England: Pergamon Press.

Maehr, M. (1992, April). "Transforming the School Culture to Enhance Motivation." Paper presented at the annual meeting of the American Educational Research Association, San Francisco.

Marshall, H. (1992). "Seeing, Redefining, and Supporting Student Learning." In H. Marshall, (Ed.), *Redefining Student Learning: Roots of Educational Change.* (1–32). Norwood, NJ: Ablex.

Mayer, R. (1983). "Can You Repeat This? Qualitative Effects of Repetition and Advance Organizers from Science Prose." *Journal of Educational Psychology* 75, 40–49.

Mayer, R. (1984). "Aids to Text Comprehension." *Educational Psychologist* 19, 30–42.

Mayer, R. (1987). *Educational Psychology: A Cognitive Approach.* Boston: Little Brown.

McCollum, J. (1978). *Ah Hah! The Inquiry Process of Generating and Testing Knowledge.* Santa Monica, CA: Goodyear.

McGreal, T. (1985, November). "Characteristics of Effective Teaching." Paper presented at the first annual Intensive Training Symposium, Clearwater, FL.

McKeachie, W., and Kulik, J. (1975). "Effective College Teaching." In F. Kerlinger, (Ed.), *Review of Research in Education* Vol. 3. Washington, DC: American Educational Research Association.

McLeish, J. (1976). "The Lecture Method." In N.L. Gage, (Ed.), *The Psychology of Teaching Methods: Seventy-Fifth Yearbook of the National Society for the Study of Education.* (397–401). Chicago: University of Chicago Press.

Morine-Dershimer, G. (1983). "Instructional Strategy and the Creation of Classroom Status." *American Educational Research Journal* 20, 645–661.

Morine-Dershimer, G. (1985). *Talking, Listening, and Learning in Elementary Classrooms.* New York: Longman.

Morine-Dershimer, G., and Vallance, C. (1976). *Teacher Planning (Beginning Teacher Evaluation Study, Special Report C).* San Francisco: Far West Laboratory.

Murdock, B. (1992). "Serial Organization in a Distributed Memory Model." In A. Healy, S. Kosslyn, and R. Shiffrin, (Eds.), *From Learning Theory to Connectionist Theory* Vol I. (201–227). Hillsdale, NJ: Erlbaum.

Murphy, J., Weil, M., and McGreal, T. (1986). "The Basic Practice Model of Instruction." *The Elementary School Journal* 87, 83–95.

Murray, H. (1983). "Low Inference Classroom Teaching Behavior and Student Ratings of College Teaching Effectiveness." *Journal of Educational Psychology* 75, 138–149.

Nickerson, R. (1986). "Why Teach Thinking?" In J. Baron and R. Sternberg, (Eds.), *Teaching Thinking Skills: Theory and Practice.* (27–38). New York: W.H. Freeman.

Nickerson, R. (1988). "On Improving Thinking Through Instruction." In E. Rothkopf, (Ed.), *Review of Research in Education.* (3–57). Washington, DC: American Educational Research Association.

Norris, S., and Ennis, R. (1989). *Evaluating Critical Thinking.* Pacific Grove, CA: Midwest Publications.

O'Keefe, P., and Johnston, M. (1987, April). "Teachers' Abilities to Understand the Perspectives of Students: A Case Study of Two Teachers." Paper presented at the annual meeting of the American Educational Research Association, Washington, DC.

Perkins, D. (1992). *Smart Schools.* New York: The Free Press.

Perkins, D., and Blythe, T. (1994). "Putting Understanding Up Front." *Educational Leadership* 51, 4–7.

Peterson, P., Marx, R., and Clark, C. (1978). "Teacher Planning, Teacher Behavior, and Student Achievement." *American Educational Research Journal* 15, 417–432.

Peterson, P., and Walberg, H. (1979). *Research on Teaching.* Berkeley, CA: McCutchan.

Porter, A., and Brophy, J. (1988). "Synthesis of Research on Good Teaching: Insights from the Work of the Institute for Research on Teaching." *Educational Leadership* 45(8), 74–85.

Pratton, J., and Hales, L. (1986). "The Effects of Active Participation on Student Learning." *Journal of Educational Research* 79, 210–215.

Prawat, R. (1992). "From Individual Differences to Learning Communities—Our Changing Focus." *Educational Leadership* 49, 9–13.

Presseisen, B. (1986). *Critical Thinking and Thinking Skills: State of the Art Definitions and Practice in Public Schools.* Philadephia: Research for Better Schools.

Raffini, J. (1993). *Winners Without Losers: Structures and Strategies for Increasing Student Motivation to Learn.* Boston: Allyn and Bacon.

Resnick, L., and Klopfer, L. (1989). "Toward the Thinking Curriculum: An Overview." In L. Resnick and L. Klopfer, (Eds.), *Toward the Thinking Curriculum: Current Cognitive Research.* (1–18). Alexandria, VA: The Association for Supervision and Curriculum Development.

Robinson, E., Wilson, E., and Robinson, S. (1981). "The Effects of Perceived Levels of Warmth and Empathy on Student Achievement." *Reading Improvement* 18, 313–318.

Rosenshine, B. (1979). "Content, Time, and Direct Instruction." In P. Peterson and H. Walberg, (Eds.), *Research on Teaching: Concepts, Findings, and Implications.* (28–56). Berkeley, CA: McCutchan.

Rosenshine, B. (1986). "Synthesis of Research on Explicit Teaching." *Educational Leadership* 43(7), 60–69.

Rosenshine, B., and Stevens, R. (1986). "Teaching Functions." In M. Wittrock, (Ed.), *Handbook of Research on Teaching* 3rd (Ed.) (376–391). New York: Macmillan.

Roth, K., and Anderson, C. (1991). "Promoting Conceptual Change Learning from Science Textbooks." In P. Ramsden, (Ed.), *Improving Learning: New Perspectives.* London: Kogen Page.

Rowe, M. (1974). "Relation of Wait-Time and Rewards to the Development of Language, Logic, and Fate Control: Part One—Wait Time." *Journal of Research in Science Teaching* 11, 81–94.

Rowe, M. (1986). "Wait Time: Slowing Down May Be a Way of Speeding Up." *Journal of Teacher Education* 37(1), 43–50.

Rumelhart, D. (1980). "Schemata: The Building Blocks of Cognition." In R. Spiro, B. Bruce, and W. Brewer, (Eds.), *Theoretical Issues in Reading Comprehension.* Hillsdale, NJ: Erlbaum.

Rumelhart, D. and Norman, D. (1981). "Analogical Processes in Learning." In J. Anderson, (Ed.), *Cognitive Skills and Their Acquisition.* (335–359), Hillsdale, NJ: Erlbaum.

Rumelhart, D. and Ortony, A. (1977). "The Representation of Knowledge in Memory." In R. Anderson, R. Spurs, and W. Montague, (Eds.), *Schooling and the Acquisition of Knowledge.* Hillsdale, NJ: Erlbaum.

Rutter, M., Maughan, B., Mortimore, P., Ouston, J., and Smith, A. (1979). *Fifteen Thousand Hours.* Cambridge, MA: Harvard University Press.

Schwarz, B., and Reisberg, D. (1991). *Learning and Memory.* New York: Norton.

Science for All Americans. (1989). Washington, DC: American Association for the Advancement of Science.

Scruggs, T., and Richter, L. (1988). "Tutoring Learning Disabled Students: A Critical Review." *Learning Disability Quarterly* 11(3), 274–287.

Sharon, S., Kussell, P., Hertz-Lazarawitz, R., Bejarano, Y., Ravis, S., and Sharon, Y. (1984). *Cooperative Learning in the Classroom: Research in Desegregated Schools.* Hillsdale, NJ: Erlbaum.

Sharon, S., and Sharon, H. (1988). *Language and Learning in the Cooperative Classroom.* New York: Springer-Verlag.

Shulman, L. (1986). "Paradigms and Research Programs in the Study of Teaching: A Contemporary Perspective." In M. Wittrock, (Ed.), *Handbook of Research on Teaching* 3rd (Ed.) (3–36). New York: Macmillan.

Slavin, R. (1980). "Cooperative Learning." *Review of Educational Research* 50, 317–343.

Slavin, R. (1986). *Using Student Team Learning* 3rd (Ed.) Baltimore, MD: The Johns Hopkins University, Center for Research on Elementary and Middle School.

Slavin, R. (1989). "Cooperative Learning and Student Achievement: Six Theoretical Perspectives. In M. Maehr and C. Ames, (Eds.), *Advances in Motivation and Achievement* Vol. 6. Greenwich, CT: JAI Press.

Slavin, R. (1990). *Cooperative Learning: Theory, Research, and Practice.* Englewood Cliffs, NJ: Prentice-Hall.

Slavin, R., Karweit, N., and Madden, N. (Eds.) (1989). *Effective Programs for Students at Risk.* Boston: Allyn and Bacon.

Smith, F. (1975). *Comprehension and Learning.* New York: Holt, Rinehart and Winston.

Smith, L., and Cotten, M. (1980). "Effect of Lesson Vagueness and Discontinuity on Student Achievement and Attitude." *Journal of Educational Psychology* 72, 670–675.

Snyder, S., Bushur, L., Hoeksema, P., Olson, M., Clark, S., and Snyder, J. (1991, April). "The Effect on Instructional Clarity and Concept Structure on Students' Achievement and Perception." Paper presented at the annual meeting of the American Educational Research Association, Chicago.

Soar, R.S., and Soar, R.M. (1978). *Setting Variables, Classroom Interaction, and Multiple Pupil Outcomes.* (Contract No. 60432). Washington, DC: National Institute of Education.

Stallings, J. (1983). *Findings from the Research on Teaching: What We Have Learn(Ed.)* Vanderbilt University: Peabody Center for Effective Teaching.

Stallings, J., Needels, M., and Stayrook, N. (1979). *How to Change the Process of Teaching Basic*

Reading Skills in Secondary Schools. (Menlo Park, CA: SRI International).

Steinberg, R. (1985). "Critical Thinking: Its Nature, Measurement and Improvement." In F. Link, (Ed.), *Essays on the Intellect.* Alexandria, VA: Association for Supervision and Curriculum Development.

Stevens, R., and Slavin, R. (1991). "When Cooperative Learning Improves the Achievement of Students with Mild Disabilities: A Response to Tateyama-Sniezek." *Exceptional Children* 57(3), 276–280.

Stipek, D. (1993). *Motivation to Learn: From Theory to Practice* 2nd (Ed.) Needham Heights, MA: Allyn and Bacon.

Suchman, R. (1966a). *Inquiry Development Program: Developing Inquiry.* Chicago: Science Research Associates.

Suchman, R. (1966b). *Teacher's Guide: Inquiry Development Program in Physical Science.* Chicago: Science Research Associates.

Taba, H. (1965). "Techniques of Inservice Training." *Social Education* 29, 44–60.

Taba, H. (1966). *Teaching Strategies and Cognitive Functioning in Elementary School Children* (Project No. 2404). Washington, DC: U.S.O.E.

Taba, H. (1967). *Teachers Handbook to Elementary Social Studies.* Reading, MA: Addison-Wesley.

Tennyson, R. (1978). "Content Structure and Instructional Control Strategies in Concept Acquisition." Paper presented at the meeting of the American Psychological Association, Toronto.

Tennyson, R., and Cocchiarella, M. (1986). "An Empirically Based Instructional Design Theory for Teaching Concepts." *Review of Educational Research* 56, 40–71.

Thelen, H. (1960). *Education and the Human Quest.* New York: Harper and Row.

Tobin, K. (1983). "Management of Time in Classrooms." In B. Fraser, (Ed.), *Classroom Management.* (22–35). Perth, Australia: WAIT Press.

Van Patten, J., Chao, C., and Reigeluth, C.M. (1986). "A Review of Strategies for Sequencing and Synthesizing Instruction." *Review of Educational Research* 56, 437–471.

Villegas, A. (1991). *Culturally Responsive Pedagogy for the 1990s and Beyond.* Princeton, NJ: Educational Testing Service.

Vito, R., and Connell, J. (1988, April). "A Longitudinal Study of At-Risk High School Students: A Theory-Based Description and Intervention." Paper presented at the annual meeting of the American Educational Research Association, New Orleans.

Voss, J. (1986). "Problem-Solving and the Educational Process." In R. Glaser and A. Lesgold, (Eds.), *Handbook of Psychology and Education.* Hillsdale, NJ: Erlbaum.

Vygotsky, L. (1978). Mind in Society: The Development of Higher Psychological Processes (M. Cole, V. John-Steiner, S. Scribner, and E. Souberman, (Eds.) and Trans.). Cambridge, MA: Harvard University Press.

Wertsch, J. (1991). *Voices of the Mind: A Socio-Cultural Approach to Mediated Action.* Cambridge, MA: Harvard University Press.

White, R. (1959). "Motivation Reconsidered: The Concept of Competence." *Psychological Review* 66, 297–333.

Wittrock, M. (1986). "Students' Thought Processes." In M. Wittrock, (Ed.), *Handbook of Research on Teaching* 3rd (Ed.) (297–314). New York: Macmillan.

Wlodkowski, R. (1984). *Motivation and Teaching: A Practical Guide.* Washington, DC: The National Education Association.

Wlodkowski, R., and Jaynes, J. (1990). *Eager to Learn: Helping Children Become Motivated and Love Learning.* San Francisco: Jossey-Bass.

Glossary

Academic rule: A relationship between concepts arbitrarily derived by people.

Active teaching: A positive and proactive approach to teaching in which teachers are directly involved in guiding learning by providing examples and representations, asking questions, guiding discussions, and monitoring student progress.

Advance organizers: Verbal statements at the beginning of a lesson that preview and structure the new material and link it to the students' existing schemata.

Arousal: A physical or psychological reaction to the environment.

At-risk students: Students in danger of failing to complete their education with the skills necessary to survive in modern society.

Automaticity: The process of overlearning information and skills to the point where they can be accessed or used with little mental effort.

Basic cognitive processes: The fundamental constituents of thinking. "Tools" for thinking.

Call-out: An answer given by a student before the student has been recognized by the teacher.

Characteristics: The defining features of a concept.

Closure: A form of review that occurs at the end of a lesson.

Comprehension monitoring: The process of informally assessing student understanding in lecture-discussion lessons.

Concept analysis: The process of describing a concept in terms of its characteristics, related concepts, examples, and definition.

Concepts: Categories, sets, or classes of objects, events, or ideas with common characteristics.

Conceptual framework: An organized and interconnected network of ideas that people have stored in their memories.

Connected discourse: Instruction that is thematic and leads to a point.

Constructivism: A view of learning that says that learners develop their own understanding of the way the world works rather than having it delivered to them by others (most commonly teachers) in an already-organized form.

Cooperative-Learning Models: A cluster of instructional strategies that actively involve students in group work towards a common goal.

Coordinate concepts: Concepts with distinct characteristics, all of which are members of a larger class or category.

Critical thinking: The process of assessing conclusions based on evidence.

Definition: A statement that includes the name of the concept being defined, a superordinate concept, and the concept's characteristics.

Direct-Instruction Model: A teacher-centered strategy that uses teacher explanation and modeling combined with student practice and feedback to teach concepts and skills.

Empathy: An individual's capacity for understanding how other people feel, what their points of view might be, or where they're "coming from."

Emphasis: Signals that alert students to important information in a lesson, which are communicated through vocal or verbal behavior and repetition.

Encoding: The process of forming representations of information in long-term memory.

Equal opportunity for success: A concept within cooperative learning suggesting that all students, regardless of ability or background, can expect to be rewarded for their efforts if they make an honest effort.

Equitable distribution: A questioning pattern in which all students in the class are called on as equally as possible.

Essential teaching skills: The critical teacher attitudes, skills, and strategies necessary to promote student learning.

Examples: Cases that illustrate a concept.

Feedback: Information about current behavior that can be used to improve future performance.

Focus: Instructional materials and techniques that attract and holds students' attention throughout the learning activity.

General Inquiry Model: A teaching strategy designed to teach students how to investigate problems and questions with facts. The Inquiry Model is implemented in five steps, which are: (1) identifying a question or problem, (2) making hypotheses, (3) gathering data, (4) assessing hypotheses, (5) generalizing.

Generalizations: Relationships between concepts that describe patterns having exceptions.

Generative knowledge: Knowledge that can be used to interpret new situations, solve problems, think and reason, and learn.

Group Investigation: A cooperative-learning strategy that places students in groups to investigate a given topic.

Group goals: Incentives within cooperative learning that help create team spirit and encourage students to help each other.

Higher-order thinking: The process of forming conclusions based on evidence.

Hypothesis: A tentative answer to a question or solution to a problem that can be verified with data.

Individual accountability: A cooperative-learning principle requiring that each individual member of a cooperative-learning group demonstrate mastery of the concepts and skills being taught.

Information processing: The way people gather and organize information from the environment in order to form useful patterns that are used to explain and predict events in their experience.

Inquiry: A process for answering questions and solving problems based on facts and observations.

Instructional alignment: The congruence, or match, between objectives and learning activities

Integration: In lecture-discussion lessons, the process of linking new information to prior learning and linking different parts of new learning to each other.

Introductory focus: The set of teacher actions at the beginning of a lesson designed to attract students' attention and pull them into the lesson.

Jigsaw II: A form of cooperative-learning in which individual students become experts on subsections of a topic and teach that subsection to others

Lecture: A form of instruction in which students passively receive information delivered in an organized way by teachers.

Long-term memory: The permanent memory store in our personal information-processing systems.

Meaningfulness: Establishment of links or associations between an idea and other ideas.

Meaningful verbal learning: The acquisition of ideas that are linked to other ideas.

Metacognition: The awareness of and control over our cognitive processes.

Modeling: The display of behaviors that are imitated by others.

Models: Representations of academic topics that allow us to visualize what we cannot observe directly (as in a *model* of the atom).

Monitoring: The process of constantly checking students' verbal and nonverbal behavior for evidence of learning progress.

Observational learning: The changes in behavior, thinking, or emotions that result from observing the behavior of another person (a model).

Precise Terminology: Teachers defining ideas clearly and eliminating vague terms from presentations and answers to students' questions.

Primary data sources: Individuals' direct observations of the events being studied.

Principles: Relationships among concepts accepted as true or valid for all known cases.

Prompt: Any teacher question or directive that elicits a student response after the student has failed to answer or has given an incorrect or incomplete answer.

Prototype: A case representing a "best illustration" of a concept.

Questioning frequency: The number of questions teachers ask during learning activities.

Review: The process of summarizing previous work that prepares a link between what has been learned and what is coming.

Rote learning: A form of learning that emphasizes the memorization of specific items of information rather than exploring relationships among topics.

Scaffolding: Instructional support that helps learners to perform skills.

Schema (Pl. Schemata): Knowledge stored in people's memories, described as sets of interconnected ideas, relationships, and procedures.

Schema theory: A theoretical view of knowledge construction that says that the information people store in memory consists of networks of organized and interconnected ideas.

Secondary data sources: Other individuals' interpretations of primary data sources, such as information found in textbooks, encyclopedias, and other reference books.

Self-regulation: An individual's conscious use of mental strategies for the purpose of improving thinking and learning.

Sensory focus: The use of stimuli—concrete objects, pictures, models, materials displayed on the overhead, and even information written on the chalkboard—to maintain attention.

Skills: Cognitive operations with three essential characteristics: they have a specific set of identifiable procedures; they can be illustrated with a large and varied number of examples; and they are developed through practice.

Social structure: The characteristics of the classroom environment necessary for learning to take place and the roles of the teacher and students in the environment.

Student Teams Achievement Division (STAD): A cooperative-learning strategy designed to teach basic facts, concepts, and skills through the use of multi-ability learning teams.

Subordinate concepts: Subsets or examples of concepts.

Suchman Inquiry: A form of inquiry in which data are gathered in a simulated setting through a process of student questioning.

Superordinate concept: A larger category or class into which a concept fits.

Task analysis: The process of breaking a skill into its component subparts.

Task specialization: A component within Jigsaw II requiring that different students have specialized roles in reaching the goals of a learning activity.

Teacher effectiveness research: A description of the patterns of teacher behavior that influence student learning.

Teacher expectations: The inferences teachers make about students' future academic achievement, behavior, and attitudes.

Teaching models: Prescriptive teaching strategies designed to accomplish particular instructional goals.

Think alouds: Conscious attempts to verbalize internal cognitive strategies.

Transition signal: A verbal statement that communicates that one idea is ending and another is beginning.

Transfer: The ability to apply a skill or knowledge learned in one setting to a different setting.

Wait-time: The period of silence both before and after a student responds.

Warmth: Teachers' abilities to demonstrate that they care for students as people.

Working memory: The portion of memory in which conscious processing of information occurs.

Zone of proximal development: A stage of learning in which a student cannot solve a problem or perform a skill alone but can be successful with the help of a teacher.

Index